THE RAF'S ROAD TO D-DAY

In Memory of my Father John Frederick Baughen.

His war ended at Anzio.

THE RAF'S ROAD TO D-DAY

THE STRUGGLE TO EXPLOIT AIR SUPERIORITY, 1943–1944

Greg Baughen

THE RAF'S ROAD TO D-DAY
The Struggle to Exploit Air Superiority, 1943–1944

First published in Great Britain in 2023 by
Airworld
An imprint of
Pen & Sword Books Ltd
Yorkshire – Philadelphia

Copyright © Greg Baughen, 2023

ISBN 978 1 39905 180 4

The right of Greg Baughen to be identified as Author of this work has been asserted by him in accordance with the Copyright, Designs and Patents Act 1988.

A CIP catalogue entry for this book is available from the British Library.

All rights reserved. No part of this book may be reproduced or transmitted in any form or by any means, electronic or mechanical including photocopying, recording or by any information storage and retrieval system, without permission from the Publisher in writing.

Typeset by SJmagic DESIGN SERVICES, India.

Printed and bound in the UK by CPI Group (UK) Ltd.

Pen & Sword Books Ltd includes the Imprints of Atlas, Archaeology, Aviation, Discovery, Family History, Fiction, History, Maritime, Military, Military Classics, Politics, Select, Airworld, Frontline Publishing, Leo Cooper, Remember When, Seaforth Publishing, The Praetorian Press, Wharncliffe Local History, Wharncliffe Transport, Wharncliffe True Crime and White Owl.

For a complete list of Pen & Sword titles please contact

PEN & SWORD BOOKS LTD
George House, Units 12 & 13, Beevor Street, Off Pontefract Road,
Barnsley, South Yorkshire, S71 1HN, England
E-mail: enquiries@pen-and-sword.co.uk
Website: www.pen-and-sword.co.uk

or
PEN AND SWORD BOOKS
1950 Lawrence Rd, Havertown, PA 19083, USA
E-mail: uspen-and-sword@casematepublishers.com
Website: www,penandswordbooks.com

Contents

Introduction vi

Chapter One   The Bomber Rules 1

Chapter Two   The Shape of Wars to Come 22

Chapter Three   Italian Lessons 40

Chapter Four   Cover for Overlord 65

Chapter Five   Bombing Versus Invasion – The Race 78

Chapter Six   Invasion Air Support 103

Chapter Seven   Italian Dress Rehearsal 129

Chapter Eight   Tedder and Coningham Take Charge 149

Chapter Nine   D-Day 179

Chapter Ten   Re-learning Old Lessons 194

Chapter Eleven   The Bomber War 212

Chapter Twelve   Breakthrough 228

Conclusion 263

Bibliography 268

Appendix 1: Aircraft deliveries July 1943–September 1944 273

Appendix 2: Aircraft Performance 276

Endnotes 281

Index 297

Introduction

The Second World War had its fair share of ironies. Britain was facing one of the most ruthless, depraved regimes any country has ever had the misfortune to endure. The horrors inflicted on its own people and the nations it subjugated were unsurpassed. Yet, in the battle to restore freedom, Britain resorted to a ruthless policy of mass destruction of enemy urban areas which involved killing civilians of all ages in vast numbers.

It was not a policy born out of evil intent or any desire to seek the most brutal, vengeful way of waging war. In the inter-war years many experts in many countries genuinely believed this was how wars of the future would be fought. As Trenchard put it, the country that squealed first, would lose The RAF Air Staff had tried to develop a more refined variant which would see bombers strike enemy war industry rather than people. This had failed and policy reverted to targeting people. It was a policy that seemed more associated with the horrors of the worst sort of tyrannical totalitarian state than, by the standards of the day, a modern, liberal democracy.

Paradoxically, Hitler's military had rejected the idea of relying on indiscriminate aerial bombardment as a way of winning wars. Although Hitler had skilfully used the bomber as a diplomatic weapon in peacetime, and had no qualms about bombing civilians in wartime, the country's military leaders recognised that there were better ways of defeating their enemies. Instead, Germany had opted for a new brand of combined arms warfare that exploited the speed and flexibility of mechanised ground and air forces to win fast-moving battles of manoeuvre. The German variant of combined arms warfare became known as 'blitzkrieg' and it set the pattern for military operations for decades to come. Ironically it was a method Britain had done so much to pioneer in the First World War.

With these methods, German forces were soon defeating nation after nation until, in the summer of 1940, Britain stood alone. These defeats did not in any way shake Air Staff faith in their bomber strategy. Nor did the

INTRODUCTION

Air Ministry feel there were any lessons to be learned from the string of rapid victories their enemy was amassing. Even when invasion loomed in Britain's darkest hour, they saw no reason why they should provide the army with the sort of direct support that was such an important component of the Wehrmacht method. As far as the Air Staff were concerned, to achieve victory, the country merely had to follow the bomber path. This had been clearly laid out by Jan Smuts in 1917 when the decision was taken to create an independent RAF. In Smuts's vision of future war, bombers would be the deciding factor. If armies and navies had any role, it would be entirely secondary. Trenchard had built his fiercely independent RAF around this philosophy.

In the desperate days of 1940, the bomber approach had not yet had time to fail. Indeed victory in the Battle of Britain encouraged the Air Staff's belief that airpower alone would be decisive. Britain just needed a powerful air force to prevail. Fighter Command had averted defeat; now it was up to Bomber Command to follow up this success and win the war. It all seemed very reasonable. Indeed, with the French Army defeated, the bomber seemed to provide Britain with the only plausible way of winning the war. Britain had never even attempted to assemble the ground and air forces that might challenge the mighty Wehrmacht. The invincibility of the German armed forces was accepted as immutable fact. Bombing the enemy into defeat would avoid the need to cross the English Channel and engage the German army. For a country tottering on the brink, Bomber Command provided hope for its people and leaders. It was easy to argue that the country had no choice but to rely on the bomber for victory.

The hope proved to be an illusion. The bomber could not turn the tide of war. Indeed it soon transpired that bombing Germany was achieving remarkably little. Far from making the key contribution to victory, the diversion of resources to the bomber project from the conventional battles raging across the globe was actually handicapping Allied efforts to contain and defeat their enemies. It was a torrid time for Britain's armed forces. The lack of effective air support on and around the battlefield was not the only area in which British military thinking lagged behind but it was undisputedly one of the reasons why Commonwealth armies were struggling. The Army had much to learn in this new era of mobile mechanised warfare, and the learning curve was very steep. The Air Ministry, however, did not feel the RAF needed to be on this particular learning curve.

The Air Ministry remained stubbornly in denial about its contribution to the difficulties Britain's armed forces faced. It resented any suggestion that the RAF was in any way responsible for any of these problems. The segregated organisation of Britain's three services made it easy to lay the blame at the door of someone else. If Britain suffered defeats on the battlefield, it was nothing to do with the Air Force; it was an Army problem.

It was difficult, not just for the Air Staff, but for Britain as a nation to accept that a method of war the RAF had been set up to develop and into which the country had invested so many of its industrial, scientific and manpower resources, was not actually a very good way of winning wars. Even when the German invasion of the Soviet Union transformed the strategic balance of power, the Air Staff persevered with the bomber project. By hook or by crook, the war was going to be won by bombing. When precision bombing failed, Air Chief Marshal Arthur Harris was brought in to implement an indiscriminate area-bombing policy.

The alternative to the bombing strategy, an invasion of France, was, however, gaining ground. The Soviets were pushing for a second front. With the bomber offensive struggling, Churchill set his planners the task of investigating possible landings on the continent. In December 1941 Normandy was mentioned in their discussions for the first time. The Americans were now in the war and they believed the sooner an invasion of France was launched, the sooner the war would be over. Much to the dismay of the hardcore bomber school, the realities of fighting a real war inevitably resulted in ever greater demands from front-line commanders for air support. Gradually, and against the better judgement of the Air Staff, Commonwealth armies began to get the air resources they needed to win crucial battles. Victory at El Alamein sent Rommel into headlong retreat. At Stalingrad the Red Army inflicted a crushing defeat on the invader. By early 1943 claiming that armies and navies were the obsolete methods of the past was becoming an increasingly untenable argument.

There was, however, still hope for the bomber hardliners. The United States entry into the war also saw the arrival of an air cohort who were just as convinced as their RAF counterparts that airpower would dominate future wars. American air commanders brought welcome support for a fast flagging strategic bombing programme. There were also political factors working in favour of the bomber strategy. Churchill needed the bomber offensive to prove to Stalin that Britain was doing its bit.

With the war into its fourth year, and no sign of bombing bringing about a German collapse, talk of an invasion of France being unnecessary was beginning to sound unrealistic. However, by rebranding the bomber policy as a necessary precursor for a successful invasion, the Air Staff

INTRODUCTION

managed to ensure the bomber remained the cornerstone of the Western Allies' war strategy. Without the bomber offensive, it was argued, defeating the Wehrmacht would be impossible. Such a crucial, central role went a long way towards meeting the aspirations of the airpower apostles. Army commanders were more than happy to go along with this. Rather than analyse why taking on the German Wehrmacht was such a daunting prospect and improving Britain's battlefield capabilities accordingly, they were quite happy to see airpower used to reduce German capabilities to a level Allied methods could cope with.

By the summer of 1943, despite the extravagant claims to the contrary, the bomber offensive had still not had any major impact on the course of the war. Germany had not been broken by the horrendous civilian casualties bombing was inflicting on the nation. The German leadership had been severely shaken by the destruction of Hamburg, Germany's second largest city, but the nation had survived even this catastrophe. Three years of steadily increasing bombing had caused considerable disruption and much personal hardship and grief but, at a national level, German war production had scarcely been affected and was still rising.

Even at the time it was clear that by the summer of 1943 the war had turned against the Axis forces. North Africa had been cleared of Axis armies and Sicily had fallen. On the Eastern Front the Germans had been turned back at Kursk and Soviet forces were sweeping westwards with their own 'Deep Battle' brand of mechanised combined arms warfare. All these victories had been won before bombing had achieved anything worthwhile. Germany was in retreat not because the country had been bombed but because her enemies possessed vastly more manpower, industrial and natural resources. The Allies were winning the war despite the effort that had gone into the bomber offensive, not because of it.

The Allies might be winning the war, but final victory still seemed a long way off. On all fronts Allied armies were now combining ground and air forces to win dramatic victories. However, whereas this was a method the Soviets were expanding and refining with an army and air force that were fully committed to the policy, in the West the process was bedevilled by inter-service disputes and a shared belief by Army and Air Force that whatever the pros and cons of tactical air support, victory by any means required a strategic bombing offensive.

Even the growing consensus that tactical air support was an essential element of modern warfare was marred by disagreement over exactly how it should help Allied ground forces. In the Middle East, the Desert Air Force seemed to be establishing a successful template in which support on the field of battle was just as, if not more, important than any indirect support airpower could provide. It was agreed in principle that the armies invading France would need a specialist tactical air force along the lines of the Desert Air Force. In March 1943 it was decided that a Second Tactical Air Force should be created in the United Kingdom to provide this support.

However, the innate air force desire to view air warfare as a separate entity was slowing progress towards a truly integrated ground/air approach. There was broad agreement between the services about the different ways in which airpower could contribute to victory on the battlefield; the differences of opinion were about which were most useful. The War Office welcomed both the bombing of industrial targets and, even more so, lines of communication leading to the battlefield. However, the ultimate goal was to defeat the enemy army and they believed that, at critical stages of the land battle, the most valuable air contribution would always be direct support on and around the battlefield. The Air Staff, on the other hand, considered the order of importance to be the reverse, with some taking the extreme position that direct support on the battlefield was a misuse of airpower and was never justified.

Attitudes were not entirely along service lines. General Alan Brooke, the Chief of the Imperial General Staff, believed an invasion of north-west Europe would be impossible unless strategic bombing significantly reduced German armed strength and this view was gaining ground in American army circles. Arguably, this assigned absolute importance to strategic bombing. On the other hand, Air Vice-Marshal Harry Broadhurst, who commanded the RAF's Desert Air Force, believed the RAF's first duty was to support the troops on the battlefield.

The reality of engaging in actual battles in East Africa and the Western Desert helped turn the Middle East based RAF into a modern tactical fighting force with interdiction, close air support and air superiority co-equal tasks. As was the case with German and Soviet offensives, there were no hard and fast pre-conditions for initiating a land offensive. There was certainly never any question of delaying an offensive until air superiority was secured; the battle in the air was fought in parallel with the battle on land; indeed, the two were interconnected. Gaining the edge in the air made it easier to advance which, in turn, caused confusion amongst the opposing air force which accelerated the victory in the air which then enabled the air force to speed the advance. Ground-based flak helped establish superiority in the air while aerial reconnaissance and air strikes helped establish superiority

INTRODUCTION

on the ground. This was the essence of combined arms warfare – different elements of the armed forces applied simultaneously to the mutual benefit of all. The success of the Desert Air Force was due to its willingness to vary the importance attached to air superiority, interdiction and close air support according to circumstances.

The lessons learned by the Desert Air Force were soon being lost. General Bernard Montgomery's methodical approach on land was being mimicked by the increasingly staged and laboured approach in the air. Air Marshal Arthur Coningham, the commander of the Allied tactical air forces in the Mediterranean, was not of the Trenchard school. He believed ultimately armies won wars and air forces had to help them do this. However, he was moving away from the Desert Air Force's pragmatic, flexible approach. In its place he introduced a ponderous, systematic pecking order. First the battle for air superiority would be fought. Once won, it would be exploited by severing enemy lines of communication to the front. Air support on the battlefield came a very distant third.

At the heart of this pecking order was the air force desire to fight their own separate, clearly defined, independent war. This frame of mind was the very antithesis of what was required to develop a successful inter-service combined arms approach. For the Air Ministry, integrating air operations with ground operations undermined the RAF's independent status. The air force preferred to keep its distance, metaphorically and physically. It would play its part by creating the circumstances in which battles on the ground could be won, rather than actually taking part in and helping to win these battles. In this way airpower could maintain its separate identity. Indeed, with typical air force swagger, success in independent air superiority and interdiction campaigns was elevated to the status of preconditions for army success on land. It was a rather watered down version of Smuts's original vision, but it was still a vision in which airpower was the dominant and determining factor. Military success depended on air force success. The USAAF, with aspirations of independence, was more than happy to fall in line with these priorities and enshrined them in its latest FM 100-20 field manual.

With Brooke demanding a fatal weakening of German forces before an invasion of France was attempted, there was no guarantee this operation would take place even in 1944. There was still time for the bomber advocates to prove they had been right all along and an invasion was unnecessary. However, with Allied armies advancing on all fronts, time was running out. Harris was still trying to destroy Germany city by city and the Americans hoped to pick apart Germany industry by industry but there was a growing danger their efforts would be overtaken by events on the ground.

The outcome of the war might no longer be in doubt, but how it would be won was very much still in the balance. As the war entered its fifth year, there was much to ponder. The Air Ministry was already looking ahead and laying the foundation for a post-war defence policy. The realities of war had forced the Air Staff to temper their vision of the bomber as a decisive war-winning weapon, in public at least. Discussions within the Air Ministry reveal the true extent to which the current conflict was influencing thinking.

Chapter One

The Bomber Rules

In the summer of 1943, after three years of bombing, there was still no sign of Germany crumbling. Civilian casualties had been heavy but morale remained unbroken. Thousands of tons of bombs raining down on a country was bound to cause much disruption but it was manageable and German forces still had the means to fight fiercely and effectively on all fronts. In Britain, despite the setbacks and disappointments, an exaggerated assessment of what was being achieved ensured the bomber policy still had pride of place in the western Allies' war winning strategy. The Casablanca conference in January 1943 set out the Anglo-American plan for defeating Germany. As the Americans had always insisted, there would have to be an invasion of northern France, despite the claims of their own band of bomber advocates and their British counterparts. Brooke, however, wanted bombing to cause 'visible cracks' to appear in Germany's military edifice before any such operation was considered.[1] Meeting this requirement could only delay an invasion of France.

The Mediterranean was the only theatre where Allied forces in the west were in contact on the ground with the enemy. The Americans had never been enthusiastic about the British Mediterranean policy; they believed a major effort in Italy would divert more Allied than German resources. American army commanders were more enthusiastic about the value of a bombing campaign. The Allied plan was, to say the least, ambitious. The aims set out in May 1943 required an 89 per cent reduction in submarine production, 76 per cent in ball bearings, 65 per cent in bomber production, 43 per cent in fighter output, a 50 per cent reduction in synthetic rubber production and the elimination of nearly all tyre output. The emphasis was on air and naval targets. For a plan that was supposed to help defeat the German army, one might expect tanks to be more prominent but they were only mentioned in passing as an element of motor transport and there was no target percentage reduction.[2] Even so, if the planned reductions were achieved, no one would be able to dispute that the bomber offensive had indeed fatally weakened German capacity for armed resistance and this ought to translate into rapid advances on all fronts.

The Americans planned to achieve these ambitious goals by targeting key industries with precision daylight bombing. Harris, the intractable commander of Bomber Command, had never believed bombing specific economic targets would achieve much. He was convinced the war would be won by the wholesale destruction of factories, housing, communications and anything else that could be destroyed. As the aim was to maximise total destruction, residential zones in big cities made the most attractive targets as all bombs dropped had a good chance of destroying something. Aiming at individual factories in the outskirts of cites would just result in too many bombs falling harmlessly in open countryside. The aim was to maximise destruction and not to worry too much about what was being destroyed. This indiscriminate approach was the Air Staff policy Harris had been appointed to implement and he had no doubt it would eventually break the German will and destroy the means to continue the struggle.

Air Chief Marshal Charles Portal, the British Chief of Air Staff, put a gloss on this area bombing policy by arguing that a third of German industry would be destroyed in the process. By a different route, the argument went, British bombing had the same objective as their American ally's. It was putting a very positive spin on British objectives. While the Americans' target figures involved German production, the British figures included people. Portal believed the bombing would kill 900,000 Germans, seriously wound another million and make 25 million homeless by December 1944. Portal considered these conservative estimates. No account, he emphasised, had been taken of the way the death toll in raids would accelerate as the average number of people occupying the surviving inhabitable buildings increased.[3] There was no doubting the ruthlessness of the policy.

The British warned the Americans that bombing by day was prohibitively expensive and, with Churchill in the vanguard, wanted the Americans to throw their lot in with Bomber Command's nocturnal area offensive. Roosevelt was close to conceding the point but an impassioned plea from Major General Ira Eaker, the commander of the American Eighth Air Force in Britain, won over the British prime minister. The idea of a 'round the clock' bombing offensive, the Americans by day and the British by night, that gave the enemy no respite, appealed to Churchill. Although this gave the bombing plan a superficial unity, operational and ideological difference meant the two bomber forces were rarely attacking the same target. The two bomber fleets were essentially going their own way.

In early 1943 the extent to which the bomber offensive was failing was not clear but it was clear that the offensive was not going to plan. The German fighter force was inflicting heavy losses on both American and British bomber fleets. Before setting about the more general reduction in German arms output outlined at the Casablanca conference, something had to be done to reduce bomber losses. The Pointblank directive, issued in June 1943, addressed this problem. It required as its primary aim,

> the progressive destruction and dislocation of the German military industrial and economic system and the undermining of the morale of the German people to the point where their capacity for armed resistance is fatally weakened[4]

The undermining morale element had been included at the insistence of the British Air Staff. After listing the key industries that needed to be bombed to fatally weaken the capacity for armed resistance, the directive added, as an 'intermediate objective', the German fighter force. This would have to be neutralised before the bomber force set to work on its main task.

The neutralisation of the German fighter would be achieved principally by bombing. American bombers would attempt precision attacks on fighter factories and any industries associated with fighter production. The latter included ball-bearing production. This had been identified as a major bottleneck with German industry heavily reliant on the factories based in Schweinfurt. Bomber Command was supposed to focus its efforts on area targets with a high concentration of fighter related industries. The problem for Harris was that these were sometimes relatively small towns like Schweinfurt where it was easy to miss the town completely. Harris always found reasons for not attacking such targets; they were either too far, defences were too strong or the weather was never right. He saw German morale as his target and saw no need to focus on any particular industry. He intended to go straight for the jugular with a direct attack on the German people. Harris's only contribution to the intermediate aim would be any fighter related targets that by chance happened to be in the area he had chosen to flatten.

The hope was that the effectiveness of the German fighter force would be reduced to manageable proportions by October 1943. From this point the American bombers would continue the offensive against the fighter industry, but would also be able to turn their attention to the main Pointblank targets. From October onwards it was expected the German fighter force would go into a dramatic decline until, by 1 April 1944, front-line fighter strength on all fronts would be down from the 3,000 fighters Allied intelligence knew the Germans were aiming for, to a mere 650. The main attack would be conducted by unescorted bombers. To distract the defences, escorted raids by fifty bombers against shorter range targets would coincide with the entry and exit of the main force into and out of enemy air space. The Americans were confident that, once daylight raids with around 200 bombers could be mounted, the defensive firepower of the main force would be too much for the defending fighters. No long-range fighter escorts were contemplated.[5]

American air force commanders, like Harris, found the war had a habit of getting in the way of their plans. In late 1942, just when the Eighth Air Force in the UK was building up a reasonable front-line strength, a large part was re-assigned to Operation Torch, the invasion of North-West Africa. With the bombers went the Lockheed P-38 Lightning fighters to escort them. Operations in North Africa were soon confirming that these escorts were needed. American commanders had to hope they were right that larger bomber formations would overwhelm defences. It seemed just as indisputably obvious to the Americans, as it had to the British and Germans, that, given the same technology, any escort fighter weighed down by extra fuel would struggle against the short-range interceptors it was supposed to deal with.

This might seem logical enough but, as the Japanese were demonstrating in the Far East, it was a flawed argument that was becoming more flawed with time. As the cruising speeds of fighters increased, so did the distance they could fly for any given endurance. Flying further was only going to get easier; time was always going to be on the side of the long-range escort fighter. Drop tanks were an instant way of enabling them to fly further. In the Far East drop tanks were enabling Japanese fighters to operate over huge distances. These could be made of any non-strategic material – wood, bamboo, even papier-mâché – and once dropped the fighter returned to its normal loaded condition. These encumbrances had to be dropped before engaging an enemy, so internal fuel had to be used for combat and the return flight. Internal fuel therefore determined radius of action in an escort role. As a rule of thumb, the external fuel could only be about two-thirds of internal fuel. Japanese long-range operations often involved flying over uncontested oceans, rather than heavily defended enemy airspace, which meant the aircraft could fly at very low but highly economical cruising speeds. Even so, the distances they were flying were impressive and an embarrassed Portal found himself struggling to explain to Churchill why RAF fighters could not do the same.[6]

American fighters tended to carry more internal fuel than British fighters but like the British, the Americans had not even attempted to build a fighter that could go all the way with the long-range bomber. The Thunderbolt could not fly much further than the Spitfire. The twin-engined Lightning could do better but could still not penetrate very far into Germany. If the bombers could not defend themselves, it would mean vast areas of Germany would be out of reach, in daylight at least.

The disastrous Schweinfurt raids still lay in the future but the writing was already on the wall. On 13 June 1943 twenty-two out of sixty American bombers were lost attacking Kiel.[7] The size of the formation was nowhere near the 200-strong force the Americans believed was necessary but, even so, it was scarcely encouraging. British calculations had suggested any loss rate above 5 per cent would be difficult to sustain over time. The loss rate on the Kiel raid was approaching 40 per cent. The heavy losses already being suffered were enough for General Henry Arnold, commander of the USAAF and an inveterate bomber advocate, to order something be done to enable fighters to escort bombers all the way. The manufacturers insisted it was impossible. Extra internal fuel tanks would affect handling characteristics and drop tanks were dangerous accessories to carry in combat zones. Arnold brushed aside these objections and the manufacturers were told to get on with it.[8]

The losses the American day bombers were suffering may have been no more than the Air Ministry had predicted, but it was no time for any smugness. After his early scepticism, Portal, who was responsible for overseeing the Allied combined bomber offensive, had decided that the Eighth Air Force had done enough to prove that precision bombing by day was possible. Portal had not really been converted; he had no intention of following the American example and switching Bomber Command to daylight operations. It was just that Portal needed the Americans to be right. His scheme for crushing Germany required a force of four to six thousand heavy bombers and Portal was hoping the Americans would provide two-thirds of them. He was willing to believe anything that gave the bomber offensive a chance of succeeding. Portal was therefore every bit as frustrated as American commanders about the diversion of American resources to North Africa and delays in making good combat losses. By the end of June 1943, he pointed out, deliveries to the Eighth Air Force were already 20 per cent down on what had been planned and by the end of September they would be nearly 30 per cent down.

> If we do not now strain every nerve to bring enough force to bear to win this battle during the next two or three months, but are content to see the 8th Bomber Command hampered by lack of reinforcements just as success is within its grasp, we may well miss the opportunity to win a decisive victory against the German Air Force which will have incalculable effects on all future operations and on the length of the war.[9]

The idea that success was 'within grasp' of the Eighth Air Force was somewhat optimistic. Losses had already been heavy and with the German decision in the late summer of 1943 to begin pulling back more fighter units from the front lines to strengthen home defence, they were likely to get heavier. On 17 August 1943, a couple of days after Portal's appeal, the Eighth Air Force suffered shattering losses attacking the Schweinfurt ball-bearing plants and the Regensburg Messerschmitt factory. A total of 230 bombers set off for Schweinfurt, of which 188 bombed their targets. This was the sort of formation that was supposed to overwhelm the defences. Instead it was the Fortresses that were overwhelmed. As soon as their Thunderbolt escorts turned back, the German fighters tore into the American bombers. Even lumbering night-fighters were thrown into the assault. Thirty-six of the Fortresses attacking the ball-bearing plants were lost.

The 146 bombers that set off for Regensburg surprised the defences by continuing to fly south once they had dropped their bombs, heading for airfields in North Africa. The German defences were indeed wrong-footed but still claimed twenty-four American bombers on the approach to the Messerschmitt factories. Overall, 20 per cent of the attacking bombers were shot down. The Luftwaffe lost forty-two single and twin-engined fighters. A downed Flying Fortress meant the loss of ten crewmen. German aircrew baling out were soon back with their squadron. The Luftwaffe lost around twenty aircrew compared to more than 550 lost by the Americans.[10] Ball-bearing production, so key to so many armaments, not just aircraft, was reduced by a worrying third but there were sufficient stocks in stores to tide the Germans over until production was restored. Indeed, the huge stocks held by various companies came as a surprise to the German authorities.[11] Allied planners would have been equally taken aback. For precision bombing to work, knowing where the enemy is vulnerable is vital, which inevitably involves a degree of guesswork. If German planners did not know about the extensive reserves held by German companies, it is hardly surprising Allied planners were unaware. The raid on the Messerschmitt factories seemed to cause German leaders less concern. Production was temporarily reduced, but again the recovery was speedy.[12] It was a decisive victory for the Luftwaffe, not the Eighth Air Force.

The Eighth Air Force did not return to German skies until 6 September. It proved to be another inauspicious mission. A total of 338 Fortresses attempted to bomb an instruments factory in Stuttgart but heavy cloud cover meant the raid was totally ineffective. Even if the defences could be overcome, European weather would often provide a last line of defence. Again, losses were heavy, forty-five bombers were lost, twenty of which had to ditch or crash-land after running out of fuel.

To get round the weather problem the Americans were forced to acquire H2S blind-bombing equipment from the British. This was first tried in an attack on Emden on 27 September, with formations dropping their bombs on a signal from the H2S-equipped lead bomber, and follow-up formations unloading their bombs on the markers dropped. Effectively the Americans were using Bomber Command nocturnal tactics by day. There appeared to be little point in exposing the bombers to daylight interception if they were bombing blind anyway. Around this time a Fortress unit began investigating the problems of operating by night by joining in several Bomber Command raids. Harris might yet get his way.

By this time the first improvised efforts were being made to increase fighter range. In July 1943 P-47 Thunderbolts began using rather clumsy 200-gallon ferry tanks. These were not intended for combat use; they could not be used above 23,000 feet and seriously reduced performance so had to be dropped before entering enemy air space. However, half-filled, they enabled the Thunderbolts to reach the enemy coast without using any internal fuel. In August an American 62-gallon metal drop tank and in September two British developed 90-gallon tanks, one metal the other papier-mâché, became available, although for some time the American tanks remained the mainstay until British production could meet demand.[13] The American tank enabled the Thunderbolts to fly almost as far as Bremen (345 miles) and the British tanks took them just beyond Bremen (375 miles). Larger drop tanks were on the way, but the petrol-guzzling Thunderbolt would never be able to carry the huge fuel load it required to fly all the way with the bombers.

While manufacturers in the United States investigated what else might be possible, the day bombers persevered as best they could. In October the Americans tried another deep penetration mission, with 300 bombers returning to the Schweinfurt ball-bearing plants. It was another show of strength, with well in excess of the number the Americans hoped would prove too much for the defending fighters. Again it was a disaster. No fewer than sixty were shot down for the loss of twenty-two defending fighters. Above key battlefields on all fronts the German fighter force was finding it increasingly difficult to make much impression on the growing Allied air forces it faced but against attacks deep inside the Reich it could still make its presence felt.

To the Germans it seemed anything could shoot down the lumbering American bombers. Once again even night-fighters had been able to play their part. New ways of maintaining this dominance were being investigated. From close range, hefty 30mm cannon only required two or three hits to bring down a bomber. From outside the range of the bomber's formidable defensive fire, twin-engined fighters could lob rockets into the American formations and trials were taking place with long-range 50mm cannon. The Blohm und Voss aircraft company suggested a small, cheap, glider, armed with two cannon. This could be towed above the bomber formations from where it would be able to pick up sufficient speed to attack. With no engine and the pilot, lying in a prone position, the small frontal area would make it a difficult target for the American gunners. Substantial armour provided further protection. Without any fighter escort to worry about, all these ideas were perfectly practicable.

While the Americans struggled, Harris believed he was well on the way to winning the war without any need to worry about any 'intermediate objectives'. In July Harris was able to use Window, metal strips dropped from bombers that gave the same radar reflection as a bomber. These had completely confused German defences, enabling his bombers to devastate Hamburg with minimal losses. The raid had seen the first appearance of the firestorm phenomenon. The heat generated by fires in the target area was so great that a chimney effect was created with a rising column of hot air sucking in the surrounding air at hurricane force speeds to feed and intensify the blaze. Firestorms, however, were not something that Bomber Command could reproduce at will. Even the heaviest concentration of incendiaries and bombs will not guarantee a firestorm.

After the 40,000 killed in Hamburg, the next major raid on a German target, Mannheim on the night of 9/10 August, caused widespread damage but there was no firestorm and only 269 people died. Nevertheless, the damage on this raid and others looked impressive enough in the photo-reconnaissance images and it seemed reasonable to assume that it must be having an effect on German output and morale. Harris's blunt, uncompromising and often outlandish claims for his bomber offensive were bound to attract all the attention but he was only articulating what many in the Air Ministry were thinking. The reality of crucial battles taking place on sea and land was forcing Portal to adopt a more balanced approach in which the bomber offensive was merely an important element in the overall Allied war-winning strategy. Nevertheless, he, and many others, still hoped that the bomber would achieve much more than this.

Portal was keen for Harris to try to do to Berlin what he had done to Hamburg. It was a big ask. Berlin was a much larger city. It was much further away so it would be more difficult to find and bomb loads would be much reduced. An attack on the capital was also bound to provoke a fierce response. So it proved on the night of 23/24 August when some 727 bombers set course for Berlin. Fifty-six failed to return, a loss rate of nearly 8 per cent. It was the highest number of bombers lost so far in a single night. Although the bombing was scattered and inaccurate, 900 civilians were killed, a figure which included one hundred foreign workers. Berliners seemed taken by surprise. The relatively high death toll was attributed to far too many failing to seek the protection of air raid shelters.[14]

On 31 August/1 September Harris tried again. Over 600 bombers set off and forty-seven failed to return, a 7.6 per cent loss rate. The bombing was again inaccurate and it would seem the local population were more prudent as there were only sixty-six fatalities. This loss compared to over 300 missing aircrew. The Halifax and Stirling squadrons were suffering especially heavy losses and for the next attack on 3/4 September, only Lancasters took part. In fact it made little difference to the loss rate. Twenty-two of the 316 Lancasters (7 per cent) failed to return. Another 400 Berliners were killed. It was proving very difficult to replicate the Hamburg success. Harris decided to suspend the attacks on Berlin until an improved version of H2S and another navigational aid, the Ground Position Indicator, became available. The former, H2S Mark III, used 3-centimetre wavelength instead of 10-centimetre, which provided a much sharper representation of the terrain below. The latter was a development of the dead reckoning Air Position Indicator, which fed wind speeds into the calculation. There was no shortage of technical innovation to help the bomber crews.

Harris was convinced that all his problems would be resolved if his entire force could be equipped with Lancasters, but even his favoured bomber was beginning to struggle. In truth the Lancaster could not fly much faster or much higher than the Stirling and Halifax and, like them, had no defence to attack from below. This lack of ventral defence was becoming a major problem. Originally, it had been planned to mount ventral turrets on the Lancaster and Halifax but this idea had been dropped partly because of the difficulties designing an efficient ventral turret and partly because it was thought attack from this direction was unlikely. Mosquito pilots, however, had demonstrated how easy it was for a night-fighter to approach the Lancaster from below without being seen and there was growing evidence that the German night-fighter force was using this tactic. Indeed, German fighters were diving below the bomber and then climbing and shooting as they climbed before breaking away.

A climbing attack with forward-firing guns was not an easy manoeuvre to perform. Attacking from below would be much easier if the guns were fixed to fire upwards. From the spring of 1943 a small number of German fighters had been experimenting with vertically-mounted guns. So successful were they, the Bf 110, Ju 88 and Do 217 night-fighters were all equipped with guns firing upwards at an angle of 60 to 70 degrees. With this weapon it was simply necessary to fly parallel and lower than the bomber. The 60-70-degree angle, rather than 90-degree, made it easier to follow evasive manoeuvres and also reduced the risk of being hit by debris from the disintegrating bomber. It was virtually impossible for the rear gunner to spot these attacks. In his cramped turret with guns and other equipment, any view was fairly rudimentary but the rotation mechanism required by a powered turret made any downward view particularly limited. Nor could the guns be depressed more than 45 degrees.

Interceptors with upward-firing guns was scarcely a new idea. British pilots had used them in the First World War against Zeppelins and aeroplanes. Interceptors like the Defiant had a turret specifically to enable the fighter to attack a bomber from any angle. The Air Ministry, however, seemed determined to believe that attacking from below would never occur to the Germans. The Air Ministry and Air Force commanders were very good at ignoring the obvious if it was convenient to do so. In an analysis of sixty-two aircraft hit by intercepting fighters, Portal pointed out that only one attack came from below 35 degrees and the vast majority came from between the horizontal and 10 degrees below.[15] It was a result that was somewhat skewed by the absence of those bombers unable to be part of the study because they had been shot down by far more effective attacks from below.

Harris insisted something be done about the problem and some sort of downward-firing gun was an obvious solution. To avoid major modifications, existing holes in the structure of the fuselage had to be used to poke the gun through. In the case of the Halifax and Lancaster these were, ironically, the positions the dispensed-with ventral turret had been going to occupy. In the Stirling the rear escape hatch was used. Plans were hurriedly drawn up for a single 0.5 inch gun to fire downward. The Stirling installation was approved in July 1943 and introduced on the production line in October. Harris raged at the delay in getting similar mountings approved for the Lancaster and Halifax, but by November production drawings for the Lancaster modification had been released and by the New Year all Halifaxes coming off the production lines could mount a ventral gun.[16]

However, in practice hardly any bombers ever carried the gun. The increasing production of H2S radar sets meant there would soon be enough for most bombers to be equipped with this priceless navigational aid. This also needed a natural hole in the aircraft structure. Without a major re-design the bomber could not carry H2S radar and the downward-firing gun. The few bombers that tried out the new gun mounting found the view was poor, the position cramped and the sight vibrated so much it was virtually impossible to aim the weapon. With Monica rearward-pointing radars giving some warning of approaching enemy fighters, there was always the option of violent evasive manoeuvres to shake the enemy fighter off, which made aiming the gun even more difficult. If the crews were given the choice of H2S or the ventral gun they preferred the former. The fear of getting lost over Germany was still greater than the fear of being shot down. The ventral gun was officially abandoned in April 1944.[17]

There would be less need for the ventral gun if the rear turret guns could be depressed more than the 45 degrees possible with the current Fraser-Nash FN20 design. A better view for the rear gunner would also be handy. The FN20 rear turret was going to be followed by the FN121, another four-gun turret that would use the blind-firing Village Inn gun-laying system. This used a radar dish that rotated with the turret to detect the enemy interceptor, with the radar-generated dot identifying the target reflected onto the gun-sight. The range would be indicated by the length of a horizontal bar running through the dot; the wider the bar, the closer the enemy fighter was. To the gunner it looked like the dot had sprouted wings and indeed, with expanding 'wings', it looked like an approaching fighter. The gunner used the gun-sight in the normal way; once the 'wings' filled the gun-sight ring, the enemy plane was within range.

The system would enable enemy fighters to be engaged long before they came within visual range and before they could occupy the blind spot below the bomber. It was hoped this would reach the squadrons in 1944 but it was extremely advanced technology and was still very much at the development stage. There was, for instance, in 1943 still no clear idea how friendly aircraft would identify themselves. If the problems could be resolved, Village Inn made the gunner's view and the depression angle less of a problem.[18] If it did not work, a better view would still be needed. A two-gun rear turret was being developed to provide this but given the choice of four guns and a poor view or two guns and a better view, Harris considered the former was the lesser of two evils.[19]

All these options used rifle-calibre machine guns, which had been considered inadequate even before the war. In 1939 there were pessimists who feared Bomber Command might enter 1943 still relying on the 0.303-inch guns. As it turned out, Bomber Command was going to enter 1944 relying on them, and indeed the plan was to continue using them for some time. The Air Ministry had done its best to play down the advantages of heavier calibre machine guns. With their lower rate of fire and the lower number of rounds that could be carried, it was argued they gave gunners less chance of hitting an enemy fighter.[20] There was perhaps a degree of wishful thinking in this analysis but it was true that even heavy calibre machine guns lacked the range of the enemy cannon, so they were scarcely a complete solution. Switching to heavy machine guns would also have implications for the bomber's offensive capabilities. The 0.5-inch Browning machine gun weighed three times as much as the 0.303 version. Replacing the eight guns of a Lancaster meant an additional 300lbs, which meant correspondingly less fuel or bomb load. This was probably the more significant disadvantage in Air Ministry minds.

Harris was determined to get his crews heavy machine guns. Two 0.5-inch Brownings delivered about the same weight of fire as four rifle-calibre guns, though with a much lower combined rate of fire. Two guns meant a less cluttered turret so there were advantages purely in terms of view and there was no reason why they could not be used with Village Inn. Fraser Nash were working on their FN82 turret with two heavy machine guns, but like all Fraser Nash designs, the guns would only depress through 45 degrees. Harris wanted the angle of depression increased to 60 degrees and was none too pleased when told the modifications needed would require a complete re-design, delaying the introduction of the turret by six months. Harris fumed at the way commanders were never consulted about what they needed until it was too late to do anything about it.[21] Harris turned to the Rose brothers, a small Lincolnshire company that had helped him out in the past, and they came up with a turret with twin heavy machine guns and the 60-degree depression he wanted. This was eventually ordered but it could not reach the squadrons until well into 1944.

A more drastic suggestion was to do away with the rear turret completely. The value of the tail turret, with its lonely occupant, provoked fierce debate. Allied propaganda rather unkindly suggested that German bomber crews had to be grouped closely together in the main cockpit, as they needed the reassuring presence of their comrades to sustain their morale. It was, however, a very practical arrangement for that very reason. The plight of the hapless British rear gunner was truly grim, isolated from the rest of his crew, left to ponder his fate for many hours as he peered into the darkness that engulfed him in the hope of making out the outline of an approaching fighter. If he spotted one he would have to do his best to fend off his cannon-armed opponent with his rifle-calibre machine guns. If his bomber was crippled. he had the task, easy in theory, not so easy in practice, of extracting himself from the confined turret he occupied.

The tail turret had always been a contentious issue. The weight of the turret, rotation mechanism and gunner so far to the rear was a headache for designers. So great were the disadvantages, before the war it had been decided that no future bombers would have one. Revised versions of the Manchester and Halifax with no tail but dorsal and ventral cannon turrets were drawn up but these proposals came to nothing. Given all the problems with the restricted field of fire and view, there was a strong case for just removing the tail turret. The weight saved would enable the plane to fly higher and faster and at least every lost bomber would involve one fewer casualty.

As a compromise, Harris was attracted by the idea of replacing the turret with a simple Perspex covering. The warning the gunner could provide was, he suggested with much justification, far more important than any defence he could provide. A couple of hand-held machine guns would provide a token defence but, more importantly, the gunner would have a much better view. The Air Ministry approved and it was decided that the Stirling, Halifax, Wellington and Lancaster bombers, in that order, would be so modified. However, no sooner had the plan been approved than protests from squadron commanders and complaints from the MAP (Ministry of Aircraft Production) that it was too complicated a change to make resulted in the idea being dropped. There was plenty of debate about bomber defence and no shortage of ideas, but very little end result.

Bomber defence was just one problem area. For some time British bomber design had been losing its way. The bombers available to Bomber

Command had their origins in specifications released in 1936. By the standards of the day, the bombers that emerged were not particularly advanced. For far too long the Air Ministry had a rather exaggerated idea about how good they were. In late 1939 the Air Ministry wanted to send a Short Stirling to the United States to give American designers an idea of what they should be striving for. At the time the USAAF were drawing up a specification that would lead to the Boeing B-29 Superfortress. Quite what the USAAF Air Staff and the Boeing design team would have made of the Stirling as a template for future bomber design can only be imagined.

Even the realisation that the Manchester and Halifax were incapable of flying the day missions they were designed for did not set alarm bells ringing. The unsatisfactory Manchester was rescued by its conversion into the reliable four-engined Lancaster. It was popular with crews, manoeuvrable for its size and could carry more bombs further than the Halifax and Stirling. This was enough for it to be rated by the Air Ministry as an outstanding design. In truth, it was only excellent by comparison with what had gone before. A 280mph bomber that struggled to reach 20,000 feet entering service in 1942 was scarcely a sensational performer. The Lancaster's poor service ceiling meant it could not fly above the worst of German flak and crews had no choice but to fly though a lot of very unfriendly weather. With its poor defensive armament, it was no more suitable for the day missions it was designed to fly than its predecessors.

Even by night it was scarcely ideal. A cruising speed of little more than 200mph meant it spent far too long in enemy air space and its top speed was inadequate to escape even some of the more makeshift night-fighters the Luftwaffe was using. It flew lower and slower and had nothing like the defensive fire-power of the American B-17E Flying Fortress, which entered service around the same time. Its one outstanding asset, compared to the Flying Fortress, was that it carried more and heavier bombs. For an Air Ministry anxious to accelerate the destruction of Germany, this outweighed all the aircraft's disadvantages. Far from being a world-leading design, the Lancaster was more a measure of how far behind Britain was slipping in the bomber development stakes.

By the time the Lancaster reached the squadrons, the Americans were preparing their B-29 for its maiden flight and it was already pencilled in to production schedules. Its 358mph top speed and 32,000-feet service ceiling was far better than the Lancaster could manage. It could carry 20,000lbs of bombs over a range of 3,250 miles compared to the 14,000lbs of the Lancaster over 1,660 miles. The Boeing bomber was at least one generation ahead of anything the British had flying and indeed it was more advanced than anything the British had on the drawing board. It was going to reach American squadrons just two years after the Lancaster had entered service. The even mightier six-engine Convair B-36 intercontinental bomber with a 10,000-mile range was set to follow. There might be doubts about the operational practicality and cost effectiveness of such monstrous bombers but there was an impressive, progressive continuity about American heavy bomber development.

Britain's aircraft industry had no such grandiose projects. For a country that set such store in the long-range strategic bomber, the story of British bomber development is a far from happy one. The seven years that had passed since the release of the specifications that led to the Stirling/Halifax/ Lancaster generation seemed long enough for a new generation to be in the pipeline. Higher speeds, greater service ceiling and better defensive armament were all urgently needed, even when bombing under cover of darkness. However, after a spate of specifications for improved bombers between 1932 and 1936, in the years that followed there was very little designers could work on as the Air Ministry struggled to work out where strategic bomber design should go next.

In 1938 the Air Ministry had spent much time trying to decide what the 'Ideal Bomber' of the future should be capable of. It was agreed that bombers had to be defended by cannon rather than machine guns, and would need armour protection, but each attempt to formulate a specification just ended in a hopeless compromise that offered no real improvement over existing designs. Specification B.1/39 was released then withdrawn then re-released, but designs never got further than models.

Attempts made to update existing designs had equally little success. The B.8/41 Super Stirling envisaged a massive 100,000lb bomber which could carry 22,000lbs of bombs over short distances and 10,000lbs over a range of 2,300 miles.[22] This scaled-up Stirling would be powered by four mighty 2,000hp Bristol Centaurus engines. The engines, however, failed to deliver the predicted power at altitude. Flying at lower altitudes meant greater vulnerability, so, to compensate, over 9,000lbs of extra armour and defensive armament was added. By this time the aircraft's predicted performance was little better than the original Stirling. Work on the project was abandoned in the summer of 1942.[23]

The Warwick was supposed to be a scaled-up more powerful Wellington. The Napier Sabre or Bristol Centaurus engines were lined up to power it but, with both hitting development problems, a first batch of 250, hastily ordered in December 1940 seven months before the first prototype flew, had to make do with American Pratt and Whitney radials. With these engines, the bomber was seriously underpowered, incapable of maintaining height on one engine and completely useless for Bomber Command. Those in production were converted to Coastal Command reconnaissance aircraft or transports.

The 1941 B.5/41 requirement for a high-altitude pressurised bomber was supposed to provide a fresh start. One response was the Vickers Windsor, a radical upgrade of the Vickers geodetic bomber family with a pressurised crew cabin and powered by four Merlin 60 engines. This was expected to be capable of 345mph at 31,000 feet with an 8,000lb bomb load and have a range of 2,350 miles with a 6,000lb bomb load. In terms of lifting capability, this was broadly similar to the Lancaster, but the bomber would be capable of flying faster and some 10,000 feet higher. However, with a proposed rear turret with four 0.303 machine guns, the design was scarcely meeting the growing demand for more defensive firepower.[24]

Specification B.3/42 tried to take the development of the long-range bomber forward by proposing a rear turret with two 20mm cannon and the Windsor was now adapted to meet this requirement. The eventual aim was for all defence to be conducted by twin 20mm cannon mounted in the rear of the outer engine nacelles and controlled by a gun-layer in the tail. Placing the gunner and the guns he controlled at different parts of the bomber eliminated the need for the bulky turrets which so characterised British bomber designs but it was another area of research the British were falling behind in. The Boeing B-29 already had excellent remotely-controlled gun turrets.

The Windsor was only expected to operate by night. The nose turret in the original proposal was considered unnecessary and dropped and the remotely-controlled armament of the Windsor only covered a 90-degree cone to the rear. The bomber's 330mph cruising speed was supposed to make interception from any angle other than the rear impossible.[25] No one seemed too discouraged by the fact that this line of logic had failed so often in the past and indeed the mounting evidence that German night-fighters were already bypassing defences that could only fire rearwards. Nor were the remotely-controlled guns particularly successful.[26] Even so, before the Windsor prototype flew, the Air Ministry had the bomber pencilled in for production with entry into service expected in 1945.

The expected speed put it in the same category as the American Boeing B-29 but in terms of range there was no comparison. The Air Ministry were only expecting the Windsor to reach enemies as close as Germany. The Americans, on the other hand, were working on the intercontinental Convair B-36, which would be able to bomb targets in Europe from the United States. Even German efforts in the long-range bomber field were putting British efforts to shame. At this time developing a long-range strategic bomber force was not a German priority, but in December 1942 the impressive Me 264 with a range of over 9,000 miles took to the air. The Air Ministry was not even speculating in these terms, even though these were the sort of ranges the RAF required to strike enemies as distant as the current enemy Japan from friendly bases.

With the failure of the Warwick, it seemed Vickers had to keep building the obsolescent Wellington until the Windsor could replace it on the assembly lines. Even then, there would be problems with the changeover. A target conscious MAP was aware that the Wellington was making a significant contribution to the bomb tonnage current production could deliver, even though the Wellington was a fast fading factor in the bomber offensive against Germany. Introducing the Windsor would cause a considerable drop in this bomb tonnage figure in 1944, followed by an even greater reduction in 1945, before breaking even in 1946. A shortage of Merlin engines ruled out replacing the Wellington with the current version of the Lancaster, but a Hercules-powered version (Lancaster II) could replace the Wellington earlier than the Windsor. This would involve a greater initial loss in bomb load in 1944, but would break even in 1945 and show a substantial profit in 1946.[27] This, however, meant persisting with the Lancaster as a front-line bomber into 1946 and beyond, a somewhat worrying prospect. It might also have worried some that bomb-dropping capability in 1946 was a consideration. It was scarcely a sign that victory through bombing was just around the corner.

As an alternative, Avro came up with a Lancaster replacement which involved upgrading the basic Lancaster airframe to take four 2,000hp engines. The MAP were not overly impressed with this proposal which, despite Avro's claims to the contrary, they believed would essentially be an entirely new design. The Avro design team were already heavily involved modifying the Lancaster to carry torpedoes as well as adapting it as a transport as the Avro York and the MAP did not believe they had the resources to tackle a complete Lancaster makeover as well.[28]

A more basic upgrade of the Lancaster by replacing the Merlin XX with the Merlin 61 would bring more immediate benefit with far less effort and disruption. This became the Lancaster IV, later renamed the Lincoln.

This ought to provide a 60mph increase in cruising speed with the same bomb load and a much higher ceiling but ventral defence would at best comprise just a single machine gun. Another option under consideration was to build the American Boeing B-29 under licence.[29] This took to the air in September 1942 and was faster than the Lincoln's predicted speed. The bomber's remotely-controlled 0.5-inch guns in two ventral and two dorsal turrets, with a cannon in the tail, provided the comprehensive all-round defence the Lancaster lacked. That a foreign design was even being considered for a type that was so central to Air Staff policy gives an indication of how far behind bomber development in the UK had managed to slip.

None of these proposals looked particularly attractive. The Boeing B-29 was clearly the most advanced option, but anglicising it for production in Britain would not be straightforward and, even assuming no problems arose, bombers would not start coming off the production line until the middle of 1946. The earliest the Windsor could possibly arrive was slipping back to April 1945 and the Merlin 61 Lancaster would not be available much earlier. All the options meant a short-term loss in bomber output and bomb-lifting capacity, a loss Bomber Command could not afford. The bomber policy was already pushing Britain's resources to the limit. Available production capacity was struggling to meet existing targets; there was no slack in the system to absorb the disruption introducing new models would involve.

Yet it seemed a new design would have to be introduced. The MAP feared the Lancaster would be obsolete by mid-1945. If the war went on longer than this and the RAF was still relying on the Lancaster, Bomber Command might find itself in serious trouble. The MAP's preferred option was the Windsor. The Lancaster IV, it was claimed, would not meet many of the requirements of the B.3/42 specification. Armour would only give protection against machine-gun fire and it would only have machine-gun rear defence, possibly 0.5 inch but equally possibly the old four 0.303-inch armament. The Air Ministry too favoured the Windsor option. Portal believed a fresh start was needed rather than a tweaked Lancaster. Such an aircraft would have more development potential and, clutching at straws perhaps, there was always the chance of a 'fluke design' which vastly exceeded expectations.[30]

In truth, in terms of defensive armament or bomb load, neither the Lancaster IV nor the Windsor offered a substantial improvement over the existing Lancaster and, whichever was chosen, it would not be available until 1945. The options were not good. Bomber Command could continue with increasingly obsolete equipment, which would inevitably lead to higher losses, making it even more difficult to expand the bomber fleet. Alternatively, a new type could be introduced which would inevitably reduce production. Optimising quality and quantity is always a delicate balancing act. When a strategy is beyond the resources of a country it becomes an impossible balancing act.

Despite the problems developing suitable bombers, the huge cost and the operational difficulties encountered, faith in the bomber strategy remained undiminished. So strong was Air Staff faith it was already assumed the bomber strategy would dominate post-war defence thinking. In August 1942 a first attempt had been made to look beyond the current conflict. A new bomber would be required around 1947 when the Lancaster IV/Windsor generation would be coming to the end of their useful lives. An aircraft with a range of 2,500 miles capable of carrying an impressive twenty tons of bombs at a cruising speed of 300mph would be required. It was still a bomber with a western European war in mind; the range would not enable the aircraft to reach the Soviet Union's 1939 frontier. The emphasis was clearly on bomb load rather than range. A huge machine was envisaged with coupled engines buried in wings so thick crews would have access to the engines in flight.

By early 1943 the problems even Flying Fortresses, with their all-round defensive armament, were having underlined the folly of relying on rear defence only. All-round defensive armament would be required with fully-automated 40mm cannon for long-range defence and 20mm cannon providing close-in defence, all operated by automatic gun barbettes. The bomber would have to be capable of flying above bad weather, which meant a service ceiling of at least 25,000 feet.[31] In many respects the B-29 Superfortress the Americans were already testing was more advanced than the bomber the Air Ministry hoped to have in 1947.

The initial response from designers were proposals in the 200,000-320,000lb weight range. Power would be provided by the equivalent of up to sixteen Napier Sabre engines.[32] This would put the bomber in the same class as the Convair B-36. It was a huge jump for British designers to make, effectively skipping the B-29 generation. It was therefore agreed that work should proceed on a smaller bomber, weighing around 160,000lb (75 tons), very much in the B-29 class.[33] British designers would be embarking on the design of a type of bomber the Americans had already ordered into mass production. Short, Bristol and Vickers were a little more adventurous and came up with a range of bomber designs powered by up to eight engines and weighing as much as 220,000lb, between twice and three times heavier than a Lancaster. However, none of these bombers would be able to fly much further than the Lancaster, even though Japan was a very real reminder that not all Britain's enemies were as close to friendly bases as Germany.

Even Churchill was expressing concern about the state of British bomber development. In November 1943 the prime minister asked the MAP what they were doing about developing replacements for the Lancaster IV/Windsor generation and reminded them that the 120,000lb American Boeing B-29 could carry nine tons of bombs, was already in production and their projected 250,000lb Convair B-36 would carry 30 tons of bombs with a 'range' (presumably he meant radius of action) of 4,600 miles and suggested Britain should be developing something similar.[34] British bomber design seemed stuck in the doldrums, although arguably, the lack of ambition was merely recognition that Britain lacked the resources to match American efforts.

The Air Ministry did not have good short-term options nor were they developing the long-term ideas for progressing a policy that was at the heart of Air Staff war doctrine. The Air Ministry was still building its future bombers around the piston engine. The stuttering progress of the Gloster Meteor jet fighter scarcely encouraged thoughts of a long-range jet bomber, but 1947 was a long way in the future. As was the case with fighter development, the MAP was taking more interest in the jet option than the Air Ministry. The new axial flow Metropolitan–Vickers F.2 jet engines (the forerunner of the Armstrong Siddeley Sapphire) promised far better fuel economy, opening up the possibility of long-range jets. Towards the end of 1942 both Handley Page and Armstrong Whitworth were putting forward plans for tailless jet bombers. The MAP gave the go ahead for the Handley Page project, an impressive looking flying wing powered by eight Metropolitan-Vickers F.2 engines and capable of cruising at 500mph. Even this, however, did not appear to get any further than the project stage.[35] In September 1943 the MAP tried to chivvy the process along by suggesting specifications should be issued for a less ambitious 30,000lb jet bomber with a 1,000-mile range and an 80,000lb jet bomber with a 2,000-mile range, but nothing came of these proposals.[36] It was about this time that Boeing began design work on a 3,000-mile-range jet bomber that would eventually lead to the B-47 Stratojet.

Britain's ability to deliver a strategic bombing campaign was on a downward trajectory and there was nothing in the pipeline to halt the decline. The longer the war went on, the more ill-equipped Bomber Command

THE BOMBER RULES

would be. If Britain was serious about pursuing the strategic bombing policy post-war, it had some serious catching up to do. Britain was slipping so far behind in manned bomber design, the Air Ministry arguably needed not just to skip the next stage in manned bomber development, but to start thinking about unmanned delivery systems. This was not alien territory for Britain. In the twenties Britain had led the world in cruise missiles, or pilotless bombers as they were then known. In 1943 the Air Ministry was being reminded about this option by developments in Germany. These included Hitler's 'revenge weapons', indiscriminate long-range weapons with which Hitler planned to avenge the horrors Bomber Command was inflicting on the German population.

Chapter Two

The Shape of Wars to Come

The evidence that Germany was planning to open a pilotless jet-propelled aircraft and/or rocket offensive had been mounting for some time. A steady stream of reports caused sufficient concern for the Chiefs of Staff to recommend, in April 1943, that Duncan Sandys, from the Ministry of Supply, should be put in charge of the investigation into possible German secret weapons. Sandys had always been fascinated by the emerging rocket technology. He had more experience than most of rocket warfare, having been put in charge of one of the first anti-aircraft Z-batteries to carry out operational trials with unguided 3-inch anti-aircraft rockets. The investigation of the pilotless aircraft threat was passed to the Air Ministry as these had wings, while Sandys concentrated on the ballistic rocket. His Bodyline Committee began meeting in September 1943. One of its members was Alwyn Crow, who, as the Controller of Projectile Development at the Ministry of Supply, was in charge of British rocket development.

Rumours of long-range German rockets dated back to 1940. British intelligence was aware that Peenemunde was the German centre for rocket research. In May and June 1943 several Mosquito reconnaissance flights were flown over the research centre. In photographs taken on the sortie flown on 23 June the V-2 (A-4) rocket was spotted for the first time. The photographic evidence caused a huge controversy within the British scientific community. To most it seemed very likely that the Germans had developed a rocket capable of bombarding London but two influential voices disagreed – Crow and Lord Cherwell, Churchill's scientific advisor. Both were convinced it was quite impossible to develop such a weapon and that the reconnaissance photographs merely showed a large torpedo, a barrage balloon or, possibly, the whole thing was simply a German hoax.[1] Part of the problem was that it was assumed by the likes of Cherwell and Crow that the Germans would be using cordite-based solid fuel, which was not as efficient as liquid fuel and would mean a truly massive missile would be required to cover even the relatively short distance to London.

Crow perhaps should have known better. He was well aware of Goddard's work in the United States in the 1920s with rockets powered by petrol and liquid oxygen. In the mid-thirties Crow was already envisaging rockets whose trajectories took the projectile as high as 300 miles into space and as far as 500 miles.[2] These ideas never got further than sketchy outline proposals; there were far more urgent rocket projects to work on. With the spectre of the knockout blow dominating all decision taking, the immediate need was for much smaller anti-aircraft rockets, for which cordite was a perfectly satisfactory fuel. Nevertheless, the idea of a rocket that could fly 100 miles should not have seemed so far-fetched to Crow.

It did not help that research in Britain into liquid-fuelled rockets was only just getting underway. In response to a 1941 Ministry of Supply requirement for a substitute for cordite as a rocket fuel, Isaac Lubbock, working for the Asiatic Petroleum Company (a Shell subsidiary), had begun developing a small liquid-fuelled rocket, the LOP (Liquid Oxygen and Petrol) engine, later named Lizzie. The aim was a rocket to help get heavy bombers into the air and planned thrust was only around 2,000lbs. In 1943 small-scale experiments were underway but the first test runs of a full-scale engine were years in the future. There was no reason to suppose German progress was any more advanced. Crow was focusing all his efforts on developing solid-fuel rockets, so it was assumed the Germans would be doing the same.

Whatever its source of power, the object in the Peenemunde photos looked menacing, A misjudgement of the size of the object resulted in its weight being estimated at anything up to 80 tons and there were fears such an object falling on the capital might cause up to 4,000 casualties.[3] Cherwell, however, argued a single-stage rocket such as the one photographed could at best only reach 40 miles.[4] To reach London Crow suggested a 230-ton four-stage monster would be needed to deliver a seven-ton payload, a little more than a Lancaster bomb load, or a smaller 33-ton rocket which might deliver one ton.[5] It was not encouraging for the future development of a strategic offensive capability that one of Britain's leading rocket experts so readily dismissed the possibility of much smaller liquid-fuelled rockets having the same sort of range.

Despite Crow and Cherwell's scepticism, the possible consequences, should the Germans develop such a weapon, ensured the threat was taken very seriously. It was more than enough to revive all the old fears of London being flattened with staggering loss of life. To slow development of these new weapons, Harris was instructed to bomb Peenemunde. This was where a long-range bomber force came into its own; the research centre was a high-value target, the destruction of which might have serious consequences. The operation was delayed until mid-August to allow the deep penetration to take place with a little more protection from the lengthening nights. Nearly 600 bombers hit the relatively small target. A 'master bomber', as used in the Dambuster operation, was used to control the raid, directing approaching crews to particular targets. The residential area, rocket factory and research facilities were all hit. Damage was particularly heavy in the residential areas with 130 German scientists and engineers and 600 foreign labourers killed but many of the research facilities escaped major damage.

The raid was considered a success, so successful a follow-up American operation was deemed unnecessary. By the standards of the day the attack was a success, indeed a very reasonable attempt at precision night bombing. The destruction was not as great as believed at the time but the raid perhaps set the V-2 programme back a couple months.[6] Whether this counted as a success depends on whether the glass is viewed as half-empty or half-full. The bomber protagonists would have been bitterly disappointed by such a poor return. Nevertheless a delay of a few months was useful. For a bomber force intent on making a useful contribution to the war effort, rather than winning the war outright, the raid was a success.

Soon after the Peenemunde raid, firm evidence began arriving of another innovative weapon, a pilotless plane, the Fieseler Fi 103, which would become better known as the V-1 flying bomb. Unlike the sophisticated V-2 rocket, the V-1 was a basic, simple to build aircraft powered by a cheap pulse jet. An example had crashed on the island of Bornholm in the Baltic and photographs of the wreck were passed to London by the Danish resistance. Remarkably, British intelligence was able to eavesdrop on German radar stations tracking test flights from Peenemunde over the Baltic Sea. These revealed that that the missile flew at altitudes between 1,500 and 4,000 feet with a speed of around 400mph. It seemed the plan was to set up around a hundred catapult launching sites along the French coast, each capable of launching a missile every twenty minutes. It was estimated that just fifty to a hundred of these sites would be sufficient to destroy London.[7] In November 1943 a reconnaissance flight over Peenemunde revealed a small pilotless plane at the foot of a ramp next to a ski-shaped building. Similar arrangements had been photographed in northern France and, rather alarmingly, the number of these 'ski-sites' was fast approaching 100.

The pilotless plane was a much more believable threat than the ballistic missile simply because it was a technology the Air Ministry had pioneered in the twenties with its own Royal Aircraft Establishment Larynx flying bomb. It had been abandoned in the thirties mainly because at the time the Air Ministry was trying to move away from Trenchard's indiscriminate bombing policies. The Larynx could never be accurate enough for the precision bombing Trenchard's successors had in mind. In 1941, as RAF bombing became more indiscriminate, the idea was briefly revived with the proposal for jet-powered pilotless bombers guided by the GEE or Oboe navigational aids developed for conventional bombers. By this time, however, Britain was too committed to the manned approach to switch horses in mid-stream.[8] However, for a country not already committed to building large numbers of heavy bombers and looking for a cheap way of dispensing indiscriminate retaliation, unguided pilotless aircraft were ideal.

Meanwhile, Cherwell and Crow were in a decreasing minority in the dispute over whether Germany had developed a ballistic missile. In October 1943 Lubbock was invited by Duncan Sandys to study intelligence photographs of suspected rockets and asked if the sort of technology he was working on could be used to propel the objects photographed at Peenemunde toward London. Based on his own research and work he was aware of in the United States, he concluded that it could. The consensus in the scientific community agreed. Delivering five to fifteen tons of explosives over a distance of 130 miles and one to five tons up to 200 miles seemed feasible. Cherwell and Crow were not persuaded, but the rest of Duncan Sandys' committee concluded it was very possible for a single-stage missile powered by liquid fuels to reach London.[9]

It did not take long for the experts to start using the sort of flawed statistical analysis that had produced such exaggerated predicted death tolls for conventional bombing in pre-war days. In February 1941 a single 2½-ton German bomb dropped on Hendon had killed eighty-eight people, and, rather unsoundly from a statistical point of view, this incident was used to justify an expected 150 deaths for each rocket hitting London. It was assumed every missile launched would hit its target, just as in the interwar years it was assumed every bomber would find its target. The possible effects of technical unreliability, inaccuracy or counter-measures tended to be discounted. The result was a prediction that if the Germans launched one missile per hour, the monthly death toll would be over 100,000.[10] The prewar nightmare of a 'knockout blow' was back with a vengeance. Evidence was mounting that the Germans were ready to launch their new weapons. The ramps in northern France and the Cherbourg peninsula were being joined by more construction sites that seemed to have little to do with coastal defences and were menacingly situated equidistant from London and, rather worryingly for D-Day planners, Portsmouth and Southampton. The new structures were the huge V-2 storage bunkers and launching sites that the Germans were building. It seemed an assault on London could take place as early as the winter of 1943/44.

This was not welcome news for the British people or their government at a time when the danger of defeat had long since passed but an end to the war seemed as far away as ever. Bombing raids on Germany were suffering heavy losses by day and night and progress in the Mediterranean was slow. At least on the Home Front the RAF appeared to have the measure of the Luftwaffe. By day no deep penetrations had been attempted by German bombers since the summer of 1940. Towns on the south coast and, occasionally, targets further inland had been the victims of hit-and-run raids by German fighter-bombers, but even these were in decline in the summer of 1943. None were flown after July 1943. Defensively, Fighter Command day squadrons had very little to do.

Even by night the skies over Britain had become a dangerous place for German aircrews. From a shaky start in the winter of 1940/41, radar-equipped interceptors had become steadily more proficient. The arrival of centimetric radar (the interim AI Mark VII early in 1942 soon followed by the fully-developed AI Mark VIII) offered greater accuracy and range, especially at lower altitudes and the Mosquito had ample performance to deal with manned bombers. The Luftwaffe had been able to deliver some sharp blows during 1942 but by the summer of 1943 only a handful of sorties were being flown and, for the most part, to avoid the prowling Mosquitoes, the Luftwaffe was reduced, even by night, to hit-and-run raids on coastal targets. By late 1943, however, rumour was already rife among the war weary citizens of the United Kingdom that they might have to endure attack by aerial robots, for which the presence of Mosquitoes would be no disincentive.[11]

Hitler initially saw the V-weapons as ways of seeking revenge, a way of showing the German people their tormenters were also suffering. However, it was soon evolving into much more than simple revenge. Defeat in the Battle of Kursk had seen Germany's already fading chances of a decisive victory on land disappear. Like Churchill in similar circumstances in 1940, Hitler was willing to consider any semi-plausible alternative way of winning the war. The V-weapons began to take on the mantle of potential war winners, although, as was the case with Harris's terror offensive, there was no clear idea of the mechanism that would convert terror into surrender. The other strand in the Allied bomber offensive, the precision bombing of key economic targets, was also beginning to appeal to German minds. Albert Speer, in charge of German war production, was impressed by the Allied choice of targets, especially with their attacks on the Ruhr dams and the Schweinfurt ball-bearing plants. Indeed he was convinced the RAF and USAAF had missed an opportunity to bring about truly decisive results by not following up the initial raids on these targets.

In 1941 the failure of the Blitz to wreck the British economy or break the will of the British people had convinced Hitler that bombing alone could not defeat a nation. No evidence to the contrary had appeared since then. Indeed, with the boot on the other foot, even the horrendous destruction of Hamburg had not forced Hitler to consider surrender. Desperation, however, can distort reason. With hindsight it is clear that at this stage of the war the Allied bomber offensive was not justifying the huge quantities of resources sunk into the project. Indeed, up to this point in the war, Germany was a net beneficiary of the Allied bombing policy, albeit at a huge price in personal tragedy and suffering. The resources Britain diverted from more useful ways of opposing German aggression had been a major factor in the Wehrmacht's rapid early victories. Persistence with the policy as the main method of bringing down the Nazi regime had provided Hitler with second chances to force a decisive victory on the Eastern Front in 1942 and again in 1943. As it turned out, Germany lacked the military power to take full advantage, but an inactive western front and an enemy waiting for bombing to win the war had gifted the Wehrmacht the opportunities to try.

None of this was obvious to the leaders of a country whose citizens were being mercilessly killed and its infrastructure devastated. As tended to happen, bomber offensives look a lot more effective from the perspective of politicians in the rear with the bombs falling around them than generals at the front trying to win a war. It was a mirror image of what happened in Britain in 1917, but on a far vaster scale. Civilian casualties during daylight Gotha raids on London had triggered a chain of events that led to the creation of the RAF and the development of the bomber strategy, even though, at the time, the Germans had soon realised the pointlessness of bombing civilians and had abandoned the policy. Now it was the Germans' turn to be impressed by a failing strategy.[12]

Speer desperately needed better protection for his armament industries and was urging that home defence and fighter production should have priority. Yet, at the same time he had no objections to awarding the V-2 rocket programme top priority, despite the resources it was sucking away from the country's other defence needs.[13] He was also beginning to argue that Germany should take a leaf out of the Allied air strategy book and build its own long-range bomber force. From the German side of the fence it was not so easy to appreciate the operational difficulties involved in implementing the strategy. The Dambusters' raid might have appeared impressive to Speer, but it required an enormous amount of training. The level of skill required could not be extended to the entire bomber force. Even when taken by surprise, German anti-aircraft defences had taken a heavy toll of the attackers. It was a method that was only going to work once.

Speer could not understand why the RAF did not set alight the scaffolding being used to repair the dams with the sort of incendiary raids that were setting fire to German cities.[14] It seemed easy enough to the economist. However, dropping incendiaries randomly over a wide area was one thing, setting fire to a set of scaffolding would require an impossible level of accuracy. Nor could he understand why all the ball-bearing plants in Germany, France and Italy had not been bombed simultaneously and the attacks repeated. If those plants had been bombed every two weeks for a couple of months, he suggested, and then perhaps every two months to halt any rebuilding the consequences for Germany would have been catastrophic.[15] He might have been right, but unacceptably high losses on such a regular basis would have been equally catastrophic for the bomber force. He was also assuming the location of all ball-bearings plants would be known.

As a civilian, the operational difficulties might not have been obvious but, as an industrialist and economist, Speer should have known that Germany did not have the resources to construct and operate a fleet of huge strategic bombers on top of its current commitments. Despite the obvious problems, he still hankered after a bomber force that would take out key Allied industrial nodal points which, he believed, would devastate Allied output.[16] To the economists of all countries, it all seemed so easy from their offices. Speer's ideas were as delusional as were Bomber Command's plans at the outbreak of war to cripple German production in months.

Nevertheless, in one of the stranger twists in the war, it was suddenly the Germans who were becoming interested in strategic bombing. The Luftwaffe, like every major air force, had its fair share of bomber visionaries. The advanced He 177 long-range bomber had always been an important part of German production plans. The emphasis on tactical air support had been forced on the Luftwaffe more by the realties of war than inspired forward thinking. The Luftwaffe had been successful largely because it had been used for what it was capable of doing rather than what some of the more imaginative theorists believed it ought to be doing. In the second half of 1943 the imaginative theorists would be given their chance.

In August 1943 Hans Jeschonnek, the Luftwaffe Chief of the General Staff, committed suicide and was replaced by Günther Korten. The new Luftwaffe chief set about re-organising and strengthening the Luftwaffe. Korten was no one-dimensional bomber ideologue. His plans for the Luftwaffe included expanding the close air support forces available to the army and home defence, both of which were in desperate need of reinforcement. Under his leadership both these branches of the Luftwaffe doubled in size by the summer of 1944.[17] However, Korten saw a strategic bombing element as just as important as any other air force role and was keen to step up the Luftwaffe's long-range bombing efforts. Like Britain in 1940, Germany was now hopelessly outstripped by her enemies in terms of resources, manpower and industry. It seemed the only way some sort of more favourable balance on the battlefield could be restored was by destroying enemy sources of production. Aircraft and tank factories along with the power stations that fed them were seen as particularly profitable targets. There was no shortage of optimism about what bombing might achieve, It was hoped to destroy 50 to 80 per cent of Soviet production capacity, an ambition that was remarkably similar to the Allied plans for dismembering German industry outlined in the Pointblank directive.[18]

It was a measure of the growing despair at all levels of the German hierarchy about the eventual outcome of the war that the idea was taken seriously. The German aircraft industry and air force training programmes had never had the resources to provide the air strength required to challenge simultaneously the enemies Germany had acquired on multiple fronts, on land, sea and in the air. Somehow, on top of these commitments, the Luftwaffe was expected to conjure up a long-range bomber fleet that would fly further than Allied bombers had to, avoid the heavy losses Allied bombers were suffering, and hit Soviet industry more effectively than the Allies were managing against German targets. Bombers were withdrawn from fronts to prepare for their new role. With the German Army struggling to hold the advancing Red Army, reducing army support in any way for the uncertain rewards of a strategic bomber offensive was the logic of the desperate. With so much expected from the offensive and so few resources to deliver such expectations, German war policy was entering the realms of fantasy.

Yet, revealingly, it was a fantasy the Air Ministry were willing to praise and applaud. In their post-war analysis of Luftwaffe operations, the Air Ministry congratulated the Luftwaffe on finally seeing the error of its ways. The Germans had finally recognised that 'after a long period of success, the whole German policy of concentration of offensive airpower in support of the Army had been rendered bankrupt'.[19] This 'long period of success' had, against the odds, taken Hitler's depraved regime frighteningly close to outright victory. It was 'a long period of success' the Air Ministry were as happy to discount in 1943 as they were when the narrative on the German Air Force was written in 1947. It was an extraordinary assessment of German policy that underlined how deeply rooted the bomber obsession had become in British thinking. Germany, like Britain, could not afford to waste resources on ambitious strategic bombing offensives if it meant more fundamental defence needs were not met.

The first victim of the Luftwaffe's new offensive policy would not be Soviet tank factories a thousand miles away; it would be London, around 150 miles from German bases. Operation Steinbock was a purely retaliatory assault; bombing London had no great military significance. The German offensive was supposed to be a joint effort by manned bombers, pilotless bombers and rockets but, at the beginning of 1944, only the conventional manned bombers were ready to go. By dint of a huge effort and by stripping other fronts, a force of over 500 bombers was cobbled together, with around two-thirds serviceable at any one time. On the night of 21/22 January, by having many crews fly twice, nearly 450 sorties were flown against the capital. However, only thirty-two of the 500 tons of bombs they carried hit the city. Eight days later another 285 bombers tried again; this time thirty-seven tons fell on the capital.[20] The number of bombs hitting a target twenty-five miles wide from airfields 150 miles away did not bode well for an offensive against Soviet factories 1,000 miles in the Soviet rear.

In two nights the Luftwaffe lost fifty-seven bombers. The German bombers dropped *Duppel*, their version of Window. Ground-based radars were severely disrupted but the American AI Mark X was less affected than British radars. Low-tech sound detectors and searchlights came to the fore and the defences continued to take a steady toll. The Luftwaffe lost 129 planes in January and February, a loss rate of 6 per cent. The focus switched to easier targets on the coast, but the loss rate increased.[21] Once again night defences had prevailed against the conventional bomber. It was not long before units were being switched back to fronts in urgent need of bomber support. The 'Baby Blitz' of early 1944 petered out completely in

May 1944. Another 1,500 civilians had been killed, a reminder for a war weary population, if they needed it, of the horrors of aerial bombardment. The offensive brought much grief to many families but it was not going to have any effect on the course of the war.

The fantasy of strikes on the Ural factories and Soviet power supplies faded almost as quickly. The He 177 long-range bombers ended up being sent out in pairs to attack advancing Soviet columns at low level, a task that could be performed much more effectively by cheaper Fw 190 fighter-bombers. As attractive as the idea of a long-range strategic bomber force might sound, and as useful as such a force can be, it was not Germany's priority need in 1943, just as such a force should not have been Britain's priority earlier in the war. Germany soon realised it was wasting resources on the He 177 bomber and production was halted. Unfortunately for the citizens of London, Brussels and Antwerp, Germany did not extend this line of reasoning to the V-2.

As the nightly raids on London faded away, Churchill felt it necessary to warn his people that the ordeal was not over yet. The Germans were preparing new means of attacking the country 'either by pilotless aircraft or possibly rockets or both, on a considerable scale'.[22] It was a particularly frightening and demoralising prospect. With piloted bombers there was some comfort in the fact that the pilot was probably trying to hit a military target. With a pilotless assault, there could be no such delusion; death would be completely random. It was an aspect of a pilotless approach that had particularly appealed to Trenchard in the twenties when Britain was developing its own Larynx flying bomb.

At least a subsonic pilotless plane could be shot down. A ballistic rocket, by common consent, seemed unstoppable. Schemes seriously considered and rejected included creating a powerful magnetic field that would draw the missiles away from London.[23] The only hope was that radar might be able to provide some warning of approaching missiles, enabling the population to take cover. Attack by ballistic missile was the last thought on the minds of the early pioneers of radar, and one of the apparently least useful characteristics of the first primitive 'floodlight' early-warning radars (where the transmissions could not be tightly focused), was that the lobes of radiation it emitted happened to be able to identify objects up to 90,000 feet over 200 miles away and objects flying at well over 100,000 feet around 100 miles away. This, however, was precisely what was required to spot a V-2. In theory this might provide four minutes warning of an approaching missile. Five Chain Home stations along the south coast from the Isle of

Wight to Dover were fitted with cathode-ray direction-finding equipment, which provided reasonably accurate information on a rocket trajectory up to 50,000 feet, which might at least enable the position of the launch site to be estimated. Throughout the winter of 1943/44, for fifteen minutes at a time, observers took it in turns to stare at their radar screens, waiting in vain for the faint tell-tale vertical trace that indicated a rocket was on the way.[24]

Shorter range Anti-Aircraft Command fire-control radars were more accurate than Chain Home radar and might be able to narrow down the threatened area, although only at a later point in the missile's trajectory. These were deployed at twenty- to thirty-mile intervals along the south coast between Portsmouth and Dover.[25] The Command also set about modifying equipment, capable of tracking an aircraft 30,000 yards away at 30,000 feet, so that they could pick up a missile 140,000 yards (eighty miles) away at an altitude of 300,000 feet (nearly sixty miles). At best this might give the population a minute's warning.[26] It was suggested that maroons would be launched and whistles blown to warn citizens a rocket was about to hit, but if a missile was arriving every hour, the disruption the warnings would cause would be enormous.[27]

The pilotless plane was scarcely less frightening. Although interception was possible, the Air Ministry were not convinced a satisfactory defence could be created. With just one launch per hour, the delivery of 2,000 tons of high explosives in twenty-four hours seemed well within the capability of one hundred launching sites. Once again civil authorities began planning to deal with the panic an aerial bombardment might provoke. Rest centres just outside London were set up for the half million terrified Londoners who might elect to flee the capital on foot.[28]

As the launch date for the invasion of France became more definite, so did fears that the rockets and pilotless planes might be turned on the concentration of Allied forces in southern England. The invasion fleet itself as it set sail might be a target. The launching sites on the Cherbourg peninsula were just 100 miles from where the invasion fleet would assemble. The exaggerated ideas of how much destruction and disruption randomly falling bombs could cause meant the possibility of such an assault making an invasion impossible was taken very seriously. Attack still seemed the best form of defence. Indeed against rockets, attacking the launching sites might be the only defence. Crossbow was the name given to the air campaign and all the suspected V-weapon sites were soon being targeted. The threat to British cities and Overlord meant suspected missile sites were soon challenging Pointblank targets for priority.

THE SHAPE OF WARS TO COME

It was not only direct attack on invasion forces that was worrying the Overlord planners. It had always been a War Office fear that crucial fighter resources might suddenly be withdrawn from an invasion attempt if London was threatened. The rocket could not be intercepted but the pilotless plane could and an assault by these would inevitably provoke pressure to move fighters from covering the invasion to defending London. It was perhaps ironic that, as Allied forces prepared to fight once again on French soil, the threat to London should rear its head once more. Four years before the RAF had been reluctant to send fighters to support the Allied armies in the Battle of France in order to ensure home defence remained strong. Indeed, not a single example of the RAF's best fighter, the Spitfire, had been allowed out of the country. Now, as the Allies tried to focus their air forces on the forthcoming struggle to regain the ground lost in 1940, once again a German aerial threat might succeed in diverting RAF resources to the defence of London.

The surest way of defeating the robot aerial offensive was to win a land battle in northern France and clear the northern coast of the launching sites. The V-weapons were yet another reason why an invasion of France could not be delayed any longer. The air defence of London and land operations on the continent were intimately linked. This had been the case ever since Zeppelins had first threatened London in 1914 and the Royal Marines and RNAS squadrons had moved into Belgium to deny the Germans bases close to the Channel coast. In 1944 the need was once again to prevent the enemy from using the same stretch of coast. The land battle on the continent that Britain had always tried to avoid had always been the best way of defending London from the aerial threat the Air Ministry and country so feared. The ground and tactical air forces, which Air Ministry thinking decreed to be superfluous in the age of aerial bombardment, were in fact Londoners' best chance of defeating another merciless assault.

It was a reminder of how Britain's defence needs were changing in the twentieth century. Being an island no longer offered the security it once had. The very bombing policy the Air Ministry had espoused meant Britain could no longer be indifferent to who occupied the territory on the other side of the Channel. It was no accident that for the second time in half a century Britain was committed to deploying substantial ground forces in the battle for Europe. Britain's first line of defence now had to be on the continent and the further east it was the better. Britain's security was now inextricably linked to the fate of continental Europe. This, however, was not how the Air Ministry saw it. They had always believed the emergence of airpower reduced the need for Britain to get involved in European battles. The new era that the pilotless plane and ballistic missile were ushering in reinforced their view that Britain could fight its wars safely from the home islands. Far from invalidating the isolationist 'limited liability' defence policies of the pre-war years, these new weapons were seen as a vindication for these policies.

How air policy might develop in the post-war era was already very much on the agenda. The Air Ministry did not think the spring of 1943 was too soon to begin planning the role that airpower would play in the next Great War. With a static Channel front it was still just about possible to view the current conflict as a bomber war in the Trenchard mould. Events elsewhere, on distant fronts in distant continents, could be viewed as local aberrations, or large-scale colonial conflicts. With the inexorable approach of Overlord, however, it was becoming more difficult to maintain the idea that these distant battles were distractions from the main event. It was a lot easier to block out these distractions from the inner sanctum of the Air Ministry. Ideas circulating behind closed doors were a much better barometer of current core thinking than the more moderate policies being forced on the Air Ministry by the realities of war.

In the summer of 1943 the planning and policy departments within the Air Ministry were both busy reviving pre-war concepts for a post-war Britain. Initially the Air Ministry Plans department assumed the enemy would again be Germany. The need to deter any future German aggression seemed an obvious post-war requirement and the best way of doing this seemed to be an air force that could inflict more harm on Germany than Germany could inflict on Britain.[29] With memories of how Britain's perceived weakness in bombers had led to the 1938 Munich capitulation still reasonably fresh, no one would question the need for a powerful deterrent as a priceless diplomatic weapon. The question was whether the same force could win a war. This had not been recognised as a consideration in pre-war thinking. Previously the military or naval force that might deter aggression had been the same military or naval force that would be needed if deterrence failed. It was just assumed the same was true of the bomber. The mass destruction bombers could deliver was a very effective peacetime deterrent but, with the war entering its fifth year, there was little evidence it could actually win a war.

This was not something the Air Ministry was prepared to accept. Air Ministry thinking was still dominated by the belief that air power was the predominant force in modern warfare and the bomber the predominant weapon. Echoing thoughts so often expressed by the likes of Harris, the plans department recalled how the RAF had saved the country in the Battle of Britain and had saved the country again in the Battle of the Atlantic. The former was undoubtedly true, although it was the fighters that the government insisted on having rather than the bombers the Air Ministry preferred that had won the battle. Airpower had also played an important role in winning the Battle of the Atlantic. However, the bomber strategy had not contributed to either victory. Victory in both campaigns came in spite of the resources invested in the bomber strategy, not because of this investment.

In these Air Ministry analyses of the form a future conflict would take, France was seen as a nation in decline. Its army would forever be a 'broken reed' and could never again be relied upon to provide a defence for western Europe. This determination to see the French defeat in 1940 as a symptom of a failing nation rather than a failure to cope with new technology and tactics underlined how little progress the Air Ministry had been made in adjusting to the way warfare was evolving in the twentieth century. There was no interest in understanding the air factors that led to the defeat in France, no proposals for a more modern air element to support a better equipped army that would avoid such defeats. Instead, the Air Ministry planners argued that Britain's mistake had been sending an army to the continent. Despatching another expeditionary force to deal with a future threat would be foolish and unnecessary. The best policy, they argued, would be to create a strong air force that would deter aggression and if necessary win a war, thereby avoiding any need for a military presence on the continent.[30] This was entirely in line with the current belief that that the bomber offensive made an invasion of France unnecessary.

A September 1943 study suggested that the reality of the current conflict was beginning to impinge on thinking. It seemed to be envisaging a more balanced air force with a tactical army support element that, amongst other tasks, would be capable of supporting an expeditionary force on the continent. Yet, it still claimed, somewhat paradoxically 'Airpower has superseded in many respects, and will continue increasingly to supersede, the cumbersome methods of surface warfare'. Physical and military obstacles could be 'overflown, out-flanked or evaded by airpower ... . Airpower will become increasingly the major guarantor of the security of the British Empire', it was boldly stated.[31] These were not sentiments that provided the foundation for balanced armed forces combining ground and air capabilities.

The study outlined how a strategic bomber force based in the United Kingdom would remain the core Air Ministry policy. A peacetime force of thirty heavy bomber squadrons would be needed, with each plane capable of dropping ten tons on a target 2,000 miles away. This was quite a quantum leap forward in capability and far in advance of anything British designers had been asked to contemplate. Enemies beyond Britain's immediate neighbours were now on the agenda. 'Certain vulnerable points in Russia' would be within range, the study suggested. Indeed, 2,000 miles put Moscow well within range of bombers operating from the United Kingdom and more targets would be within range of British bases in India and the Middle East. Even this dramatic increase in capability would still leave many Soviet targets beyond the range of the bomber force. Without fighter escort, it was recognised that a fleet of such bombers would initially have to operate by night, but eventually it ought to be able to operate by day. This was in line with the still commonly held belief that bombers on their own could win air superiority. It would be a force capable of 'sinking a Navy, paralysing an Army or razing the industrial potential' of an enemy.[32] This could all have been taken from documents from the twenties, or indeed Smuts's original 1917 prognosis for the future of warfare. Trenchard would approve.

Although it was conceded that a tactical air force would still be needed, for minor conflicts throughout the Empire, in the Middle East and indeed even in Europe, in peacetime it would be restricted to a 'Nucleus Tactical Air Force', largely for training and developing tactical fighter support, fighter-bomber, tank busting and tactical reconnaissance duties. This was a significant advance on the post-First World War attitude to tactical airpower, when any mention of battlefield air support in a major conflict was considered heretical. At least some research and development would continue. Nevertheless, it was of clearly secondary importance and scarcely reflected the way the Second World War was panning out. There was no suggestion of building an air force that could contribute to a post-war European defence policy based on the sort of mobile mechanised armies that the western allies were now creating to win the current conflict. In 1943 the Air Ministry was still a long way from embracing, or even understanding, the way war was evolving in the twentieth century.

During the course of 1943 there was the opportunity to take such ideas outside the confines of the Air Ministry. In 1942 the Norwegian government in exile had triggered a debate on western European post-war security by suggesting an international pact to secure the North Atlantic with forces based in Norway, Iceland and Greenland, a suggestion that would eventually lead to the creation of NATO.[33] This initiative led to a broader look at Britain's post-war strategy and military requirements. Various inter-service committees (The Future Operational Planning section, a 1943 Military Sub-committee followed by a Post-Hostilities Planning Sub-committee) were set the task of investigating a wide range of post-war security issues and scenarios,

James Spaight was brought out of retirement to represent the Air Ministry in the last two of these. Spaight had been principal assistant secretary in the Air Ministry from 1934 to 1937. The retired civil servant was seen by some as being somewhat out of touch with modern developments but, as the Air Ministry he represented seemed determined to retain the policies of the past, he was from their point of view the ideal choice.[34] He was an ardent and outspoken supporter of the bomber strategy and the author of many books on the subject. He was about to publish *Bombing Vindicated*, a fierce defence of Bomber Command's area bombing policy. Even in this book there were signs of the lessons of the current conflict breaking through Trenchardian dogma. The book was full of praise for the contribution the tactical air forces were making in their support of Allied ground forces in the Mediterranean. Yet the author had no time for German 'air-land' war philosophy, and proclaimed that 'the bomber has really killed the old kind of war'.[35] For the Air Ministry, he was a safe pair of hands.

These various committees initially saw a resurgent Germany as the most likely enemy. There was broad agreement that this should be nipped in the bud by possessing a strong aerial striking force 'and the will to use it ... ruthlessly ... against targets necessarily civilian in character'.[36] Initially it was thought this force would require bases on the continent but the Air Staff view that this could be delivered from the UK soon prevailed. One of the problems foreseen was that a future government might not have the will to use it. This was always the problem with a weapon as blunt as the bomber. There would be many situations where it would clearly be a disproportionate use of brute force. If the bomber could not be used, Britain might end up facing a German threat 'comparable on the scale of 1939', although whether this meant the very real threat the Wehrmacht posed rather than the imaginary threat of the aerial knockout blow is not clear.[37]

Proposals put to the Post-Hostilities Planning Committee, chaired by the Foreign Office, for the peacetime policing of a defeated but hostile Germany outlined how ruthless the subjugation of the German people might be. If the Germans did not behave as required, aircraft could be used to destroy crops or bomb towns depending on the level of misdemeanour, just as uncooperative factions in the British Empire had been punished in decades past. The economic advantages were clear but the committee feared that the British public would not accept the random hardship inflicted and loss of innocent life involved in such punitive bombing. 'In well developed and civilised countries, therefore, airpower is not the most useful instrument to maintain control', the committee concluded, suggesting that perhaps in less well developed countries it was.[38]

Portal had no such qualms, pointing out that with no air defences to worry about his bombers could operate from low levels with extreme precision. The use of airpower was no more indiscriminate than the use of ground forces, he insisted, which seemed to suggest a fairly heavy-handed Army response to any misbehaviour by a subjugated people. There was no opposition from the Army to such ideas. Indeed, Brooke was in complete agreement, claiming that airpower would be even more cost effective than the committee believed. (Someone scribbled in the margin of the minutes 'What has come over the Field Marshal!')[39] Brooke seemed rather keen to offload the cost of rather mundane policing duties.

To Portal and Brooke the real future danger was not Germany, it was the Soviet Union and they deplored the Foreign Office reluctance to even consider this possibility while the country was a current ally. No one seemed in any doubt about the nature and scale of the threat. There were many casual references to the Soviets having overwhelming strength on the ground which would enable them at any time to conquer western Europe, if they so chose. Intelligence reports spoke highly of the quality of Soviet weaponry especially tanks, and the proficiency of army air support.[40] Although recognising the Soviets as a threat, Brooke did not seem interested in even speculating about the steps Britain might need to take to deal with this level of military hardware and expertise.

Intelligence assessments also emphasised that, even though there was no existing Soviet strategic bomber threat, there was no reason why the Soviets would not at some future point be as capable in this sphere as they were in land warfare. The bomber strategy was so embedded in British military thinking that it was assumed that any nation that had not placed its faith in long-range weapons of mass destruction as a war-winning method would soon realise their mistake and do everything to make up for lost ground. It was the Soviet aerial threat Britain had to guard against and prepare for. The committee suggested that technical developments, especially in the field of radar, should be vigorously pursued. A skeleton air defence system should remain in place, with the capability of being expanded into a comprehensive system in the two years warning a deteriorating political situation was likely to provide.[41] The Air Staff thought this risky and believed some sort of system would have to be up and running to deal with a surprise attack delivered when there was no international tension. A hypothetical future Soviet bomber threat was causing far more concern than the very real threat the Soviet Army already posed.

Brooke was no more interested in promoting a more active army role in European defence than he was in policing a defeated Germany. There was vague talk of the need for the nations of Europe to come together to defend their interests. Indeed, the three Chiefs of Staff came to the unpalatable, from the Foreign Office's point of view, conclusion that Germany as an ally would be vital to stiffen the defences of Western Europe. This, they insisted, should be borne in mind when considering plans to dismember and de-industrialise the country.[42]

With the War Office reluctant to push the need for a modern mechanised army to deter the Soviet Union, the way was left for airpower to dominate the military scenarios. Strategic air defence and offence would be the lynchpins of Britain's future military strength. Both could be conducted from within the United Kingdom. There was no need to get involved on the continent. Four years of conflict, with crucial land battles raging across four continents, was having surprisingly little effect on Air Ministry ideas about how future wars should be fought.

While the Air Ministry began to look to a post-war era in which Britain would want to avoid at all costs sending an army to the Continent, in the current conflict this was precisely what Britain was preparing to do. Nearly two and a half years after the most recent expeditionary force had been evicted from Greece, British forces were setting foot once more on mainland Europe.

Chapter Three

Italian Lessons

For those planning the invasion of France the landings and fighting in Italy should have provided useful lessons. By the summer of 1943 Allied air forces had established air superiority in the Mediterranean. The theatre had always been of secondary importance to Hitler. Ever since the invasion of the Soviet Union, relatively few Luftwaffe resources had been available for any other front. Luftwaffe strength in the Middle East had never been overwhelming; the German Air Force had been successful in the region because of the low number of aircraft and, even more significantly, the inferior quality of the fighters Britain had chosen to send there. It was March 1942 before the first Spitfires were deployed as fighters outside the United Kingdom. Now the quality gap was closing and a slight Axis numerical superiority had been turned into a huge numerical inferiority. What had sufficed to torment Allied forces in the first two years of the Mediterranean war was no longer capable of making much of an impression against the Anglo-American aerial armadas. Only the ever present, and still very effective, German flak was challenging Allied control of the skies. For those contemplating an invasion of France, the fighting in Italy would provide an excellent opportunity to discover how best to exploit air superiority.

The Allied ground forces in the Mediterranean were led by General Dwight Eisenhower. For Eisenhower, airpower was the Allied ace in the pack. He had been enormously impressed by the carpet bombing of the island fortress of Pantelleria in June 1943, a bombardment which had brought about the island's surrender without a shot being fired. This barnstorming air effort attracted far more attention than the more refined but less spectacular close air support organised by Broadhurst's Desert Air Force. In the dramatic victory at Tebaga in Tunisia a few months earlier for three hours waves of fighter-bombers had swamped the battlefield, picking off individual enemy positions, enabling Commonwealth forces to punch through German defences. This would turn out to be a more instructive demonstration of what airpower could contribute.

Eisenhower's deputy, Air Chief Marshal Arthur Tedder was the most senior RAF commander in the theatre and is often seen as the architect of the Desert Air Force's rise to fame. He was, however, far from being a confirmed advocate of battlefield air support. Pressure from the War Office, not to mention political pressure from the leaders of the Commonwealth countries whose troops were fighting in the Middle East, had rather forced his hand. Like so many air commanders, Tedder always worried about the Air Force becoming a mere adjunct to ground forces. He was not impressed by either the Tebaga or the Pantelleria type air support, both of which he saw as the Air Force doing the Army's work. In line with traditional Air Staff thinking, he believed air forces should confine themselves to targets beyond the battlefield and entirely backed Coningham's air superiority/interdiction/close air support order of priority. The invasion of Sicily had reminded the Allies of the German ability to mount powerful counter-attacks, with the Americans nearly being pushed back into the sea. Despite this near disaster, Coningham's mission priority had been rigorously applied and it had been left to naval firepower to come to the rescue of the struggling Americans.

In the summer of 1943 General George Marshall, the American Army chief, still wanted an invasion of France to follow the capture of Sicily. However, with Italy on the brink of collapse and Allied forces in place in the Mediterranean ready to take advantage, it was always going to be difficult to argue against an invasion of Italy. On 25 July, as the fighting in Sicily raged, Mussolini had been deposed and, although the new Italian government pledged to continue the fight at Germany's side, they were soon sending out peace feelers. For the Allies, the opportunity to eliminate Italy and continue the advance into southern Europe seemed too good to miss. It was agreed that the announcement of the Italian surrender should coincide with the main Allied landings around Salerno.

For the bomber advocates, the Italian surrender was a clear result of the softening up of Italy by the British and American bomber fleets. From October 1942 a series of area attacks on northern Italian cities by Bomber Command had the specific aim of terrorising the local population in order to destabilise the regime and encourage surrender. These raids included a daylight Lancaster attack on Milan on 24 October 1942 in which 172 people died. Those casualties did indeed provoke considerable resentment against the authorities, mainly for their failure to organise more effective civil defence. However, there was no question of the attacks bringing down the government.

Rome had so far been exempt from any bombing because of its cultural status. On 13 July 1943, however, USAAF bombers launched a heavy daylight raid against the San Lorenzo and Littoria marshalling yards, attacks in which as many as 2,000 civilians were killed.[1] It was part of a general campaign against Italian communications and particular care was taken to hit purely military targets. Nevertheless, the aim was also to intimidate and encourage a desire to surrender.[2] This was all the more effective precisely because it did not seem to be a deliberate terror attack. The bombing was accurate enough for it to be clear that marshalling yards were the target and the civilian deaths just an unfortunate by-product. In these circumstances, a government determined to continue the war can be seen as at least partly responsible for the casualties. Blatant terror attacks on residential areas are more likely to focus resentment on the attacker.

It was easy to see Mussolini's fall from power a few days later and the new government's desire for peace as a direct result of these raids. They were no doubt a factor but perhaps not the primary factor. The bombing was much heavier in the summer of 1943 and the civilian casualties were far higher than in the autumn of 1942. However, the more significant difference was that the previous autumn, the Italian Army had been at the gates of Alexandria, and the country on the verge of a glorious victory. Nine months later, Allied forces were fighting on Italian soil and defeat was looking increasingly inevitable.

Bombing might accelerate surrender by a country already suffering major military defeats, but it is unlikely to compel a country buoyed by victories and winning a war to suddenly decide to concede defeat. For bombing to have any effect on a political decision to surrender, a necessary precondition is that the country's armed forces must already be losing the war. Even then bombing civilians might well have the opposite effect and stiffen the determination to carry on the fight. Intimidating civilian populations is at best an unpredictable method for accelerating victory when that victory already seems inevitable. It is not at all obvious that Italy would have carried on fighting if Rome had not been bombed.

A land campaign in Italy was never going to be easy. Churchill famously explained his Mediterranean strategy to Stalin by drawing a crocodile across Europe, with Italy the soft underbelly. Politically this might have been a reasonable analogy, but the mountainous and easily defended terrain of the Italian peninsula was anything but a soft option for an army trying to advance, especially when compared to the open plains of north-west Europe. It seemed more like the crocodile was lying on its back. For the USAAF,

ITALIAN LESSONS

invading Italy offered one major advantage. From North Africa, American long-range bombers were largely confined to tactical communication targets. However, an invasion of Italy would be a golden opportunity to capture the extensive complex of airstrips in the Foggia region. With these airfields, strategic targets deep inside occupied Europe would be well within range. With the Eighth Air Force threatening Germany from bases in the UK, the German air defences would be split between the west and the south.

The Allied plans for invading Italy involved two stages. First Montgomery would cross the Straits of Messina and hopefully draw in German reserves. Six days later an Anglo-American force would land in the German rear at Salerno, take Naples and cut off the German forces engaging Montgomery. There were no particularly suitable sites for an amphibious assault along the Italian coastline; all were overlooked by mountain ranges that gave defenders an advantage. The best site was Gaeta, north of Naples, but this was thought to be too far for effective fighter cover. Beaches south of Naples, around Salerno, were chosen instead.

On 3 September 1943 Montgomery's forces landed on the toe of Italy. Fighter protection for the landings was a relatively easy task from airfields in Sicily; around 500 fighters covered and supported the landings on the first day. Italian airfields in the area were primitive and had been heavily bombed in the previous days. The only attempt to disrupt the landings came from around fifty Italian and German fighters and fighter-bombers. By this stage of the war Broadhurst's closely co-ordinated air support was a smoothly functioning operation. In North Africa Army Air Support Controls (later renamed Air Support Signals Unit) had been set up, with radio links enabling commanders at the front to call in air support. These were often referred to as 'tentacles'. At the battle at the Tebaga Pass Broadhurst had added a forward air controller as part of the tentacle system. This was an RAF pilot who could communicate directly with the pilots above and direct then to their targets. Using an experienced pilot to pass on instructions ensured they made sense to the pilots in the air. This idea would evolve into joint army/air force teams attached to forward army headquarters. In Italy these were known as Rovers. Ideally, they would be located where the battlefield could be viewed.

From midday on the first day of the invasion, fighter-bomber P-40 Kittyhawks and North American A-36s (the dive-bomber version of the P-51 Mustang fighter, unofficially known as Invaders) together with light bombers (Baltimores and Bostons) were seeking out targets ahead of the advancing forces, while B-25 Mitchells and Liberators struck further inland.³ With attention of the top commanders focused on the upcoming Salerno landings, Broadhurst had more freedom to use his air force for direct battlefield support. The Germans had no intention of mounting a major stand so far south and targets were hard to find amongst the rapidly withdrawing German forces. Demolitions were the main obstruction to Allied progress. However, where the Germans did make a stand, light bombers and fighter-bombers attacked a range of tactical targets including troop concentrations and targets as small as individual pillboxes and mortar positions.⁴ To many airmen such apparently trivial targets seemed unworthy of air attack but for the troops on the ground the support was very welcome. For commanders they were another valuable way of providing fire support to help maintain the momentum of an advance, especially when artillery could not keep up with an advance.

The Air Force always made much of the fact that low-level attack was a dangerous occupation. Indeed, it often was, but it tended to be less dangerous against enemy positions in the front line. The sort of strongholds that might be blocking an immediate advance were not likely to have their own anti-aircraft defences. These tended to be focused on targets further to the rear or particularly high-value targets such as panzer divisions. The further to the rear aircraft operate, the more dangerous the mission becomes. This is particularly true of armed reconnaissance missions where time is spent in enemy air space looking for targets, increasing the chances of interception.⁵ These were lessons learned in the First World War.⁶

It was not therefore surprising that the humble Auster observation aircraft was so successful. These slow-flying, unarmed observation aircraft, flown by Army pilots, were intended principally for directing artillery fire but also provided useful information on enemy positions. Flying low and within range of friendly anti-aircraft fire to ward off any enemy that appeared, losses in combat among these AOP (Air Observation Post) squadrons were low. Their ability to operate from the smallest of airfields was priceless. The first RAF aircraft to operate from mainland Europe was a flight of No. 651 Squadron Austers that landed at Reggio Calabria the day after the initial landing.⁷

There were not many problems for Montgomery's troops but, when one emerged, the Desert Air Force was on hand to help deal with it. On 8 September a small force landed in the port of Pizzo, ahead of the main body of Montgomery's army. This soon found itself in difficulty against unexpectedly fierce German counter-attacks. Kittyhawks came to the rescue, flying around 100 sorties against German positions in the vicinity.⁸

It was a minor example of how airpower could provide immediate support where it was most required. For Broadhurst it was just another run of the mill application of airpower.

Ground-attack was far more in evidence in the Calabrian campaign than it had been in Sicily. In the nine days from 31 August to 8 September the Allies flew around 2,400 fighter and 1,000 fighter-bomber sorties in the Calabrian peninsula, compared to 7,000 fighter and 270 fighter-bomber in the seven days following the landings in Sicily.[9] It may not have been the direction Tedder wanted the Air Force to go but, under Broadhurst, the close air support expertise developed in North Africa was still very much alive and kicking. The Army could not order close air support; it could only request it. This was not ideal for an army commander but could be made to work if relations and communications between the two services were good, and Montgomery had great faith in Broadhurst. However, co-ordination was not helped by the fact that, being a separate service, the RAF had to have its own headquarters, and the two headquarters did not always manage to move together.[10]

For the main assault on Salerno, the air superiority/interdiction/close air support order of priority was more in evidence. The Air Ministry liked to emphasise the role the bomber played in establishing and maintaining air superiority by destroying aircraft on the ground but it was the fighters that were proving to be the critical factor. The Allies had nearly 1,700 combat planes to support the landings, of which over 600 were fighters or fighter-bombers.[11] The Luftwaffe had fewer than 600 in the entire Mediterranean theatre, of which under 200 were fighters. Less than 450 aircraft (with no more than 300 serviceable) were available for operations in southern Italy.[12] The distance over which Allied fighters would have to operate reduced the advantage to an extent but Allied superiority was still overwhelming.

Even so, with major naval units involved, no chances were going to be taken; air defence had absolute priority. The Allied airfields in Sicily were around 170 miles from Salerno. Fighters would have to fly far further than the 110 miles required for an invasion of Normandy. The American Lockheed P-38 Lightning, with long-range tanks, could stay over the landing zone for at least an hour. At the last minute it was decided to use A-36 Mustang dive-bombers as conventional fighters and these could also manage an hour over the beachhead. The fighter with the least range was the Spitfire. The Air Ministry, however, had despatched 1,800 90-gallon drop tanks for Spitfire squadrons to use, which, it was hoped, would allow the fighter to patrol the beachhead for twenty-five minutes from airfields in Sicily. In practice, thirty-five, even forty-five, minutes proved possible, which, with hindsight, led to speculation that the landing could have taken place at the more favourable Gaeta site to the north of Naples, some 230 miles north of Sicily.[13] Five escort carriers with around 100 Seafires would help provide extra cover for the northern end of the beachhead. With pilots flying two sorties a day, it was possible to have forty-eight fighters over the bridgehead from dawn to dusk.[14]

It was the classic air umbrella, although this was a term that seemed to attract the same irrational abhorrence in Air Ministry circles as the despised 'dive-bomber' term. The Army and Navy had never understood why having fighters patrol close to a target that needed defending was such a bad idea. For the Fleet Air Arm the 'combat air patrol' was a standard defensive procedure. However, for many air force purists, being restricted to a particular zone did not fit in with their idea of a free-wheeling air force fighting its own war independently of what was happening on sea or land. When the Navy was involved, it tended not to be so controversial; it seemed the air marshals were more reluctant to argue with the admirals. It was not as restrictive as air force commanders would try to make out. Radar enabled fighters to be vectored towards incoming raiders as soon as they were detected, but the target area was always a sensible place to await instructions.

Army commanders were told that, with air defence the priority, there would be no fighter-bomber support in the first days of the landings. There was no need for this hard and fast delineation. One of the reasons for the success of the Desert Air Force was a willingness to switch from air defence to ground-attack or vice versa, according to the situation, even in mid-mission on occasion. There was no reason why the patrolling fighters could not be used for ground strafing if the need arose. Air Support Parties, the American equivalent of the British Rover, providing basic forward control, were supposed to go ashore with the first wave so that they would be in position to request air support as soon as it did become available. It was hoped that a small airstrip at Montecorvino would be in operation on the first or second day of the landing, which would make providing air support easier. As it turned out, the air support parties got lost in the confusion of the invasion.[15] The whole close air support mission was stymied by a lack of urgency, which reflected the low priority it had been accorded. If the troops landing at Salerno encountered the same problems as those landing at Pizzo, they would not have the same access to air support.

The lack of battlefield air support in the invasion plans was not a concern to Tedder; he was, however, worried about the shortage of heavy bombers to attack targets in the rear. To bolster his already rather substantial forces, Tedder was rather hoping that American bomber units in the United Kingdom might be temporarily transferred to the Mediterranean for the invasion. A doubling of bomber strength, he believed, would ensure the German Air Force in the region was paralysed and potential German ground reinforcements immobilised. Far from getting these reinforcements, Tedder was ordered to transfer three American heavy bomber groups and three Wellington squadrons to the UK to bolster the faltering strategic air offensive. This amounted to around a third of his long-range bomber force. Tedder had a reputation for fitting in rather compliantly with Air Ministry priorities but his growing status within the Allied high command was allowing a more forthright Tedder to emerge. He was furious at the suggestion; it would threaten the maintenance of air superiority and the pre-invasion interdiction programme. The transfer Portal was demanding might result in the whole operation being cancelled, he melodramatically insisted, and threatened to take the matter to Eisenhower.[16]

Such threats made little impression on Portal. The strategic bombing offensive was not going well and Portal feared that, unless the heavy losses the Luftwaffe was inflicting on RAF and USAAF heavy bombers could be made good, the offensive was in danger of failing. He boldly claimed that the aerial superiority Tedder's air forces now enjoyed was the direct result of the destruction the strategic air offensive was wreaking inside Germany. The Allied bombers were also pinning down key fighter resources that might otherwise be used to reinforce the Mediterranean front. The bomber offensive would be even more effective if the Mediterranean did not hog all the resources, he suggested. The overwhelming air superiority the Allied air forces possessed in the Mediterranean was 'headline news which had not escaped the notice of our bombers here'.[17] Even without the transferred Liberators and Wellingtons Tedder would still have a 'very great numerical superiority'. It seemed to be a case of reinforcing failure at the expense of a theatre where Allied forces were enjoying some success.

There was a degree of irony about Portal's suggestion that Tedder owed air superiority to the bomber offensive. For years the Middle East had suffered because of the huge investment in the bomber programme and indeed the need to hold back fighter resources to defend Britain from the ever-expected German knockout blow. The Allies had established air superiority in the Mediterranean by 1943 because the theatre was finally getting the high-quality fighters it had been denied for so long, not because Germany was being bombed. It was noteworthy that one of the reasons

Tedder wanted to keep the Liberators and Wellingtons was because he believed that they were key to maintaining air superiority. At the heart of their disagreement, both Portal and Tedder found common ground in their Trenchardian belief that the bomber was the route to air superiority.

Tedder had no doubts about the value of strategic bombing but even he was outraged by Portal's claim. He may not have expressed himself as forthrightly as some other senior RAF commanders but, coming from one who had so often been more than willing to toe the Air Ministry line, his words perhaps carried more sting. He confessed to being 'a little surprised to see it is considered that bomber offensive from UK is largely responsible for our local superiority', especially, Tedder continued, as the Air Ministry's own assessment had claimed that German fighter losses in the Mediterranean in July were the heaviest of the war so far, amounting to three quarters of German output. In the face of Tedder's indignant response, Portal felt obliged to withdraw his claim.

Tedder argued that a successful invasion of Italy was crucial for the strategic air offensive as the capture of the airfield complex around Foggia would open up a second front for German air defences. It was an argument designed to appeal to Portal's determination to see the bomber offensive succeed, but also reflected Tedder's own belief in the strategic bomber as a decisive war winning weapon. Tedder prevailed and the bombers stayed. From the RAF perspective, three squadrons of Wellingtons scattering bombs by night over German cities or Italian airfields was not going to make much difference to the prospects for the strategic air offensive or the establishment of air superiority over the Italian mainland. Portal and Tedder were attributing bombers with powers of destruction they did not possess. Eisenhower was falling into the same trap. He was increasingly subscribing to Tedder's view that the bomber was capable of paralysing enemy movement and this was the decisive contribution from the air that Eisenhower was seeking, not closely co-ordinated air support on the battlefield.

On 9 September Allied forces went ashore at Salerno and, as had been agreed, the Italian government immediately surrendered. The Italian defences ceased to exist and it was hoped that the Germans would be too distracted by the need to disarm their former allies to offer serious resistance. During the day there were continuous patrols of twelve A-36 (Mustangs) at low altitude, twenty-four P-38 Lightnings at medium altitude and twelve Spitfires as top cover, with Seafires providing additional support. In all over a thousand fighter sorties were flown over the beachhead

(199 A-36, 309 P-38, 288 Spitfire and 265 Seafire).[18] Throughout the day small Luftwaffe formations carried out hit-and-run raids on the beaches. In total the Luftwaffe managed twenty-six fighter-bomber sorties covered by eighty-two fighters.[19] By this stage of the war this was a rather typical scale of effort in the Mediterranean theatre. Even these light attacks provoked complaints that they had interrupted unloading. The subsequent history of the operation by the Anglo-American Western Naval Task Force, responsible for delivering and supporting the invasion forces, melodramatically claimed that 'the scale of these attacks has never before and has never since been equalled'.[20] Bombing often attracts a stronger reaction than other forms of enemy fire – there is always something particularly unnerving about being fired on from above. Even so, on the face of it, it seemed a remarkable overreaction.

It was a reaction that reflected the distrust that had built up over the years between the air and land services, British and American. The policy that airpower should be used principally against more distant targets beyond the battlefield and a dislike of 'aerial umbrellas' was all too easily seen by Army and Navy commanders as an air force wanting to be somewhere else rather than where it was needed. For the soldiers and sailors in battle, the absence of any visible friendly air presence was bound to lead to the perception that their fellow air force combatants were not pulling their weight. This had of course always been completely unfair; the aircrews were under orders to be somewhere else, but the seeds of distrust had been sown. These feelings of mistrust could only grow stronger as the Allied numerical advantage increased and the excuse of air inferiority was no longer valid.

On the ground, this distrust tended to manifest itself as discontent with the level of protection against air attack rather than a lack of air support on the battlefield. Being bombed was a far more obvious air force failing than the absence of close air support. In past battles ground forces had a lot to complain about, but for the Salerno landings the fighter cover was focused and comprehensive. Complaints reflected past rather than present failings. It only took the lightest of attacks to re-ignite the criticisms of the past. This was all rather ironic given that the tactical air policy hammered out by Coningham and Tedder had air superiority as the absolute first priority.

The level of Luftwaffe activity was so low it made it difficult to justify the number of fighters used for defensive patrolling. Some fighters were soon setting off with bombs to attack ground targets before beginning their patrol and even, on occasion, being briefed en route on targets to attack.[21] However, it seems for the most part, fighters freed from the air protection role were switched to the second priority task of attacking communications in the rear. On 10 September, the A-36 Mustang/Invader dive-bombers previously used as fighters were attacking targets in the Potenza area, fifty miles behind the front line.

It did not take much to cause these fighters to be pulled back to air defence duties. The Luftwaffe started deploying a new generation of guided weapons against naval vessels: the Fritz X guided glide-bomb and the Henschel Hs 293 guided missile. The former was a free-fall weapon for use against heavily armoured warships while the latter was rocket-powered and used for attacking smaller vessels. Both weapons were guided by radio, enabling aircraft to launch accurate attacks from safer altitudes and distances. The effectiveness of Fritz X was dramatically demonstrated on 9 September when the Italian battleship *Roma* was sunk and her sister ship badly damaged as they attempted to make for an Allied port. On 11 September the American cruiser USS *Savannah* was seriously damaged by a guided bomb. This immediately brought demands for all fighters to return to defensive duties. On 16 September HMS *Warspite* was seriously damaged by a Fritz X guided bomb.[22] Despite these successes, the scale of attack was never sufficient to threaten the invasion.

The Allies soon discovered the landing was not going to be the formal occupation of a surrendering country. Any hopes that the Germans would be too busy disarming their former allies proved well wide of the mark. The landings were greeted by fierce resistance and progress from the bridgeheads was slow. This was where close air support could help eliminate strongpoints and help maintain the momentum of the advance. The advance was not just slowing, in places local German counter-attacks were soon pushing the Allied troops back. Despite the growing difficulties the troops on the ground found themselves in, there was still no great urgency about providing them with any air support.

The bombing of communication targets throughout southern Italy was thorough and destructive. Nevertheless, by the 12th, the Herman Göring Division had arrived from Naples and 29th Panzer Grenadier division from Calabria. The Herman Göring Division struck the British from the north, driving them out of the Molina Pass and blocking the path to Naples. Even more dangerous was a counter-attack launched on 12 September by the 16th and 19th Panzer Divisions, exploiting the gap between the American and British bridgeheads. The British were driven out of Battipaglia and the next day the Americans lost possession of Persano. The situation in the American beachhead was critical, with German forces at one point just half a mile from the beaches. Unloading was halted and evacuating the southern beachhead was being considered.

As in Sicily, the initial response was to rely on naval bombardment to support the hard-pressed ground troops. Fighters finishing their defensive patrols were encouraged to use up any remaining ammunition on targets of opportunity in the battle area. However, on the 12th, A-36 dive-bombers were still attacking targets around Potenza and Sapri, up to sixty miles behind the front line, and the light, medium and heavy bombers were operating even further afield. On the 13th the growing crisis at the beachhead resulted in more effort being focused closer to the front with Baltimores, Mitchells, Liberators and Fortresses bombing lines of communication in the Sala Consilina, Auletta and Torre del Greco areas. However, on the evening of the 13th, it was decided that the situation had become serious enough for all air effort to be focused in the battle area.[23]

On 14 September, around 1,200 bomber light, medium and heavy bomber sorties struck targets within a twenty-five-mile radius of Salerno, with some as close to the front line as the recently vacated town of Battipaglia. This was virtually obliterated by Fortress and Marauder bombers. Flying Fortress were scarcely the ideal tactical bomber; from the altitudes they operated, hitting individual battlefield targets was impossible. However, flattening a town was an effective way of blocking movement and an enemy massing their forces for counter-attacks made a reasonably large target for carpet bombing. Baltimores and Mitchells were also used from lower altitudes against troop concentrations in the battle zone. Around 1,000 fighter and fighter-bomber sorties were flown, with many fighters on defensive duties bombing targets of opportunity before beginning their patrols. The Desert Air Force also flew fighter-bomber sorties from airfields in Calabria. During the night of the 14th/15th, 200 night bombers, including 126 Wellingtons, kept up the pressure on German forces, by flying low over the battle zone and bombing any target that presented itself. For the Wellingtons this was a much more useful contribution to the Allied cause than attempting to drop bombs on German cities. On the 15th the assault continued with 550 of the 850 fighter sorties involving ground-attack and over 400 bomber sorties.[24] By comparison, German effort in the battle area does not appear to have exceeded 200 sorties in any one day.

Naval artillery also played a critical role. American and British warships benefitted from the presence of the Austers of No. 654 Squadron. These landed on D-Day and by the following morning were operating from a landing ground 150 yards from the beach. During the German counter-

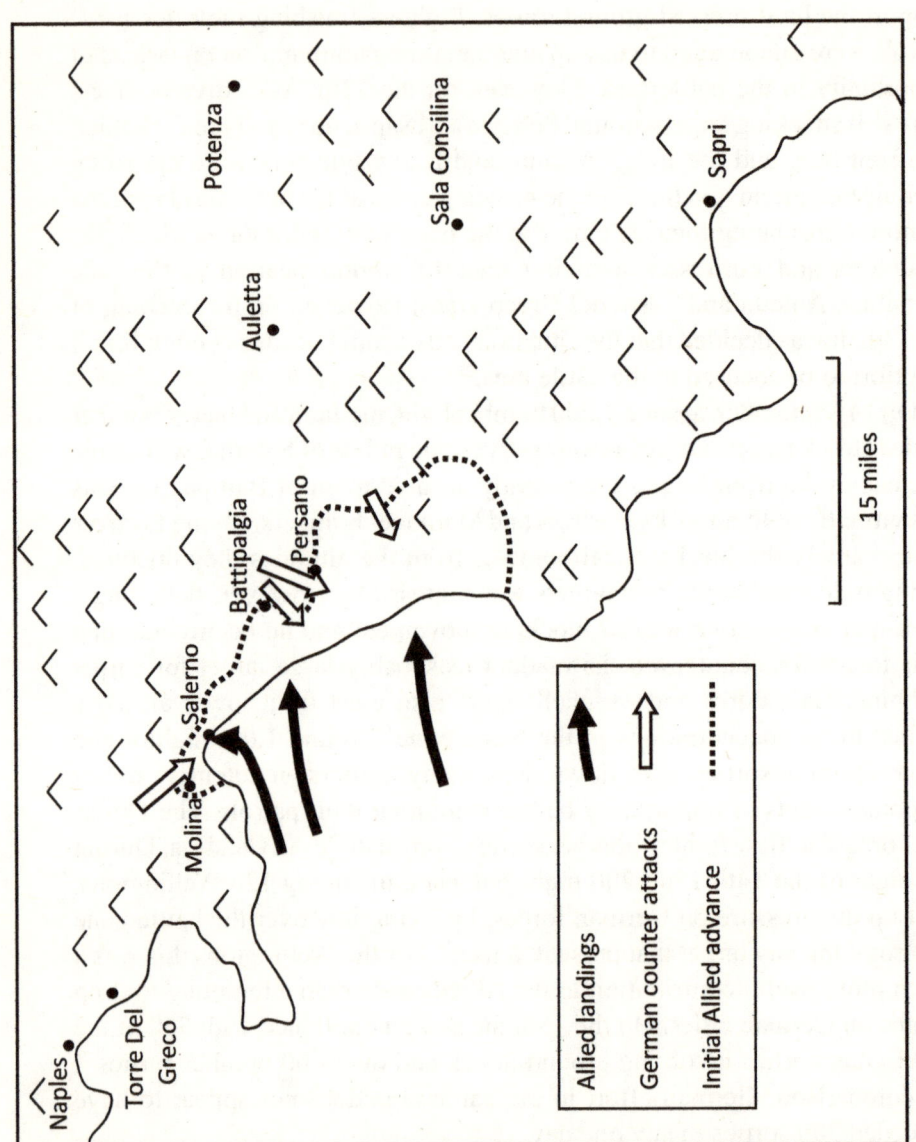

Salerno landing September 1943.

attacks they played a key role directing naval fire on to the advancing German forces.[25] Without functioning forward control posts the air support the bombers provided lacked this sort of precision but it was effective by sheer stint of scale. In the end, air power, the naval guns and fierce resistance on the ground had combined to save the day. Eisenhower was again greatly impressed by the impact airpower had on the course of land battle, but perhaps a little too impressed by the bludgeoning blows the heavy bombers could deliver.

It was still a defensive use of airpower, rather than the offensive use made of close air support by the Desert Air Force in its heyday. Airpower could do much more than save the day; it was a key means of creating and maintaining the momentum of an advance, especially when, for whatever reason, the army's normal artillery was not available. In an amphibious assault naval firepower would always be available, but air support could provide greater precision and was always a boost to morale.[26] Allied indirect air support had failed to prevent the Germans mounting dangerous counter-attacks, but switching bomber support to the battlefield had done much to defeat these attacks. An earlier application of battlefield air support might have helped the invading forces keep the initiative and made it more difficult to organise these counter-attacks. Unless there was some flexibility about the air superiority/interdiction/close air support order of priority, the Allies were not going to get a good return on their overwhelming numerical superiority in the air.

A final effort to eliminate the bridgehead was made by the Germans on the 16th but in the face of stiff resistance this made no progress. The next day the advance guard of Eighth Army made contact with patrols pushing out from the Salerno bridgehead and the German forces began a phased withdrawal. This was also the first day a request from a forward controller for air support was met.[27] It was this sort of directed precision support that had been needed from the very first day.

All the organisations in the United Kingdom involved in preparing for Overland were watching events in Italy closely. There was much to ponder. A bridgehead on an enemy coastline had been established but it had been contained. Indeed, the Salerno landings had come close to failing and had most certainly not achieved the decisive strategic impact anticipated. In the end it was only the largely unopposed advance of Montgomery's Eighth Army from the south that persuaded the Germans to withdraw from the Salerno area to defensive positions north of Naples. None of this was encouraging for those planning an invasion of France.

The air support Broadhurst's Desert Air Force was providing was one bright spot and the War Office were enthusiastic about developing it further. A War Office note in September 1943, passed on to the Overlord planners, the Second Tactical Air Force and Air Ministry, emphasised how experience in Sicily had already demonstrated that:

> if Rover tentacles are always kept with the leading bdes [brigades] on the axis of advance, supporting air formations should be very well in the local picture and able to give quick and intimate support against resistance which might otherwise demand a full-scale attack and an elaborate artillery plan.[28]

This, however, was not the Montgomery way. He did not see 'quick and intimate' air support as an alternative to his meticulously planned set-piece battles. The War Office alternative required initiative and boldness at all levels of command, a willingness to seek and exploit opportunities that arose. These were qualities that Montgomery did not believe could be inculcated in a conscript army. He believed his troops needed the certainty of victory that meticulous planning and preparation could provide, not the uncertainty bold risk taking involved. The flexible and rapid response air support could provide was not required by Montgomery's methods.

There was no shortage in the Mediterranean of aircraft capable of providing close air support. As the German forces pulled back from Salerno, they were hounded by Allied Lightning, Mustang dive-bomber and Kittyhawks, with the long-range Lightnings proving particularly useful as the distance between the retreating German forces and the available airfields grew. By the end of September, most American and British air units were operating from mainland Italian airfields, allowing the shorter range fighters to play more of a role. With Rover tentacles attached to each of the two Eighth Army divisions advancing along the eastern coastal plain, the provision of close air support seemed well catered for.[29] It would soon be needed to avert a mini-crisis.

The Germans initially had no plans to make a major stand in central Italy. Hitler planned to withdraw to defensive positions in northern Italy, where the Gothic Line was already being prepared. German holding positions on the Volturno in the west and the Biferno, Trigno and Sangro rivers in the east were merely intended to buy time for the completion of the Gothic Line. The Biferno line was soon under threat. On the night of 2/3 October, commandos landed at Termoli, a port just north of the Biferno.

Three days later, these forces were taken by surprise by a fierce German counter-attack supported by tanks and fighter-bombers. The Allied forces were pushed back to within half of a mile of the sea. Poor weather had limited air operations up to this point but over the next two days around 950 sorties were flown in and around the battle zone. Their intervention helped break up the German attack and won warm praise from army commanders.[30]

Montgomery had a bridgehead across the Biferno but he showed little inclination to take advantage with the imaginative offensive air/ground partnership the War Office in London seemed to be envisaging. As soon as any serious resistance was encountered, it was time to regroup and take stock. Overcoming each German holding position seemed to require a period of preparation and a set-piece battle. A bolder approach, with maintaining momentum more important than guarding against failure, might have helped keep the advance going. The well-established ability of the air forces to intervene when unexpected resistance arose should have provided some re-assurance. On the other hand, army commanders would argue they could scarcely count on this support as poor weather had a habit of intervening and there was no shortage of poor weather in Italy around this time. If the aircraft were not actually grounded, finding targets became problematic. Poor visibility had led to some friendly fire incidents, which did little to encourage requests for more air support. Procedures were tightened up with no close support being delivered unless there were clear landmarks or the target was clearly marked by smoke shells or some other indicator.[31]

Nor was the air support always as prompt as it might have been. Poor communications meant that some attacks were delivered up to two hours after the troops at the front had been told to expect them. The physical damage inflicted on the enemy was not always great either. However, the psychological boost to advancing troops of fighter-bombers attacking targets ahead of them was enormous, and this alone made them worthwhile. Equally significant was the demoralising effect on the enemy, especially as there was often little sign of similar support from the Luftwaffe. Indeed the absence of German activity in the air was freeing more Allied aircraft for ground attack. From 29 October Spitfires were switched to the fighter-bomber role.[32] There was no shortage of ways of providing close air support but there was still much to be done to ensure it was always delivered it in a timely and accurate fashion.

Closer co-ordination ideally needed a more integrated Army/Air Force set up. The Austers of the Air Observation Post squadrons were showing the way. These were under Army control which made them much more responsive to Army needs. They had no offensive capability but this did not stop them having a major influence on the struggle on the ground. The very presence of a snooping Auster could induce the enemy to cease fire for fear of becoming the target of Allied artillery. During the crossing of the Volturno, a continuous watch by Austers of No. 654 Squadron was enough to halt troublesome German mortar fire while a bridge across the river was completed. They were also providing information on the position and progress of friendly forces as well as identifying enemy positions and carrying out a host of often unglamorous but vital liaison/communication tasks, including taking army commanders into the air to see the lie of the land. The commander of 7th Armoured Division, operating with Clark's Fifth Army on the other side of ther Apennines, described how a flight of Austers attached to his division had proved priceless in speeding the division's advance by providing warning of and helping to deal with problems ahead.[33]

However, having an air force that was part of an army was no guarantee of close co-operation. The USAAF was part of the American Army but the friction caused by an air force trying to establish its right to independence could be just as great as one trying to justify independence. While Broadhurst was doing his best to close the divide that separated Army and Air Force, the gap between Clark's largely American Fifth Army and its XII Air Support Command (ASC) seemed to be growing ever wider. This, like Broadhurst's Desert Air Force formed part of Coningham's First Tactical Air Force, which in turn was an element of Tedder's Mediterranean Air Command. USAAF commanders were more than happy to follow the steer provided by their British commanders. Indeed, without Broadhurst as a counterweight, Tedder and Coningham's ideas were probably more influential within Clark's Fifth Army than Montgomery's Eighth.

Clark's commanders were constantly demanding far closer support than his tactical XII ASC was willing to provide, with frustration growing on both sides. The air force were not impressed by the army's shrill demands for better air cover every time the Luftwaffe managed any sort of attack. For their part the army felt the air force was showing too much interest in targets too far beyond the battlefield to be useful. Air commanders did not endear themselves to the army commanders by insisting they needed twelve hours' notice for any requested air strike. On 13 October troops came under Luftwaffe attack but when they requested their own air support they were told the weather was too poor. It seemed to the Army that the weather affected the USAAF more than it affected the Luftwaffe. Four requests made for air support between 14 and 17 October were all turned down. The poor weather on the 14th and 17th was undoubtedly a factor but, on the 16th, with fine weather, XII Air Support Command did not enhance its reputation by turning down one request because flak concentrations in the area were considered too strong.

Neither side had much faith in the other's willingness to play their part. The British system of having a forward controller to guide the attacking aircraft in was tried and worked well when used on 23 October, when the American troops being supported took their objective with few casualties. However, there did not seem to be any attempt to make this practice widespread.[34] The Tedder/Coningham philosophy of focusing air effort beyond the battlefield seemed to be prevailing on the western side of the mountains. In the east, Montgomery seemed happy enough to have Broadhurst's air units supporting him, but his efforts were going against the grain of official air force thinking.

From 20 November Allied forces were across the River Sangro at several points but it was the 27th before a full-scale crossing was underway. Montgomery's refusal to be rushed might be justified by logistical factors, but battlefield air support is most useful when the situation on the ground is fluid. Montgomery's methodical approach provided least opportunity for tactical air support to make a difference. Nevertheless, Broadhurst was stepping up his efforts to refine what he could offer. He was concerned by the relatively low number of requests for support from forward troops, which meant the majority of sorties were still being flown against targets in the rear. Enemy artillery and communications were important but Broadhurst wanted more air involvement much closer to the front line, with aircraft engaging targets as small as machine-gun nests or anti-tank guns holding up the advance. He was also unhappy with the time taken for the air support to arrive.

For the crossing of the Sangro, Broadhurst instituted a new system, devised by Wing Commander David Haysom, which soon became known as Rover David. The basic difference was that the forward controller would not just guide the attack in, he would also nominate the target and issue the instructions. A flight of six fighter-bombers would take up a position in the vicinity of the front line where they would await instructions from the forward controller. When a suitable target appeared the squadron would be briefed in the air and then deliver the strike. The whole process was expected to take little more than ten minutes from request to attack. If no target appeared, at the end of the patrol the flight would attack an alternative pre-determined secondary target. They would then be replaced by the next flight on the 'cab rank'.[35] It was by no means a new idea; Air Marshal John Slessor had organised a similar arrangement while commanding air units in India in the thirties.[36]

The main advantage was not so much having the fighter-bomber in position over the front ready to strike – the airfields they were operating from were only some fifteen minutes flying time away from the front. The key advantage was that it cut out the Army/Air Force request/deliberation/authorisation process. Army commanders could nominate targets and, if the RAF officer with the forward control thought it was a reasonable task, these would be passed straight to the pilots flying above. Effectively, the Army had direct control of the fighter-bombers flying above them. The Army was getting the decentralised control the Air Ministry had so often ridiculed as the 'penny packet' approach and it was getting it without upsetting Air Force sensitivities over control and ownership.

On the first day of the Sangro offensive only one request was made but more came in on following days with enemy 'forward defended localities' and machine-gun nests among the targets engaged. These was a clear clash of priorities here between Broadhurst, who was keen to take on these relatively minor targets on the battlefield, and Coningham, who felt such targets should not be the business of the Air Force. The experiment, however, was declared a success. There were problems to overcome. Forward troops were often unaware that air support had been called in and so did not indicate their position This did not prove to be too much of a problem in practice – pilots were sufficiently familiar with the terrain and briefing sufficiently detailed for serious errors to be avoided – but clearly this was an area that needed to be improved for rapid advances into less familiar terrain. Also, the transport the Rovers were using lacked the cross-country capability to keep up with the advance. It was very much a work in progress but the advantages and potential of this cab-rank system were clear, to the Army and Broadhurst at least.[37]

As pilots became more involved in the land battle there was a new awareness among them of the dangers the foot soldier faced. This encouraged a sense of solidarity with the infantry and a greater willingness to accept the dangers close support sometimes involved. Soldiers, too, were becoming more aware of exactly what aircraft could and could not do.[38] It was becoming a genuine joint effort. During the drive towards Orsogna in December, in order to counter heavy German flak, artillery engaged known flak sites before the fighter-bombers attacked.[39] The need to work together was producing the sort of unity of purpose that had always existed in more tactically orientated air forces, where the Air Force and Army were part of the same force, both in body and in spirit, rather than separate often quarrelling services.

Decades of inter-service bickering, empire building and, on the air side, a mistaken assumption that airpower decided wars, had left their mark. At lower levels at least, the divisions were being healed and the bitterness of the early war years was dissipating. However, the significance of the close co-operation that Broadhurst was encouraging was least well understood at the higher levels of both services. For air force commanders, supporting the army on the battlefield did not fit in with their conception of an all-conquering air force. If tactical air support had been delivering dramatic, war-changing results, air commanders might have been more enthusiastic but this was an unrealistic expectation. The reality was that close air support was just one small part of the military jigsaw puzzle Britain's armed services needed to piece together. For the apostles of air power this was all rather underwhelming. As far as Tedder and Coningham were concerned, the failure of close air support to produce any obvious, clear-cut results merely confirmed their belief that this was not a useful way of supporting Army operations.

For Eisenhower, the failure of Allied air power to make much difference was rather puzzling and extremely frustrating. He, too, was being sucked into the notion that airpower was all conquering. In Italy, the Allies had total control of the skies. The Luftwaffe had almost disappeared. The Allies could bomb any targets as far behind the front line as they liked. Yet there was no sign of the German army disintegrating or even buckling. Montgomery's quote 'If we lose the war in the air we lose the war and we lose it quickly.' is still often trotted out as a self-evident truth.[40] The German forces in Italy were not losing the war very quickly.

It was as mystifying to many then as it is to some even now. Throughout the early victorious German campaigns of the Second World War, Germany's adversaries had blamed overwhelming German airpower for their defeats. Possessing air superiority became the Holy Grail. Its mere possession was supposed to solve all problems. Now the Allies possessed it, the anticipated easy victories were not materialising. In truth, Allied commanders had never understood why Blitzkrieg worked. Allied thinking had been distorted by the indelible image and sounds of nerve-shattering Stuka dive-bombers, which seemed to suggest German success was all about airpower. In fact, the method had worked not because the Germans had air superiority but because they knew how to exploit air superiority. It was not just the mobile firepower the Luftwaffe offered, it was the freedom air superiority granted German army commanders and the way they exploited this freedom that made the German Wehrmacht so effective as an offensive force. German commanders at all levels were masters at combining what was available to deal with a particular situation. Luftwaffe air superiority had provided the ideal conditions in which these attributes could flourish. The German Wehrmacht remained formidable because these qualities were not going to disappear just because air support was not as plentiful as it had been. The lack of air superiority might constrain German forces and limit their offensive options but it was not going to reduce their effectiveness as a fighting force.

It was this ability to combine different arms and grasp opportunities that Allied commanders needed to try and match if they were to take full advantage of air superiority. Allied commanders at all levels had to start seeing the opportunities instead of being put off by the dangers. They had to stop fixating on stopping the enemy air force from intervening and focus more on using the available air power to serve their own forces. Simply having air superiority will not bring victories on the battlefield but, if exploited to the full, it can help achieve those victories. It was very much a virtuous circle. Air support makes bolder action on land easier and the bolder the action on the ground, the more useful and indeed critical effective air support becomes. If the Italian campaign established anything it was that just possessing air superiority does not guarantee rapid advances, and not having it does not necessarily condemn armies to instant defeat.

As if to emphasise the laboured advance of the Allies in Italy, the Germans gave a demonstration of what bold action with air support could achieve. Following the Italian surrender, both Hitler and Churchill were anxious to occupy the Dodecanese, the Italian garrisoned islands strung out between Crete and Turkey. Churchill was still harbouring hopes of bringing Turkey into to the war. Hitler wanted to secure his southern flank and keep Turkey neutral. The local Italian garrisons had no interest in defying their new pro-Allied government, but the geography was on the side of the Germans. Rhodes with its three airfields was quickly occupied by the Germans, while Kos, with a single airfield and Leros were taken by the British. Airfields on Cyprus were 350 miles away, a distance American P-38 Lightnings could cover, but not British fighters. The Americans had made it very clear they had no interest in an operation they saw as a political move by Britain to influence the make-up of the post-war Balkans rather than accelerate the defeat of Hitler and Eisenhower rejected requests to transfer USAAF Lightning squadrons to the Eastern Mediterranean.

The Luftwaffe concentrated around 300 aircraft in the area. The airfield on Kos was bombed, the Spitfire strength gradually whittled away and, on 3 October, 4,000 German troops were landed by sea and air. For one last time on the Western Front the Ju 87 screamed into action as a dive-bomber and the 5,000 British and Italian troops surrendered the next day. Leros fell almost as swiftly early in November. The Royal Navy lost five destroyers to air attacks during the campaign, one of which was a victim of the Henschel HS 293 air-to-ground guided missile.

There was much here to ponder. The long-range fighter cover the Lightning could have provided might have made the difference. Eisenhower's refusal to help was a reminder of how dependent Britain was becoming on the United States. It was also a reminder of the vulnerability of warships to air attack and a demonstration of how dynamic, decisive and effective even small numbers of German troops could be. None of this bode well for the Normandy landings, nor indeed proposed amphibious landings in Italy. The speed and efficiency of these German conquests made Allied efforts in the Mediterranean look rather clumsy by comparison. Churchill and Brooke were as frustrated as Eisenhower by the slow progress in Italy. Frontal assaults were clearly not the answer; Brooke felt the Allied armies had to exploit their superiority at sea and in the air by outflanking these defences with an amphibious assault in the enemy rear. The Anzio landings were beginning to crystallise in the minds of Brooke and Churchill.

Meanwhile, in Italy the lack of progress on the ground was encouraging a significant shift in the type of operations the tactical air forces were engaged in. Throughout September, October and November battlefield gun positions had been top of the Allied list of targets but, in December, they were replaced by marshalling yards to the rear.[41] It was a shift in emphasis which reflected the growing stalemate on the ground but also hinted how air commanders thought this stalemate would be broken. Instead of frontal assaults or outflanking amphibious landings, air commanders argued that starving German front-line troops of supplies would alone force a retreat to the Po Valley, an idea that would soon become a reality in the shape of Operation Strangle.[42] This was the air purist's dream of airpower winning wars without any need for forces on the ground. Tedder was certainly impressed by the idea and, with the advice and support of his scientific adviser Solly Zuckerman, was already considering similar ideas for his next great task, the invasion of France. Tedder spoke of his pride in the ability of his tactical air forces to support the Army by attacking enemy lines of communication by night and day 'from the Brenner to the front' but the emphasis was moving towards the former rather than the latter.

The move away from Broadhurst's emphasis on battlefield air support was part of a general shift in Mediterranean priorities. With the occupation of southern Italy and in particular the complex of airfields in the Foggia region, the American heavy bombers could now switch their focus from tactical communications to strategic Pointblank targets. The change in emphasis was underlined by the regrouping of the American bomber squadrons into the new strategic Fifteenth Air Force, formed in October 1943 as a parallel formation to the UK-based Eighth Air Force. Britain did not have the resources for a second Bomber Command in Italy, but Portal was encouraging Tedder to switch the handful of night-bomber squadrons of No. 205 Group, mostly equipped with Wellingtons, from tactical targets to fighter-related industries in southern Europe.[43]

Tedder needed little prompting. He rather optimistically claimed a recent attack on the Messerschmitt Wiener Neustadt factory 'had the immediate effect of halting deliveries of much needed engines' and enthusiastically set about organising more strategic operations against southern Europe.[44] He described the attack as 'our raid'. Tedder had made much of his desire not to refer to the Americans as 'you' 'From now on it is "we"', he had proudly proclaimed in North Africa, but there was very little 'we' about the strategic air operations from Italy.[45] Tedder was overseeing a largely American effort but happily embraced and approved of the greater strategic emphasis the Fifteenth Air Force was bringing to the theatre. Army commanders were not so happy as the resource hungry strategic bombers ate into the supplies available for operations on the ground.[46]

In December 1943 all air units in the Mediterranean were brought together in the Mediterranean Allied Air Force (MAAF). The priority was supporting the Pointblank strategic offensive, still struggling to complete the preliminary task of crippling the German fighter force. Coningham was infuriated when he was told that his fighter-bombers were going to be redeployed as bomber escorts. His three P-38 Lightning groups, along with a Thunderbolt group were all transferred to the Fifteenth Air Force, denying Coningham a much valued long-range fighter-bomber capability.[47] Tedder might be happy with the direction air policy was taking, but it was becoming too strategic for Coningham.

By this time both Tedder and Coningham had already been lined up for key commands in the Overlord operation. The American General John

Cannon, Coningham's deputy, took over the tactical air forces. Ira Eaker, the commander of Eighth Air Force in the UK, took over from Tedder. Air Marshal Slessor, an ardent supporter of the bomber strategy, became Eaker's deputy and the most senior RAF officer in the Mediterranean. The Mediterranean air commands were now dominated by bomber advocates.

Coningham and Tedder were leaving an Air Force that had been transformed from a predominantly tactical force into one that was much more strategically orientated force. At the beginning of the war, Allied air forces in the Mediterranean had not been able to pursue a strategic bombing policy because there were no major suitable targets within striking distance. The limited available resources had to be used tactically. By late 1943 the Allied advance had brought German industrial targets within range. With the vast resources available to the Americans there was no problem maintaining strategic and tactical air forces in the region. However, the desire for more independently orientated air operations was also dragging tactical airpower away from the battlefield. Despite the efforts of Broadhurst, the balance between indirect and direct tactical support was becoming ever more weighted in favour of the former. There was no doubting the increasing sophistication in the way close air support was being delivered. History, however, was repeating itself. Much of the unity of purpose on the battlefield that had characterised early operations in East Africa and the Western Desert, had disappeared by the time the Allies invaded Sicily. It was beginning to re-emerge in Italy, but once again it was draining away.

This left Burma as the one RAF theatre where the value of battlefield air support was still fully appreciated. Here, too, enemy industrial targets remained well out of range so there was no such temptation to muddy the waters. The focus remained on winning the land battle. As was the case in the Middle East, pre-war colonial operations meant there was some tradition of air and ground forces working together. Lieutenant General William Slim, the commander of ground forces in Burma had a more mobile, flexible approach to ground operations than Montgomery, and this encouraged and indeed required a more pro-active battlefield role from the air force. As far as Slim was concerned, close air support was just as important as interdiction and there were no fleets of bludgeoning heavy bombers to distract attention from the precision that low-level attack and dive-bombing could provide. The RAF was also needed for supplying surrounded forces and ferrying out casualties, two roles which were crucial in difficult jungle and mountainous terrain and which, even more than active combat support, helped bond the two services. There was a unity of purpose in the Far East at all levels of command that was growing stronger as the war progressed. The opposite was happening in Europe.

The command positions for Overlord would be dominated by Mediterranean commanders. Eisenhower became the supreme commander for the invasion and Tedder his deputy. Montgomery was to command the British and Canadian armies, which together formed 21 Army Group. Montgomery brought with him Lieutenant General Miles Dempsey to command the British Second Army. Coningham replaced Air Marshal John D'Albiac as commander of the Second Tactical Air Force. Broadhurst stayed in Italy for the time being. It was argued that the Italian theatre should not lose all its command assets but, given their different attitude to battlefield air support, for Tedder and Coningham it was no great loss.

Eisenhower, Tedder and Coningham brought with them their interpretation of the lessons learned in the North African and Italian campaigns. In Britain Lieutenant General Frederick Morgan was already hard at work laying the foundations for the invasion they would lead.

Chapter Four

Cover for Overlord

Morgan had been appointed as Chief of Staff to the Supreme Allied Commander (COSSAC) in the spring of 1943 and since then had been working on a detailed invasion plan. Stalin had hoped the invasion of France would take place in 1941 and had been led to believe it would take place in 1942. He was then assured that it would take place in 1943. It seemed inconceivable that he would be denied again in 1944. Yet, with Brooke insisting the bomber offensive must first seriously weaken the German Army, and the problems the bomber offensive was having trying to achieve this, there was already a strong case for a further postponement.

Morgan and his staff had decided on Normandy for the landing. Here the German defences would hopefully be less well developed than in the Pas de Calais region, which was a much more obvious invasion route. The Normandy beaches were reasonably easy to land on and the hedgerow countryside to the south and west, with its sunken narrow lanes lined with trees and hedges, was relatively easy to defend. The proximity of a major port, Cherbourg, was another advantage.

In Morgan's original plans the initial landing would consist of just three divisions on two stretches of beach totalling eighteen miles. Within hours of landing, these forces would be expected to capture Caen and establish a bridgehead six to ten miles deep between that city and Bayeux. It was, Morgan conceded, a rather narrow front to land on, but, given the resources he had been asked to work with, it was about the best that could be managed.[1] The short range of RAF fighters dominated planning. The terrain eastwards towards Caen and beyond was more favourable for a rapid advance and the building of airfields. With this territory gained, Cherbourg would be the next key objective. Within a couple of weeks it was hoped to capture the entire Cotentin peninsula and have advance units pushing as far as the line Mont St Michel-Alençon-Falaise-Trouville, a bridgehead sixty-five miles deep. There was always a strange mix of deepest despair about the prospects of an invasion and wild optimism about how quickly territory could be captured.

Morgan was already anticipating massive air support; initial planning assumed 660 squadrons of all types would be available, of which 144 would be fighters. This amounted to a total force in excess of 10,000 aircraft, which indeed was the approximate size of the Allied air forces on D-Day. They would be tasked with maintaining air superiority, attacking reinforcements heading for the front, and providing indirect and direct support for the troops in the beachhead. The latter included air strikes on the beach defences as the troops landed. He was expecting aircraft of widely different types and capabilities to perform the many different roles expected of them. No doubt wishing to make a point, he used a 'tank-buster' as an example of the specialist aircraft that would be required.[2]

A joint services committee set up in August 1943 under the head of the COSSAC Air Branch, Air Vice-Marshal Ronald Graham, to study fire support for the landing, assigned air support a leading role in the elimination of beach defences. Naval artillery would be needed to knock out the more heavily protected gun emplacements, but against less well protected front-line defences air support was considered the better option. Fighter-bombers would also have a key role attacking targets of opportunity in the battle zone as the troops pushed inland.[3] Naval and air fire-power were seen as complementary, not alternatives.

The staged approach that was now characterising operations in the Mediterranean was much in evidence. Air superiority was first priority and had to be achieved before the invasion was launched. Morgan seemed to be assuming that the Luftwaffe would be able to respond on a vastly greater scale than it had been capable of mustering in the Mediterranean. There was very little appreciation of the degree to which the limited resources of the Luftwaffe were already stretched covering the vast frontages the German army was now trying to defend. The exaggerated ideas of what the Luftwaffe might be capable of was a misconception of Britain's own making. By choosing to oppose the Luftwaffe in earlier campaigns in Norway, France and Greece with Gladiators and Hurricanes instead of Spitfires, they had helped create the myth of an all-conquering, invincible Luftwaffe. The second priority was lines of communication. The ability of the Germans to move reserves to an invasion front faster than the Allies could land troops had always been a major concern. Levelling the playing field by attacking enemy communications to slow their arrival was considered vital. Morgan had made it clear that close air support had an important part to play, but the overriding importance of securing air superiority and slowing the movement of reserves was already beginning to dominate thinking.

The absolute importance of air superiority had always been a fundamental tenet of Air Ministry thinking and had become a pre-condition for just about any action. It had never been a German prerequisite. The only occasion in which Germany had attempted to establish air superiority in advance of an assault on the ground had led to the Battle of Britain, which was not Germany's finest hour. One of the unfortunate consequences of the Battle of Britain was that it reinforced Air Ministry ideas that airpower was all decisive. It was believed that just possessing air superiority saved Britain from occupation. This was patently not the case; Spitfires dominating the skies over southern England could have done nothing to stop panzers advancing on London. As the Allies were discovering in Italy, having air superiority does not guarantee anything: it is having the means to exploit air superiority that counts. However, in Air Ministry circles there was a belief that just having air superiority in 1940 made a successful German invasion impossible. By extension, only having air superiority made a 1944 invasion of France possible.

It did not help the Allied cause that the Army and Navy shared this obsession with air superiority. Their demands that air superiority be a precondition were driven by the ghosts of campaigns past, where the RAF's belief that they could do more good by being somewhere else had persistently left their sister services in the lurch. The relatively light naval losses in the landings in Sicily and Italy should perhaps have eased concerns but the arrival of weapons like the guided Henschel Hs 293 and Fritz X suggested the danger was increasing rather than decreasing. Both these weapons enabled bombers to deliver attacks from outside the effective range of naval anti-aircraft fire, leaving the Navy more reliant on fighter cover. The RAF would not be allowed to take any chances with Royal Navy battleships. The War Office also had bitter memories of the constant hammering the Luftwaffe had handed out to British forces in so many campaigns, not least in the 1940 French campaign in which Brooke, as a corps commander, had experienced Luftwaffe hammerings first-hand. Army and Navy commanders accepted losses in battle but, like all commanders, they resented unnecessary losses. With little control over how the RAF should be used, the only sure way of providing protection for their forces was to set air superiority as a hard and fast pre-condition.

The Air Ministry was more than happy to comply. It gave airpower the key central role its commanders craved. Only the air force could make the invasion possible. An air only battle for air superiority unfettered by army or naval considerations was precisely the way the air force wanted to fight wars. It was a role worthy of the air force, and they would be fighting this battle at the request of the Army and Navy. For entirely different reasons the air commanders and their sea and land counterparts were in complete agreement. It was, however, a frame of mind that encouraged the idea that air superiority was the goal rather than simply a means to an end.

Since the 1920s the Air Ministry method for achieving air superiority had been the bomber. Control of the skies was won by bombing enemy aircraft factories, enemy airfields and any other air related target. This was the thinking behind the combined bomber offensive. However, as the war progressed, and theoretical analyses were replaced by practical realities, there was a growing realisation that the fighter had a key role to play. In Air Ministry thinking the fighter had not yet overtaken the bomber as the primary means for establishing control of the skies, but by 1943 it was undeniably an important factor. It was no longer any good just thinking of the fighter as a bomber interceptor. In 1942 Portal had underlined this shift in thinking by requiring a specialist air superiority fighter, the capabilities of which would be determined by what enemy fighters could do, not the performance of enemy bombers. His F.6/42 specification never got off the ground but it was a sign of changing attitudes. When enemy fighters were captured the top priority was to see how they compared to Allied fighters, not how good they were at shooting down Allied bombers. The air superiority fighter of the First World War was back.

In the fighter battle for air superiority, tactics, numbers and quality all come into play. Tactically, it had taken the RAF a long time to switch from the tight 'vic' formations tailor-made for bomber interception to the looser pair and 'finger four' formations that were more suited to fighter-versus-fighter combat. By 1943 the gap in tactical expertise between RAF and Luftwaffe pilots was finally closing. As far as numbers were concerned, the Allies had possessed numerical superiority for some time. The Luftwaffe had thrown away its numerical advantage the day it invaded the Soviet Union. When the Soviet nation did not collapse, numerical inferiority became a fact of life for the Luftwaffe for the rest of the war. Even with the production capacity of an enslaved Europe, Germany was never going to match the aircrew training and aircraft production rates of the British Commonwealth, the United States and the Soviet Union. In the summer of 1943 the RAF alone already had had a two-to-one advantage in fighters in North-West Europe and the Allied advantage was rapidly growing with the arrival of Eighth Air Force fighters.

In terms of quality the situation was also improving. Perhaps more than any other country, British fighter design had been stymied by the focus on the bomber interceptor role. The country had been lucky with the Spitfire. The fighters that were lined up as alternatives or replacements underlined how lucky. Aircraft like the Typhoon, Whirlwind, Beaufighter and Defiant would all have been successful against the unescorted bombers they were designed to shoot down but were hopelessly outmatched when confronted by fighters designed for air combat. Even the Spitfire had not been designed with fighter-versus-fighter combat in mind. First the Bf 109F and then, even more dramatically, the Fw 190, proved superior. In 1943 the appearance of the Bf 109G, accompanied by rumours of a revised Me 209, not to mention second-generation turbo-supercharged and inline-engined Focke-Wulfs (Fw 190B, C and D), the Air Ministry believed it had plenty to worry about.

British fears were eased considerably by a remarkable stroke of good fortune. American fighters had always been superior to British designs in terms of high-speed handling and manoeuvrability. On the other hand, American designs had always suffered from the poor performance of American engines at higher altitudes. Combining American high-speed handling characteristics with British engine technology had resulted in the North American Mustang P-51B, without doubt the best all-round Allied fighter of the war so far. Thanks to a radiator system that was particularly efficient at turning engine heat into forward thrust, a low-drag laminar flow wing and overall better aerodynamics, the Mustang was around 40mph faster than the similarly powered Spitfire IX. It had a similar speed advantage over the Fw 190. Even the Mustang could not match the superb manoeuvrability of the German fighter. The Focke-Wulf would always be a tricky opponent but the Mustang's speed ensured Allied pilots would always have the initiative. The only problem with the fighter had been persuading the Americans how much better it was than the officially favoured P-47 Thunderbolt and P-38 Lightning. By 1943 the Americans had been convinced.

To keep pace with the Merlin 61 Mustang, British designers were having to make use of more powerful engines. The Spitfire provided two options.

The Spitfire 21, the definitive and final version of the classic fighter, would be powered by the much larger, more powerful Griffon 61 engine. It had an entirely new, stiffer wing to improve high-speed manoeuvrability and there were also plans to use a Mustang-style laminar flow wing. It was such a radical re-design it was briefly given the new name of Supermarine Victor. As an alternative there were also hopes that the existing Spitfire VIII airframe could be updated. (The Spitfire VIII was the fully-developed Merlin 61-powered version of the Spitfire, generally used overseas as opposed to the more makeshift Spitfire IX.) With a laminar flow wing and the new, more powerful Merlin 100 series engine replacing the Merlin 61, it was hoped that this would also match the Mustang's speed. Both of these Spitfire variants had a good chance of being available for a 1944 invasion.

The first Spitfire 21 prototype, without all the planned improvements, flew in December 1942. Performance exceeded expectations with a top speed of 455mph, which was faster than the Mustang. However, rather worryingly, it proved to be a handful to fly. Indeed the first prototype crashed. An anxious MAP urged Vickers to get a second prototype into the air as quickly as possible, but clearly there were going to be delays.[4] Meanwhile, to get a bit more experience of flying the Griffon 61, Vickers took six standard Spitfire VIII airframes and made the minimum modifications to allow them to take the larger Griffon engine. In April 1943, extending this idea, the MAP decided to order a batch of fifty, later increased to 100, of these conversions so that a couple of squadrons could get some operational experience with Griffon 61-powered Spitfires.[5] This conversion became the Spitfire XIV.

Initially Air Marshal Trafford Leigh-Mallory, in charge of Fighter Command, saw no need to rush this interim version into service. He did not believe the performance advantage would be so great and, without the extra fuel planned for the Mark 21, the higher fuel consumption of the Griffon would reduce endurance. His first priority was to get the obsolescent Spitfire V out of the front line. It was the Merlin 61-powered Spitfire IX he desperately needed and he did not want deliveries of these to be affected by efforts to get the makeshift Spitfire XIV into production.[6]

At this point, the tried and trusted Spitfire VIII with the more powerful Merlin 100 seemed a safer option. However, doubts about the Spitfire VIII/Merlin 100 were soon growing. The larger Griffon seemed to be offering better climb at medium altitudes and slightly higher speeds than the Merlin 100 could offer.[7] It also transpired that fitting the laminar flow wings to the existing Spitfire VIII fuselage was impossible without a complete redesign.[8]

Indeed, attaching the laminar flow wing to the Spitfire 21 fuselage proved just as problematic and incorporating it would lead to the completely revamped Supermarine Spiteful. The definitive Spitfire 21, without the laminar flow wing, flew in May 1943 and, although the handling problems had not disappeared, such was the urgency it was rushed into production in the hope that any required modifications could be applied as the fighters were being built. Even with this rather desperate measure, the first could not arrive before January 1944 and at best only twenty were expected before the end of April. There did not appear to be much chance of many being available for a 1944 invasion. Indeed there might not be any if the handling problems could not be sorted out.

The good news was the performance of the makeshift Spitfire XIV. In trials held in September 1943 the Spitfire VIII/Griffon 61 combination exceeded all expectations. It possessed a huge advance in performance over the Spitfire IX, as dramatic an advance as the Spitfire IX had been over the Spitfire V, it was claimed. Speed was increased from 409mph to 446mph, service ceiling increased to 44,000 feet and climb rate was also much better at all altitudes. All this was achieved without any deterioration in manoeuvrability.[9] It offered the RAF an immediate home-grown alternative to the Mustang P-51B. The Spitfire XIV had approximately the same horizontal speed, could climb much faster and was far more manoeuvrable. In trials with captured enemy fighters it proved superior to the Bf 109G in all respects, superior to the Fw 190A in all respects except rate of roll and there was every expectation it would be at least a match for any improved versions of the Fw 190 that might appear.[10]

With fears that these and the Me 209 might appear at any moment, the Air Ministry were anxious to get the Spitfire XIV into large-scale production as soon as possible. To the relief of the Air Ministry, Leigh-Mallory completely changed his tune once he heard what his pilots thought of the fighter and was soon appealing for as many as possible before the spring of 1944.[11] As first deliveries of the Spitfire 21 drifted further into the future, orders for the Spitfire XIV were increased and, like the Spitfire IX before it, it became much more than an emergency interim. The first squadron started re-equipping with Spitfire XIVs in January 1944, a month after the first Merlin 61-powered Mustangs entered service. The decision to adopt the Spitfire XIV proved to be doubly fortuitous. The teething problems with the Spitfire 21 could not be sorted out. The fighter's handling characteristics were so poor the fighters coming off the production lines were declared unusable in their existing form.[12]

Once again, as with the Spitfire IX, the problem was getting the updated Mark XIV to the squadrons in numbers. The bomber programme was placing huge demands on Rolls Royce production capacity. There was still a shortage of Merlin 61s, never mind Griffon 61s. Leigh-Mallory worried that, come the spring of 1944, some of his squadrons would still be equipped with the Spitfire V, a fighter that had been outclassed by the Bf 109F ever since it entered service in 1941. Spitfire V production was being phased out in the summer of 1943 but such was the shortfall in Merlin 61 production that engineless Spitfire IX airframes were piling up in storage units.[13] In November 1943 an exasperated Air Ministry was bitterly complaining that the Germans seemed to manage to get their latest types into service much quicker than Britain seemed capable of doing. German units on the western front, they pointed out, appeared to have been exclusively equipped with the latest versions of Fw 190 and Bf 109 for some months. The contrast was indeed striking. The Spitfire IX entered service in July 1942, but sixteen months later there were still only two Spitfire IX squadrons to every three Spitfire V squadrons in the United Kingdom.[14] Indeed, remarkably, as late as March 1944, on the eve of Overlord, squadrons equipped with Spitfire IX were having to convert back to the Spitfire V because of the shortage. In June 1944 eleven of the fifty-five Spitfire fighter squadrons were still equipped with the Spitfire V.[15]

Rolls Royce were partly to blame with their determination to maintain their reputation for quality craftsmanship. The two-stage Merlin 61 and Griffon 61 were complicated engines to build, but Rolls Royce abhorrence of mass production methods using semi-skilled labour was not making it any easier to produce them. The Rolls Royce factories (along with the Ford shadow factory) were supposed to be turning out nearly 3,000 engines a month. The extra complications in the manufacture of the two-stage Merlin 61 and Griffon 61 engines meant targets had to be cut back, but even these lower targets were not being met. In May 1943 total monthly production was little more than 2,000 engines a month.

The Air Ministry, however, were scarcely entirely innocent victims. Production was falling behind schedule but it had always been the plan to re-equip Spitfire V squadrons at a leisurely rate so as not to affect the output of Merlin XX engines required by bomber production. It was a question of priorities. The Germans were quicker at getting the latest fighters into large-scale service because that was their priority. The Air Ministry was very happy to celebrate the way Germany was being forced to focus production on what it saw as defensive fighters at the expense of offensive bombers, but they were not so happy when they did not get the fighters the RAF needed.

Leigh-Mallory might fret at still having to use Spitfire Vs instead of Spitfire IXs and be pushing for the rapid introduction of the Spitfire XIV, but his problems paled into insignificance when compared to the plight of RAF and Commonwealth fighter squadrons in other regions of the globe. In Burma, the RAF was just happy to get Spitfires of any mark. No Spitfires reached Burma until November 1943 and these were the second-generation Spitfire Vs Leigh-Mallory was so anxious to be rid of. These went into action for the first on 26 December, just as the first fourth-generation Spitfire XIVs were reaching RAF squadrons in the UK. Commanders in Burma rejoiced at finally having a fighter with the speed and altitude performance to intercept the previously uncatchable Japanese Mitsubishi Ki-46 Dinah reconnaissance planes.[16] The history of Spitfire deployment within the RAF was indeed a very sorry tale.

The shortage of Rolls Royce engines was also affecting the options open to Hawker for their Tempest programme. This refined version of the Typhoon was supposed to eliminate the persistent aerodynamic and structural problems that plagued Camm's original offering. However, the fighter's Napier Sabre II engines were just as troublesome as the Typhoon airframe. The more advanced Sabre IV that was supposed to power the Tempest I had been abandoned entirely. The Bristol Centaurus radial-engined Tempest II was lined up as the alternative but it was becoming clear there would be no Centaurus engines until 1945. Rolls Royce Griffon IIb and Griffon 61 were in production and had been proposed as Sabre alternatives with the Tempest III and Tempest IV respectively, but the shortage of Rolls Royce engines scuppered these plans. The Tempest had to go into production with the Typhoon's original Sabre II engine as the Tempest V. Only this version was going to be available in time for an invasion.

Given the troubled history of the Typhoon/Tempest project, expectations were not high. However, with its thinner wing and a redesigned tail, most of the aerodynamic problems had been resolved and, with English Electric now running the Napier development programmes, the Sabre II was a much more reliable engine. Trials early in 1943 reported the Tempest V was manoeuvrable and pleasant to fly with no major handling difficulties.[17] With the same engine as the Typhoon, it was up to 30mph quicker in level flight and climbed far faster. With a clear all-round-view bubble canopy, the Tempest had turned into a very reasonable combat aircraft.

Even so, it was less manoeuvrable than the Spitfire XIV and had nothing like its rate of climb. The Tempest could dive faster, was faster in level flight below 10,000 feet and was even credited with a better high-speed rate of roll. Above 20,000 feet the Spitfire was far superior and above 30,000 feet the Tempest could scarcely operate at all. It was far less manoeuvrable than the Fw 190 but its higher speed would always give its pilot an advantage.[18] It was still a rather typical British oversized interceptor, scarcely the nimble air superiority fighter Portal had wanted with his abandoned F.6/42 specification. (The Hawker Fury with a much reduced wing span was an attempt to bring the Tempest more in line with what Portal wanted.) Despite its disadvantages, it gave the RAF another 430mph-plus fighter to supplement the P-51B Mustang and Spitfire XIV. The first Tempest reached the squadrons in January 1944.

With no sign of more advanced versions of Fw 190 and the increasingly mysterious Me 209 (it was a failure and had been cancelled), the Air Ministry was becoming more relaxed about the quality of the available British fighters. The Spitfire IX was a competitive opponent for current Luftwaffe fighters, especially with the tinkering inspired by trials with a captured Fw 190. The fighter was now appearing in two versions. The Spitfire IX LF (low fighter) which had a Merlin engine that gave maximum power at lower altitudes specifically to deal with the Fw 190. This was the version that would equip Second Tactical Air Force. The Spitfire IX HF (high fighter) had a Merlin optimised for high-altitude operations, making it more suitable for dealing with the Bf 109G. A smattering of Spitfire XIVs, Tempest Vs and Mustang IIIs (the RAF designation for the P-51B), provided some insurance against the appearance of a new generation of German piston-engined fighters.

In terms of quality, despite the disappointingly high number of Spitfire Vs still in service, there was no reason for Morgan to be overly concerned. Nor need he worry about numbers; for some time the Allied fighters in the UK had vastly outnumbered those available to the Luftwaffe. His main concern was not so much how good the fighters were or how many there were, but how far they could fly. All the information he was getting from the Air Ministry suggested that the 110 miles that separated Britain from the Normandy coast posed insuperable problems for British fighters.

Ever since a landing in France had first been considered in late 1941, the limited range of British fighters had been portrayed as a major, possibly insoluble, problem. All sorts of frightening charts were made available to Morgan to underline how precarious the fighter protection would be because of these range limitations. These were accompanied by stern warnings that it was simply technically impossible to do any better. Yet events in the Far East had already clearly demonstrated it was possible to do far better. Japanese fighters seemed capable of operating over vast distances, much further than the 100-odd miles that separated the British and Normandy coastlines. Churchill was furious at having been misled, but Portal stuck to his guns, insisting carrying extra fuel was simply out of the question.[19]

Portal was grossly exaggerating the problem. It had always been possible to increase Spitfire fuel capacity. Long-range unarmed reconnaissance versions of the Spitfire, with additional rear fuselage and wing leading-edge tanks, had been carrying vastly more internal fuel since 1940. There was nothing to stop some of these modifications being used by armed fighters. Indeed such modifications had been under consideration since 1940.[20] The Air Ministry's subsequent objections to increasing the Spitfire's internal fuel seemed to reach fever pitch when covering an invasion was being discussed. Whenever there was any other reason, the Air Ministry did not hesitate to insist the Spitfire carry more fuel.

This had happened with the Spitfire VIII. The Merlin 61 consumed fuel faster than previous versions of the engine. To compensate room was found for two leading-edge wing tanks, with an additional twenty-six gallons, and a larger fuselage tank with an extra eleven gallons), increasing internal fuel by over 40 per cent. It was felt that these modifications could not be applied to the Merlin 61 Spitfire IX, although much later it would transpire that it was perfectly possible. The Spitfire 21 was another example. In the autumn of 1942 the MAP were taken by surprise by an Air Ministry demand that the endurance of the Spitfire 21, the prototype of which was about to fly, should be increased by 25 per cent. The fact that this came in the words of the MAP 'like a bolt from the blue' underlined how little pressure the MAP were under to do anything about increasing fighter range.[21] The request was not made with a future invasion of France in mind or the need to escort bombers further or in response to complaints from the Far East. The Air Ministry was worried that the fighter would not have enough fuel to intercept bombers attacking at altitudes in excess of 30,000 feet and wanted wing tanks installed to increase internal fuel from 96 to 120 gallons. It might seem an odd priority when there were scarcely any daylight bombing attacks on the United Kingdom. At a time when Churchill was demanding increased fighter range to avoid being 'helpless in the West and beaten in the East', the only justification the Air Ministry could come up with for increasing endurance was to ensure the fighter could stay in the air longer to intercept high-altitude bombers.[22]

In the summer of 1943 Morgan asked both the Americans and British for their latest assessments on fighter endurance, emphasising that he only wanted to know what might be possible the following spring, not what was actually possible at that time. The British response was rapid and not very encouraging. The information Morgan was provided included what the Spitfire could do with 30-gallon and 90-gallon drop tanks. However, the Air Ministry made it clear that the 30-gallon drop tank, with the eighty-five gallons of internal fuel the Spitfire IX carried, was the 'ideal' ratio of external to internal fuel, and so Morgan based his plans on this. With this, the Spitfire IX could patrol for just fifteen minutes at a range of 140 miles, about twenty-five miles inland from the Normandy coast.[23] It was far from ideal. Morgan was grimly warned that there was likely to be very little improvement on what was currently possible 'unless there is some radical change in engine and aircraft design'.[24]

The Air Ministry were clearly misleading Morgan. While Morgan was being told the 90-gallon slipper tank would not be suitable for extending the endurance of the Spitfire for a Normandy landing, Portal had decided it was entirely suitable for the Salerno landings which involved an even longer sea-crossing. Indeed, he was proudly taking credit for despatching the 1,800 90-gallon tanks the invasion required.[25] It is hard not to link the determination to make the invasion of France seem as difficult and dangerous as possible with the desire to prove the bomber offensive was a better way of winning the war. There may not have been a conscious conspiracy but, clearly, the longer an invasion of France was delayed the more time there would be for the bomber to prove an invasion was not necessary.

While Morgan was looking at the Air Ministry assessment on what was possible with existing fighters, he might have noticed tucked away at the bottom of the list was a fighter being used for tactical reconnaissance, which, without any drop tanks, could fly further than the Spitfire IX could manage with a drop tank. This was the Allison-powered P-51 Mustang, the fighter that would ultimately demolish Air Ministry claims that high-endurance single-seater fighters were an impossibility.[26]

With air cover such an apparent problem, the need to establish airstrips within the bridgehead as quickly as possible had always been a major factor in Morgan's planning. The hedgerow countryside of Normandy had been deliberately chosen to make it easier to defend the bridgehead but it also made it difficult to construct airfields. The coastal belt north of Bayeux did not pose insuperable problems for airfield construction but the airfield-friendly terrain south-east of Caen provided a lot more room for airfields and the plan was to capture this within days. Within a couple of weeks, it was planned to have between twenty-eight and thirty-three squadrons operating from eighteen airfields within the bridgehead.[27]

While Morgan grappled with the problems of air cover, the bomber barons were setting about achieving the other primary pre-condition Brooke had laid down for any successful invasion – the crippling of the German arms industry. This was not just about meeting the expectations of army commanders. If the bombers could achieve the level of destruction outlined in the Pointblank directive, it would, the bomber advocates believed, surely go a long way towards proving an invasion was not needed.

Chapter Five

Bombing Versus Invasion – The Race

Brooke had always insisted that the invasion of France would only be possible if bombing had caused 'visible cracks' to appear in Germany's military edifice.[1] This requirement was confirmed at the January 1943 Casablanca conference. The expectation was that bombing would leave Germany's 'capacity for armed resistance fatally weakened'. Everyone was happy with the plan. For the Army and Navy, a successful bombing campaign would at the very least make the invasion easier. For the air forces it provided plenty of time to prove a full-scale invasion would not be necessary. Once German industry had been devastated, a simple policing operation to disarm an already beaten enemy would suffice, the bomber barons suggested. It was an approach that put airpower at the heart of Allied strategy. It gave the air force a vital, clearly defined role that did not require any inter-service co-operation. The visionaries might see this as the way of future wars but it was an approach that owed more to a First World War way of thinking. Instead of artillery obliterating the enemy front line as preparation for an unhindered advance on land, bombers would obliterate an entire country and make the invasion of continental Europe a mere formality.

Militarily, a successful bombing campaign might be a pre-condition but politically it was difficult to see how an invasion could be put off beyond 1944. Indeed, a 1944 invasion was acquiring an unstoppable momentum. The Trident conference in May 1943 had declared that the invasion of northwest Europe should take place within the following twelve months. At the Quebec conference in August 1943 a date of 1 May 1944 was set for the landings. Target dates had been suggested before and then abandoned but this one was beginning to look increasingly definite. With the Red Army regaining vast swathes of their country, if the invasion was delayed until 1945 the troops landing in France might find themselves being greeted by the Soviet Army.

Brooke had no reason to believe the bombing was not causing the 'cracks' he wanted. The American daylight offensive might be running into difficulties, but it was not quite so obvious that Bomber Command's nocturnal offensive was failing. Indeed with Harris declaring his offensive was on course to win the war on its own, and many in the Air Ministry backing these claims, there seemed good reason to believe it was well on the way to achieving Brooke's more limited aim. Harris was not short of photographic proof that his bombers were turning large tracts of German cities into rubble. It seemed impossible that this scale of destruction was not having a disastrous effect on German output. Indeed, It was having an impact, although nowhere near the catastrophic impact Harris was claiming and Brooke was expecting. Steel production in the Ruhr region was down nearly 15 per cent in the summer of 1943. At a national level the reduction was more than 6 per cent.[2] This was impressive but it was not translating into a reduction in arms output, which continued to rise.

British estimates of the damage the RAF was inflicting were now far more realistic and accurate than they had been earlier in the war. It was necessarily a crude process. The overall damage inflicted on German cities was compared to damage to British cities and the lost production in the latter gave a guide to lost production in the former. The actual estimates of overall lost production, civil and military, were not that inaccurate. There was disappointment at how low this figure was, but at least the bombing seemed to be making some impression. As it turned out, even this estimate was misleading. The effect on military production was lower than the effect on overall production. Furthermore, the degree to which Germany relied on production in major German cities was overestimated and the level of military production outside Germany was underestimated. Even from the optimistic Air Ministry assessment, it was clear that the bombing was nowhere near achieving the ambitious Pointblank targets, but there was plenty of scope to spin the results. Margins of error and 'immeasurable effects' could always be exploited to the full. Estimated losses tended to be described as minimums, which always left room for optimists to add some. Morale was one of the 'immeasurables'. There were all sorts of inaccurate reports of German civilians refusing to help control fires and workers refusing to return to their factories.

At every stage from initial intelligence analysis to final reports to the Combined Chiefs of Staff, the interpretation of results achieved was tweaked in the same positive direction. In September 1943 the Joint Intelligence Committee claimed Germany was already in a state of collapse similar to the situation existing in the late summer of 1918. In their report to the Combined Chiefs of Staff in November 1943 Portal and Eaker rather vaguely claimed that 10 per cent of 'total war production' had already been destroyed and this figure could only increase as the bombing continued. Once this figure reached 30 per cent the consequences might be fatal, it was suggested.[3]

In a way, the 10 per cent claim was correct. Post-war American studies suggested that in the last three months of 1943 output was nearly 10 per cent lower than it would have been had there been no bombing.[4] With the Americans temporarily out of the battle, a lot of the credit for this has to go to Harris's Bomber Command. German arms production was still increasing but bombing was reducing the rate of increase quite considerably. Given the huge cost of the bomber offensive, whether this achievement would survive a rigorous cost-effectiveness analysis was another matter, but nobody could claim Bomber Command was not achieving something.[5] Indeed, if the bomber disciples had not had such grandiose ideas about winning the war, they might justifiably have hailed this achievement as a triumph. However, the bombing was not reducing output. On a three-month rolling average, between May 1943 and February 1944 output increased by 15 per cent.[6]

Harris was convinced he was already doing much better than just slowing the increase in German output. With the American day bombers beaten out of German skies, there was an opportunity for Harris to demonstrate his area bombing approach was the only way forward. In October 1943 Harris sent Portal his assessment of what had been achieved so far. Harris admitted the first three years of bombing operations against Germany had achieved little, but the previous seven months of intensive operations had produced quite a different picture. Success was measured by acres flattened. Seventeen cities had been destroyed, eight of them among the fifteen largest cities in Germany. By 'destroyed' Harris meant they were now more of a liability to the German economy than an asset. Another fifteen had been seriously damaged and still required a substantial effort before they could be added to the list of destroyed. The results of these attacks, he boldly claimed, could clearly be seen at the front, where German forces were now in retreat everywhere.[7] For Harris, no further evidence was required; the fact that the bombing was occurring as the German army retreated was proof enough.

In fact, as was the case with other claims, there was no causal link. The victories in Russia, North Africa and the Atlantic in 1942 and 1943 had been achieved before the bombing had made any impact on German production. Harris claimed that once 40 per cent of urban areas in major German cities were destroyed capitulation would follow. He had little faith in his Stirlings or Halifaxes contributing much to the offensive, but he believed his Lancaster force alone would be sufficient 'to produce in Germany by April 1 1944 a state of devastation in which surrender is inevitable'.[8] It was a date determined more by the knowledge that at this point Bomber Command would be expected to switch its efforts to supporting an invasion than any detailed analysis.

A rasping response from Deputy Chief of the Air Staff Norman Bottomley demonstrated how frustrated some were becoming with the area bombing approach. He pointed out that most Germans did not live in Harris's target cites. The bombing would only 'dehouse' 11 per cent of the total German population and these could easily be re-housed in other parts of the German empire. Warming to the task of putting Harris in his place, Bottomley continued,

> The grounds for assuming that the degree of destruction suggested would necessarily result in capitulation, are therefore not entirely clear ... . The Air Staff must take a somewhat less confident view than that expressed in your letter of the possibilities of causing the enemy to capitulate by reason of your attacks alone.[9]

Harris was told he should stop attacking targets where he could maximise acreage destroyed and concentrate on targets where fighter production and ball-bearing plants were situated, as required by existing Pointblank priorities.

Harris, however, was not fighting a lone battle. Air Commodore Frank Inglis, the Assistant Chief of the Air Staff for Intelligence, was furious that Bottomley had not consulted him before sending his missive. He insisted Harris's area bombing campaign was a perfectly legitimate contribution to the Pointblank objectives as any city bombed was bound to have some connection with fighter production. Furthermore, his department were in complete agreement with Harris that area bombing was the strategy most likely to break German resistance and warned that Harris was bound to be puzzled by Bottomley's contradiction of the encouraging evidence his intelligence department was providing. He also objected to Bottomley taking it upon himself to speak on behalf of the 'Air Staff'.[10] Bottomley's riposte was that since Portal had provided input for the letter, he was perfectly entitled to claim to be speaking on behalf of the 'Air Staff'.

Perhaps the obvious question was why Portal did not send the letter he had played a part in composing. In truth Portal was in a quandary. Part of him wanted Harris to be right. However, the need to deal with the other services and confronted by the realities of a multi-faceted war meant he was more in touch with reality than Harris in his High Wycombe bunker. His views on the post-war air force role made clear that he still saw the bomber as the central war-winning pillar of future British defence policy, but he was not as confident as Harris about this being the case in the current conflict. It was hard to ignore the fact that events at the front were beginning to overtake the bomber strategy

It looked like the invasion of France would be one of those events. Preparations were moving forward apace. In October Admiral Bertram Ramsay was assigned command of the naval forces. It had been agreed in principle in the spring of 1943 to create the Second Tactical Air Force to support the invading forces. In November 1943 it was finally created in practice. The Americans agreed to form a parallel tactical Ninth Air Force, under Lieutenant General Lewis Brereton.[11] In August Air Marshal Trafford Leigh-Mallory had been put in command of the Allied Expeditionary Air Force (AEAF), which would combine these two tactical air forces. In December the appointments of Eisenhower as Supreme Commander and Tedder as his deputy seemed to end any chance of a further postponement. The bomber strategy was running out of time.

The heavy losses suffered during the second Schweinfurt raid had underlined how far the Americans were from achieving even the preliminary goal of taming the German fighter force. Instead of moving to the second stage and creating the fatal cracks Brooke was expecting, no American bombers dared enter too deeply into German air space. This gave Harris the chance to seize centre stage; the success of the strategic air offensive might depend on his Bomber Command. The Pointblank directive had diplomatically left open both Harris's indiscriminate and the American precision approach as ways of achieving Pointblank objectives. The question was whether Harris should use his bombers to attack cities containing the industrial Pointblank targets that the Americans could not attack or continue his attempts to undermine German morale.

By the end of 1943, with the American precision bombing offensive so far behind schedule, any chance of their approach being decisive before an invasion seemed to be fast disappearing. The only way bombing could possibly win the war outright in the short time available was by terrorising the German population into defeat. Production could not suddenly collapse, but morale could. There were no obvious indications this was about to happen but there was always a chance that collapse would be as sudden and unexpected as it had been in 1918. The intelligence community was already suggesting the early signs were there. Harris was convinced that he could trigger this collapse by 1 April if he was allowed to continue his attacks on large cities. Victory might come even quicker if he focused his efforts on Berlin. Portal was not going to stand in his way, not yet at least.

Berlin was on Harris's list of 'seriously damaged' cites. With the long winter nights providing more protection, he would now return to Berlin and fulfil Portal's, and indeed Churchill's, desire to finish off the German capital. He pleaded for the Americans, licking their wounds after the beating they had taken over Schweinfurt, to throw their Fortresses and Liberators into the night offensive. 'It will cost between 400-500 aircraft, it will cost Germany the war', Harris boldly proclaimed. It was Harris now who was seeking a panacea target. Just destroying the German capital would be enough to win the war. Harris may have been certain of the outcome; for Portal it was a final throw of the dice.

The Americans did not come in, but this did not dampen Harris's optimism. The first major raid of this latest offensive against the capital was launched on the night of 18/19 November by 440 Lancaster led by four pathfinder Mosquitoes. The weather was poor which made it difficult for the defending fighters and attacking bombers. Only nine bombers were lost, just 2 per cent of the attacking force. The target was covered by cloud and marking was done blind with the help of H2S. Although a large number of bombs fell on the city there was little concentration. Only 169 houses were destroyed and 145 people were killed or missing. There was little evidence that the Lancasters could win the battle on their own. On the second raid on the night of the 22nd/23rd, Halifaxes and Stirlings joined the Lancasters, boosting the strike force to 764 bombers. Although the weather was again poor, far more destruction was inflicted with fires raging uncontrollably in parts of the city. Some 2,000 Berliners lost their lives and no fewer than 175,000 were bombed out of their homes. It was not, however, another Hamburg. There was no firestorm.

Despite the poor weather again keeping many fighters on the ground, bomber losses were already rising; 3.4 per cent of the bombers failed to return from the 22/23 November raid. The Stirlings suffered most, 10 per cent failing to make it back. In the previous three months the average loss rate of the Stirlings had risen to 6.4 per cent. The losses suffered in this latest raid were the last straw for the Stirling; the bomber would not be employed over Germany again.

The distances were huge, the problems of even finding the target immense and the weather often atrocious. In fact, the odds were far more heavily stacked against the attacking bombers than any of the aircrews realised. Window was becoming less effective. The new Lichtenstein SN2 airborne radar operated on a longer 3.3-metre wavelength and was not affected so badly by the length of Window strip the RAF was using. Like all German radars it required a complicated array of transmitting and receiving aerials, which increased drag and reduced top speed. A disadvantage of early models of the radar was that it lost the signal while it was still out of visual range and another shorter-range radar had to be added to complete the interception. This meant more weight and required another set of aerials, with more loss of speed. However, the British bombers were flying so slowly this posed no major problems for the defence. The Lancaster might lift more bombs than the Stirling and Halifax but it was scarcely any faster.

More German fighters were equipped with the vertically-firing cannon. The 65-70 degrees the Germans had decided was optimum for aiming purposes also put the fighter below the vertical traverse of the rear turret and outside the field of fire of any ventral guns the bomber might be carrying. German fighters attacking from below were also outside the effective scanning cone of the Monica early-warning radar. The tale of woe did not end here. The scientists had constantly warned the Air Ministry that any active radio or radar device could be used by the enemy as a homing signal. Carrying any device over enemy territory inevitably ran the risk of that device falling into enemy hands and the Germans had been in possession of the H2S navigational aid and Monica early-warning equipment for some time. The Germans were horrified to discover the British had leapfrogged them in the high-frequency radar used by H2S, but were soon introducing Naxos, which could detect and home in on its centimetric emissions. In early 1944 this would be followed by Flensburg, which could home in on the transmissions of the metric Monica radar. At least with jamming it was obvious it was happening. With homing there was no indication it was taking place. Despite the warnings the Air Ministry chose to hope for the best. Aircrew were totally unaware of the dangers. Navigators were regularly turning their H2S sets on as they set off for Germany and keeping them on and Monica was constantly scanning the skies for the dreaded night-fighters. Monica and H2S, which had done so much to raise the confidence of bomber crews, were both guiding the German fighters to their prey.

Both sides were making extensive use of decoys. Berlin was ringed by decoy sites, including one massive affair to the north-west of the city which was effectively a plywood copy of Berlin. Bomber Command used various deception tactics to disguise the bombers' true destination. To keep the Germans guessing, Berlin was not always the target. Pathfinders might drop decoy markers on one city while the bombers headed towards another. The main bomber stream might feint towards one city then veer towards another. Operational training units might head en masse across the North Sea towards northern Germany, before turning back just short of the coast, thereby attracting the attention of the German defences while the main force approached from a completely different direction. Sometimes these deceptions worked and sometimes they did not, but for the Germans a huge advantage was again the low speed of the bombers. The defending fighters could afford to wait to see where the main bomber force was heading for and still have time to intercept.

Escorts were tried. By chance the metric AI Mark IV picked up the Lichtenstein B/C emissions. Used as a receiver it could identify the direction of a German fighter and, by switching to normal transmissions, could establish distance. Beaufighters were used initially, but these proved too slow. Mosquitoes were tried and achieved some early successes but by early 1944 Lichtenstein B/C was being phased out and the wavelength of the latest German radars was unknown. The bombers were at a hopeless disadvantage. There could be no formation flying to multiply the defensive fire. Each bomber was on its own and would always be outgunned by the cannon-armed interceptor. Darkness was providing more protection for the attacker than the attacked. The Air Ministry was forced to recognise that even Harris's favoured bomber, the highly prized Lancaster, had little chance of survival if intercepted.

Bomber Command monthly loss rates steadily rose; 3.1 per cent in November 1943, 4.1 per cent in December, 5 per cent in January. The success of the second raid on Berlin was rarely repeated. As bomber losses rose, German civilian casualties fell. In the three attacks in five days at the end of November, more than 4,000 people lost their lives. In two raids on 1/2 January and 2/3 January around 100 Berliners died for a loss of nearly 400 aircrew in the fifty-five Lancasters shot down. Industrial plants were hit but production in Berlin continued to grow. It was not a battle Bomber Command was winning on any count.

Desperation was beginning to creep in. Bomb loads were increased, which reduced the altitude at which the bombers could fly and made them even more vulnerable to German defences. For crews who were far from convinced their attacks were having much effect on the course of the war, it was becoming very demoralising. The number of crews finding reasons to abort a mission increased. Many more dropped some of their bombs into the North Sea in order to gain the altitude they needed to have a chance.[12] It was difficult to gauge how much impact the raids were having as the constant poor weather limited photo-reconnaissance. One fact, however, was beyond all dispute. Germany had not surrendered.

Meanwhile Arnold was growing increasingly frustrated by the progress the combined bomber offensive was making. The theory that large formations of day bombers would make any defence futile was proving hopelessly wrong. No matter how many bombers attacked at once, the fighter defences could not be overwhelmed. The conclusion was obvious. American bombers had to be escorted. The P-38 Lightning was the American fighter with most range and Arnold was directing as many as possible to the UK. Lockheed were persuaded to fit extra fuel tanks in the leading edge of the wings, increasing fuel capacity by 92 (110 US) gallons. With 75-gallon wing drop tanks the P-38 escorts reached 350 miles. By February 1944, with two 90-gallon tanks, it could go all the way to Berlin (585 miles). It was a remarkable achievement.

However, the twin-engined Lightning could not compete with the single-engined Fw 190 and Bf 109. Like the Bf 110 in the Battle of Britain, it could only achieve the first objective of an escort fighter, the still very useful feat of occupying enemy interceptors that might otherwise be shooting down bombers. At the altitudes the Fortresses were operating, the Thunderbolt was perhaps a more formidable foe, but the rate at which its Pratt and Whitney engine burned up fuel meant it could never have the range to reach Berlin. Neither fighter could match the fighting qualities of the P-51B Mustang.

Even by American standards the Mustang in its original configuration already had a very creditable range. It carried 150 gallons of fuel internally, nearly twice the standard Spitfire IX. Thanks to its all-round better aerodynamics, with the same Merlin 61 as the Spitfire IX, and therefore the same fuel consumption, the Mustang had a much higher cruising speed, which meant it flew further per gallon. A 74-gallon tank was installed behind the pilot bringing internal fuel up to 224 gallons and with this the fighter could fly further than the P-47 managed with two 90-gallon drop tanks. When the P-51 was also fitted with 62-gallon wing drop tanks it could penetrate further than the P-38. With two 90-gallon drop tanks it could fly almost anywhere in Germany.

Fully loaded it was a handful to fly but pilots would have to get used to it. Even basic manoeuvring was difficult until it had burnt off some fuel, but this could be done crossing the North Sea. Once some of the extra fuselage fuel was consumed and the drop tanks were jettisoned, the fighter's outstanding combat capabilities were restored in full and it still had the internal fuel to make it home. This was the fighter the RAF had wanted the United States to build in large numbers, not because of its exceptional range but because of its exceptional qualities as a fighter. For the American bomber offensive, it was an extraordinary piece of good fortune. It was an American design that only went into production because in 1940 Britain had been willing to order just about anything on offer. The RAF had ordered it as a bomber interceptor, but with an engine it was not designed for, and a fuel load it had never been built to carry, it could more than hold its own against the best the Luftwaffe could muster over virtually the entire Third Reich.

In November 1943 the first P-51B unit arrived in Britain. It might seem rather perverse that it should be a fighter group assigned to the forming tactical Ninth Air Force rather than the strategic Eighth. It was in fact a clear statement of American priorities. These supposedly tactical fighter groups were going to be used for long-range escort rather than prepare for their army support role.[13] The Air Ministry decision to send part of its Mustang III (P-51B) allocation to India and use a substantial proportion of the rest to re-equip Allison-powered Mustang I/II) tactical-reconnaissance squadrons was a little more difficult to explain. In total, just twelve UK-based RAF squadrons were to be equipped with the fighter, eight tactical reconnaissance and four fighter. It could be generously interpreted as a belated realisation that overseas commands and Army tactical-reconnaissance squadrons in the UK deserved the best available rather than home command rejects. With Overlord approaching, the equipment of tactical-reconnaissance squadrons in particular was beginning to attract more attention. It would also be more straightforward for tactical-reconnaissance squadrons to convert from the Allison-powered Mustang to the Merlin-powered version of the same aircraft rather than some entirely new type. As for the allocation to India, where possible, it was standard practice for American aircraft to be used abroad to save on shipping. It made no sense for the Americans to ship their aircraft to Britain and Britain to ship British aircraft overseas. There was a logic about shipping Mustangs to India. Even so, both deployments were surprising ways of using a fighter the RAF had fought so hard to acquire, as an irate Leigh-Mallory at Fighter Command would soon be pointing out.

Arnold was soon eyeing up the RAF Mustangs as escorts for his bombers. Late in September 1943 he wrote to Portal, explaining that the only fighters with the range to protect his bomber force were the P-51B Mustang and P-38 Lightning and production of neither was sufficient. He was redirecting all available Lightnings and Mustangs to the Eighth Air Force but, he reminded Portal, 1,200 Mustangs were due to be delivered to the RAF. He also reminded Portal of his declaration that the American Eighth Air Force must not be 'hampered by lack of reinforcements, just as success was within grasp' and how an opportunity might be missed with 'incalculable effects on all future operations and on the length of the war'. Portal now had to do his bit to make sure the USAAF was not hampered, the American air force chief suggested. Arnold asked if the RAF Mustang squadrons could be put under the operational control of the USAAF. Alternatively, he was willing to exchange the British Mustangs for an equal number of Thunderbolts.[14] Portal promptly promised to let Arnold have the four fighter Mustang squadrons until the invasion was underway. He could also have the eight tactical-reconnaissance P-51B squadrons on a more occasional basis as they would be required for pre-invasion training with the Army.[15]

This exchange seemed to bring to Leigh-Mallory's attention how the Air Ministry planned to deploy the Mustang III. He was horrified that tactical-reconnaissance squadrons would be getting the priceless American fighter while his fighter squadrons would have to persevere with Typhoons or indeed Spitfire Vs. He wanted the tactical-reconnaissance squadrons to make do with these fighters and was more than happy for all the Mustang III squadrons to gain combat experience escorting American bombers.[16] Leigh-Mallory got his way, the tactical-reconnaissance squadrons lost their Mustang allocation and the Far East got Thunderbolts instead of Mustangs. Arnold was told he could now count on the full time services of twelve Mustang III fighter squadrons as soon as they were available. Even so, Arnold was not impressed that the delivery of 1,200 Mustangs was only going to yield twelve fighter squadrons. Portal's response 'was not on the scale or at the time I had hoped', he informed the RAF chief with thinly veiled frustration. He was pulling in every Mustang from every theatre to help the Eighth Air Force and clearly believed the RAF could make more of an effort. Nevertheless, the British offer would help 'in a small way'.[17]

It was not the only British contribution Arnold considered 'small'. He was none too pleased that the 'thousands of fighters' available to Fighter Command were not contributing more. He could not understand why Fighter Command could not increase the range of its fighters as the Americans were doing. If his Thunderbolts could be modified to fly 200 miles from their bases, what was stopping Spitfires from flying similar distances? In a detailed and lengthy response, Portal described the many ways Fighter Command was involved on the fringes of the battle. He dismissed the claim that Fighter Command had 'thousands of fighters'; it only had 1,400, he insisted. Unabashed by their failure to contribute more, Portal insisted that British fighters were specialist interceptors and therefore very different to the much larger American 'general purpose' fighters. The Spitfire was far too small to accommodate the extra internal fuel required for long-range escort, he argued.[18]

The idea that there was no room inside a Spitfire for more fuel was clearly absurd, as demonstrated by the various reconnaissance versions of the fighter. Portal's lack of enthusiasm for providing the escorts Arnold needed might seem strange given the importance he attached to the American offensive succeeding. In a way Portal had been hoist with his own petard. Morgan had been told that only some dramatic technological breakthrough would enable single-seater fighters to fly further. Portal could hardly now agree that Spitfires were capable of flying deep inside Germany, far further than required to cover the Normandy landing and to do this all that was required was adding a few additional fuel tanks. A frustrated Arnold decided to take the law into his own hands and instructed American engineers in the United States to see what they could do with the Spitfire.

Portal might not be embarrassed by the inability of Fighter Command to contribute more, but Leigh-Mallory, while still in charge of Fighter Command, was becoming acutely embarrassed by the impotence of his force. Way back in 1939 Slessor had spoken of the embarrassment of having 600 fighters based in the United Kingdom unable to intervene in a potentially decisive battle in France.[19] History was repeating itself, except the battle was now taking place over Germany and the number of single-seater fighters was more than a thousand. In the summer of 1943 Leigh-Mallory's fighters had been escorting American medium bombers on attacks on German airfields along the coastal fringe, which was as far as they could go. However, by August German units were only engaging daylight bombers further inland, after their escorts had been forced to abandon them. Leigh-Mallory's fighters, with their standard 30-gallon drop tanks, could not now even fly far enough to make contact with the German air defences.

Fighter Command needed larger drop tanks. Leigh-Mallory had agreed to adopt the 45-gallon drop tank the Fleet Air Arm wanted, but only as a concession to standardise and simplify production and supply. Suddenly Leigh-Mallory urgently needed the extra 15 gallons. However, needing it did not mean he was going to get it. Trials with a Spitfire equipped with the 45-gallon tank were only just getting under way and in any case the Fleet Air Arm, having instigated the development of the tank, was hardly likely to concede priority.[20] Even with the 45-gallon drop tank, the Spitfire would not have anything like the sort of range Arnold desperately needed. Nor was 45 gallons the most the standard Spitfire could carry on escort missions; 60 gallons would be closer to the ideal external/internal fuel ratio with its existing 85-gallon internal fuel capacity. The 90-gallon drop tank two-thirds full could have been used, but this was not an option Fighter Command were interested in, not yet anyway. There was some justification for this reluctance to use the 90-gallon slipper tank. Although it looked like a clever way of carrying extra fuel and, as a ferry tank, it was reasonably efficient, in its expendable mode the fit with the fuselage was poor, creating a lot of additional drag. Teardrop- or torpedo-shaped drop tanks hanging below the fuselage or wing were far more efficient, as indeed had been demonstrated during experiments conducted by the Royal Aircraft Establishment in 1943.[21] Leigh-Mallory believed it was so bulky and such a handicap it would have to be jettisoned as soon as fighters entered enemy airspace, as indeed American Thunderbolts were doing with the even bulkier improvised ferry tanks they were using. In September 1943 Fighter Command made it clear that it had no 'bulk demand' for the 90-gallon drop tank. It might be needed for 'special operations', such as missions over Norway, but it seems that as yet the invasion of France did not count as one of those 'special operations'.[22] The 90-gallon tank had, of course, been used by Spitfires operating from Sicily, for the invasion of Italy. Until there was a realistic assessment of the fuel loads UK based fighters could carry, both internally and externally, British fighters were not going to be able to play any part in the American daylight bombing offensive or indeed provide an invasion of France with the best possible air cover.

Whether escorts were the solution to the Eighth Air Force problems remained to be seen. What was clear was that the daylight bomber offensive was not achieving what it had set out to achieve. The initial aim of neutralising the German fighter force required the reduction of German fighter strength on all fronts from an expected 3,000 on 1 April 1944 to just 650. The latest intelligence forecast in November 1943 suggested that the Luftwaffe was still on target to reach 3,000.[23] The Allies were approaching 1944 without having made any progress in their initial aim, never mind the main goal of devastating German armaments production.

The Pointblank offensive was going nowhere. In the United States Arnold was expressing his discontent. He raged at the failure of the Eighth Air

BOMBING VERSUS INVASION – THE RACE

Force to focus its effort on what he saw as the key targets. Eighty per cent of effort, he claimed, had been wasted on what he considered unimportant targets. In the latter he included targets like U-boat construction, which not all would agree was so unimportant. The creation of the Fifteenth Air Force in Italy ought to open up new possibilities for intensifying the offensive, he suggested. Poor weather was not an excuse; maximum use was to be made of blind bombing. Arnold wanted a major review of the entire bombing programme and gave Portal until 15 December to do this.[24] Portal, desperately hoping Harris's offensive against Berlin would soon produce dramatic results, played for time.

The lines to and from Washington were buzzing. Portal saw no reason for any major change in Pointblank objectives. However, there was not even agreement about what those objectives were. The messages from Washington pointedly excluded the phrase in the Pointblank directive about undermining enemy morale. The replies from London pointedly reinserted the phrase.[25] What was agreed was that there was no question of yet another invasion postponement. It was inconceivable that Stalin would be asked to wait until 1945 for the second front he had been demanding since 1941. It was no longer a case of the successful completion of Pointblank being a condition for an invasion; the invasion was going to take place in 1944 regardless of how successful the bomber offensive had been. It was becoming a question of what bombing could realistically achieve before Overlord took place.

The goal posts were already on the move. Bottomley was alarmed by Archibald Sinclair, the Secretary of State for Air, claiming that the preliminary aim of destroying the German fighter force had now become 'our supreme objective'. Bottomley reminded everyone that defeating the German fighter force was just 'a necessary preliminary to the full achievement of our main aim', which was still 'destroying and dislocating the enemy's war economy and undermining the morale of the German people'.[26] He was fighting a losing battle.

Arnold's 15 December deadline passed with no review but a persistent Arnold set a new 20 January deadline. Arnold made it clear that the first priority had to be the German fighter force and the industry that supplied it.[27] Like Sinclair, Portal was coming round to the view that this was now all that could be achieved in the time available. He called all the interested parties together for a crisis meeting. He made it clear that he had by no means given up hope of breaking the will of the German people. However, ten major raids on Berlin had made no impression and Portal had to admit that there was 'uncertainty' as to whether this could be achieved before

Overlord.[28] Even more unlikely to occur was a fatal weakening of German military strength. The aim had to be less ambitious. Switching the focus to oil was considered but Air Ministry intelligence was adamant that this was not an attractive target. The threat German V-weapons posed to invasion forces along the south coast was a far more worthy target. With what was left it seemed sensible to continue with the current aim of trying to destroy the German fighter force. However, this was now all that could be expected before Overlord. What had been an intermediate objective had now become the 'main aim'.

It seemed a logical decision that met the requirements of all the interested parties. These included Lieutenant General Carl Spaatz, commander of the American Eighth and Fifteenth Air Forces. Spaatz was another firm believer in the bomber as a war winner. He and Harris still hoped to achieve their respective Pointblank aims (the crippling of German industry and the demoralisation of the German people) before Overlord was launched and indeed both still believed bombing would make a full-scale invasion unnecessary. Portal, however, more realistically, now saw the bombing campaign as a parallel operation to Overlord. Air superiority was the common factor in this dual approach. Both Overlord and the bombing offensive needed control of the skies. The bomber remained the tool for achieving this; the destruction of the factories and associated industries involved in the manufacture of fighters would simultaneously deliver air superiority over Germany and Normandy.

This Douhet-style idea of aerial warfare was not how the war was panning out. Nor was it how Morgan envisaged achieving air superiority over the invasion forces. He was assuming fighters would win control of the skies, as was happening in the Mediterranean. This was in fact how air superiority had been achieved in every Second World War campaign to date. The bomber advocates liked to promote the idea that air superiority had been achieved by wiping out air forces on their airfields. Attacks on airfields made a contribution, on rare occasions an extremely useful contribution. The attacks on Soviet airfields on 22 June 1941 and American airfields on 7/8 December 1941 spring to mind as examples. But bombing airfields could only achieve a very temporary advantage; aircraft lost on the ground are much easier to replace than aircrew lost in action. Sustained air superiority was only achieved by having more and better fighters. By this stage in the war this was appreciated by the more enlightened RAF commanders and Portal, after his attempts to get a specialist air superiority fighter developed with his F.6/42 specification, could count himself among those. However, even Portal still saw the bomber as at least as important as the fighter in the struggle for air superiority. The bomber mentality was deeply ingrained and very difficult to shift.

The claim that fighters would never have the range to provide adequate air cover over the Normandy landings arguably justified the belief that only the bomber could guarantee the air superiority Morgan needed. There was, however, now an obvious inconsistency in the evolving strategy. If long-range fighters were required to enable the bombers to establish air superiority then those same long-range fighters could far more easily provide air cover over the shorter distances required for Overlord. If the range of existing fighters could be extended to protect the long-range bombers, Overlord no longer required the bomber offensive to win the air superiority it required.

Air commanders did not see, or did not want to see, this. The British Air Staff and their American counterparts continued to claim that a successful bomber offensive against German fighter production was absolutely essential for a successful invasion of France. There was a stream of dire warnings from British and American air commanders that, unless the bomber offensive succeeded, Overlord was doomed to failure. 'It is conceded fact that Overlord and Anvil [the invasion of southern France] will not be possible unless the German Air Force is destroyed' and the bomber offensive would do this, Arnold insisted with Harrisesque certainty.[29] It was all straight out of the Trenchard/Billy Mitchell school of bombing.

Simply aiming for air superiority rather than bringing down the entire German military edifice seemed on the face of it a major downgrading of what was expected of the bomber offensive. It was not seen like that by the bomber purists. Air superiority had always been their Holy Grail. There could not be a purer or more worthwhile aim. This was what aerial warfare was all about, the battle for control of the skies fought between rival air forces, a battle conducted independently of armies and navies. Admittedly, by day at least, it seemed fighters would be required to enable the bombers to do their work but, in true Trenchardian, style, it would be bombers that would win air superiority.

Arnold had not mentioned Harris or Bomber Command in his tirade against those running the Combined Bomber Offensive. It seemed he had given up on the British bomber force contributing anything. Harris had taken little interest in the battle for air superiority when it was a preliminary step; he was no more interested now it was the main aim. He saw no reason why he should divert his bombers from their current objective of battering the German nation into defeat. However, with Portal now joining those who doubted it was possible before Overlord, Harris was directed to focus his efforts on cities like Leipzig, Augsburg, Gotha and Schweinfurt where aircraft or ball-bearing manufacturing was taking place, even if it meant more bombs missing built-up areas and fewer acres destroyed. Berlin was only to be bombed if weather prevented raids on other targets. Portal passed on to Arnold, without comment, Harris's claim that bombing Berlin would not involve any less effort against fighter related targets because, for reasons that Harris did not go into, bombing Berlin was usually only possible when Pointblank targets could not be bombed.[30]

With Arnold baying for action, an attempt had to be made to bring Harris in line. On 14 January Bottomley ordered Bomber Command to bomb Schweinfurt at the first opportunity and to keep bombing it until it was destroyed.[31] Harris explained why this was not possible or desirable and, on 20/21 January, launched 769 bombers against Berlin. The crews reported a successful mission but there is no mention in German records of a raid taking place and it seems that the entire phalanx of bombers missed the target completely.[32] On 27 January Harris was ordered to follow up the next American attack on Schweinfurt, without waiting for ideal weather.[33] His response was another assault on the German capital with three raids in four nights. The second of these caused widespread destruction, with 180,000 people bombed out of their homes. The third was probably the most successful of the three with the bombers inflicting serious damage and killing over a thousand. There followed another two-week break but Harris's next major attack was again against Berlin. It was the heaviest yet with nearly 900 bombers taking part. Again extensive damage was inflicted on the capital, but there was not even a suggestion that the raids would bring down the Nazi regime.

Harris finally and begrudgingly obeyed the order to bomb Schweinfurt, but he was treading a fine line between exercising his right to use his own judgement and outright insubordination.[34] The raid on 24/25 February was part of Bomber Command's contribution to the American 'Big Week' all-out offensive on the German aircraft industry. (Bomber Command also attacked Leipzig, Stuttgart, and Augsburg as part of this offensive.) A fair amount of damage was inflicted on the various ball-bearing factories in Schweinfurt. Ironically, all Harris's warnings about the futility of the attack were correct. The Germans had plenty of ball bearings in the pipeline, there were always other sources of, or indeed alternatives to, ball bearings and, following the earlier American attacks, dispersion of the Schweinfurt factories was already well underway. German arms production was never affected by a lack of ball bearings.[35] Both Portal and Harris were right about each other's approach. Bombing an entire country into submission and crippling a country by bombing a single key industry were both equally unlikely to succeed.

As Portal and Harris battled over where the bombers should be sent, the crews were fighting a losing battle against the elements and determined defences. With the Stirlings withdrawn, the Merlin-powered Halifax II and V squadrons were now suffering the most, with loss rates rising to nearly 10 per cent. On the night of 19/20 February, 16 per cent of the Merlin-powered Halifaxes were lost. These, too, were now withdrawn from operations over Germany, leaving just the Lancasters and Hercules-powered Halifax IIIs to soldier on. Even these were already joining the Stirlings and other Halifax bombers on less taxing raids against targets in occupied France. Harris had one more crack at Berlin. On the night of 24/25 March, 577 Lancasters and 216 Halifaxes bombarded the German capital. Forty-four of the former and twenty-eight of the latter failed to return, an 8.9 per cent loss rate. Twenty thousand were made homeless but only around 150 Berliners were killed. The scattered bombing killed another thirty in the towns and villages around Berlin.[36]

The 1 April deadline was approaching with no sign of the victory Harris had promised. In one final fling, on the night of 30/31 March 1944, Harris switched his effort to the city of Nuremburg. Evidence from weather reconnaissance suggested that the predicted high cloud that was supposed to block out the light of a full moon was unlikely to materialise. Nevertheless, the attack went ahead anyway. Throwing all caution to the wind, there was no major effort to deceive the German defences in the long run in to the target. Bomber Command had been reduced to a punch-drunk boxer caught on the ropes, risking all for the knockout blow that would justify all the suffering. Eight hundred bombers carried 2,500 tons of bombs to the city. The highest loss rate of the war, 11.9 per cent, was recorded as the German fighters savaged the bombers. In the light of a full moon, crews watched in horror as, one by one, ninety-five bombers fell from the skies. As a terror raid it failed completely. Sixty-seven civilians lost their lives in the city and the surrounding villages. As fate would have it, 120 bombers struck Schweinfurt, fifty-five miles away, by mistake. Two people were killed.[37] Such low casualties would have seemed inconceivable to the pre-war prophets of doom. Far more Bomber Command aircrew died in the Nuremburg operation than German civilians.

Harris had abandoned subtlety in much the same way as commanders had in the First World War with their frontal assaults on machine-gun-covered barbed wire. It was the type of warfare the brave new world of the bomber was supposed to have consigned to the history books. Harris always derided the idea of panacea targets that would bring quick results. However, the bomber itself was the ultimate panacea weapon, the government's supposedly cheap alternative way of fighting a war that avoided expensive conventional armies having to fight another Somme or Passchendaele. It was ironic that the closest British fighting forces in the Second World War came to the horror and futility of trench warfare was Harris's bomber offensive. With unintended irony, Harris spoke movingly of the courage of his aircrews 'daily "going over the top"'.[38] The sacrifice in human life could never match in scale the horrors of the Somme but both were equally courageous but futile attempts to overcome defences that had too many advantages.

Harris lost his predicted 500 bombers in the raids on Berlin along with 2,600 aircrew killed and 1,000 taken prisoner. Some 8,000 Berliners died.[39] It was a grim death toll but it was not going to break the nation. Physical destruction was widespread but the raids had nowhere near the impact of the attacks on Hamburg. Like London during the Blitz, the huge metropolis of Berlin seemed to be able to absorb the bombing. Just as the Luftwaffe failed in the winter of 1940-1941 to break the British will to fight on, so in the winter of 1943-1944, Bomber Command did not even come close to forcing Germany out of the war. The bomber advocates had been given another chance to prove their case and once again they had failed.

From the German point of view, however, it was scarcely a victory worthy of celebration. Nor was there much rejoicing at the technical innovation that had helped inflict so many losses on Bomber Command. On the contrary, there was despair at the huge technical lead the Allies possessed in high-frequency radar technology. There were no winners in the Battle of Berlin. The Air Ministry might argue this made the battle a tactical draw, but in terms of what Bomber Command had set out to achieve, it was a crushing defeat.[40]

In early 1944, even the more limited aim of destroying the German fighter force seemed a distant prospect. In the escort role, the P-47 Thunderbolts, and the P-38 Lightnings were doing their best but it was the arrival in late 1943 of the P-51B/Mustang IIIs that proved decisive. They were used in the long-range escort role for the first time on 5 December, accompanying US bombers to targets in France. Six days later the single-seater fighter appeared in the skies over Emden in Germany. Two days later they were over Bremen. The numbers were small but the writing was on the wall. Suddenly lumbering night-fighters and single-seaters weighed down by hefty 30mm cannon found themselves having to deal with Mustangs. By removing the cannon the Bf 109G and Fw 190 could still compete with the Mustang, but the Luftwaffe now needed two versions of its fighters, a lighter one to take on the escorts and a heavily-armed one to tackle the bombers. The strategic balance was shifting dramatically. The Americans had large numbers of P-47 fighters that could escort the bombers during the initial stages of their penetration of German airspace. P-38s could then take over and deal comfortably with the twin-engined fighters the Luftwaffe had been throwing at the bombers and at least occupy the attention of the more dangerous single-engined fighters. However, the P-51s had the ability to take on all comers.

With more effective escorts, the bombers now resumed their attempt to bomb the German fighter force out of existence. The meteorologists declared that the week beginning 19 February would provide the seven days of continuous fine weather the Eighth Air Force required. Operation Argument, better known as 'Big Week', was set in motion. In a single week, 3,800 sorties were flown by the Eighth and Fifteenth Air Forces against fighter factories the length and breadth of Germany. By night, Bomber Command flew another 2.700 sorties against aircraft industry related cities. There were still only two Mustang groups to protect the American bombers and even these were hampered by technical problems. American losses were still heavy; over 200 Eighth and Fifteenth Air Force bombers were lost, a loss rate of over 6 per cent.[41] Bomber Command lost another 150 in its nocturnal attacks. These losses were not sustainable, but the Allies believed a crushing blow had been delivered to the German aircraft industry. If this was the case, the loss of nearly 400 bombers was perhaps a price worth paying.

At the end of the assault, as Speer and Erhard Milch, responsible for German aircraft production, surveyed the scenes of devastation, both would have agreed with the Allied assessment. Milch gloomily predicted that March production would be reduced from the anticipated 2,000 to just 800 fighters. But, yet again, once the dust settled, the situation seemed a lot less gloomy. Buildings had been destroyed, but the American bombs had been too light to destroy the vital machine tools. With a resourcefulness that took even Speer and Milch by surprise, German fighter production was soon increasing again. After dropping from 1,555 in January to 1,104 in February, it increased to 1,638 in March and would continue to grow for the next six months.[42] Once again, the bomber had failed to deliver the results expected.

While the bombers struggled to live up to expectations, the American fighter escorts were more than living up to theirs. The Americans had always hoped that combat losses inflicted on the intercepting German fighters would accelerate their defeat. Originally it was the defensive fire of the bombers that was supposed to achieve this. Now, high quality escorts were proving a far greater danger for Luftwaffe pilots. Fighter losses over the Reich rose from eighty-eight in December 1943 to 177 in January and a staggering 379 in February. It was far from a one-sided battle; the Americans were paying a huge price. Around 250 Eighth Air Force bombers alone failed to return in February, along with nearly 100 of their escorts. Significantly, the Americans were beginning to appreciate that it was the escorts, rather than the bombs dropped by the aircraft they were escorting, that was doing the most damage. There was a suspicion the Luftwaffe was starting to be selective about the raids they chose to oppose in order to reduce their losses. The Americans countered by choosing targets the Germans would feel obliged to defend. Berlin had no major industries but attacking the capital would surely force their fighters to mount a defence. It was the same logic the Germans had used in September 1940 for bombing London when the Battle of Britain seemed to be reaching a decisive climax.

It was a dramatic change in approach. The escorts would not now be there to allow the bombers to establish air superiority; the bombers would be there to allow the fighters to win air superiority. This rather undermined the idea that one of the aims of the bomber offensive was to establish air superiority for Overlord. This made sense while the aim was to bomb the German aircraft industry out of existence; this would affect equally the balance of power over Normandy and Germany. It made far less sense now that the fighter was recognised as the principal tool for establishing air superiority. It was far more difficult for fighters to control the skies over central Germany than it would be over northern France. Deep inside Germany, the defence had the advantage of engaging fighters operating at the limit of their endurance, far from friendly airspace and their own airfields. The German defences only had to deal with the relatively small proportion of the Allied fighter force that could fly that far. It would be very different over northern France where the entire Allied fighter force could operate and patrol there for far longer. Clearly, the American strategic bombers needed a degree of air superiority over Germany if they were to operate freely against German industry. However, just as the Germans did not need air superiority over central London to invade Britain's south coast in 1940, even more obviously in 1944 the Allies did not need air superiority over Berlin to invade Normandy. The air commanders were right that air superiority over Germany would guarantee air superiority over Normandy, but air superiority over Germany was not necessary for air superiority over Normandy.

Whichever way the decision to bomb Berlin is viewed, it looked like American bomber policy was losing its way. If the aim was to intimidate, then the Americans were just following the rather questionable Harris path. If they were bombing Berlin to provoke a fighter-versus-fighter battle then they were allowing air superiority to become the aim and forgetting the bombers were there to attack German war production. Every bomb on Berlin was one less on a more important industrial target.

Just as Bomber Command was beginning to accept it was not going to win its Battle of Berlin, on 6 March 1944, 730 American bombers headed for the German capital in broad daylight. It would be the first of five major raids delivered against the capital by Eighth and Fifteenth Air Forces in March. The Americans were joining Harris's assault after all. For the 6 March raid some 615 Thunderbolts were able to escort the bombers as far as Brunswick on the outward and return legs. At this point eighty-six longer range P--38s and a hundred Mustangs took over the escort role, covering the bombers as far as Berlin. More fighters rendezvoused with the returning bombers in the Brunswick region. These included three RAF Mustang squadrons, which, without the rear fuselage tank the American version carried, could not fly as far as Berlin.

The bombers were hampered by cloud in the Berlin area and none of the primary targets were hit. Most bombs were dropped through any gaps that appeared in the cloud and fell fairly randomly over a large area. The aircrews could at least claim they had aimed visually rather than blind, even if what they were aiming at was not necessarily a particularly worthwhile target. It helped improve the percentage of visually aimed bombing and fend off accusations of indiscriminate bombing. For Berliners it was undoubtedly a demoralising experience. They were used to being bombed by night but not by bombers brazenly flying in formation over the capital in broad daylight.

Fighter cover for the final approach and departure was still thin and German fighter controllers were becoming expert at identifying which formations had no escort and concentrating on those. Sixty-nine American bombers were lost, the highest number in any one raid by the Eighth

Air Force in the Second World War. However, the Luftwaffe lost sixty-six fighters, twenty-four of which were twin-engined fighters still pointlessly being risked by day. The Mustang was now asserting its authority. Although little more than 10 per cent of all sorties were flown by the P-51 they were responsible for more than half the claims for Luftwaffe fighters destroyed.

The German fighter force was beginning to struggle. Lightened versions of the Bf 109 with fewer guns and boosted engines were able to restore technical parity and provide some protection for the heavily-armed and armoured bomber destroyers, but the numerical balance was shifting fast. On 18 March more than 200 Mustangs escorted the bombers. On bombing missions the primary aim of protecting the bombers would never be forgotten. Initially, with escorts scarce, pilots were instructed to stay with the bombers. If the German interceptors were chased away that was job done. However, as escorts grew in size, pilots could give chase to a fleeing enemy in the knowledge that there was still plenty of cover for the bombers.

Mass head-on attacks were another reason for escorts leaving the immediate vicinity of the bombers. These were proving particularly effective and there was little the immediate escort could do about the fighters hurtling towards them. To counter these and with intelligence providing the rendezvous points, some of the escorts flew ahead of the bombers to break up the German forces as they assembled. As the number of escort fighters increased it became standard to assign a proportion to close escort while others were given more freedom. Having the numbers to allow more fighters to leave the immediate vicinity of the bomber stream was a measure of the growing superiority and an ominous sign for the Luftwaffe. Air commanders always like to extol the advantages of the offence, but there was more method in the American escort policy than simple unbridled aggression.

Everything seemed to be going against the German pilots. Allied pilots were benefitting from the new computerised gyroscopic gun sight (GGS) which doubled the accuracy and effectiveness of air-to-air gunnery. The pilot just had to keep his sight trained on the enemy aircraft. An analogue computer measured the rate of turn, even took into account gravity drop and the air density at the altitude the fighter was flying, and told the pilot where to aim. Suddenly the most average fighter pilot had a chance of matching the skill of the aces. No equivalent technology was available to German fighter pilots.

Another 347 German fighters were lost in March, bringing losses to 900 in the first three months of 1944. Nor was there much advantage in the losses occurring over home territory; nearly 500 German fighter pilots had been killed or wounded.[43] Yet the factories and training schools kept turning out replacement fighters and pilots. Front-line strength was maintained, even if pilot training courses had to be shortened to keep up with the losses. For all the question marks about the quality of fighters like the P-47 and P-38, there was no doubting the thoroughness of American pilot training. It was an extraordinary success story. The American escorts were not only enabling the bombers to penetrate German airspace on a regular basis, they were taking on the German fighter force in its own backyard and winning. It was still far from a one-sided struggle. American Eighth Air Force bomber losses in March rose to one short of 300, with escorts not returning nearly doubling to 167. Those were heavy losses but it was the Luftwaffe that was now on the back foot.

Despite the dramatic success of the American escorts, when Pointblank officially came to an end on 1 April 1944, the combined bombing offensive could not claim to have achieved any of its objectives. Far from decimating Germany production, output was still increasing in all categories. Nor had the aim of reducing fighter strength on all fronts to just 650 been achieved. On 31 March 1944 the Luftwaffe possessed 2,545 fighters.[44] Nor could the offensive claim to have paved the way for Overlord. On 30 June 1943 there were 791 single-engined fighters defending western Europe. At the beginning of 1944, when air superiority became the main aim, this had grown to 871. By 31 March there were 1,019.[45] As the Luftwaffe had discovered in the Battle of Britain, it is extremely difficult to win a complete victory in an air-only war of attrition. In March 1944 there was no doubt that the USAAF was winning but the Luftwaffe was far from defeated and still extremely active. Bomber Command was suffering unacceptably high losses by night and by day the American air forces were suffering losses that would probably be beyond the means of most countries to replace.

The combined bomber offensive may not have achieved what it set out to achieve, but it was by no means a failure. The day and night bombers were inflicting significant damage on German industry. In the first three months of 1944 German war production was still increasing but the difference between what was being produced and what would have been produced without bombing had increased to 12 per cent. This was a notable achievement. It would have been even better had Harris and the Americans not diverted so much effort into bombing Berlin and other city centres. However, even if more effort had been focused on more important industrial targets, the bombing would still not have come anywhere near achieving the original Pointblank objectives. By any reasonable criteria what the bombers were achieving was remarkable. The Pointblank bomber offensive was only a failure in terms of the unrealistic targets that it had been set. Whether it was a good return on the resources invested is another matter.

Earlier in the war the principal damage inflicted on the Allied cause by the bomber strategy had been the diversion of resources from more crucial battles. With the seemingly bottomless industrial resources of the United States, and indeed a mighty Soviet Army with no strategic bombing distractions in the east, this was no longer the case. The western Allies could afford to experiment with strategic bombing offensives without risking defeat. However, bombing had not brought the expected rewards. The British believed they could break German morale, the Americans that they could cause armament production to nosedive. Both believed bombers could make an invasion of France unnecessary. They were wrong on all counts. They assured the generals that, at the very least, bombing would seriously weaken the enemy forces they would face. The generals were misled. Delaying the invasion to give the bombers time to succeed had just delayed the decisive battle. Even worse, it had given the Germans time to fortify the Channel coast.

With Allied politicians no longer willing to brook further delay, nothing was going to stop the invasion happening in 1944. However, as D-Day approached, the bomber would continue to cast an adverse shadow over Allied thinking and planning.

Chapter Six

Invasion Air Support

While Arnold was gearing his fighter force up for the struggle over Germany, Morgan was still poring over maps of northern France with what he described as 'the depressingly small' radii of action of the fighters available to him.[1] The response from the British to his request on what might be possible in the spring of 1944 had been rapid and extremely disappointing. In contrast, when the American view on what might be possible finally arrived in October 1943, the figures revealed a very different story. The American aim of having fighters escort the bombers all the way to Berlin had, coincidentally, solved all Morgan's problems.

The Americans informed Morgan that with a 75-gallon drop tank the P-47 had a 350-mile radius of action. This increased to 385 miles with a 108-gallon tank and a new 164-gallon tank would push the P-47 radius of action up to between 420 and 440 miles. The P-38 could manage 300 miles without drop tanks and 510 miles with a couple of 150-gallon tanks. The Mustang would soon be arriving and this could manage 600 miles, with two 75-gallon tanks.[2] He was also told of the plans to increase further the range of the Mustang with more internal fuel. With their bomber offensive dominating American thinking, the figures they were providing were escort range rather than patrol times over the French coastline, leaving Morgan to work this out. In fact presenting the information in this way undervalued what the Americans were offering. As the note explained, the radius of action of the P-38 with two 150-gallon tanks was limited to 510 miles by the internal fuel the fighter could carry. It had the external fuel to fly further but not the internal fuel to get back. The low proportion of internal fuel would not be a factor when it only had to fly back over the Channel.

The American were offering more than twice the endurance the Air Ministry thought possible. The American offer put the Normandy beachhead comfortably within range. For Portal the game was up. The Americans were clearly demonstrating that no new dramatic technological breakthrough

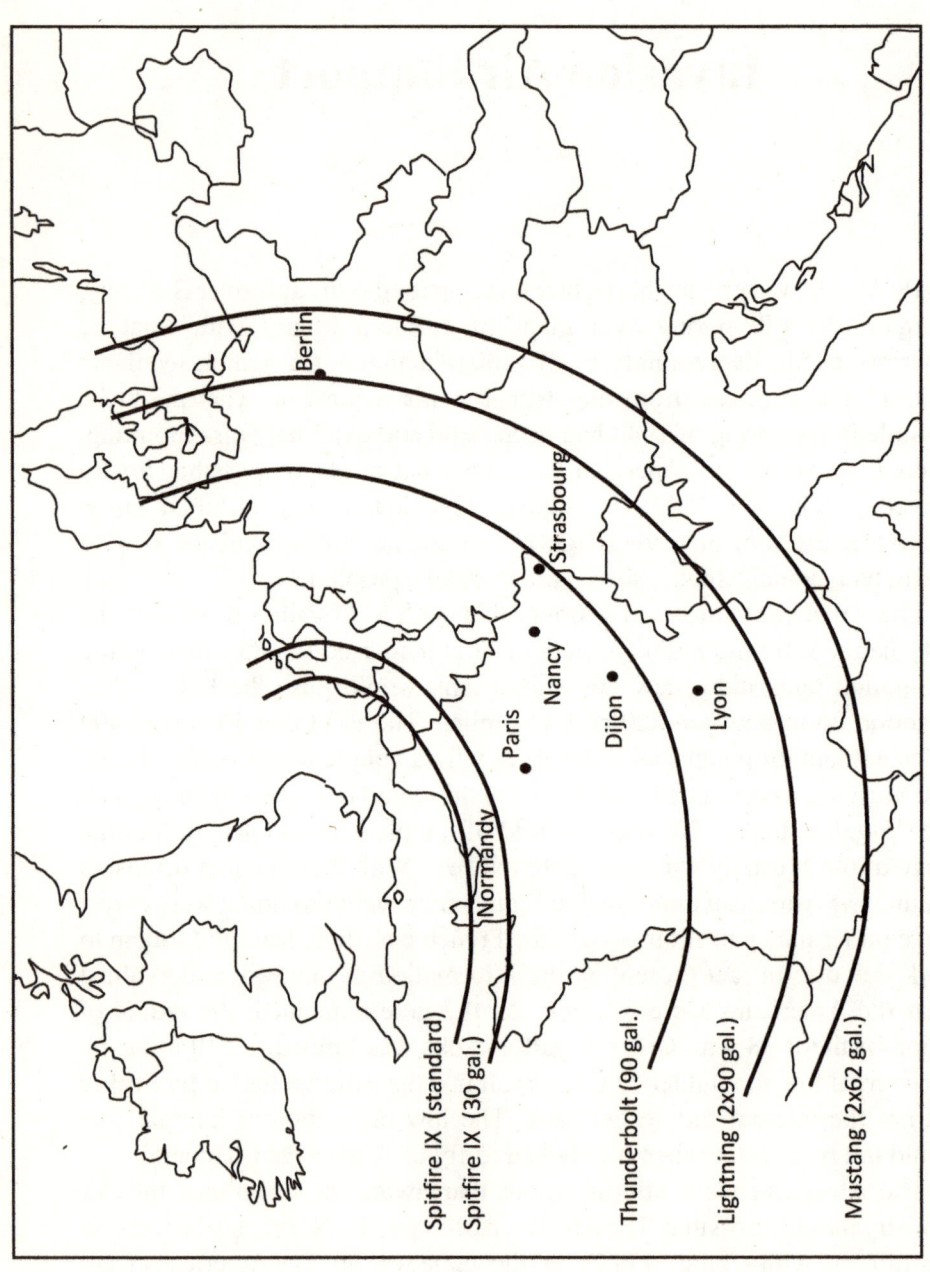

Fighter radii of action figures supplied to Morgan in 1943.

INVASION AIR SUPPORT

was required to extend the range of the single-seater fighter. It was no use pretending any longer that the Spitfire could carry a 90-gallon drop tank to cover the Salerno landings but it could not do the same to patrol over the Normandy landings.

Leigh-Mallory was already rethinking drop tank policy. In December he took over as commander of the Allied Expeditionary Air Force although, even in his new role, it was still escort range rather than patrol time over the Normandy beaches that was his main concern. He now accepted that even the 45-gallon tank he had changed his mind about was not good enough. The AEAF correctly assessed that with 85 gallons of internal fuel the Spitfire could use a 60-gallon drop tank for escort. This pushed the radius of action of the Spitfire up to 240 miles, still much less than the Thunderbolt and Lightning. However, there was no such drop tank, so the only option was to use the 90-gallon tank two-thirds full. There was, of course, nothing to stop the tank being filled to the brim and used to extend patrol time over the Normandy coast. By a somewhat tortuous route, fighter squadrons were going to get the 90-gallon tanks they needed to cover Overlord.

The 90-gallon Spitfire slipper tank had been available since an invasion of France had been first considered in 1942. At the time Portal had even given Churchill the impression they were being stockpiled with a future invasion in mind.[3] This was not the case. Nearly two years later there was no readily available supply and the sudden demand for the tank took the MAP by surprise. There was no way existing production could meet the needs of UK squadrons on top of existing Mediterranean and Far East requirements.[4] Overseas theatres had led the demand for more range but it was the air forces tasked with covering the invasion that would now benefit from their demands. Overlord had absolute priority over all other operations and theatres. A batch of tanks that were actually about to be despatched to India was immediately recalled.[5] When the MAAF said they would need more than they had originally requested because of the continuing need to patrol the Anzio bridgehead they were told they would have to make do with 45-gallon tanks.[6] Despite these measures, it was February 1944 before there were enough for operations using the tank to begin from UK bases.[7]

Still nothing had been done about increasing the Spitfire's internal fuel. There seemed to be a feeling that matching American achievements was beyond the wit of British aircraft designers and engineers. The Operations department were in awe of the Mustang. 'The distance covered by the single-engined aircraft is beyond anything that the Royal Air Force has ever attempted or indeed even considered possible.'[8] The Americans had overcome all the supposed problems with not just endurance but navigation and pilot fatigue. Yet, instead of a desire to make up for lost time, the Air Ministry seemed paralysed by hopeless despair. In March 1944, Vice-Chief of Air Staff Air Marshal Douglas Evill was still lamenting the lack of a British Mustang type fighter and wanted to know what was in the pipeline. The answer he got suggested very little. Neither the Spitfire IX nor Spitfire XIV would ever be able to manage a 500-mile radius of action, never mind the 722 miles they were told the Mustang was capable of. The Spitfire simply lacked the internal capacity to fly any further. Evill showed no desire to question this assumption. Creating a single-engined fighter with the range of the Mustang, he believed, would mean starting a fighter design from scratch.[9]

Belated efforts were being made to insert an additional fuel tank in the Tempest fuselage, a modification Second Tactical Air Force considered urgent.[10] When this request was passed on to Hawker, they, rather revealingly, considered it to be fairly straightforward, undertaking.[11] The problem seemed to lie entirely within the Air Ministry. Having convinced themselves the Spitfire could not fly further, they found it impossible to break free from the myth they had created. It seems that news the Americans were investigating what could be done with the Spitfire prompted Vickers to be asked to have a go but it does not seem much was expected of this initiative.

In the meantime, as far as the invasion was concerned, the news that American fighters would soon be able to fly as far as Berlin made the short range of British fighters an irrelevance. Compared to Berlin, the beaches of Normandy were a mere stone's throw away. By the New Year, plans to use the Spitfire with a 90-gallon slipper tank meant this, too, would have no problem patrolling the Normandy coast for a reasonable length of time. In January, as Portal was coming to the conclusion that establishing air superiority for Overlord was all the bombers could achieve, Overlord planners were told they could expect 2,500 American Thunderbolts Lightnings and Mustangs along with over a thousand Spitfires to be available for the invasion, all with more than enough endurance to cover the Normandy beaches. Even the most dire fears of a 3,000 strong German fighter force by 1 April 1944 only envisaged fewer than 900 German day fighters being available on the western front. The 4 to 1 advantage in fighters seemed ample. There was no need for the bomber offensive to win air superiority for the Normandy landings. The air superiority the bomber commanders were promising was something Morgan could already count on.

INVASION AIR SUPPORT

Indeed, the Allies had possessed the fighter resources to secure air superiority over northern France for some time. The myth that there was a problem had only been sustained by the claim that the existing 90-gallon drop tank could not be used and a stubborn refusal to admit the Spitfire could accommodate more fuel internally. RAF Mustangs were soon demonstrating the absurdity of the claim that, as yet unimagined, new technology was required for single-seater fighters to fly further. RAF pilots were roaming as far as the Swiss border. On 19 April Mustangs damaged an He 111 near Lyons; on 22 April three Bf 109s were claimed in the Nancy-Strasbourg region; on 23 April, six out of a formation of eight He 111s were claimed twenty-five miles south-east of Dijon.[12] The Allied fighter force had the numbers, the quality and the range to secure the skies over the invasion.

There was just one dark cloud on the horizon. Evidence was mounting that by the spring of 1944 Germany might be deploying a dangerous new generation of jet aircraft, perhaps even rocket-propelled aircraft, that might transform the balance of power. Since early in the war British intelligence had been compiling evidence of German progress in the development of jets and rocket-powered aircraft. The British had known about the Heinkel He 280 jet fighter since 1940. In May 1942 a reconnaissance plane photographed what was believed to be the prototype at the Heinkel factory at Rostock. Intelligence reports credited the fighter with a top speed of between 490mph and 530mph, a service ceiling of over 49,000 feet and an impressive climb rate of 5,900 feet per minute. There were also reports that both Heinkel and Messerschmitt were developing rocket-powered aircraft.[13]

Most of these early reports were accompanied by re-assuring suggestions that the Germans were finding it difficult to develop a practical warplane using these new forms of propulsion. The problems Gloster were having with their Meteor seemed to support the idea that the jet-powered combat plane was still a rather distant prospect. However, in the summer of 1943, evidence was growing that the Germans were close to overcoming these problems and jets would soon be in service. The Air Ministry were aware that the He 280 had now been joined by the Messerschmitt Me 262 and this was apparently capable of 527mph. A captured German airman rather indiscreetly reported that Adolf Galland, in charge of the German fighter force, was, equally indiscreetly, promising front-line pilots that the Heinkel jet fighter, with speeds in excess of 500mph, would be in service in 1944.[14] Some estimates put the He 280 top speed as high as 620mph.[15]

This was all very worrying for Leigh-Mallory, as he took over the reins of the new Allied Expeditionary Air Force in late 1943. Suddenly the 440mph of the Mustang III, Spitfire XIV and Tempest V did not look so impressive. German jet performance was far in advance of any British jet, never mind conventional piston-engined fighters, and, he feared, might easily win back air superiority. He suggested as a first step setting up a unit equipped with jets and piston-powered aircraft to see how they would fare in opposition.[16] Churchill was also urging Portal to step up British efforts in jet development.[17] Portal assured everyone every effort was being made to match German progress but, given the problems Britain's own jet programme was encountering, he was not so convinced the Germans were really that far ahead.

There was indeed no chance of any British jets becoming available in time for the Normandy landings. In early 1943 just getting a jet into the air was an achievement. The first Meteor prototypes were powered by Whittle's Power Jet W2, which became the Welland when Rolls Royce took over development. This was not even developing enough power to get the Meteor safely airborne. Frank Halford, working for de Havilland, came to the rescue with his 1,500lb thrust Goblin engine. The engine was intended for the twin-boom DH 100 (the future Vampire) that de Havilland were working on. For this single-engined fighter, the Goblin would have to develop the full 3,000lb thrust Halford was aiming for but, in March 1943, an early version developing 1,500lb thrust at least enabled the twin-engined Meteor to get into the air, this version becoming the Meteor II. Its first flight did not last long; serious control problems forced an immediate return to earth. They were problems that would prove difficult to eradicate.[18] By June the Welland W2B was producing sufficient power (1,600lb thrust) to allow a second prototype, the original Meteor I, to take to the air, but, as was the case with the Goblin-powered version, the fighter did not handle well. Nor was performance particularly impressive. Just 403mph was possible and even when the engine had been boosted to its planned thrust of 1,700lb no more than 424mph was expected.[19] This was slower than the Spitfire XIV/Tempest V generation of piston-engined fighters. It was hoped that 2,000lb thrust might eventually be possible with the Welland, which ought to push the top speed of the Meteor beyond 460mph. This version became the Meteor III, but this was a much more distant prospect.

These disappointing results were not causing too much concern in Air Ministry circles. The jet engine was particularly efficient at high altitude and the Air Ministry had been mainly interested in the jet as a way of dealing with the high-altitude bombers the Germans were believed to be developing. However, the threat had never materialised and the specialist twin-engined piston-powered Westland Welkin was flying and provided some insurance should this threat emerge. The need for a jet fighter did not therefore seem so urgent. In the summer of 1943 the MAP were considering an order for 300 Meteors (twenty Meteor Is for training, fifty Meteor IIs and 230 Meteor IIIs), but at this stage, within the Air Ministry there was not much interest in going beyond the ten pre-production Meteors already on order.[20] Indeed, given the problems the Meteor programme was encountering, the Air Ministry began to wonder if it was worth persisting with the fighter. It was probably not going to become available in any useful form until the end of 1945 and the Gloster workforce could be more usefully employed producing something else. Germany, fighting a defensive war, might need jet interceptors, the Air Ministry argued, and this might not be good news for the USAAF long-range bombers, but the priority for the Allies now was offence and the short-range jet did not lend itself to offensive operations. It was an argument that emphasised the strategic bias in all Air Ministry thinking. The effect jets might have on the tactical air battle was not a consideration. Jets may not have sufficient range for offensive operations over Germany but they had ample range to operate over the battlefield.

News that once the Goblin was producing the promised 3,000lb thrust, the Meteor ought to be capable of speeds close to 500mph was enough to keep Air Ministry interest alive.[21] The emergence of the V-1 threat provided more reasons. The low-flying 400mph V-1 posed problems for piston-engine fighters as they generate their highest speed at medium altitudes. The Meteor might only have a marginal advantage over the Spitfire 21/ Spiteful generation of fighters at medium altitude but the Welland-powered Meteor III was expected to be around 50mph faster at sea level and the Goblin-powered Meteor II ought to be 100mph faster.[22] In November 1943, Portal ordered an Aircraft Development Unit for jet-propelled planes to be set up as soon as the pre-production Meteor 1s became available in order to investigate how they might be used against the V-1.[23]

Meanwhile, the MAP had already set in motion the development of a second generation of jet fighters powered by a single engine. With weight concentrated near the centre of gravity this ought to result in a far more manoeuvrable fighter than the twin-engined Meteor, making jets a much better like-for-like replacement for single-engined piston-engined fighters. The lack of Air Ministry interest meant jet specifications were written by the MAP around experimental proposals from industry rather than being fully-fledged Air Ministry requirements, but they were being designed as fully-armed combat planes. The MAP saw this second generation of jets primarily as dog-fighting air superiority fighters, whereas Air Ministry suggestions that they carry six cannon and have a pressurised cockpit still put the jet firmly in the high-altitude bomber destroyer category.[24] Amendments to the specification variously described the jet as a 'fighter', or 'high altitude interceptor', depending on whose thinking prevailed at the time.

Technically, a single jet engine posed a dilemma for designers. For maximum efficiency, the jet pipe carrying the exhaust away needs to be short, which was not a problem if the engines were mounted under the wings but it became a problem if the engine was mounted centrally in the fuselage. To get round this, de Havilland opted for a twin-boom design with the engine in a truncated central fuselage. Specification E.6/41 was written around the de Havilland project, the target speed being set at 490mph and a service ceiling not less than 48,000 feet.[25] The prototype DH.100 flew in September 1943. With their second-generation single-engined Ace fighter, Gloster accepted the disadvantages of mounting the engine in a more conventional central fuselage. Specification E.5/42 was written around their proposal requiring a maximum speed of at least 485mph and a service ceiling of 50,000 feet with an armament of four cannon.[26] This, however, could not be expected to fly until 1944.

The alarming feature about all these proposals was that they were slower than the Me 262 which was expected to enter service imminently. Coningham was as alarmed as Leigh-Mallory about the prospect of having to deal with jets.[27] As the invasion approached with still no sign of them entering service, fears about them being an immediate factor eased, but they remained a long-term threat. On the eve of the invasion a blunt memo from the Executive Committee of the Army Board to Evill, the Vice-Chief of Air Staff, made their concerns clear.[28] Even Portal was beginning to appreciate jets might be a significant tactical factor.[29]

Jets aside, with the fighter range myth demolished, there was absolutely no reason to believe the air situation over an invasion of Normandy would be any different to the superiority the Allies had established over the landings in Italy. The key question for Morgan was no longer how to win air superiority but how to exploit it. From the very beginning, Morgan had seen air support as vital if a repeat of the disastrous Dieppe raid was to be avoided. This had demonstrated all too tragically the dangers of attacking a well-defended port and Morgan's invasion plans had always involved landing on open beaches. In the summer of 1943 the Normandy beaches were still only nominally defended but feverish activity along the French Channel coast suggested it was not going to stay this way for long. Indeed, by 1944 there would be no beach where the landing would be largely unopposed; the entire French coastline had been turned into a defended zone. Wherever troops landed, the resistance would be stiff and well organised and the firepower so obviously lacking in the Dieppe raid would be crucial if these defences were to be overcome. Every means possible had to be assembled to give the initial wave the best chance of establishing a bridgehead.

By August 1943 the initial bombardment had evolved into a plan for drenching the beach defences to a depth of 1,000 yards with fire from battleships and cruisers. This would be preceded by Bomber Command assault during the hours of darkness and a concentrated bombardment by American day bombers at first light. How effective the aerial bombardment would be was open to question. Pinpoint accuracy was impossible by night and, even by day, so inaccurate were the American day bombers expected to be, this bombardment was to take place when the assault forces were still six miles from the shore. Naval guns were far more accurate but even these would have to halt their assault on front-line defences before the landing craft hit the beaches.[30]

The most critical phase of the landing would be the time between the lifting of the naval and aerial bombardment and the Army being able to get its own artillery into action. Landing craft would be armed with rocket projectiles and light artillery. However, the fire from supporting ships and landing craft would, in the words of one Army assessment, 'obviously not' be sufficient if the beaches were well defended.[31] Air support would also be required and would be particularly vital while the first wave of amphibious tanks were getting their bearings and would continue to be crucial until the Army got its heavy weapons ashore. Morgan was expecting precision close air support, as well as naval fire, to compensate for the lack of Army firepower. This would need to react to requests for support as rapidly as possible. Fighter-bombers on standby in the UK might require an hour to respond but aircraft either already crossing the Channel or on patrol near the beachhead would be able to intervene much quicker.[32] This was all pretty much in line with what the War Office believed was the norm in the Mediterranean.

For the Air Ministry, however, it was a norm that they had sought to avoid at all costs throughout the war. Battlefield close air support was not even a third priority requirement in Air Ministry thinking; it was a straightforward misuse of air power. Since the outbreak of war the Air Ministry had fought tooth and nail to limit the resources invested in army air support. The British Expeditionary Force in 1940 had been supported by the tactical 'British Air Forces in France'. This rather unfortunate title made it easy to disband once it was forced to retreat from France, even though such a force would obviously have been needed had Britain been invaded. Having abolished the means to resist an invasion, they then set about delaying for as long as possible the creation of an air force that could support an invasion of France. It was very different in the Middle and Far East where the reality of fighting real battles had ensured effective tactical air forces had come into being and stayed in being.

Army demands early in the war for something like the Stuka led to the MAP ordering American Vultee Vengeance dive-bombers, much to the annoyance of the Air Ministry. The RAF rejected these for use by UK-based squadrons and they were shunted off to the Far East, where they performed very successfully. When War Office pressure forced the Air Ministry to develop a specialist low-level armoured assault plane, they made sure it could double as a long-range bomber. The result was the Bisley, a converted Blenheim, which was neither suitable for long-range bombing nor low-level ground attack. In the Middle East the fighter-bomber had become the standard way of delivering army support and all fighters could be used in this role. However, both the Army and Air Force had doubts about the accuracy and effectiveness of the bombs they delivered. The 250lb and 500lb general-purpose bombs were still the primary standard RAF battlefield weapons. Even with 60-degree dive-bombing, accuracy left a lot to be desired. Nor were the bombs particularly effective. A bomb could land fairly close to a tank without inconveniencing it. In soft ground bombs buried themselves before exploding, cushioning the blast. Low-level attack on hard surfaces often resulted in the bomb bouncing past the target.[33] For some time the War Office had been pressing the Air Ministry to make more use of cluster bombs that could spread smaller bomblets over a larger area, which would be far more effective against dispersed soft targets. By 1944 a 500lb weapon with twenty-eight 20lb bombs had been developed and a new version which carried fifty-six 8lb bomblets was on the way. However, even on the eve of the invasion, the War Office was struggling to get these delivered in sufficient numbers.[34]

Much was expected of the air-to-ground rocket. These had been designed to shoot down bombers, and had also been considered as air-to-air weapons, but proved far too inaccurate for either role. The same was true in an air-to-ground role. The RP-3 (Rocket Projectile 3) version, with a 60lb warhead, was devastatingly destructive. Early trials also demonstrated its potential to demoralise. It generated a frightening noise, flew slowly enough to be seen and gave the appearance of a 'flame thrower-cum-rocket'.[35] However, the RAF's own operational research teams assessed the weapon as hopelessly inaccurate and probably only capable of hitting something as big as a ship. In their view, the most effective method of attack was still strafing with fixed machine guns and cannon.[36] These were indeed the only weapons accurate enough to hit small battlefield targets, The RAF's standard Hispano-Suiza 20mm cannon was a particularly effective ground-attack weapon against lightly-armoured targets. Hurricane tank-busters armed with the Vickers 40mm cannon had impressed Rommel with their ability to knock out anything up to a Panzer IV tank.

Rather than develop specialist aircraft to carry these weapons, the Air Ministry and MAP preferred to rely on fighters that had either failed in their intended role or were becoming obsolete. The Typhoon was an example of the former and the Hurricane the latter. In mid-1943 the rugged Hurricane was still seen as the best available ground-attack fighter and indeed in this role it had a lot going for it. Its four 20mm cannon alone gave it an excellent built-in ground-attack capability. It could also carry bombs or rockets and the Mark IID version carried two 40mm anti-tank guns. The specialist close-support Mark IV had a universal wing that enabled it to carry bombs, rockets or 40mm cannon. High value targets such as Panzer divisions were bound to bring their own anti-aircraft defences with them, so to deal with these the Hurricane IV carried 350lb of protective armour. This was rather skimpy compared to the 800lb of the German Fw 190F/G, the 1,500lb of the Soviet Shturmovik and over 2,000lb of the twin-engined German Henschel Hs 129. Even so, the Hurricane IV was the nearest the RAF had to a specialised armoured close air support aircraft.

There were, however, no plans to build this version in great numbers. Despite its obsolescence, even in late 1943 the Hurricane was still needed as a fighter in overseas theatres. Over 200 Hurricane IIs but only a little over thirty of the armoured Hurricane IV were coming off the production line each month. It was planned to phase out the fighter version, with the last Hurricane IIC due to be delivered in December 1944. However, even though at this time the MAP was envisaging the Hurricane as the RAF's standard ground-attack aircraft into 1945 and beyond, there were no plans to step up production of the armoured Mark IV. Indeed planned monthly production through to the end of 1945 was reduced from sixty to thirty-five.[37] Nor was there any specialist replacement in the production pipeline.

The rocket projectile and the 40mm cannon both reached UK-based squadrons in the summer of 1943, and there was considerable debate about which was the better. Leigh-Mallory was anxious to keep the 40-mm cannon because it was so much more accurate than the rocket projectile.[38] The gun only fired a couple of rounds a second so slow speed was essential if the pilot was to get any rounds on target. The Hurricane was the best available platform for the weapon. The laws of flight make it very difficult to design an aircraft with a high top speed and a low minimum speed. The faster an aircraft can fly, the higher its minimum speed tends to be. The Hurricane was not famed for its speed, but the ability to fly fairly slowly combined with excellent handling at these speeds was just what was needed for the 40mm cannon. The Air Ministry always saw low speed as a disadvantage and indeed it was for deep penetration missions where the aim is to spend minimum time in enemy airspace. This was not the case for battlefield air support where no deep penetration of enemy airspace was required. However, air commanders in the Middle East were adamant that single-role aircraft like the anti-tank Hurricane were not required. Even Broadhurst thought it was a rather extravagant luxury.[39]

The final straw for the 40mm-cannon-armed Hurricane 'tank-buster' was the appearance of the Panzer VI Tiger with its much thicker armour, much too thick for a 40mm cannon shell to penetrate. The 57mm Molins cannon, an adaptation of the standard army 6-pounder anti-tank gun, was available but this had an even slower rate of fire than the Vickers cannon. It also weighed an enormous 1,800lb, compared to the 300lb Vickers gun. It seemed only a large twin-engined aircraft like the Mosquito would be able to carry the weapon and such a high-performance aircraft would only be able to get two or three shells on target during a pass. Ideally, the gun required a smaller slower aircraft if it was to be of any use on the battlefield. Martin-Baker came up with such a plane. Their compact twin-boom pusher design was built around the huge cannon.[40] With its fixed undercarriage and a top speed of 270mph it was not the Air Ministry's idea of a modern, high-performance combat plane. However, with its pusher engine, it provided the pilot with a much better view forward and also offered the protection of an impressive 5,000lb of armour. It was precisely the sort of specialised 'tank buster' Morgan had mentioned when outlining his air requirements for the invasion.

It was, however, instantly rejected by the MAP; Martin was told that the Air Ministry had no interest in such a highly specialised weapon although, as James Martin pointed out in his reply, destroying tanks surely required a specialised weapon.[41] It was also somewhat unfair to claim tanks were the only targets it could attack. The Air Ministry's real objection was that it was clearly a battlefield weapon and that was not where they wanted their air force operating. The more versatile, higher performance fighter-bomber, capable of deeper penetrations, was the preferred option. In August 1943 the Air Ministry armaments department, basing their opinion on a rather liberal interpretation of the trials' results and operational experience (mostly against shipping and locomotives) suggested that 'there was little to choose' between the rocket and 40mm cannon in terms of accuracy as the latter was 'only' 4.5 per cent more accurate.[42]

By September 1943 Leigh-Mallory had been persuaded. The heavy cannon, either 40mm or 57mm as an anti-tank weapon, was abandoned in favour of the rocket projectile. For high-speed attacks a salvo of inaccurate rockets each with a deadly 60lb explosive head seemed a better bet than two or three accurate 6lb shells. It was perhaps a rather hasty decision. Both the German and Russian air forces continued to use 37mm cannon for ground-attack until the end of the war. Indeed the RAF's own 20mm Hispano-Suiza cannon continued to be one of the most effective RAF ground-attack weapons.

Abandoning the anti-tank cannon meant there was less need for the slow-flying Hurricane. Leigh-Mallory was already unhappy with its low performance. Armed with eight rocket projectiles, the Hurricane IV, even with its special low-level 1,620hp Merlin 27 engine, managed a top speed of just 284mph. The commander of No. 83 Group, Air Vice-Marshal William Dickson, complained that the Hurricane was too slow and had inadequate range, both criticisms reflecting where Dickson was expecting his squadrons to operate. In December No. 184 Squadron suffered particularly heavily in low-level rocket attacks on suspected flying-bomb launching sites.[43] Pilots were understandably not enthusiastic about using such a low performance aircraft on long-range missions. The highly-trained crews of No. 184 Squadron were simply being wasted flying such an obsolete machine, Dickson insisted.[44] Against distant, well-defended targets, Dickson was right. Leigh-Mallory was now anxious to replace the Hurricane before the Normandy landings took place.[45] Everything seemed to be falling into place. The Typhoon had the performance to operate deeper in the enemy rear and it could carry rockets. It was already in service in large numbers with fighter squadrons but was of limited value as a fighter. The Typhoon was the obvious candidate for the tactical ground-attack role.

Even the perennial problems with the Typhoon airframe and its Sabre engine seemed to be easing. By September 1943 almost all operational Typhoons had been re-engined with the latest more reliable version of the Napier engine. Fighter Command had seen too many false dawns with the engine to be anything other than sceptical. When asked to comment on the performance of the modified engine they reported over one fifth of the new engines had failed after an average of sixty hours, although only two were the result of problems with the Achilles heel of the engine, its sleeve valves.[46] It was hardly a ringing endorsement. Indeed, problems would re-emerge with a vengeance when the Sabre engine was exposed to dusty Normandy landing strips.

The flutter problem with the Typhoon was resolved by fitting the Tempest tail plane, a modification that would appear on production machines early in 1944 and would be retrospectively fitted to all aircraft in service.[47] The same bubble cockpit canopy used for the Tempest gave the pilot a much better all-round view. A useful combat plane was finally emerging from the problem-strewn Typhoon saga. The Typhoon's poor high-altitude performance need no longer embarrass its pilots in its new low-level ground-attack role and the hefty airframe gave the plane an inbuilt ruggedness even without any armour. Its liquid-cooled engine was an obvious vulnerability but, as a readily available interim, it was a very handy fighter-bomber.

It was ironic that now that a useful role had been found for the Typhoon, production was due to end. From the spring of 1944 the Tempest II was supposed to take its place. With a genuine fighter capability and a Centaurus air-cooled engine that was less vulnerable to ground fire, it was a far superior fighter-bomber. In December 1943 the first Tempest II was still rather optimistically expected in March 1944. The Meteor was pencilled in to replace the Typhoon on Gloster production lines, but problems with the Meteor were delaying production, so an additional 500 Typhoons were ordered to keep the workforce occupied. This would extend production at a hundred a month until the summer of 1944, with production finally fading out entirely in May 1945.[48] It would prove to be a fortuitous decision.

The Hurricane was now very much an unwanted aircraft. The Far East was the only command making substantial use of the fighter. In November 1943 the first Spitfire Vs reached Burma, the last front on which the Hurricane was being used as a fighter. Thunderbolts were earmarked to replace the surviving Hurricanes in the fighter-bomber role.[49] There was little interest in extending the operational career of the Hurricane. In December 1943 the Air Ministry finally informed the MAP that the RAF had no further need for any Hurricanes.[50] The MAP immediately set about winding up Hurricane production, the last one coming off the production lines in July 1944. Production of the low-level Merlin 27 for the ground-attack Hurricane IV was immediately suspended, freeing production capacity for other versions of the engine.

Since being ordered in 1936 the Hurricane had led a charmed existence. Fortunate to be ordered in such large numbers when the contemporary Spitfire was vastly superior, and described as approaching obsolescence even as it was entering service, a combination of circumstances, including an inexcusable shortage of Spitfires, had contrived to keep it in production as a fighter until the last year of war. The fighter and its pilots had performed miracles, but its continued use as a front-line fighter so long into the war was an indictment of Britain's air procurement policy. The fighter was probably most useful in the short-range ground-attack role, but this was the role the Air Ministry was least interested in pursuing.

This, however, was very much what the War Office was interested in. Direct support on the battlefield would be especially crucial as the troops went ashore on D-Day. Ever since the Dieppe disaster, the problems involved in landing on heavily-defended beaches had generated a lot of imaginative thinking in War Office research and development departments. A whole range of weird and wonderful amphibious, even submersible, tanks were developed, or at least investigated, under the stewardship of Major General Percy Hobart, to bulldoze and flail their way through beach obstacles and minefields and engage beach defences. Ways in which air power could help were also being investigated. Major General Kenneth Crawford's Land/Air Warfare Department, usually referred to as the 'Air Department', had been created in 1942 to advise the General Staff on air matters. They were in no less imaginative mood, albeit not always with the backing of their head of department. In the early summer of 1943 Crawford's team was outlining the air options they believed the Army needed to give the invasion the best chance of succeeding.

They were already assuming the Allies would possess air superiority and argued that it ought therefore to be possible to take greater liberties with the types of aircraft deployed. Using heavily-armoured autogyros to land troops behind enemy lines, in addition to the gliders already earmarked for these operations, was one of their proposals. It was also suggested that 'flying tanks' could glide into the landing zone, jettisoning their wings on landing. Even more outlandishly, they proposed tanks, equipped with rotating foldable aerofoils, that could briefly hop into the air to pass an obstacle. The Army's detachment from mainstream aeronautical thinking was certainly allowing some blue water thinking but even they would concede that 1944 might be a little too soon for many of these ideas.[51]

One proposal, however, ought to be realisable in time for the invasion. It involved yet another War Office attempt to get a purpose-built close air support aircraft. The War Office were constantly frustrated by the Air Ministry tendency to push 'close support' ever further into the rear, to the point where it included targets as far as fifty miles beyond the front line. In an effort to reset Air Ministry thinking, the Air Department emphasised they wanted more than 'close support', they wanted 'intimate support' and they wanted a different sort of aircraft providing it. They did not want a high-performance aircraft that made a high-speed pass, launched a lightning strike then exited the battlefield as quickly as it had arrived. They wanted a more permanent offensive aerial presence over the battlefield.

They explained how traditional means of providing close support, epitomised by the German Stuka, Russian Sturmovik and British Hurricane tank-buster, were not what was required. They were too vulnerable, too fast to aim their guns accurately and lacked hitting power. Most of all they lacked the ability to sustain their attack. Bombs were considered a particularly unsuitable weapon. They were far too inaccurate; indeed, they posed as much danger to friendly forces as they did to the enemy. Aimed fire which could eliminate armoured vehicles and strongpoints would be much more effective. Suitable weapons might include recoilless anti-tank guns, rockets, cannon and heavy machine guns.[52]

High speed was both unnecessary and undesirable. On short-range missions over the battlefield there was no need to minimise the time spent in enemy airspace. Indeed they wanted the aircraft to stay as long as possible. What was required was an 'assault aircraft' that flew as slowly as possible, ideally under 100mph, so that gunners could take aim at targets. With the Luftwaffe on the wane, it was German flak that was becoming the main threat, so the aircraft would have to be sufficiently armoured to withstand anything up to 20mm cannon fire. At least five crew members were envisaged, a pilot, radio operator and three gunners. The machine should be designed with the best possible view for the occupants, the ability to fire in all directions and the endurance to cruise over the battlefield for at least thirty minutes. Such a platform would also be ideal for observing the enemy. With this in mind, later proposals included an endurance of three hours over the battlefield. If more substantial air support was required, targets could be marked with radio beacons (the Rebecca transceiver/Eureka transponder

INVASION AIR SUPPORT

system) so that aircraft could home in on their objectives. It was not just during the early stages of an invasion that such machines would be useful, it was emphasised. Indeed, 'It is difficult to foresee any situation in which this aircraft would not be of immense value' they ventured to suggest.[53] Looking even further ahead to post-war military requirements, such a machine would also be ideal for dealing with troublesome rebellions in far-flung corners of the Empire.

This was all in the rather grey area, between Army and Air Force spheres of interest and responsibility. What they were suggesting, they made clear, was an Army rather than an RAF item of equipment. It was more a vehicle that could fly rather than a conventional combat plane. As far as the War Office Air Department were concerned, the sort of craft they were describing was no more part of the Air Force than the submersible tank was part of the Navy. These 'intimate support' aircraft had to be an integral part of the Army. An armoured division for example, might benefit enormously by having a permanent allocation of such aircraft.[54]

To ensure these slow aircraft could intervene rapidly, they would need to operate from basic forward airstrips very close to the front line, just as the Auster artillery observation aircraft did. They would not need to have a high service ceiling; all their missions would be conducted at low altitude. A return to the biplane format, even the triplane, might help achieve the required low speeds and short take-off and landing runs required. They did not see any reason why such an aircraft should not be available in time for a 1944 invasion.

Much to the disappointment of his subordinates, Crawford, was not impressed. He reminded them of the scathing Air Ministry reaction to previous Army proposals for slow-flying close-support aircraft. Such aircraft had been described as 'death traps' and the War Office had been ticked off for trying to 'distort the natural attributes of aeroplanes to fulfil unsuitable and limited roles'.[55] The Air Department were well aware of the potential problems with their proposal; they realised it would be difficult to armour wings and tail planes and still have an aircraft that could get into the air. Beyond the technical difficulties, however, there was the far greater problem of persuading the Air Ministry there was a need for such a platform. They were very aware that they were asking for a machine that would attack targets that were already within range of ground-based army weapons, an argument the Army always felt rather vulnerable to.[56] There was no need to feel defensive. The advantages of a gun platform that could rise quickly into the air from improvised airstrips near the front line and race to where it was required at 100mph had such obvious military advantages, it scarcely needed much explanation or justification, as subsequent history would demonstrate.

As for the technical means for achieving the required performance, talk of biplanes and triplanes might seem like the ideas of an Army department that had lost touch with reality, hopelessly trapped in a Biggles-esque bygone era. In fact, having two or three aerofoils to provide more lift was a perfectly efficient and effective way of flying slowly. Replace the two or three fixed aerofoils of the biplane and triplane with two or three rotating aerofoils and the idea looks a lot more familiar. The Air Department was essentially describing a helicopter gunship. The War Office might fear ridicule but it was the disdainful, dismissive Air Ministry attitudes to slow-flying combat aircraft that would prove so embarrassingly incorrect.

Autogyros and helicopters had been suggested as the means by which some of their other proposals might become realty. Indeed there was frustration within the Air Department that Britain had abandoned helicopter development in 1940 and handed over everything it knew to the Americans. By 1943 the first practical helicopters were emerging in the United States and the Admiralty were certainly aware of the possibilities. As early as January 1941 news that an American autogyro could carry depth charges had attracted the attention of the Admiralty and by 1943 they were working closely with the Americans on autogyro and helicopter development.[57] A similar open mind and a different set of priorities might have seen a similar initiative to investigate how the helicopter could meet Army requirements. Unlike the Navy, with its Fleet Air Arm, there was no equivalent Army Air Arm which might have provided a framework for investigating the options. The War Office was totally reliant on the Air Ministry and helicopters had never had a place in their strategically-orientated thinking and their 'higher, faster, farther' mantra for combat aircraft development.

So fearful was Crawford of another scathing response, he elected not to pass his department's proposal on. It was a measure of just how dominant the Air Ministry had become that the Army lacked the confidence to push their ideas. One has to have some sympathy for Crawford. The Air Ministry were still struggling to understand how the 100mph Auster could be useful, although perhaps the fact that the War Office had won that particular battle should have encouraged a more confident approach. First use of an armed helicopter, by the French in Algeria, was still more than a decade away. A more closely integrated defence community might have seen Britain emerge as a pioneer in the field. As it turned out, the Air Ministry was still deriding the idea of a combat helicopter well into the 1960s. The Air Ministry always liked to ridicule the other services for their lack of vision, but it was the Air Ministry's pre-occupation with strategically-orientated warfare that was limiting horizons.

Instead of specialist slow-flying attack aircraft, the Army would have to rely on the high-speed fighter-bombers the Air Ministry had in mind. Eighteen Typhoon squadrons would be assigned the ground-attack role. This was the maximum number of squadrons that planned Typhoon production could support. Two would remain attached to Air Defence of Great Britain (ADGB), the air defence element of the disbanded Fighter Command, to help deal with V-weapon launching sites.[58] Of the sixteen attached to the Second Tactical Air Force, eleven would carry rocket projectiles and five bombs. A programme was put in hand to modify the Typhoons for their new specialist role. This was supposed to include fitting armour. Details of how the Typhoon should be armoured had been outlined as early as November 1942. In July 1943 the fitting of 780lb of armour, some permanent, some attachable, to all Typhoons to protect the engine and pilot had been approved. This was about the same as the armour carried by the ground-attack versions of the Fw 190. However, this was stretching even the robust Typhoon to the limit and there were concerns that the undercarriage would not be able to support more than two 500lb bombs with so much armour.[59]

It had been agreed that, to speed up the conversion of the Typhoon to the ground-attack role, the first hundred to be converted would not have the extra armour. There followed a somewhat muddled and contradictory attitude to the issue, as the Air Ministry wrestled with the balance between armour, manoeuvrability, range and weapons load. In the spring of 1944 there were constant reminders about the need to speed up the modifications required by the Typhoon, and the forthcoming Tempest, for its new role. These included reminders about the armour, but the armour aspect seemed to be quietly forgotten and no substantial armour was ever fitted.[60] It was all rather reminiscent of the Fairey Battle/armour saga in 1940, and the issues were essentially the same.[61] The Air Staff wanted to use the Typhoons over the greatest possible range with the greatest possible bomb load. Drop tanks and weapons load were more important than armour.

There do not appear to have been any major concerns within Leigh Mallory's AEAF about the plans to replace the Typhoon by the Meteor on the Gloster production lines. Early in 1944 they were still rather optimistically expecting the Centaurus-powered Tempest II to become available in the summer. There was also the Sabre-powered Tempest V to fall back on, although the AEAF were well aware that the first hundred of these were going to be delivered as pure fighters and there were no immediate plans to ensure subsequent deliveries could carry rocket projectiles.[62] There does not appear to have been any pressure from the AEAF to extend Typhoon production. The MAP were only doing this to keep the Gloster workforce occupied until the Meteor III was ready. Indeed, ironically, in view of future events, on the eve of the Normandy landings, with some 300 airframes in storage awaiting engines, the concern was that no use would be found for all these Typhoons.[63] As was the case with other unwanted fighters, tactical-reconnaissance squadrons seemed a suitable home for them

As with battlefield air support, from within the Air Ministry bubble it was difficult to appreciate the critical value of battlefield reconnaissance. For an army commander, finding out where the enemy was and what he was doing was arguably the most important contribution an air force can make. This did not just mean the enemy's strategic intentions; knowing the location of enemy positions on the battlefield and, when advancing, knowing what lay around the next corner were at least as valuable as any aerial bombardment. The confusion during the disastrous Dieppe raid over exactly where the Germans were firing from had not been forgotten. Ideally some sort of permanent 'eye in the sky' was required.

Reconnaissance, and tactical reconnaissance in particular, had always had the lowest priority in Air Ministry eyes. Any aircraft that did not drop bombs or shoot down enemy aircraft tended to be seen as a waste of resources. Air Ministry attempts to pack all army requirements (artillery observation, reconnaissance, ground-attack, dive-bombing) into a single aircraft had resulted in the unfortunate Lysander. The 'army co-operation' squadrons (a term that emphasised the Air Staff hope that these would be the only squadrons co-operating with the Army) were constantly being dipped into to reinforce bomber squadrons. By 1943 the authorised strength of a squadron had been trimmed down to just ten aircraft. Even then the Air Ministry still expected those that remained to fill the ground-attack as well as the information-gathering role. It took three years of war to disentangle the 'army co-operation' concept into its artillery-observation, tactical/strategic reconnaissance and close air support components. Even then, no specialist aircraft were developed; squadrons always had to make do with any aircraft not wanted by other commands. The only aircraft that was not an Air Ministry reject was the Auster AOP. Why the Army would want an unarmed 100mph aircraft had been a complete mystery to the Air Ministry, but it required little development (it was based on an existing light aircraft) and was cheap to build. For the Army it was a priceless asset.

Crawford's War Office Air department were in no doubt about the need for effective observation and were already working this requirement into their slow-flying 'army support' plane. Ideally, the Army needed something that approached the near total coverage corps aircraft and, in particular, observation balloons, had provided in the First World War and, as had been the case in 1914-1918, they needed these resources to be under Army control. The system of requesting and having to justify an RAF reconnaissance mission could never provide the instant response and comprehensive, overall picture the Army needed. Commanders could not rely on odd snippets of information gathered by 'half-fledged airboys'.[64] The War Office Director of Research (General Alfred Goodwin-Austen) returned from a conference with No. 84 Group so depressed about the fleeting observations high-speed aircraft could provide, he insisted the previously proposed 'support aircraft' was needed purely for the observation role.[65] By late summer of 1943 the idea had evolved into a nine-seater which the War Office were describing it as in 'the class of a heavy bomber'.[66] This 'super AOP' would operate from behind friendly lines to avoid enemy anti-aircraft fire, from where it would observe and direct operations. What was being proposed was in essence a proto-AWACS.

There was enormous frustration within the Air department that once again Crawford refused to pass on their ideas. He insisted that there was no need for such an aircraft; existing RAF arrangements met all Army requirements and there was no demand from front-line Army commanders for a high duration observation capability. His subordinates pointed out that it was the Air Department's job to lead the way, not react to suggestions. It seemed to his team that years of 'knocking our heads against a brick wall' had taken its toll and the Army had given up even trying to explain to the Air Ministry what they needed. Unless the Army was more willing to challenge Air Ministry hegemony, Crawford's team feared, the advantages of air superiority were not going to be fully exploited.[67]

Again, the Army might be accused of lacking in self-belief by failing to pursue a very legitimate requirement. Whether it be by an early twentieth-century observation balloon or a late twentieth-century drone, a real-time view of the battlefield is priceless. Just outlining the requirement might have got a serious discussion going about how the Army's short-range tactical requirements could be best met with the available technology. Indeed it might have led to even more. The RAF would soon be experimenting with their own primitive AWACS, a Wellington with a rotating radar scanner mounted above the fuselage, to direct fighters against aerial threats, especially low-level threats flying under the cover provided by ground-based radar. A closer spirit of collaboration and a more integrated defence establishment might have seen a start made on providing an advanced airborne system for directing and controlling ground and air operations in the battle zone.

In the short term, the best option available to the Army was to make more use of the humble Auster. These were not an Army entitlement; they were issued at the discretion of the Air Force. An Army corps might be assigned one squadron, which meant a flight of four aircraft per division. However, once assigned, these were effectively part of the Army. They moved with the Army and were in a better position to respond to Army needs. A more generous allocation might have been useful – it would scarcely have cost much – but, in Air Ministry eyes, doling out air units to Army control was a dangerous, precedent-setting practice that needed to be kept to an absolute minimum.

The War Office were not without a sympathetic ear in Air Ministry circles. The development of the tactical-reconnaissance squadrons was one of the top priorities for Air Commodore Andrew Geddes. He had started his career in the Army but had been regularly seconded to the RAF and indeed in 1939 became the commander of Lysander equipped No. 2 Army Co-operation Squadron. Although still technically in the Army, he served on the staff of the RAF Army Co-operation Command and became the deputy Senior Air Staff Officer at Second Tactical Air Force when this was formed in 1943. As was the case with Broadhurst, his Army roots gave him a different perspective on army air support. Geddes would perhaps have had some sympathy for the ideas on short-range observation circulating the War Office, had such ideas ever reached his desk.

Geddes was in no doubt about the importance of tactical reconnaissance. He anticipated, quite logically, although given the way future events initially panned out, somewhat optimistically, that the campaign in north-east Europe would be very different to the battle in Italy, where the fronts, constrained by sea and mountains, were very narrow. In northern France there would be more opportunities for outflanking movements and effective reconnaissance would therefore be even more important. If pilots were to provide the necessary information they would need the best possible aircraft. Equipping reconnaissance squadrons with anything but the best was a false economy, he insisted, as more missions would be required to gain the same information. [68]

This was all contrary to existing policy which was to use any aircraft unwanted by other commands for tactical reconnaissance. There were, however, some pretty impressive cast-offs. Early in the war, tactical-reconnaissance squadrons acquired the excellent American P-40 Tomahawk. They were even luckier with the Allison-powered Mustang I, 'discovered like a good meal in a dustbin' as Geddes put it.[69] Their luck had continued when they had rather surprisingly been assigned the much vaunted Merlin 61-powered Mustang III. It seemed too good to last. And so it would prove.

Perhaps surprisingly, the Mustang III was not seen as a particularly attractive acquisition, certainly on the basis of the information Geddes was getting. The first 140 would be 30mph slower than the Mustang I at sea level and would remain slower up to 10,000 feet, he was warned. Subsequent aircraft would only match the performance of the Allison-powered Mustang at these lower altitudes. This was indeed true if the Allison-powered Mustang was also lighter, and therefore more manoeuvrable, which was a useful asset.[70] So strong was the preference for the Allison version of the Mustang, there were plans to acquire as many Allison engines and P-51 airframes as possible from the United States before production ceased completely.[71] Rather disparagingly the Mustang III was considered just about better than the only other readily available alternatives, surplus Typhoons or 'time expired' Spitfire Vs.

Leigh-Mallory's intervention would make sure no Mustang IIIs were delivered to tactical-reconnaissance squadrons. Undeterred by the change in fortune, Geddes suggested the new much-improved light-weight Mustang F and G as future replacements, while the Tempest II was perhaps the best British option. He also suggested it was about time Britain developed a specialist reconnaissance aircraft, a single-seater with the best possible performance at low altitude, rather than relying on discards from other commands.[72] There was no doubting his determination to see tactical-reconnaissance squadrons get the best equipment, but he was competing with fighter and fighter-bomber squadrons for the limited slice of the industrial cake allocated to fighter production.

When the Second Tactical Air Force was formed, it only possessed nine reconnaissance squadrons (seven on the Mustang and two with the long-range Spitfire IV and XI reconnaissance variants). With a front-line strength of fewer than a hundred aircraft, it was scarcely a huge force to maintain in the overall scheme of things. However, with no supposedly sub-standard American fighters to fall back on, equipping this handful of squadrons was becoming a problem. Two of the Mustang squadrons were re-equipped with the strategic reconnaissance Spitfire XI. To keep the remaining five Mustang squadrons going for as long as possible, squadrons were instructed not to stray from their primary reconnaissance role by getting involved in dangerous extra-curricular air combat or ground attack. Eventually, however, the RAF would run out of Mustangs.

Of the British alternatives, the Typhoon was the initial choice; in late 1943 it seemed a good way of using up the growing surplus of engineless airframes. Indeed with the Normandy landings rapidly approaching, the task of converting the Typhoons to the tactical-reconnaissance role managed to acquire an especially high priority. At the time infantry shortages were forcing a major review of all production programmes, and those working on non-crucial aircraft that were not 'designated', were likely to be called up to the Army. The main designated types were the Halifax, Lancaster, Spitfire, Tempest and Mosquito, but the photo-reconnaissance version of the Typhoon had been added because of the acute shortage of tactical-reconnaissance aircraft.

Reconnaissance squadrons were used to getting by on what other commands did not want but engineless airframes seemed to be taking this to another level. Even with an engine the Typhoon was scarcely ideal. Conversion of a first batch of twenty Typhoons to carry cameras was approved early in 1944 and by the beginning of May cameras were being installed in 200 of the Typhoon airframes in store. As for the engines, in March 1944 it was hoped a predicted small surplus of Sabres would allow the delivery of twenty photo-reconnaissance Typhoons a month, beginning in July 1944.[73] A more immediate solution was to use Spitfires and, indeed, not 'time expired' Spitfire Vs but its successor the Spitfire IX. This was suggested early in 1944, to the horror of the Air Ministry. They pointed out that ADGB were already having to convert Spitfire IX squadrons back to the Spitfire V and, with the forthcoming invasion, fighter losses were bound to be heavy. The Air Ministry demanded to know what exactly was wrong with using Typhoons, to which the obvious answer was that they did not have engines.[74]

The MAP chipped in with a claim that the Spitfire IX could not take a vertical camera, a strange claim given that the Spitfire XI, the photo-reconnaissance version of the Mark IX, did and a claim soon refuted when the manufacturers were contacted. The MAP admitted that they really just meant it was difficult to fit vertical cameras. Coningham wanted five tactical-reconnaissance squadrons converted to the Spitfire IX and he offered to have his own maintenance units fit the cameras if the MAP found

INVASION AIR SUPPORT

it so difficult. If there was a shortage of Spitfires, he suggested a couple of ADGB Spitfire IX squadrons could be converted into the more useful fighter-bomber role with Typhoons and their Spitfires passed on to a couple of tactical-reconnaissance squadrons. Coningham's proposal was rejected, and in June 1944 the plan was still to convert the five Mustang tactical-reconnaissance squadrons to Typhoons between July and November 1944.[75]

All these problems were concerning a remarkably small reconnaissance fleet. For the invasion Second Tactical Air Force would still only have four long-range reconnaissance squadrons, now equipped with a mixture of photo-reconnaissance Mosquitoes and long-range Spitfire XIs, and the five tactical-reconnaissance squadrons with the Mustang I/II. A little more than one hundred aircraft were supposed to provide the needs of the British and Canadian forces. This was little more than 3 per cent of the total UK RAF strength. Seven Auster AOP squadrons, each with a normal strength of twelve aircraft, would eventually be fed into the Normandy beachhead, as soon as airstrips became available. Even so, it was scarcely a generous allocation. The Americans were planning to commit a similarly limited number of aircraft to tactical reconnaissance. For the German invasion of France in 1940, nearly 20 per cent of the Luftwaffe combat force were short or long-range reconnaissance aircraft. It was perhaps too easy for the western allies to rely on intelligence gathering by other means, especially with the wealth of information the code breakers at Bletchley Park were providing. Arguably, this made air reconnaissance less crucial. However, these intelligence sources could not always provide ground commanders with the immediate information they needed. Sometimes there is no substitute for physically seeing what is happening, as events in Normandy would demonstrate.

The Allies were approaching the forthcoming invasion of France with a massive but rather unbalanced air force. In January 1944 it was anticipated that, by May 1944, there would be more than 9,000 combat planes ready to participate, more than twice the number available the previous spring. However, 40 per cent of these aircraft would be heavy bombers while only 7 per cent were medium, and 5 per cent light bombers. Nearly 30 per cent would be fighters. Including seventeen fighter squadrons provided by ADGB, fifty-nine pure RAF fighter squadrons would be available for operations on the other side of the Channel. With the American contribution, the total fighter strength would be around 3,500.[76]

Despite all the dire warnings about how disastrous invading France would be if the bomber fleets did not first establish air superiority, controlling the skies was never going to be a problem. The Allies had ample fighter resources. There was also no shortage of aircraft to attack targets in the rear. It was battlefield support, both in terms of reconnaissance and ground-attack, that was lacking. In the spring of 1944, the Typhoon squadrons were the only dedicated ground-attack force. However, there was plenty of scope for last minute adjustment. The fighter is a remarkably versatile weapon. It is relatively easy to switch it to other roles. Much would depend on how many fighters the Allies felt they could free from air defence duties.

As the commanders made their plans in the UK, Italy continued to be the only front in Europe where British and American forces were in action. All eyes turned to the Mediterranean for clues on how the enormous air forces being assembled in the UK could best be used to support the invasion of France

Chapter Seven

Italian Dress Rehearsal

Brooke and Churchill still believed there was much to be gained by an Allied drive north through Italy. It was not just a question of pinning German forces down; there were still hopes of an advance into Austria trapping German forces in the Balkans. At the Tehran conference in December 1943 Brooke managed to persuade the Americans to delay the invasion of Normandy by a month to ensure the Italian front had the resources for the next attempt to advance.[1] Stalin had no major objections. With the Soviet Army driving German forces back over the Dnieper, a second front was not as crucial as it had been. Indeed, the longer it took for his western allies to establish themselves in western Europe, the more time he would have to establish a firm grip on eastern Europe.

For Brooke everything seemed to be falling neatly into place. The German army was seriously stretched on its southern and eastern fronts. He scoffed at Harris's claims that the advance of the Allied armies was a result of the bomber offensive and the bomber could win the war on its own. Nevertheless, he was sufficiently persuaded by Harris's brash claims to believe the bomber offensive was well on the way to creating the major cracks in German military strength he deemed so necessary for an invasion.[2] Not that Brooke was convinced the invasion of northern France had ever been necessary. With Harrisesque bluster, he believed that if his Mediterranean policy had been pursued with more vigour instead of a 'nebulous 2nd front', the war would have been over in 1943.[3]

Portal might still hope the bomber offensive would decide the outcome of the war but the realities of fighting a real war and the obvious air needs of the other services for air support were forcing a more realistic appraisal. The positions of Portal and Brooke were converging. Both saw the bomber offensive as crucial and both rather reluctantly accepted an invasion of France was going to happen. There was a lot they could agree about. The joint fishing trips and other social events that followed the various inter-Allied conferences were perhaps now that much more cordial. However, it was a consensus that concealed fundamental flaws in the way the western Allies were trying to win the war.

With the Italian surrender, Hitler had initially decided to make a stand in northern Italy. Work began on the Gothic Line running across the Apennines to the north and east of Florence and Rommel was put in charge of the forces assembling there. However, so slow was the Allied progress northwards, Hitler decided that a stand could be made much further south. Construction work on the Gothic Line was put on hold and the main defence became the Gustav Line south of Rome, with the defences at Cassino blocking the most obvious path to the capital. It was an Allied Army Group exhausted and much depleted by three months of bitter fighting that finally made contact with these defences in January 1944.

The obvious way round the German defences was to exploit Allied control of the air and seas and launch an amphibious assault in the enemy rear. Brooke and Churchill favoured a landing fifty miles beyond the Gustav line at Anzio. The problems encountered landing in Sicily and Salerno did not encourage much enthusiasm for the plan. It was an odd reaction from two global naval superpowers. With control of the seas and skies, amphibious assaults should have been opportunities for the Allies to strike anywhere they chose, not options to be approached with trepidation. With literally thousands of miles of European coastline to defend, it was the Germans who had most to fear.

For the Allies the Anzio operation should have provided an opportunity to put right what had gone wrong in previous Allied amphibious operations. With the landings on Sicily and mainland Italy there had been no major problems protecting the invading forces from enemy naval and air attack. The serious problems had started once the troops were ashore and found themselves dealing with fierce counter-attacks. In both cases close air support for the landings had not been part of the plan. The air forces only became involved on the battlefield when things started to go wrong. If this was to change Allied air forces had to be more flexible about the air superiority/interdiction/close air support order of priority. Crucially, the Army had to make it clear they wanted the balance rethought. There were nearly 4,700 Allied aircraft in the Mediterranean, compared to fewer than 600 German. Around 2,500 of the Allied aircraft were capable of intervening in central Italy, compared to fewer than 400 German.[4] The Allies had to start making this advantage count.

The landings at Anzio, Operation Shingle, would involve British and American forces from Clark's Fifth Army, with General John

ITALIAN DRESS REHEARSAL

Lucas leading the landings. Neither was enthusiastic about the plan. The immediate objective was supposed to be the Alban Hills, about twenty miles inland from Anzio, which dominated the two major routes leading south from Rome to the Gustav Line. The plan was to launch an all-out attack on the Gustav line just before the landing. This would drive up the Liri valley towards Anzio. The reinforcements drawn in to counter this advance would ease the path for the forces landing at Anzio. By advancing inland, Lucas would cut supply lines to the German forces farther south and ultimately block their retreat. Those planning the Normandy landings looked on with interest.

The offensive against the Gustav Line was launched on 20 January 1944 but made little significant progress. Since a rapid link up with the Anzio bridgehead was part of the plan, the operation was already in trouble. For the amphibious assault, there was no major rethink about air support; air defence, interdiction and close support were the priorities in that order. The involvement of naval units inevitably pushed the focus in the direction of air defence. The beachhead and the convoys approaching were covered by permanent patrols, the RAF and USAAF flying around 650 sorties during the course of the first day. However, there was clearly excess fighter capacity for other roles. Thunderbolts were flying speculative sweeps as far afield as Rome. Heavy bombers struck targets in the rear along which reinforcements from the Cassino front would have to pass. The Desert Air Force played its part by flying 145 Spitfire, Kittyhawk and Baltimore sorties against 26th Panzer Division as it started to move towards Anzio from Eighth Army's front. A-36 Mustang dive-bombers joined B-17 Fortresses, B-24 Liberators in attacks on communication targets around the Alban Hills.[5]

The British and American forces stepped ashore in the early hours of 22 January. The Germans were taken completely by surprise. They had been anticipating a landing somewhere along the Italian coastline, but it was not expected imminently. The German cause had not been helped by a particularly effective raid by twenty-eight Liberators just three days before the landing on the airfield at Perugia, the base for the only available long-range reconnaissance squadron in the region. This put the airfield out of action and no sorties were flown for four days.[6] There were scarcely any German forces in the area and the landing was virtually unopposed. The Luftwaffe did not react until around mid-morning, sending around fifty Fw 190 fighter-bombers against the bridgehead, none of which were able to break through the fighter shield. The first successful Luftwaffe attack came on the evening of 23 January. About half of a force of fifty bombers broke through the defences, attacking shipping with torpedoes, Fritz X guided bombs and Henschel Hs 293 guided missiles, sinking the destroyer HMS *Janus*. The attacks continued on the following day. However, the Luftwaffe suffered heavily, losing some thirty aircraft in two days and subsequent Luftwaffe efforts were on a much reduced scale.[7] The defending fighters had successfully seen off the threat.

By the end of the first day 36,000 troops and 3,000 vehicles had already been landed and only thirteen casualties had been suffered. Here was the perfect opportunity to display some dash and drive and strike inland. The Allies had the air resources to provide an adventurous advance with all the protection and close air support it required. For the time being, however, Lucas's priority was to consolidate the bridgehead. From the second day of the landing the defensive fighter patrols began to be used more offensively. Fighters arrived with bombs and before taking up their patrol lines the control ship or the forward controllers within the bridgehead could direct them towards targets. If there were none they attacked any target of opportunity that presented itself. If, at the end of the patrol, they had any unused ammunition, they would strafe more targets of opportunity before returning to base. Maximising defensive and offensive capabilities in this way was now the norm in Italy and it was the sort of air support the War Office were assuming would be available for Overlord. The Allies ruled the seas and ruled the skies. The question was could the Army take advantage.

The question soon became would they even try. Even in the overwhelmingly favourable circumstances the Allied forces found themselves in, Lucas failed to take the initiative. The American commander had never been happy about his allocation of just two divisions and Clark gave Lucas maximum discretion on deciding when he had sufficient forces to make the move towards the Alban Hills. Indeed Clark's parting advice was not to stick his neck out as he had done at Salerno. First Lucas should secure his base. Lucas took note of this advice and waited for the rest of his 75,000 troops to land, and made sure he had supplies for fifteen days. Only then would he advance. In the meantime his forces were to dig in and wait for the German counter-attack.

In the air above them, the fighters armed with bombs were arriving, effectively forming a cab rank available to support any advance inland, or help stop any German counter-attack. But there was no advance to support and no German counter-attack to counter. The fighters bombed and strafed any targets they could find, usually having to fly well inland to find

ITALIAN DRESS REHEARSAL

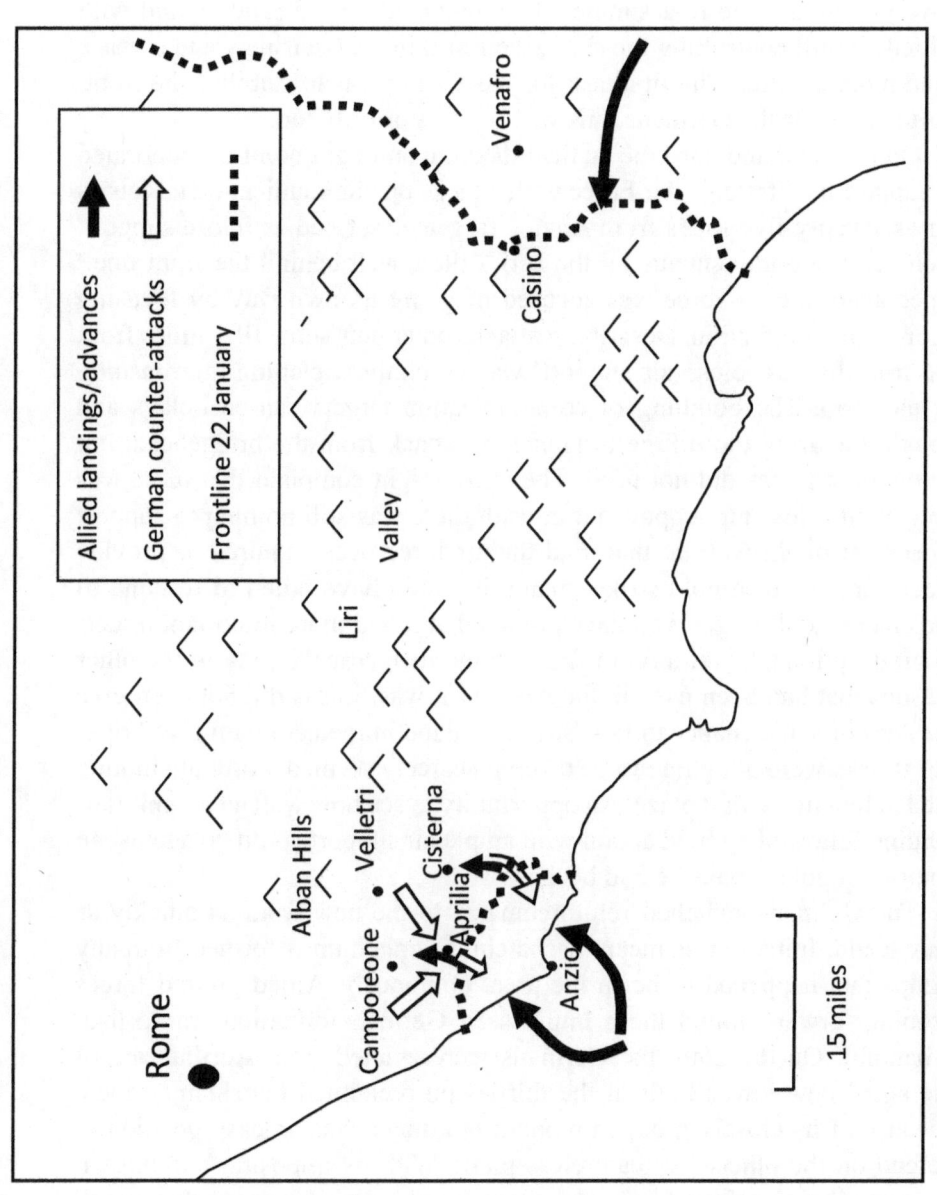

Anzio landing, January 1944.

them. The Allied domination in the skies was as great as the Allied lack of initiative on the ground. Lucas had good reason to fear the German ability to organise effective counter-attack, but the air resources available should have provided some re-assurance. Outnumbered on the ground, and with Allied aircraft controlling the skies, the last thing Kesselring wanted was a fluid mobile battle. The first task for Kesselring was to stabilise the front. Fortunately for the Germans, this was Lucas's priority too.

On the 22nd and 23rd the tactical medium and light bombers continued to support the Strategic Air Force with attacks on communication targets as far as seventy-five miles from Anzio. Targets described as 'close support' included troop movements up the Liri Valley, well behind the front line.[8] Once again the air force was accused of going its own way by focusing entirely on interdiction. Describing attacks on targets some fifty miles from the front line as 'close air support' was certainly stretching the meaning of the term. The bombing of communication targets caused delays and bought the army more time to launch an attack from the bridgehead, but it was time Lucas did not need. The army might complain that there was no genuine close air support but in truth there was still nothing to support closely. It might well be that, had the air force been required to provide close support for a bold strike inland, it would have failed to respond to the challenge. It might well have argued that it had more important targets to hit deep inland, anti-aircraft fire was too dangerous, or any of the other reasons that had been used in the past. As it was, Lucas did not even give the Air Force the chance to fail. Striking inland immediately involved risks but if risks were not going to be taken it scarcely seemed worth attempting the landing in the first place. An opportunity to see how well an amphibious landing followed by bold action with ample air support could do against an enemy caught off balance had been missed.

The Germans switched reinforcements to the new front as quickly as they could. Initially this meant despatching scratch units formed from any troops that happened to be in the area. Ominously, Allied ground forces probing forward found these improvised German formations more than a handful. On the 25th, the Germans were evicted from Aprilia, one of the small new towns built in the thirties on reclaimed marshland which, because of its closely grouped modern buildings, was an easy position to defend on the otherwise featureless plain. With its imposing buildings it was soon being referred to as the 'Factory'. Realising the significance of the 'Factory' the Germans launched a counter-attack on the 26th, supported by tanks, a heavy artillery bombardment and even some air support. It was a typical example of the Germans effectively combining the limited resources available. Ironically, given the overwhelming Allied air superiority, the defending British ground forces received no such air support, even though plenty was close at hand. The German counter-attack was repelled and the 'Factory' remained in Allied hands, but it was an ominous warning of what was to come.[9] The first request for direct support was made next day, 27 January, five days after the landing. Predictably, it was provoked by a German threat rather than an attempt to exploit German weakness. The fearsome collection of artillery the Germans had amassed around the bridgehead, expertly directed by observation posts in the surrounding hills, needed to be dealt with. The targets attacked on the 27th were gun positions in the Cisterna and Lanuvio regions. The following day Kittyhawks bombed artillery in the Cisterna and Velletri areas.[10]

It was the night of 29/30 January, a week after the initial landing, that the first serious attempt to advance got underway. The Americans struck towards Cisterna and the British towards Campoleone railway station, two miles south of Campoleone. By this time German forces were in place. Both prongs of the attack made some initial progress but, against stiff resistance, both were held just short of their objective. Air support provided on the 30th is not clear. Bad weather ruled out support on the 31st but on 1 and 2 February XII Air Support Command managed nearly 650 sorties, many against enemy ground troops seeking to recover the ground lost. The initiative was now with the German forces. Aprilia was recaptured and, by mid-February, the Germans had more troops surrounding the bridgehead than the Allies had managed to land and were ready to launch the first serious attempt to push the Allies back into the sea. This was precisely the nightmare scenario the Overlord planners feared.

The Allies had established a bridgehead but it was a hollow achievement. Far from making a breakthrough of the Gustav Line easier, the landings at Anzio now required a renewed effort further south in order to relieve the pressure on the bridgehead. Here the powerful defences around Cassino continued to pose a formidable obstacle to any Allied advance up the Liri Valley. In particular, the abbey perched on top of Monte Cassino appeared to offer the Germans the perfect location from which to direct artillery fire on the Allied forces below.

In fact the Germans had no need of the abbey, observation posts elsewhere were perfectly adequate, if perhaps less convenient. The Allies were convinced otherwise. Even if the Germans were not occupying the abbey, it was argued they might choose to move in whenever it suited them to do so. In any case, the building was such an imposing structure and had such a depressing effect on the Allied troops below, just the sight of it being destroyed would boost morale. General Bernard Freyberg, whose corps had been given the task of occupying the mountain top, demanded that the monastery be eliminated before his troops made any more attempts to advance.

For Arnold, Cassino provided an opportunity for the USAAF to make its mark. Arnold was becoming as frustrated at the dawdling progress in Italy as he was with the slow progress of the bomber offensive. Like Eisenhower and Churchill, he could not understand how the Allies could be held when they had such an overwhelming advantage in the air.[11] Arnold had not lost faith in the bomber as a strategic weapon, but, with his strategic bomber fleets struggling to achieve their Pointblank objectives, he needed something to justify the huge resources being invested in the bomber project. Punching a hole in German defences and paving the way for a decisive, possibly even bloodless, victory just as had happened with the island fortress of Pantelleria, would be an opportunity to demonstrate that the bomber was indeed the decisive weapon in modern war.[12]

There was not a great deal of enthusiasm for bombing the abbey from General Harold Alexander, commanding Allied ground forces, or General Henry Wilson, Eisenhower's successor in the Mediterranean. Destroying a target as politically and culturally sensitive as an ancient abbey with the possible loss of priceless treasures, not to mention innocent lives, was bound to be controversial, especially as the evidence that Germans had occupied the abbey was rather flimsy. Nevertheless, Wilson was sufficiently persuaded to order Eaker to temporarily turn his bombers away from German industry and direct it at the Benedictine monastery. Eaker argued that reducing the monastery to rubble would just make it easier to defend. Eaker was right but, to a suspicious Freyberg, such objections were just more evidence of an air force unwilling to co-operate with ground forces. There was little sympathy with the argument that this was not what strategic bombers were designed to do. Both the USAAF and RAF had often used the argument that there was no need to develop specialist tactical bombers because the heavies, if required, could do it just as well if not better. This was their chance to prove it.

For Eaker it was at least an opportunity to silence his critics, which by this time included an increasingly irate Arnold. However, the operation was not seen as an act of air/army co-operation; the bombers had the task of destroying the abbey and this they would do in their own time. Weather forecasts suggested it would be better to bring the bombing forward and this was done even though there was no way of bringing forward the ground assault the bombing was supposed to support.

On 15 February, 224 heavy and medium bombers dropped 450 tons of bombs and incendiaries on the ancient abbey. For the soldiers, the bombing was a not to be missed spectacle. They took any vantage point available and cheered as the bombs fell. But when the dust settled the edifice was still looking down on them. Most of the bombs had actually missed, which, against such an easily identifiable target, was scarcely a good advertisement for precision bombing. An Indian company in the front line suffered twenty-four casualties from wayward bombs. Artillery attempted to finish the job. The inside of the abbey was completely gutted but many of the 15-foot thick outer walls remained in place. Two hundred and thirty civilians seeking refuge in the monastery were killed. The only Germans killed were victims of the bombs that missed the abbey.

The next day all air force operations had to be diverted to counter a German attack on the Anzio bridgehead, but Desert Air Force squadrons based in eastern Italy stepped in, sending seventy-two fighter-bombers across the Apennines to attack the ruins. Around half made it through poor weather.[13] Freyberg's New Zealand Corps were not in position until the night of the 17th/18th. By this time any advantage the bombardment might have achieved had been lost. No German forces had been in the monastery when it was bombed but, by the time the New Zealanders attacked, the Germans had moved in to the excellent defensive positions the rubble provided. Freyberg's soldiers were repelled and a frustrated Alexander called off the attack 'until a bombardment worthy of the name' could be organised.[14] It would seem Freyberg saw nothing wrong with the approach; it was just a question of dropping more bombs and firing more shells.

The controversy over whether there were actually any Germans in the monastery and whether targets of cultural value should be bombed tended to distract attention from the military value of the bombing. Using heavy bombers to destroy an abbey scarcely constituted the sort of genuine combined-arms warfare support Broadhurst was trying to promote. It was very much the 'first destroy everything, then advance' mentality that dominated the fighting for much of the First World War. It had not worked then and it was not working in the Second World War. The Cassino affair tended to have a negative impact on close air support in all its guises and indeed on army/air force relations in general. The army had expected a more thorough demolition of the abbey, and stray bombs killing Allied troops did nothing to improve the army mood. The air force were equally unimpressed with the performance of the army. A failure to understand what was possible and what was required on both sides was deepening suspicions and mistrust.

Meanwhile, the Anzio bridgehead was under serious threat. On 16 February, with the support of 250 Luftwaffe aircraft dive-bombing, strafing and scattering 2kg anti-personnel bomblets on Allied forward positions, powerful German forces struck south on either side of the Campoleone-Anzio axis. There were no grandiose long-term plans for establishing air superiority as a prerequisite for taking the offensive. The Luftwaffe was just doing what was most likely to be useful with what was available in the prevailing circumstances. From forward command posts overlooking the battlefield, ground-attack aircraft were expertly directed towards their targets. Too often Allied troops had to wait until they were in retreat before they got such support. The Allies were flying more than a thousand sorties a day on a regular basis in the theatre while the maximum the Luftwaffe could manage was 250, but on this particular day it was debateable which army was benefitting most from airpower.

Throughout the day the Germans made steady progress towards the coast. There was a real danger that the Allies might be forced to evacuate the bridgehead. The situation was desperate enough for the Allied air forces to be called in. Fighter-bombers were in action against the advancing Germans on the 16th but it was the following day before the Allied response got into its stride. All Allied airpower in the region was focused on the battle for the bridgehead, with 248 fighter-bombers, 152 medium bombers, sixty light bombers and no fewer than 288 heavy bombers joining the naval and artillery bombardment of the advancing German columns. The four-engined heavies concentrated on communication targets to the rear of the battle zone, the mediums struck targets as close as 400 yards to the front line while low-level fighter-bombers operated even closer to friendly troops. Mistakes were made and there were losses among Allied forces, generally from bombers operating at higher altitudes rather than the low-level fighter-bombers. The material damage inflicted on the enemy was perhaps less than estimated at the time, but the operation of air forces in such close proximity to the front, as always, lifted the morale of the hard-pressed defending forces, a factor at least as significant as the damage inflicted.[15]

Yet still the Germans pushed on, through the night of the 17th/18th until by dawn they were on the final Allied defensive position. The weather closed in on the following days, making air support more difficult but 160 aircraft, mostly fighter-bombers, braved the conditions on the 18th to attack the advancing Germans.[16] Equally valuable was the contribution of the British Auster and American Piper Cub AOP flights operating from within the bridgehead. Just before midday on the 18th, an American Cub spotted a concentration of 2,500 advancing German troops and within twelve minutes the fire of over 200 guns was brought to bear on the target. In the next fifty minutes four further concentrations of enemy troops became the targets of artillery barrages.[17] Although close to victory, the endless bombardment from sea, land and air finally told and the German attack was broken off. Utilised earlier in the Anzio operation, this sort of aerial assault might have helped sweep aside any German opposition.

Further south plans were being laid for a fresh attempt to link up with the beleaguered Anzio bridgehead. The failure of the Monte Cassino carpet bombing did not discourage anyone from trying this tactic again. It was hoped more bombs, more closely co-ordinated with the attack on the ground, would bring more success. This time it would be the town of Cassino in the valley below the monastery that would be the target. It would be 15 March before weather conditions over the battlefield and Allied airfields would allow a second attempt. A huge artillery barrage on the town would be backed by 500 medium and heavy bombers, along with 200 fighter-bombers. The aim was to saturate an area 1,400 yards by 400 yards in a four-hour-long bombardment, during which nearly 1,000 tons of bombs would be dropped. To avoid friendly casualties, troops pulled back 1,000 yards from their forward positions. It was not the most encouraging way of beginning a forward advance, but if this was the only way heavy bombers could be used without inflicting casualties on their own side, then that was how it had to be. Again Eaker and others warned that turning the town into rubble would just slow the advance but Freyberg, with bulldozers ready to clear a way through, had no such concerns.[18]

Only half the bombs dropped fell in the proscribed area. Despite the precautionary withdrawal, many of those that missed fell among Allied troops, killing or wounding around one hundred. Sixty civilians were killed in Venafro, eleven miles away. Eighth Army HQ was among other friendly targets the bombers hit.[19] Nevertheless, enough bombs hit the town to create the required level of devastation. Losses among German forward units were heavy and command posts in the rear were completely cut off. As Eaker had predicted, however, as the Allied infantry advanced, the tanks were not able to follow over the mounds of rubble. It is one thing to obliterate a town in a defensive situation where the advancing enemy have the task of clearing a path through the debris but it is quite another when your own advancing forces have to do the bulldozing. If the Germans had been taken aback by the severity of the aerial/artillery assault, the Allied commanders were just as astonished to find German infantry emerging from the rubble to offer the fiercest of resistance.[20] Those with longer memories might not have been quite so surprised; in the First World War, weeks of artillery bombardment had also often not had the desired effect on well dug in troops.

As soon as the aerial bombardment of Cassino itself ceased, eight fighter-bombers were taking off every ten minutes to support the advance by attacking German artillery in the rear. Over the next few days fighter-bombers together with light and medium bombers continued to attack tactical targets up to ten miles away but there was no genuine close air support. It was argued that once the Allied advance had started, the fighting was at such close quarters and so confused it was impossible to intervene any closer. There were clearly problems, but the Rover arrangements with forward controllers guiding the air strikes in provided the basis for solutions. As was so often the case, difficulties were seen as reasons for not providing close air support rather than problems that needed to be overcome. Inroads were made into German defences but, aided by some atrocious weather, which turned bomb craters into mini lakes, German forces managed to hold on. Used defensively, carpet bombing can be useful. Offensively, the case is not so strong. There is nothing fundamentally unsound about dropping, even rather randomly, a lot of bombs on strong enemy defensive positions. It is, at the very least, an excellent way of ensuring enemy heads stay down. However, it is difficult to organise, co-ordinate and execute safely, especially with heavy bombers operating from higher altitudes. Used to excess, it tends to create more problems than it solves. The lack of success saturation bombing was having should have been food for thought for those planning the Normandy landings.

The tactical efforts of the heavy bombers in Italy provided plenty of mud for the two sides to fling at each other. Coningham, watching events from Britain, believed this misuse of airpower was simply exposing the Air Force to unwarranted criticism. Having met the Army's requests for carpet bombing, the Air Force was now being blamed for the failure of the Army assault. For Coningham it just confirmed that aircraft should not be used for close support. 'If ever the Army press me to take wrong air action near the front line, I shall use the word "Cassino" and say "No"', Coningham warned.[21] In fact Coningham's Second Tactical Air Force did not have any heavy bombers, so it was not the sort of operation anyone could ask him to lay on. It was more a justification in advance for not using his more tactically orientated forces in a way he felt was inappropriate.

Similarly, Slessor believed operations in Italy proved that he had been right all along in his belief that the bomber was not a battlefield weapon. It had been a frustrating year or so for Slessor as the success achieved by the Desert Air Force seemed to contradict his oft-stated view. Every good rule, he was willing to concede, had an exception, and the exception for this rule was the desert, 'where', as he put it, 'there was about as much cover as on the floor of a bird-cage.'[22] Here there might be occasions where, like Tebaga, it might be necessary to get armour through a defile, but in general 'the immediate battlefield is not the place to use the bomber or even the fighter-bomber'. Effectively, both Coningham and Slessor were using the disadvantages of heavy bomber close support to blacken the name of all close air support. Precision fighter-bomber support and saturation heavy bomber support were at opposite ends of the close air support spectrum but both were being tarred with the same brush. To Slessor, the whole idea of the Air Force contributing on the battlefield was simply the Army expecting the Air Force to fight their battles for them. Slessor was particularly unimpressed by the apparently light casualties suffered by the attacking New Zealanders on the first day of the recent Cassino offensive, which Slessor suggested, implied the Army was not attacking with sufficient vigour. It was scarcely an attitude that was likely to go down well in Army circles.

Slessor stuck to his belief that eliminating enemy strongpoints and gun positions was the job of the artillery. The bomber should concentrate on paralysing the movement of enemy supplies and reserves to the rear, not get involved with day-to-day events on the battlefield.[23] Indeed, Slessor believed that his sort of indirect support could be decisive on its own and he would now have the chance to prove it. With Arnold baying for some return on the enormous air resources tied up in the Mediterranean, and the obvious lack of success on the ground, Spaatz, Eaker and Slessor came up with an alternative way in which the tactical air forces might bring about the defeat of the German Army in Italy, without any help from the Allied armies.

Throughout the fighting in North Africa, cutting Axis lines of communication had played a key role. The air offensive against sea lanes between Italy and North Africa had been particularly rewarding. With the island of Malta providing a base for attacks and Ultra intercepts providing the shipping schedules, Axis convoys had suffered grievous losses. During the campaign in Sicily and Italy, attacking communications had remained a key part of the preparation for landings or ground offensives. The aim now was to take this one step further. With the Anzio and Cassino fronts quiet and with the full backing of General John Cannon, Coningham's American successor, all Allied tactical light, medium and fighter-bomber units in Italy would focus their efforts entirely on enemy communications in central Italy. Their target zone would be anything from the front to a line running through Florence, from Pisa to Pesaro. Pointblank targets remained the priority for the heavies, but these too would on occasion join on the offensive with attacks on communication targets north of this line.

The aim was not to help the ground forces by reducing the supplies reaching the enemy. The plan was to reduce the supplies getting through to the German front line to the point where holding their current positions would no longer be possible and the German army would be forced to evacuate the Italian peninsula. This was airpower being used as Trenchard had always envisaged. Airpower would simply make it impossible for an army to function. Like the strategic air offensive, this would be an independent campaign with its own well-defined objectives and would offer an alternative to bloody indecisive battles like the one for Cassino. The aim was not to support the army, the aim was to demonstrate that armies were not needed. This was pure Trenchardism. Slessor had always believed firmly in the Trenchard philosophy; indeed, as his right-hand man he had penned many of his pronouncements. Now he was going to get a chance to prove Trenchard had been right. It was to be the death of an army by strangulation.

On 19 March Operation Strangle was set in motion. The problems with the plan soon became apparent. The first was the weather. Poor weather would always provide the Germans with a breathing space to effect repairs and transport materials unhindered, and there was no shortage of poor weather even in an Italian spring. The weather prevented the mediums from operating on about half the days between 19 March and 10 May. Fighter-bombers, operating at lower altitudes, were able to fly more often and for this reason soon became a crucial element of the offensive. They also proved more effective than medium or heavy bombers. Dive-bombing Thunderbolts were more likely to destroy a bridge than bombers flying level at medium altitudes.

It was soon becoming clear that the offensive was not having the desired effect. There were no targets as attractive and rewarding as naval convoys. Over land, there were too many alternative ways of getting supplies through. Whatever the damage inflicted on marshalling yards, railway lines and bridges, it could always be repaired and the Germans became very

ITALIAN DRESS REHEARSAL

efficient at organising repairs. These took time and resources, but arguably not the time, energy and resources the Allies had invested in the forces carrying out the attacks. Most discouraging of all, it soon became apparent that German front-line units did not need the huge quantities of material it had been assumed they needed. As Slessor ironically noted at the time, German troops could do without chewing gum, Coca-Cola, entertainment and masses of motor vehicles 'without which it is assumed the modern British and American soldier cannot wage war'.[24] Even at the time it was estimated that German divisions were getting by on a quarter of the supplies required by an Allied division.

There was an air of desperation about Slessor's complaint that the Army was not playing its part. He fully supported the view put by Cannon that 'In this phase it is not a question of the Air supporting the Army – the Army must support the Air'.[25] The most effective way of doing this, Slessor suggested, would be for the Army to be more aggressive and force the enemy to use their ammunition. On the face of it, it was an outrageous suggestion. The Army might reasonably expect the Air Force was there to reduce their casualties, not to ask them to deliberately bring fire down on themselves just in order to aid an air interdiction programme. Yet in essence Slessor was right. Interdiction cannot be expected to have much effect on front-line strength when a front is not active and resources are not being consumed. Interdiction is most effective when the front is under attack and needs re-supply and reinforcements. The Army and the Air Force could only succeed by working together. Blaming the Army for the Air Force's failure to achieve the decisive results it had believed it could achieve on its own was scarcely likely to create the spirit of co-operation this required. Any offensive action the army took had to be part of a long-term plan to defeat the enemy and win the war, not an attempt to come to the rescue of a failing air force interdiction programme.

Over 20,000 sorties were flown as part of the campaign, but the effort never came close to bringing the level of German supplies below the minimum they needed. In May, as the German armies prepared to meet another Allied offensive, Kesselring did not consider the levels of supplies at the front a major concern.[26] There was never any chance that the Allied advance would merely be a question of occupying territory vacated by a starving, defenceless and helpless army. Operation Strangle had failed. It was one thing to cut off supplies across a narrow sea, with naval support and Ultra intercepts; it was quite another to achieve the same result against lines of communication on land where the air force really was on its own.

With similar plans in place for the run-up to the Normandy landings, a chastened Slessor warned Portal not to expect too much from attacking enemy communications.[27]

An important part of Brooke's Overlord strategy was to keep as many German units as possible pinned down in Italy. Another costly frontal assault on the Gustav Line was therefore unavoidable. By this time the majority of the Eighth Army had joined Clark's Fifth Army to the west of the Apennines for the assault. It was an assault that would see a much more effective utilisation of air power.

Just before midnight on 11 May the attack began with an artillery barrage provided by some 1,600 guns. The following morning Allied air units joined the offensive, flying around 3,000 sorties during the course of the day. About half of these were in the battle zone and the other half ports, airfields and lines of communication leading to the battle zone. The heavies were used tactically, but only to attack German command centres in the rear. There was no saturation bombing of the front line; fighters rather than heavy bombers were used to attack targets close to the front. Extensive use was made of the cab-rank system. Targets were provided by forward troops, as well as reconnaissance and artillery observation aircraft.[28] Among the most feared Allied aircraft were the Auster, Piper Cub and Stinson Sentinel observation planes circling unopposed above. Strategic reconnaissance squadrons were switched to tactical reconnaissance for the duration of the assault to help provide a clearer picture of what was happening on the ground.[29] A forward control perched on Monte Trócchio helped guide the fighter-bombers on to targets. Throughout the battle the Germans could not escape the feeling of being constantly watched.[30]

On both the 13th and 14th around 2,500 sorties were flown; the Luftwaffe struggled to fly 100 sorties on any one day. On the 13th, nine times in five and a half hours, fighter-bombers took up position in the cab rank and awaited instructions on targets to attack. On the 14th it was filled ten times in five hours. Between the 15th and 18th, fighter-bombers responded to fifty calls from ground units for support. Tanks assembling for counter-attacks, troublesome mortar positions and artillery were amongst the targets. Even twin-engined Marauders were used to attack targets just 400 yards ahead of friendly troops. Fighter-bombers swarmed over the front and light and medium bombers disrupted the rear while the medium and heavy bombers restricted the flow of supplies and reinforcements to the front. This was when interdiction counted. With the battle raging, even temporary delays in reinforcements arriving or re-supply could be crucial.[31] It was a stunning display of tactical Allied airpower, applied equally on and beyond the battlefield. It was what the War Office was expecting for the landings a few weeks later in Normandy.

However, even this impressive display of strength did not guarantee success. Once again, the German ground forces at the entrance to the Liri Valley were under extreme pressure but still they refused to crack. On the southern side of the valley, however, French forces, mostly Moroccan and Algerian, with little direct air or artillery support, had broken through. Advancing through terrain the Germans believed impassable, by the 17th they were well to the rear of the main German defences. Outflanked, Kesselring was forced to order a general withdrawal, a retreat made more difficult by the Allied air forces. A fallback position soon had to be abandoned. Allied forces linked up with the Anzio bridgehead and the German forces began a long retreat to the Gothic Line in northern Italy.

The French had undoubtedly benefitted from the enormous pressure Allied ground and air forces had exerted all along the front and in the rear. The Germans had been forced to focus attention on the centre. When the danger the French posed was realised, the attacks on German lines of communications made it more difficult to mount a response. However, the actual breakthrough had come not by the massive application of artillery or airpower but by troops attacking with guile, flair, skill and courage, willing to take opportunities as they arose.[32] It was a reminder that air superiority is not a panacea. Defeating the well-organised German army was always going to be a challenge. Air superiority will always give ground forces a better chance; it might provide opportunities that can be exploited but it guarantees nothing.

The retreat saw ever more sophisticated targeting, with fighter reconnaissance planes alerting the Rover Forward Air Controls to new targets which were then passed on to fighter-bombers on cab-rank duty. As the front lines became more fluid, so the risk of hitting friendly forces increased. A 'close co-operation' bomb line was set up that might change as often as ten times a day in order to ensure the latest position of friendly forces was known.[33] Even so there were tragic errors. Genuine close support required good organisation, intensive training and strict discipline. It was not something that could be thrown together overnight. Mobility was still a problem. The Forward Air Control Posts had grown into substantial organisations, which was not a problem when front lines were fairly static or in the early stages of an advance but the advance was soon moving too fast for the Rover air controls to keep up.[34] Ways had to be found of enabling them to stay in touch. There were still lots of problems to sort out but in Italy good progress was being made. Battlefield air support was not a cure-all but it was an option any army commander would not want to be without.

The Cassino front had been broken, but the Allies were denied a complete victory. The forces in the Anzio bridgeheads were well placed to cut off the retreat, which had been the original intention of the landing, but Clark decided to go for glory and take Rome. Instead of the Army surrounding and capturing the German forces that had held the Cassino front, the air forces were left with the task of destroying as much as possible before they could reach their new defensive positions. Forced out of their Gustav Line strongpoints and with little Luftwaffe to protect them, the retreating German forces seemed ripe for attack. However the disorganised retreat soon became an organised withdrawal. The retreating columns were fairly compact targets for flak to defend and this was soon proving very effective. It was a sufficient deterrent to limit low-level fighter-bombing operations and the German forces were able to withdraw in reasonable order.[35]

It was another reminder that the struggle for air superiority is not all about the battle in the skies. Air commanders might like to see this struggle as a battle between rival air forces, but ground-based weapons also play a part. Air superiority means an air force being able to operate where it chooses without suffering unacceptable losses. German flak was preventing this. Ground defences were creating local air superiority. Air and ground warfare are more entwined than the apostles of independent airpower like to imagine.

The Air Ministry never tackled the flak problem with the same urgency as an aerial threat because it was not seen as a bona fide aspect of the air war. If Allied air forces wanted to operate wherever they chose, the problem of ground fire had to be faced and dealt with. Solutions might be tactical or technical. Assigning some aircraft the task of flak suppression, using army artillery to suppress fire, hitting the target as quickly as possible and escaping, sacrificing accuracy in order to fight another day, were among the tactical ways of tackling the problem. However, the problem was as worthy of a technical response as any other obstacle the air force faced. The Soviets and Germans had provided their assault aircraft with heavy armour. The Germans were using stand-off weapons that could be guided to their target from outside the range of enemy anti-aircraft fire. The War Office appreciated it was a problem that needed solving but the Air Ministry were happy to use the problem as a convenient reason for not using aircraft in ways they disapproved of.

ITALIAN DRESS REHEARSAL

Once again, the Germans had been pushed back but had avoided encirclement and had prevented an organised retreat turning into a disorganised rout. They were achieving this despite the Allies' overwhelming numerical superiority in the air. Slessor was as puzzled by this as anyone else. He warned Portal not to expect too much from the air superiority the Allies would have for Overlord but he could offer no real explanation, beyond his belief that Germans were 'the world's finest ground soldier'.[36] Allied air and ground commanders needed to think about why this was the case rather than explaining it away as a genetic trait.

Slessor was presiding over the force that could help dent this imagined superiority of the German race. The way the Allied air forces were used in the recent hard-fought Cassino victory was the most comprehensive since the Desert Air Force achievements in its North African heyday. Nevertheless, a negative attitude to battlefield air support was still very much in evidence in the final report to reach Overlord planners from the Mediterranean before the Normandy landings. It was intended as a summary of lessons learned in the previous six months of tactical air operations in Italy specifically for the benefit of those preparing for the invasion. It was signed by Wilson, the Supreme Commander, but written by Lieutenant General James Gammell, Wilson's Chief of Staff. Gammell was relatively new to an active front and certainly no Desert veteran. He had spent most of the war serving in the United Kingdom, before being transferred to the Mediterranean in January 1944, at the same time as Slessor, whom he knew and got on well with. It is therefore perhaps not surprising that his report passed on many of Slessor's views. In many respects the contents were remarkably similar to Air Staff pronouncements just before the German invasion of France in May 1940, which Slessor had also been responsible for drawing up.

The report contained some interesting and useful warnings. On the basis of the fighting in Italy, 'air superiority should not be overrated' was perhaps a conclusion the planners in Britain had not been expecting, but was a welcome breath of fresh air in Allied thinking. For interdiction to work, enemy forces had to be engaged in action, using the supplies the enemy was trying to get to the front, was another useful comment. In an emergency, heavy bombers might be used on the battlefield but the report emphasised that in normal circumstances the heavy bomber was not a battlefield weapon. It went into detail about how rubble in flattened urban areas aided the defence and slowed the advance of tanks and infantry. In the countryside, huge bomb craters created natural anti-tank obstacles. This was all sound advice.

However, the report also insisted that 'Even light and fighter-bombers will usually afford more valuable assistance in the rear'. The success of fighter-bombers in the North African desert was misleading, the report explained. The very different geography in mainland Europe meant that tactical targets were not nearly so exposed to air attack. 'As a general rule' aircraft should not attack enemy positions within range of friendly artillery. The morale-boosting effect of fighter-bombers attacking targets immediately ahead of advancing troops was recognised but even during an assault, such close support should be reduced to 'the absolute essential minimum' so that fighter-bombers could concentrate on targets in the rear.[37] This was not such sound advice. It was almost a word for word restatement of Air Staff opinion on close air support on the eve of the 1940 Battle of France. This assessment though was ostensibly coming from the Army. It was all grist to the mill for the air elements planning air support for the Normandy landings.

The report arrived in London with less than a month to go to the invasion. This was rather late in the day but it ought not to have been too late to have some influence on thinking and planning. As it turned out, it was remarkable the extent to which the good advice was unfailingly ignored and the bad advice religiously followed.

General Arnold (left) and Air Chief Marshal Portal in discussion. (Crown)

From left to right, Air Marshal Coningham, Air Vice-Marshal Broadhurst and Air Chief Marshal Tedder. (Crown)

The Avro Lincoln, due to enter service in 1945, was little more than an upgraded Lancaster. (Crown via BAE Systems)

The Vickers Windsor was a far more advanced design but even this possessed a pedestrian performance when compared to foreign equivalents. (Crown)

The German Me 264 flew in 1942 and was in many ways more advanced than anything on British drawing boards.

The backwardness in British bomber design led to serious consideration being given to the licence production in Britain of the American Boeing B-29 Superfortress as the successor to the Lancaster.

The diminutive Blohm & Voss BV 40 glider armed with a couple of 30mm cannon. With no escorts to worry about it was a viable bomber interceptor

Mustang IIIs from No. 19 Squadron. In April 1944. The appearance of the Mustang ended such hopes. Early versions did not have the all-round vision canopy that characterised later models. (Crown)

A Bf 110 with a dazzling array of aerials. The low frequency radar used by German night fighters required large, complicated aerial arrays which seriously reduced performance.

Mosquitoes with Serrate radar attempted to emulate the success of the Mustangs but the German night-fighter proved elusive. Darkness was providing more protection for the German interceptors than RAF bombers. (Crown)

The cramped FN.20 rear turret of a Lancaster. (Crown)

The Village Inn scanner was housed in the radome at the base of the Lancaster tail turret and rotated with the turret. (Crown)

Above: Juvisy marshalling yards, before and after the raid on the night of 18/19 April. The concentration of bombs looks impressive but the background in the image below gives some idea of the level of destruction outside the target area. (Crown)

The Gloster Meteor III powered by a couple of Rolls Royce Derwent I engines. The twin engine layout inevitably reduced manoeuvrability. (Crown)

All early British intelligence reports on German jet development focused on the Heinkel He 280. Problems with its Heinkel-Hirth engines were never fully resolved and the aircraft never went into production.

The de Havilland Vampire powered by a single Goblin engine. The single centrally mounted engine made the Vampire far more manoeuvrable than the Meteor. The twin-boom layout was chosen to ensure the best distance between air input and thrust output. (Crown)

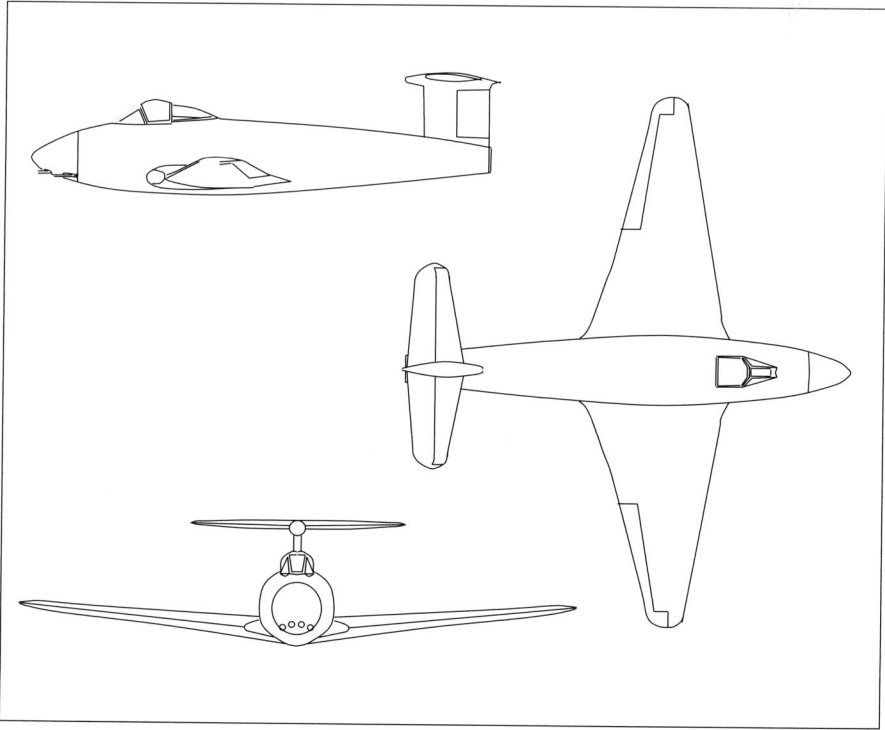

The original version of the Gloster Ace, also powered by a single Goblin. With a more conventional fuselage this was viewed as a more conservative back up to the unconventional de Havilland project. The worrying feature of all these projects was that the Germans were known to have superior jets that were about to enter service.

A Spitfire IX with a 30-gallon slipper tank, the tank the Air Ministry considered 'ideal'. This could be carried with relatively little effect on handling and performance. (Crown)

An RAAF Spitfire IX with a 90-gallon slipper tank. As a drop tank it was not ideal and was not popular with pilots. (Crown)

The Spitfire IX modified by the Americans. The teardrop shaped wing tanks were aerodynamically far more efficient than the standard RAF slipper tank. (Crown)

HMS *Implacable* Seafires with teardrop shaped 90-gallon drop tanks. The pilots got to learn of some abandoned RAAF 90-gallon tanks intended for P-40 Kittyhawks and managed to acquire 100 in exchange for a crate of Scotch whiskey. (Crown)

A V-1 flying bomb with its He 111 carrier, pioneering air-launched cruise missiles. The closing two years of the Second World War saw technologies emerge that would shape wars for decades to come.

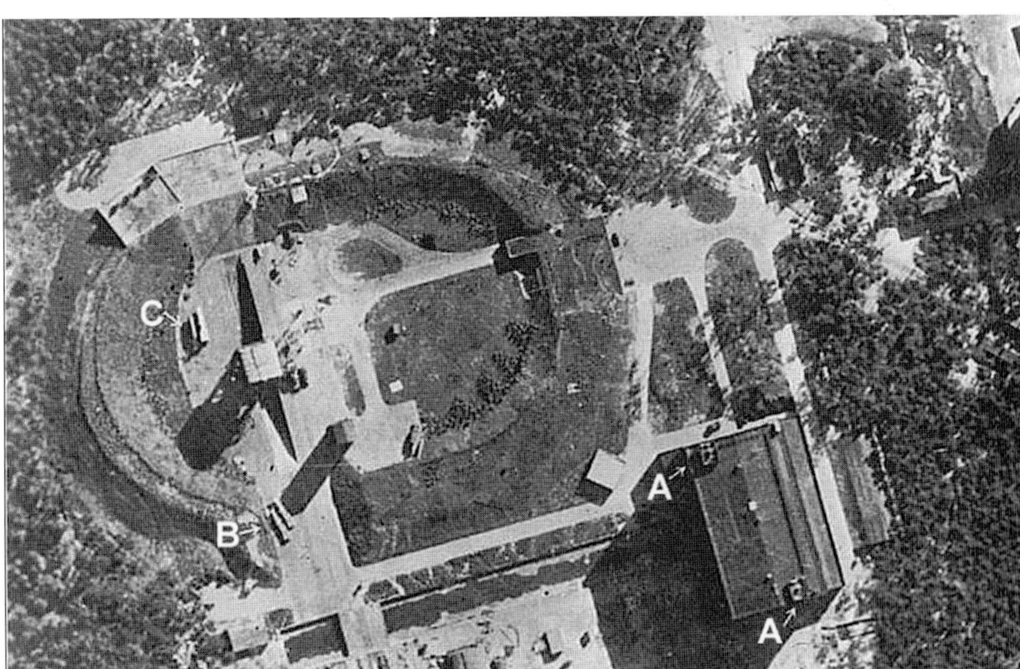

The photo of Peenemunde taken on 23 June 1943 of the V-2 launch site. A is the storage unit, B and C show V-2 missiles. (Crown)

A He 111 launches an air-to-ground Henschel HS 293 guided missile. The ability of aircraft to launch these missile from outside the range of anti-aircraft defences was one way of tackling the ground fire problem. The appearance of these missiles would prompt the Navy to investigate the possibility of ground-to-air guided missiles.

A first attempt at an AWACS. A Wellington with its rotating radar scanner without the benefit of a streamlined radome. (Crown)

Many of the thick outer walls of the Monte Cassino monastery survived the carpet bombing and continued to make an imposing impression on the Allied troops below. Where the walls were reduced to rubble, they made excellent defensive positions.

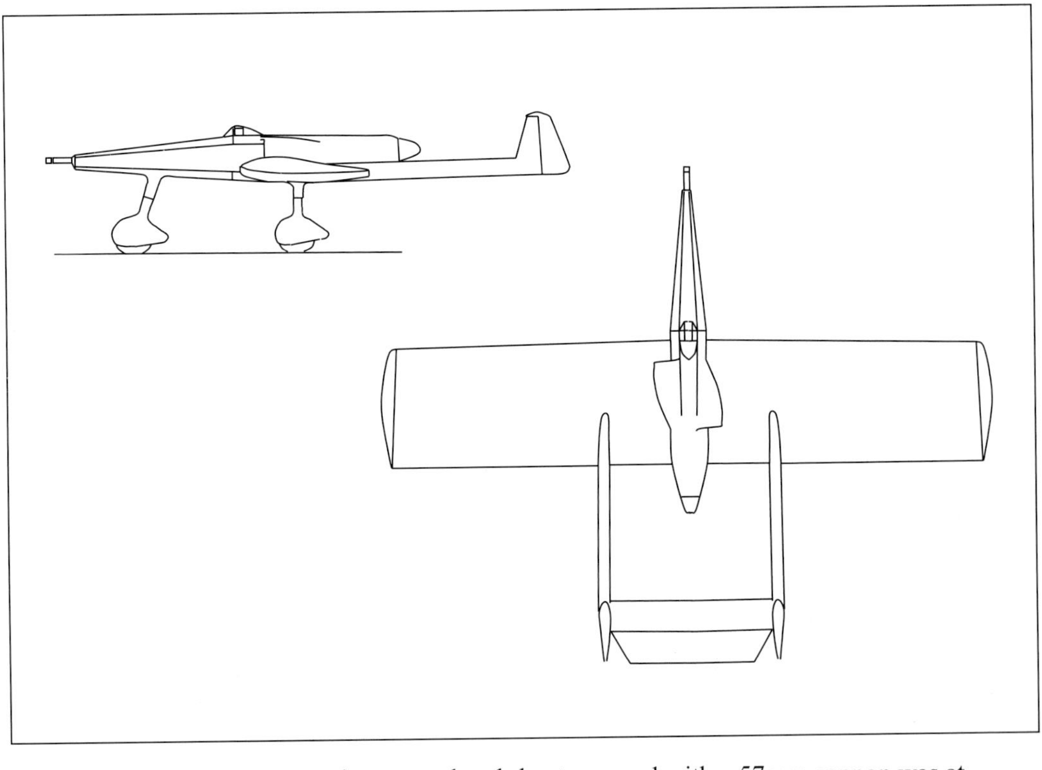

Martin Baker's proposed armoured tank-buster armed with a 57mm cannon was at the other, more discriminate, end of the close air support spectrum.

Army and RAF combine to guide attacking aircraft onto their target. A Forward Air Control operating from an armoured car. (Crown)

Austers did the same job for the artillery. An Auster IV of No. 652 Squadron flying above a 25-pounder in Normandy in July 1944. (Crown)

The desire to attack more distant targets meant Typhoons had to reduce their offensive load to just two rockets under each wing to accommodate a drop-tank. (Crown)

Carnage around Falaise. Research teams discovered most of the damage had been inflicted by machine gun and cannon fire, not rockets. (Crown)

Chapter Eight

Tedder and Coningham Take Charge

With no active front in north-west Europe, and Brooke insisting a successful strategic air offensive was necessary before any such front existed, it had been easy for the Air Staff to pursue its bombing policy without worrying too much about other ways of using its bombers. At the Casablanca conference in January 1943 it had been agreed that the strategic air forces would be available to Army commanders a month before and during the invasion of France. At the time that still looked a very distant prospect. The bomber advocates believed bombing would have won the war long before then. As 1943 drew to a close, it was becoming clear that this was not going to be the case. With the invasion of France increasingly becoming an operation that was going to take place in 1944 regardless of what bombing achieved, and the commanders who would direct it taking up their positions, deciding how strategic bomber forces should support the operation could not be put off any longer.

With their reputation for leading the revival of RAF tactical air support, Tedder and Coningham were perceived to be the experts in the field. They tended to bring their own teams with them. Air Vice-Marshal James Robb, part of Tedder's Mediterranean team, became head of the SHEAF Air Branch, rather than Graham, who had headed Morgan's Air team. Graham, who had chaired the committee which had assigned a key role to close air support in the initial assault, was packed off to West Africa.

The Mediterranean commanders arrived in Britain to find the creation of the tactical air forces to support the invasion, the RAF Second Tactical Air Force and the USAAF 9th Air Force, was only just getting under way. Both would form part of Leigh Mallory's Allied Expeditionary Air Force (AEAF). Leigh-Mallory had a strong background in air/army co-operation, dating back to his work developing air/tank co-operation in the First World War.[1] Since then his field of expertise had been largely air defence, but he had not forgotten his Army roots and still firmly believed that air forces existed to support armies. Interestingly, Leigh-Mallory appears to have been one of the few who recognised that a successful Pointblank offensive was not necessary to secure air superiority required for a successful invasion. He correctly assessed that the Allies would have ample fighter strength to deal with anything the Luftwaffe might be able to muster whatever the bombing might achieve.[2] This heretical stance alone was enough to put him at loggerheads with the American bomber apostles.

While the Second Tactical Air Force came into being with a reasonably strong frontline strength, in single-seater fighters and fighter-bombers at least, Colonel Lewis Brereton's Ninth Air Force was starting virtually from scratch. Arriving rather late on the scene, Brereton rather resented the way his force was being grafted on to an essentially British organization. Leigh-Mallory's rather stiff personality did nothing to ease inter-ally tensions.[3] Tedder's arrival as Eisenhower's deputy meant he was the most senior RAF officer in the invasion command set up. He was not actually in command of anything, but it put Leigh-Mallory in an awkward position. With the British and American tactical air forces having their own established commanders there really did not appear to be an obvious need for Leigh-Mallory's post.

As the initial landings would be conducted by a relatively small fraction of the ground forces available, Montgomery was given temporary command of all the forces involved. These largely comprised the Americans of Lieutenant General Omar Bradley's First Army and the British and Canadians of Dempsey's Second Army. Eisenhower and Montgomery were soon making radical changes to the plans Morgan had drawn up. They quickly agreed that the Allies could only win the race to build up forces if the first wave established a much broader bridgehead, which meant landing more troops. Montgomery wanted separate landings from Dieppe to Brittany, but it was felt this would stretch available air and naval resources. The final plan involved landing six divisions along a sixty mile front from the base of the Cotentin Peninsula in the west to the mouth of the River Orne in the east.

Although the actual combined width of the individual beaches where the landings were to take place would only be some twenty miles, this was still a considerable increase on Morgan's original plan. Even with the massive heavy bomber fleets available to the Allies there were fears that such an extended frontage could not be thoroughly 'drenched' with bombs. The fighters assigned the defence of the beachheads also seemed more thinly stretched. Such fears were scarcely justified by the huge air resources available, but it gives some idea of how powerful many still imagined the

Luftwaffe to be and how perilous many still viewed the entire Overlord operation.

Montgomery seemed to be trying to throw off his cautious image. He constantly spoke of the need for a rapid advance, especially on the first day. 'We must blast our way ashore...Armoured columns must penetrate deep inland and quickly on D-Day...We must gain space rapidly and peg out claims well inland'.[4] He seemed to foresee a key role for the air forces. He bemoaned the way air and ground forces were not 'one fighting machine'.[5] He urged his army commander to do everything in their power to improve air/ground planning. Montgomery was certainly talking the talk. His plan was not much different to Morgan's. British and Canadian forces in the east would capture Caen on the first day and then push on to take the airfield friendly country beyond. The Americans in the west would swing round to take Cherbourg and push south out of the Cotentin peninsula. If all went well, within twenty days of the landing, the British and Canadians would be beyond Falaise and the Americans would be beyond Avranches and out of the bocages. In less than a month the Americans would be well on their way to capturing the Brittany Atlantic ports. This advance would be covered by a defensive line along the Loire. With the Atlantic ports in Allied hands, the Americans would form up on the right flank of the British and Canadians for an advance towards the Seine.[6] There were no plans to out-manoeuvre and envelop the enemy. Just as Montgomery had been doing since El Alamein, the aim was to push the enemy back. The plan was more concerned with gaining territory than defeating the German Army.

Despite the disappointing returns air superiority in Italy had brought, Eisenhower still saw airpower as vital to the success of the Normandy landings. As he later explained to Churchill, 'one of the fundamental factors for undertaking 'Overlord' was the conviction that our overpowering Air Force would make possible an operation which might otherwise be considered extremely hazardous or even foolhardy'.[7] However, by 'overpowering airpower' Eisenhower had in mind the huge fleets of four-engined bombers the RAF and USAAF possessed. These would be needed for the preparatory pre-invasion air offensive, the actual landings and the subsequent drive inland. The Casablanca conference had assured him he would have full control of these bombers and he had no intention of letting this control slip.

There was little enthusiasm from Harris and Spaatz about passing control of their bomber forces to Eisenhower. With the USAAF still part of the Army, Spaatz had little option but to fall in line, ostensibly at least. Harris, as a commander in an independent air service, was in a stronger position to resist and initially had the support of Churchill. However, ultimately he too had to agree to cede control of Bomber Command to the invasion forces. Eisenhower agreed to have 'direction' rather than command of the strategic air forces, a sop to the feelings of Harris and Spaatz, but effectively Eisenhower had got what he wanted. Who exactly would control them within the invasion command set up was still up for discussion. Anxious to assert his authority as commander of all invasion air forces, Leigh-Mallory insisted the strategic air forces assigned to Overlord should come under his jurisdiction. The Americans did not trust Leigh-Mallory and ensured Tedder would be given responsibility for coordinating their use.

From 14 April, the two strategic bomber fleets officially became part of the invasion forces. However, neither Spaatz nor Harris saw the new arrangement as necessarily tying the strategic bomber forces to tactical targets. A more liberal interpretation of supporting the invasion might see the bomber fleets carrying on as before. The aim of the Pointblank offensive was, after all, to make the invasion possible. Spaatz in particular could point out that his current priority of destroying the German fighter force was a crucial contribution.

Both would claim that using their bomber fleets to support an invasion directly was a misuse of their resources. Harris and Spaatz suggested that any discontinuation of the Pointblank bombing offensive would give Germany a breathing space to recover from the damage the bombers were inflicting. Spaatz exploited Allied commanders' anxieties to the full by insisting that if the Eighth Air Force offensive was interrupted, the power of the Luftwaffe would be restored, and this might spell disaster for an invasion.[8] Any mention of the Luftwaffe appearing over the invasion fleet in numbers immediately sent shivers down the spines of Navy commanders in particular. There seemed to be two parallel realities coexisting. In one, War Office planners were assuming that the Allied air superiority established in the Mediterranean would continue in northern France. The expected availability of 3,500 Allied fighters provided reassuring confirmation. In the alternative reality, senior commander seemed to believe the securing of air superiority hinged entirely on the outcome of the bomber offensive and this outcome hung very much in the balance. It is possible that the likes of Spaatz were just scaremongering to ensure the strategic bombing offensive continued uninterrupted but it also possible that the bomber advocates were so steeped in their own bomber mythology they genuinely did not see that the same long-range escort fighters they needed to pursue their bomber offensive were also capable of securing the skies over the French coast. When fundamental beliefs are involved, there is always a temptation to believe what is convenient.

Harris did not have such a strong case as Spaatz. His programme of attempting to flatten one city after the other could not have the same direct relevance to an invasion. All Harris could claim was that if he could continue bombing Germany, an invasion would not be necessary. Portal had some sympathy for this argument. Even at this late stage he still clung on to the belief that if the bombing created air supremacy, a full-scale invasion would be unnecessary, a small scale policing operation would suffice.[9] In true Trenchardian style, he still believed just having control of the skies made effective opposition on the ground impossible. Events in Italy seemed to be passing Portal by.

Even without the strategic bomber fleets, Eisenhower was scarcely short of air resources. The Ninth Air Force was expanding rapidly. By April, the British and American tactical air forces boasted over 900 light and medium bombers, mostly American it has to be said. There were also over 300 dedicated fighter-bombers and over 1,000 fighters with a ground-attack capability. An additional 3,500 heavy bombers scarcely seemed necessary. With D-Day now put back a month to June, Eisenhower would have these forces for the best part of two months before the invasion was even launched. Paradoxically, having these forces for so long helped solve the problem of what to do with them. One of the problems with launching the tactical air offensive so far in advance of the landings was that a large number of unnecessary targets would have to be bombed to conceal where the landing was going to take place As early as 10 April, batteries along the Atlantic Wall came under attack. For every battery attacked along the Normandy coast, two had to be bombed in the Pas de Calais region, where the Allies hoped to persuade the Germans the landings would take place. Others would have to be attacked to ensure the Germans could not narrow down the invasion to these two localities.[10]

Leigh-Mallory added airfields to the pre-offensive target list, even though he was not expecting to find many Luftwaffe aircraft there. Leigh-Mallory caused a few more raised eyebrows in American circles by suggesting it might not be possible to establish air superiority before D-day by any method, fighter or bomber. He did not think the Luftwaffe would make the mistake of committing its reserve until the invasion was underway and predicted a week of intensive air operations over the bridgehead before air superiority was established. Indeed, in the best traditions of the Wehrmacht, he believed the invasion would provide the perfect opportunity for the Allied air forces to engage and defeat the Luftwaffe. Like any good commander, he saw the opportunity, rather than feared the danger.[11] With a predicted 3,500 fighters available Leigh-Mallory had every right to be confident he would win this battle. The Americans, however, were aghast that anyone should be contemplating launching an invasion without establishing air superiority first.[12]

In fact, fighting the battle in the air simultaneously with the battle on land was just normal practice for the Wehrmacht. Indeed earlier in the war, when the struggle in the air hung in the balance, it was standard practice for Commonwealth and Soviet forces. Where Leigh-Mallory turned out to be wrong was in believing that the Germans were capable of secreting away a vast reserve. All the Luftwaffe could do at this stage of the war was switch its air resources from one front where they were desperately needed to another where they were even more desperately needed. The bulk of the German fighter force in Western Europe was defending the Reich and they would continue doing this until the invasion was underway, at which point this battered force would be switched to northern France.

The German reluctance to commit this reserve did not, in Leigh-Mallory's view, rule out the possibility of ensuring the Allies had a significant advantage on D-Day. The German reserve would still need airfields to fly to and if these could be destroyed. Leigh-Mallory proposed denying the Luftwaffe the use of any airfields within 110 miles, if possible, 130 miles, of the landing zone, Effectively this would force the German fighters to operate from airfields as distant from the beachhead as Allied fighters operating from the United Kingdom. It was to be a thorough demolition. Attacks on German airfields would begin three weeks before the invasion with the destruction of installations that could not easily be repaired. Five days before the invasion anything at all on these airfields would be targeted.[13] Again this would have to be done across the whole of northern France to conceal the location of the landing site.

Fears the V-weapons would disrupt the invasion ensured the suspected launching sites absorbed a fair proportion of the remaining available bombers. That still left a lot of spare capacity. More targets were required and Solly Zuckerman provided them. All Allied ground offensives were now routinely preceded by extensive interdiction programmes and Zuckerman had been heavily involved in the planning of them in the Mediterranean. These included the ambitious 'Strangle' operation. In February 1944 he proposed something similar for northern France. The aim would be the complete destruction of all major rail centres within 150 miles of the landings. This would force the Germans to use road transport for the remainder of the journey. Closer to D-Day, attacks on bridges and other vulnerable points on the road network would complete the dislocation. Again, in order to conceal where the landing was going to take place, the plan necessarily involved destruction on a massive scale across a vast tract of Northern France and Belgium. By the end of the campaign, the Allies would have created a 'railway desert', to go along with Leigh-Mallory's airfield desert. It was an enormous undertaking and Zuckerman believed his plan would require three months to complete. Leigh-Mallory was impressed. With only three months to the invasion, there was little time to lose.

It was another example of the application at a tactical level of Harris's philosophy of mass destruction. This was not about preventing trains from reaching their destination. The aim was to make sure there was no railway system for the trains to use. It also meant bombing marshalling yards in the middle of French and Belgian towns and cities with obvious risks to their inhabitants. Tedder and Eisenhower were entirely in favour despite these risks. It would be the Italian Operation Strangle on an even vaster scale. At least with the transportation plan, as it became known, it was part of an overall land/air strategy. No-one was expecting the bombardment to force the Germans to abandon their coastal defences. The aim was to help the ground forces by preventing reinforcements from arriving when the time came for the invasion

Harris did not believe his command was capable of contributing to such a campaign. His bomber crews were trained to inflict indiscriminate destruction on cities; they could not possibly hit targets as small as marshalling yards by night. Bombing by day was not an option as his crews lacked training in formation flying, and, even more difficult to put right, his bombers flew too slow, too low and lacked adequate defence. Letting his bombers loose by night on targets in occupied countries would inevitably lead to heavy casualties among the friendly civilian populations, he warned. Harris's reasoning was sound enough. It was more the sort of task RAF's day bomber force should have been taking on, but the priority Harris's night bomber force was getting ensured little effort was being made to increase this force. No. 2 Group was fixed at just twelve squadrons, six light bomber squadrons equipped with the outstanding Mosquito and the other six medium bomber squadrons with whatever the Americans could spare. Bostons were being slowly replaced by B-25 Mitchells.

Spaatz could probably have put an equally strong case for his bombers not being accurate enough, given the reputation they had acquired in Italy, if he had been so inclined.[14] Instead, he insisted his attempts to whittle down the German fighter force was a much more useful contribution than bombing railway lines. In addition to this he proposed to attack the German oil industry. These were not unrelated targets. The German fighter force was becoming increasingly selective about the American raids it chose to oppose. The Americans needed a target that would force the German fighters to fight and Spaatz believed that oil was such a target. Attempts to defend these installations would give his fighter escorts the chance to complete the defeat of the German fighter force, thereby ensuring air superiority for the invasion. Spaatz claimed the bombing would reduce German oil output by 50 per cent in six months.[15] The shortage of fuel would further reduce the effectiveness of the Luftwaffe as well as limit the German Army's ability to manoeuvre. Privately, Spaatz and his staff thought the air offensive against oil alone might bring Germany down.

The wheel seemed to be turning full circle. In the spring of 1940 as the Allies awaited the German offensive against France, the great debate was whether to use the heavy bombers (Wellingtons, Hampdens and Whitleys in those days) to attack communications leading to the front as the British and French army commanders wanted, or whether they should be used against the German oil industry. Four years later the bomber forces available were immensely more powerful than those available in 1940, but the choices were the same and so were many of the arguments for and against the two alternatives.

The oil versus transportation debate was intense and bitter. Both sides assembled experts to support their case. Doubts were expressed that it was even possible to destroy a system as complex as a rail network. There was too much spare capacity in any railway system and such a small proportion was required for military purposes that what survived would always be enough to move troops and military supplies. Advocates of the transportation plan collected colourful accounts of the success achieved in Italy but information reaching the War Office suggested events in Italy were proving quite the opposite. Claims that the bombing had isolated the Anzio area for eighteen days were considered well wide of the mark. There was evidence that two divisions dispatched to seal of the Anzio bridgehead, one from Genoa and the other from southern France, had not been delayed at all by the massive Allied bombing of communications. Another was forced to detrain and complete its journey by road, but by no stretch of the imagination had the battlefield been isolated.[16]

Then there was the problem of the inevitable French and Belgian casualties. Major rail centres were often situated in built-up areas. Initial estimates put the expected civilian death toll at between twenty and forty thousand. The Foreign Office worried about the political consequences of this in a post-war Europe.[17] There were already signs of a leaning towards communism; many of the more effective resistance movements within Europe were communist. There was also the question of whether the Allies really wanted to try and destroy so thoroughly a railway system they would later need to supply their own advance.

The problem with Spaatz's oil alternative was that it would take time for the results to work their way through the system. Nobody believed it would have any effect on Overlord. This of course assumed, it was possible for bombing to reduce oil production. Tedder for one did not think it was possible. 'We have been led up that garden path before', was his curt response to Spaatz's plan.[18] There was, he believed, no reason to believe an attack on the oil industry would be any more successful than previous attempts. Indeed since these earlier efforts, the Germans would have had plenty of time to disperse production and make some effort to bomb proof plants. Portal was undecided. He had been in charge of Bomber Command in 1940 when the first attempt was made to destroy the German oil industry. Four years later he still believed it was the Achilles heel of the German economy.

Attacking targets in Germany rather than communication targets in occupied Europe had the advantage that bombs missing their target would kill German rather than French or Belgian civilians, although in truth, with the huge number of non-Germans working in Germany, this was not as true as it had been. Limiting the attack on communications to cutting railway lines and blowing bridges and other targets outside major built up areas would reduce civilian casualties. These were targets fighter–bombers could best deal with. The effects might be shorter term but it would also leave the network in better shape for future Allied use. The heavies would then be free to continue their attacks on the German aircraft industry or Spaatz's offensive against oil.

This was the approach favoured by Brooke. Indeed, many in the War Office were dubious about the advantages of a lengthy attack on communications. A short sharp offensive coinciding with the invasion that would disrupt rather than obliterate seemed perfectly adequate. A counter argument was that a spell of poor weather might enable the Germans to repair the relatively light damage fighter-bombers could inflict. Indeed poor weather might prevent the air forces from inflicting any damage, allowing German forces full freedom of movement. With tides restricting the days on which an invasion could take place, postponements were not so easy. In any case, it was argued, with the vast fleets of bombers available, the Allies did not have to take a chance with the weather; they could just ensure the railway network was permanently out of action. Why go for half measures when such mighty bomber fleets existed?

Tedder argued that, in the interests of focusing effort, it was better to have a target system which fighter-bombers, light, medium and heavy bombers could all contribute to. Rail communications offered such a target with the heavy bombers hitting the marshalling yards and the rest attacking smaller targets outside built areas. There was an academic neatness about this approach, although it seemed to be taking to extremes the idea that airpower has to be focused. Aircraft are deliberately deigned to be different to make them more suitable for different tasks. There was something somewhat perverse about seeking a target system that got round the apparent problem of different aircraft having different attributes. With the massive aerial resources available such focus was unnecessarily restrictive.

The debate aroused strong passions with what seemed like very different views about how the Allies should apply their advantage in the air, but the transportation plan and the oil plan were both products of the same mindset. Both envisaged air power operating independently, yet achieving results that would have a decisive influence on the land battle, perhaps even making the land battle a mere formality. Both were campaigns where air force commanders could get on with the task on their own, with none of the messy, nitty-gritty, inter-service involvement required for integrated air/land operations. They were both campaigns that would appeal to air commanders who saw air power as an independent entity.

The grim warnings about civilian casualties worried Churchill. Thirteen of the seventy-five marshalling yards in the plan were considered relatively low risk and in March Portal instructed Harris to experiment by bombing six of them. Harris had good reason to doubt nocturnal bombing could be accurate enough; this was why his Bomber Command had switched to area bombing. However, precision bombing was not entirely alien to Bomber Command. The Peenemunde raid had improved accuracy by using master bombers to provide incoming aircraft with a running commentary on where they should direct their bombs. Also, there was nothing new about bombing targets in occupied countries. These raids had always required a greater degree of care and the weaker defences had often enabled bombers to attack from lower altitudes. In the six experimental attacks ordered by Portal, civilian casualties were usually well below fifty, which, in the mayhem of total war, was considered acceptable. Harris expressed surprise at how accurate the bombing had been. Civilian casualties in subsequent raids would demonstrate Harris had good reason to be surprised. These initial successes reassured Portal and he gave the plan his full backing. Indeed even Harris developed some enthusiasm for the plan. It was, after all, still an opportunity to demonstrate how decisive independent bombing operations could be.

Outside Air Force circles there was a healthy air of realism about what the transportation plan might achieve. It might not wipe out the rail network as the optimists claimed, but Eisenhower did not mind how much it helped, as long as it helped. 'Some reduction, however, small', in military movement would justify the plan, and at the end of March, Eisenhower gave the transportation plan the go ahead.[19] Ironically the night following Eisenhower's decision, the first really serious civilian casualties occurred when 252 Belgians died in a raid on the railway yards in Courtrai. The station was severely damaged but Belgians were put to work to repair the damage and within three days the line was open again.[20] There had to be questions about whether the advantage gained justified the casualties.

Churchill was still far from convinced. Given the failure of Allied bombing to achieve much against the more basic Italian railway system, he doubted much could be achieved against the more sophisticated French system. Any slight advantage gained did not justify 'the slaughter of masses of friendly French Allies'.[21] His cabinet were equally concerned and only gave approval for Bomber Command to attack the thirteen low-risk targets while the War Cabinet Defence Committee studied the plan in more detail.[22] At their meeting on 5 April, the Foreign Secretary, Anthony Eden, Wing Commander Sydney Bufton, the Air Ministry Director of Bomber Operations, Lord Cherwell, the prime minister, his deputy Clement Atlee and perhaps most significantly of all, Brooke, were amongst those who doubted the transportation plan was worth it. Portal and Tedder, however, insisted that this was the only way the bombers could be used to prepare the way for Overlord. There was no alternative. And here was the nub of the argument. The bombers that Eisenhower had gone to so much trouble to acquire, had to be used.

On the night of 9/10 April Harris launched a fresh series of raids on French and Belgian rail stations. In the first of these attacks on the Lille-Delivrance marshalling yards, severe damage was inflicted but over

450 civilians were killed and more than 5,000 homes destroyed, causing much resentment within the town. The following night marshalling yards in Ghent were severely damaged but over 400 Belgians died and the 600 buildings destroyed included seven schools, two convents and an orphanage.[23] It was a heavy price to pay for raids that had the sole intention of misleading the Germans about where the landings were likely to take place. The night of 18/19 April saw particularly severe raids on Rouen (900 killed), Juvisy (400 killed) and Noisy-le-Sec (over 450 killed).

The continuing uncertainty about the policy meant the first directive to Spaatz and Harris issued under the aegis of AEAF on 17 April sent rather mixed messages. Although emphasising the need to focus all effort on making Overlord a success, in view of the difficulties of hitting marshalling yards Harris was to continue with his main aim of 'disorganising German industry'.[24] Spaatz's top priority was to remain the German fighter force with attacking enemy rail communications just a secondary aim.[25] It was hardly surprising many thought the transportation plan had been abandoned. Harris took full advantage by launching heavy raids on eight major cities between the nights of 20/21 and 27/28 April. Spaatz had never abandoned his daylight offensive against Germany and the new instructions merely confirmed he should carry on as before.

By this time Portal had received Slessor's warning from Italy that Operation Strangle was producing disappointing results. Nevertheless, in May both Bomber Command and the Eighth Air Force were ordered to step up their efforts in support of the tactical light and medium bombers already attacking communication targets. Even then the debate continued. Both those favouring the transportation plan and those wanting to continue strategic bombing were issuing dark warnings that Overlord would be a disaster if their preferred strategy was not followed. Churchill was only partially appeased by a revised programme which reduced estimated civilian deaths to a maximum of 10,000.[26] Estimates of casualties inflicted so far conveniently suggested they were lower than expected, but reports from the French resistance emphasised the ill-feeling the bombing was causing. Churchill appealed to Roosevelt to intervene but this had no effect and de Gaulle seemed resigned to the casualties his people were suffering so the programme continued.[27]

The ability of RAF bombers to carry much greater bomb loads than American heavies, ensured their raids were more destructive. Unfortunately this was as true outside the target area as inside. Everything was done to improve accuracy. Target flares were often obscured by the bombs raining down on them. To get round this problem flares were deliberately aimed wide of the target and the bomb aimers fed in a false wind speed to compensate for the distance between the marker and the true target. More distinctive and longer lasting flares also helped bomber crews. Mosquitoes in low-level dives marked targets more accurately than level-flying Lancasters. Initially the average error was 680 yards but by May this had been reduced to 285 yards.[28] Getting half the bomb load within three hundred yards of the target was a remarkable achievement, but it also meant the other half were missing the target, some by quite some distance. It was not just a British problem. American daylight bombing, from higher safer altitudes by day, was often more inaccurate than Bomber Command efforts by night. Bombing was still a very blunt weapon. Fifteen thousand French civilians lost their lives in the two months that preceded the invasion as a result of British and America bombing.[29]

Eisenhower was right that there was no better way of using the heavies tactically if results were expected in time for Overlord. Whether this justified the transportation plan is another matter. Spaatz and Harris were equally right that switching effort from Germany to occupied countries took the pressure off German industry. German armaments output continued its remorseless rise in the second quarter of 1944, and would have done so whatever decision had been taken about where the bombers should operate. However, post-war studies suggested the loss compared to potential output had been reduced to little more than 6 percent, half of what it had been in the first quarter. This was the price paid for the switch in effort to the French and Belgian rail networks. It was not a huge price and certainly not enough to affect the outcome of the invasion. In this respect Spaatz and Harris were wrong. Nevertheless, the attacks on French and Belgian marshalling yards enabled the Germans to produce more weapons and ammunition and this has to be taken into account when assessing the overall value of the transportation plan.

No-one doubted the value of attacking enemy lines of communication, but given the wealth of more accurate air resources, not to mention the efforts of the French resistance, it is difficult to justify such a prolonged assault on targets amidst a friendly population. Eisenhower, however, had the bombers and he was determined to prove his claim over them was justified, whatever the casualties. It was an attitude entirely in keeping with the overall ruthless, Allied brute force approach to winning the war.

The campaign inflicted huge damage on communications in France. As in Italy, however, the Germans had time to adapt. Smashed marshalling yards could be made to function. It required the diversion of manpower from other tasks and could not eliminate the disruption but the disruption lost its surprise value. Delays were still delays but the Germans were beginning to work them into their calculations. The sudden violence and shock value of blitzkrieg was entirely absent in the methodical Allied approach. As was the case with the strategic air offensive, grinding down the opposition in a war of attrition always gave the enemy time to adjust. The same was true of the campaign against airfields. The pummelling inflicted on major aerodromes just forced the Germans to switch to auxiliary airstrips. These were stocked and ready to take the Reich defence force when the time arrived. It was not ideal but it had to do. Just as the German civilian population, for all the horrors involved, were learning to live with Allied bombing and German industries had to accept the need for constant repair, so German forces in the tactical zone were adjusting to the new normal. The Allies were slowly inoculating the Germans to the effects of their massive superiority in the air.

The Luftwaffe made very little effort to halt the air assault on northern France. In two months the RAF and USAAF lost around 400 aircraft in daylight operations during the course of over 84,000 sorties, a 0.5 per cent loss rate.[30] Most of these losses were due to flak rather than fighters. There was perhaps a message here for Allied planners; while there was no fighting on the ground, the Luftwaffe was willing to concede this particular round. Over the Reich it was very different; here German fighter resistance remained fierce. The strength of the long-range Mustang force was growing apace. By early May as many as 700 escorts were accompanying the bombers of which up to 300 were the deadly long-range Mustangs. Yet Eighth Air Force bomber and escort fighter losses over Germany in April were even heavier than they had been the month before, with over 350 bombers and nearly 250 fighters failing to return. In May the Eighth began to focus more on Overlord targets but still lost nearly 250 bombers over Germany along with over 150 escorts.[31] The Luftwaffe, however, had suffered even more grievously, losing 900 fighters in these two months with around 500 pilots killed or wounded.[32] Unlike the assault on French and Belgian railway junctions, this was a battle the Luftwaffe felt it had to fight.

In five months the Luftwaffe had lost 1,800 fighters and 1,000 pilots had been killed or wounded. As is normally the way in air warfare, losses among the inexperienced were disproportionately high. Even so, the overall experience level was in decline. However, it had cost the Eighth Air Force 1,300 bombers and nearly 700 escorts with all the aircrews lost. In addition, many bombers were returning with dead and wounded crew members in aircraft so badly damaged they had to be written off. It was a battle the Americans were undoubtedly winning but at a huge cost and it was still a battle far from won. The Reich day defence force had about the same frontline strength in May as it possessed at the beginning of the year.

The American escorts had achieved what they had set out to do. They were making it possible for their bombers to strike any target in Germany without suffering a scale of losses that would force the offensive to be suspended. It was a remarkable achievement. However, the claim that the escorts were establishing the air superiority required over the Normandy beaches was entirely bogus. The battle for air superiority over all fronts was a battle the Commonwealth, American and Soviet air forces had won long before the American strategic bombers set about trying to achieve it over Germany. The withdrawal of fighter units to defend the Reich accelerated the decline of the Luftwaffe over the front already in progress but it did not trigger the decline. Ironically, the front that benefitted least from this withdrawal was the Normandy front. The Reich was not far from northern France and the fighters defending it provided a conveniently positioned reserve. There were more fighters in western Europe in the summer of 1944 than there had been in the summer of 1943.

Even if the Allies had not already established air superiority over the frontline, trying to defeat the German fighter force over central Germany was scarcely the most efficient way of achieving it. In early 1944 the Allied superiority on all fronts east and west was so vast the distribution of the entire 1,000 Reich day fighter force around the various fronts would not have done much to alter the balance of power. Indeed, under far less favourable circumstances over the front, German fighter losses would probably have been even heavier, at far less cost to the Allies. As a way of securing air superiority over the battlefield taking on the German fighter force over the Reich was simply not a sensible way of going about it. But that was not why the escorts were there. They were there to ensure the daylight bomber offensive could continue and this they were doing with spectacular success.

So far the benefits of the bomber offensive had been useful rather than decisive. However, they were about to become a lot more than useful. On 12 May nearly 900 bombers set course for various synthetic oil plants in the Ruhr. Spaatz's oil campaign was underway. A savage German response saw forty-six bombers fail to return, a reminder the German fighter force was far from beaten, over home territory at least. A large proportion of the bombs dropped were still missing the target but enough were hitting to devastate the plants. It marked the beginning of an astonishingly successful phase of the bomber offensive. The next few months would demonstrate that the American day bombers were indeed capable of achieving what they were designed to do. As Portal and Tedder correctly predicted, however, it was far too late to affect Overlord. In the end, the effect the strategic bombing offensive had on Overlord was marginal. Lost German production was not on a scale that would make a significant difference to German fighting strength. Brooke never got his 'cracks'. Nor were the benefits of the bombing campaign against northern France and Belgium proportionate to the effort expended.

The debate over how the heavy bomber could best support the invasion had consumed a huge amount of time and energy. It had totally dominated the air aspect of Overlord planning. The debate was full of dire warnings about the disastrous consequences if this or that policy was not pursued. The controversy went right to the top, with political as well as military leaders involved. Amidst the furore, however, the application of air power that would be most useful on D-Day was scarcely getting a mention. Securing air superiority and paralysing the enemy rear would all be for nothing if the troops landing on D-Day could not take advantage on the battlefield. This was where air power could be really decisive. This was where it would be most needed on D-Day.

Montgomery was expecting rapid advances on D-Day. The War Office had constantly pointed out that substantial and effective air support on the battlefield was one way of aiding such an advance. The landing troops needed an air force that could that could swarm over the battlefield as the Desert Air Force had done at Tebaga in 1943 and more recently in the Cassino battle. Army commanders needed an air force that would observe the enemy, identify threats and strike wherever resistance was holding up the advance.

The first task was to get the troops ashore. With Rommel busying himself strengthening the defences all along the French coast there would be no unopposed landing as there had been at Anzio. How effective the 'drenching' of the coastal defences would be was open to question. The track record in this war and indeed the First World War for massive barrages actually destroying defences, rather than distracting defenders, was not encouraging. The 1943 Pantelleria aerial assault might have been the inspiration behind the 'drenching' policy but it should also have been a warning. Post bombardment surveys revealed surprisingly few guns had been put out of action on the Italian fortress island.

Every available heavy bomber would be thrown into the initial assault. The night before the invasion Bomber Command was tasked with eliminating ten key coastal artillery batteries in the Normandy area. Hitting a target as small as an artillery battery from altitude required a degree of luck. It was estimated that it would require one hundred bombers to offer a reasonable chance of eliminating one battery, so 1,000 sorties were required in all. This was a notable increase on the twenty-four sorties directed at two batteries in the Dieppe raid. Indeed, it seemed to be a case of going from one extreme to another. Starting with a blank sheet of paper, deciding on the best method to knock out ten artillery batteries would probably not involve creating a force of one thousand four-engined bombers. But the bombers existed and this was a way of using them.

The American Eighth Air Force would attack the coastal defences, just before the first troops landed. There was no indication day bombing was getting any more accurate. In a D-Day practice run at Studland Bay on 26 April, army commanders and VIPs were alarmed to see bombs dropping well short of the beaches they were aiming at. The Air Ministry hurriedly issued an explanation to all British, American and Canadian commanders. For the purposes of the demonstration, it was claimed, the bombers were flying lower than normal where their bombsights were not as accurate. Operating from their normal higher altitude, they would be much more accurate.[33] How convinced the observers were by this explanation is not recorded. What was clear was that the bombers would have to drop their bombs long before the landing craft were anywhere near the beaches. It was far from ideal. As tactical heavy bombing in Italy had demonstrated, defences did not stay disoriented for long. Once again the heavy bomber, and Eisenhower's determination to make full use of them, were dominating planning. In many ways the Allies might have been better off if these bomber fleets had not existed. More effort might have been focused on more useful ways of providing the invasion with air support.

The naval bombardment could continue a little longer than the aerial assault but this too would have to switch to targets further inland as the troops landed. Naval fire was more accurate than heavy bombers flying at altitude and there would be plenty of support to make sure it was as accurate as possible. Fleet Air Arm Seafires, with some help from RAF Mustangs, would be on hand to help the naval guns to zero in on their targets and thirty-nine naval forward observers would be going ashore in the first wave to direct fire. However, battleships firing from ten miles off shore could not safely engage targets immediately in front of the advancing troops.

Ramsay, in charge of the naval operation, feared disaster if the landing craft fell behind schedule and reached the beaches long after the bombardment ended. To guard against this he suggested that the landing craft should aim to be in position before the naval bombardment lifted and if necessary wait for the bombardment to end. This would leave the troops dangerously close to the bombardment for longer but the friendly fire casualties might be fewer than advancing against a defence that had had time to recover from the shelling.[34] Such a suggestion underlined how seriously the threat was viewed. Everyone was very aware of the dangers the first wave of infantry would face.

The Army were packing landing craft with all sorts of weapons to engage the defences with direct fire and tanks were supposed to lead the charge across the beaches but the War Office had always made it clear that they expected the air forces to play their part, with low-level or dive-bombing attack and forward observers to guide the aircraft in. Innovation was not required; it was just a case of applying the experience and expertise gained in the Mediterranean.

The early signs were that the Army were going to get this sort of support. In Leigh-Mallory the War Office believed they had someone sympathetic to their cause. Two decades of Trenchardian doctrine had rather dimmed Leigh-Mallory's air/ground tactical instincts but there was still more than a residual trace of the young officer that had pioneered air/tank co-operation in 1918. He had been impressed by recent developments in the Pacific. The battle for Tawara Atoll in November 1943 had demonstrated the value of air support once the landing craft were too close to the beaches to be covered by naval fire.[35] The US Marine Corps were indeed using the sort of intimate air support many in the War Office wanted and in the process demonstrating what was possible when air and ground units were part of the same service, with the mutual trust this engenders. At Bougainville, an island east of Papau New Guinea, a US Marine landing in December 1943 had been supported by air strikes never further than 500 yards and some closer than 200 yards to forward troops. The capture of one well defended ridge was greatly assisted by Grumman Avengers attacking, from a height of 50 feet, enemy positions as close as 75 yards to friendly forces.[36] This was the sort of support the troops landing in Normandy would need not just to overcome beach defences but to push inland and reach their assigned first day targets.

Towards the end of 1943, before Coningham arrived back from the Mediterranean, the AEAF, Second Tactical Air Force and 21 Army Group began discussions on how close support could be co-ordinated. Dive-bombing and low-flying fighter–bombers and even low-flying Mosquitoes were considered suitable for hitting targets close to friendly forces. Knowing the precise position of friendly and enemy forces would be vital. Coloured smoke-shells fired by mortars or artillery would indicate the positions of enemy targets with different colours marking friendly positions. The AOP Auster would be crucial for effective ground-air co-ordination. The Army was very keen to get these short-range aircraft ashore as soon as possible, even suggesting they operate from aircraft carriers if necessary.[37]

How close to friendly forces aircraft dare operate was a key question. Draft proposals in January 1944 emphasised the need for this bomb line to be as close to the front line as possible for the rather obvious reason that the further from the front line aircraft operated the more enemy forces in contact with Allied troops would escape attack. The War Office believed that, in static warfare, the bomb line should simply be the front line. If operations were mobile, it should be the line friendly troops were likely to reach in the following two hours. The War Office proposed two-hourly up-dates on the position of the bomb line throughout D-Day to ensure air support was as close as possible. Initial drafts called for a 100-yard safety margin. No one was under any illusions about the risks involved in having the bomb line so close. Commanders should be warned that they had to balance carefully these risks against the likely reward, when deciding whether to call in air support.[38]

Subsequent drafts saw some watering down of these requirements. Heavy and medium bombers were incorporated into the plan as possible battlefield air support weapons which inevitably led to pushing the bomb line to a safer 500 yards beyond friendly forces. For low-level fighter-bombers 500 yards was a reasonably comfortable safety margin; it was possibly even sufficient for low-flying light and medium bombers but was hopelessly optimistic for heavy bombers flying at their normal altitude. Right up until D-Day the Army continued to insist that it was important for the air support to be as close to the front line as possible. Much would depend on the type of aircraft being used and the systems in place to ensure accuracy.

Early discussions suggested adequate systems would be in place to control close air support. As had been the case during the Dieppe landing, the air support for each division in the assault would initially be controlled from a headquarters ship. While the divisional commander was operating from this ship, an RAF officer alongside him would operate an Air Support Signals Unit (ASSU) and would pass on requests for air support direct to Uxbridge. Divisional commanders would want to go ashore as soon as possible. It was appreciated that, in the early stages of the operation, a standard ASSU might be a clumsy unit to land on the beaches. It was therefore proposed that requests for close support would come from special assault tentacles with lighter more mobile radio equipment that would go ashore with the divisional commander. If this equipment lacked the range to reach Uxbridge directly, messages would be relayed via the HQ ships. Commanders on board the HQ ships could veto the requests or decide if alternatives, such as naval gunfire support, was more appropriate. The Army G (Air) representative at Uxbridge would get clearance from 21 Army Group HQ and then the request would be passed to AEAF, who would assign squadrons to the task. [39]

It was a somewhat cumbersome process. Air Vice-Marshal Victor Groom, who had been D'Albiac's Senior Air Staff Officer and had kept the post when Coningham took over, worried that passing requests to Army HQ would inevitably result in delays and wanted Army representatives at Uxbridge to have more responsibility.[40] Perhaps the more fundamental problem was requests going via Uxbridge. As had been pointed out in the post mortem that followed the Dieppe raid, such a distant centralised control centre was not ideal and more responsibility needed to be delegated to commanders further down the chain of command and closer to the action. Success in Italy had been achieved by cutting out lengthy communication channels.

Nevertheless, early in 1944 Leigh Mallory's AEAF seemed to be in tune with Army needs and the War Office were confident close air support would be rapid and substantial. In February 1944 the 'Air Branch' at Eisenhower's headquarters set out their understanding of what ground forces could expect during the initial stages of the assault. Much was expected of Bomber Command and American Eighth Air Force heavies. It was anticipated that Second Tactical Air Force aircraft would be on standby on airfields in Britain, but also support would be closer to hand with aircraft patrolling within radio range of the headquarter ships available for a more immediate response, effectively operating a cab rank. Regular Army/RAF ASSUs would go ashore as soon as possible to replace the temporary assault signals units. Ideally, squadrons setting off to hit a particular target could be redirected to a new target as they crossed the Channel. This would also in effect be a cab rank. Getting details of a target while halfway across the Channel might mean a slight delay compared to getting instructions when loitering off the French coast, but in practice it just meant the attack going in a little later.

War Office studies of Army operations in Italy had underlined the importance of guiding the attacking aircraft towards the target. For D-Day they wanted special landmark parties to go ashore to display prominent artificial indicators to help the incoming planes. Forward controllers in Visual Control Posts operating from the beachhead would help direct attacks onto enemy positions.[41] The American XII Air Support Command in Italy had improved the mobility of their forward observers by using jeeps with radio equipment to guide fighter-bombers in to targets, which the Army stressed seemed a practice worth copying. Other lessons from Italy included the use of fighters on 'short-range missions' to bomb 'designated enemy positions' before they began their defensive patrols.[42]

Initial drafts of what Leigh-Mallory's AEAF was willing to offer seemed to meet Army expectations in full. It was agreed pilots sent to attack specific targets could be re-briefed and redirected by the control ships as they crossed the Channel. Aircraft held on patrol within radio range of the HQ ships would be available for more immediate support. When the Army expressed concern about how calls between American and British requests for direct support would be prioritised, they were assured that this was unlikely to be a problem as resources would be so ample.[43] What the Air Force was offering was, in the view of the Army, 'a great advance on anything offered in the past'.[44] Quite unused to such riches, it seemed somewhat extravagant to have aircraft permanently on call but 'If the Air Force think they can do it, we shouldn't look a gift horse in the mouth'.[45] It seemed too good to be true. And so it proved.

A closer reading of the AEAF reply reveals there was perhaps a degree of wishful thinking about what exactly they had been offered. The Army were warned that Visual Control Posts would not be effective in the early stages of the assault because the initial beachhead would not provide ground from which the enemy could be observed, which was reasonable enough. However, the Air Force was not planning to maintain squadrons on call continuously. Indeed the document emphasised that such patrols would be of 'restricted scale and limited periods'.[46] Much would depend on how 'limited' and how 'restricted'. There was no suggestion of an Italian-style cab rank. All the Air Force intended to do was to have fighter-bomber squadrons engaged in the initial strike coinciding with the landing to be on call for twenty minutes before delivering their attack. There would be no subsequent patrolling aircraft on call, although aircraft that happened to be crossing the Channel en route to a particular target could be redirected.

The War Office had mentioned the use of fighters on 'short-range missions' to bomb targets before beginning their patrol. Indeed by this time it was standard in Italy for Spitfires to fly with 250lb bombs under the wings as well as a slipper tank. This was considered perfectly feasible even over the distances involved in a Channel crossing and the MAP was trying to modify as many Spitfires as possible for the fighter-bomber role in time for D-Day.[47] Spitfire squadrons were given training in dive-bombing, the first such mission being flown on 8 April.[48] Even without bombs, the Spitfire's 20mm Hispano-Suiza cannon was an extremely effective ground-attack weapon, as indeed reports from Italy were emphasising.[49] There was no reason why fighters on defensive patrols would not be available for ground strafing before returning home, as was standard practice in Italy. Longer range American fighters could carry more fuel and bombs. Their heavy calibre machine guns were also an effective weapon against soft targets. There were plenty of ground-attack options for D-Day.

Unfortunately, the arrival of the Mediterranean commanders did nothing to encourage greater close air support for the invading forces. The animosity between them did not help. Relations between Tedder and Coningham on the one hand and Montgomery on the other had been in decline for some time. Like many, Tedder and Coningham found Montgomery insufferable. They might have been able to live with this if they had any respect for Montgomery as a commander, but during the Mediterranean campaigns both constantly derided his over-cautious approach. Coningham, in particular, resented the cult celebrity status Montgomery had acquired following his victories over Rommel in the desert. Coningham did not believe the Air Force and, more importantly, he as commander of that air force was getting enough credit and was not afraid of letting his feelings be known. 'It's always "Montgomery's Army", "Montgomery's Victory", "Montgomery strikes again". You never say "Coningham's air force"', he complained to the press.[50] His desire for more personal glory could only intensify the determination that his air force should play a more clearly defined, independent role that would be more likely to attract attention and praise.

Montgomery seemed happy dealing with Leigh-Mallory. This might have proven fortunate if the AEAF commander had not been moving towards Tedder and Coningham's position on close air support. AEAF trials in the UK were suggesting that finding battlefield targets was not as easy as the US Marine Corps was apparently finding it in the Pacific. Pilots found it virtually impossible to identify camouflaged targets even if they were given precise co-ordinates. They had no more success identifying the positions of friendly forces. Indeed, such were the problems that it was suggested close air support could only be risked in an emergency.[51] This was just what those fundamentally opposed to battlefield close air support wanted to hear. The problems were real. As Slessor had pointed out, concealment was much easier in a non-desert environment; misidentification was a problem. However, there was no great urgency about tackling these difficulties. If anything stood in the way of the bomber offensive, the country's resources and top scientists were thrown at the problem. Problems with close air support were just taken as more evidence that it was a misuse of airpower. From the frozen wastes of northern Russia to the jungles of the Far East the problems were bring overcome and close air support was paying useful, sometimes handsome, dividends. In north-west Europe, however, overcoming the difficulties seemed to be too much trouble.

The problem for the Army was that Montgomery was not challenging these ideas. The War Office and many in the Army might appreciate the importance of close air support but Montgomery did not. He constantly spoke of the importance of airpower, the need 'for the full support of the air, all the time, and laid on quickly'. One can even find references to the need for aircraft 'coming right down and participat[ing] in the land battle by shooting up ground targets' all of which suggested he wanted Army-requested close support, but in reality it was all talk.[52] He was far too willing to accept without question the views of air commanders and was soon rather lamely falling in line with Air Ministry policy.

While still in Italy Montgomery had proclaimed

> I hold that it is quite wrong for the soldier to want to exercise command over the air striking forces. The handling of an Air Force is a life-study, and therefore the air part must be kept under Air Force command.[53]

This was an abdication of duty. An army commander might not feel that something as different as naval warfare was sufficiently relevant to be worthy of their attention, but air warfare had a huge impact on the way armies fought. Army commanders had to make air support part of their 'life study' if they were to integrate it into their thinking. In the Mediterranean, with Broadhurst to guide him, it was less of a problem. With air commanders more imbued with the Trenchardian independent spirit, it became more of a problem. Montgomery might speak about the importance of air support, welding the Army and Air Force into one and having the air force heavily involved in the land battle, but did nothing to bring this about and indeed did little to demonstrate that he understood what this entailed.[54] Instead he was quite happy to leave to air force commanders what targets should be attacked.[55] Montgomery liked to keep everything simple in his battle planning and allowing air commanders to use air power to 'hold the ring' kept things simple. In truth, while very happy to accept pre-planned air and naval fire support, improvised impromptu air support did not lend itself to Montgomery's meticulously ordered and controlled approach.

Much is made of the deteriorating relationship between Coningham and Montgomery. The two no longer worked side by side as they had in the desert. With Montgomery commanding all Allied troops for the opening phase of the invasion, he no longer considered Coningham to be an equal. Montgomery complained to Eisenhower about having to co-ordinate with two air commanders, Leigh-Mallory and Coningham, and made it clear he preferred to work with Leigh-Mallory, whom, as commander of the AEAF, he saw as his equivalent in rank on the air side. Montgomery was instructed to work through Coningham, but did not attend conferences with Coningham, preferring to send deputies, and carried on dealing with Leigh-Mallory. It is easy to blame the deteriorating relationship with Coningham for Montgomery's attitude but he was not making any great effort to get close air support from the more favoured Leigh-Mallory. Coningham and Tedder may have been at constant loggerheads with Leigh-Mallory and Montgomery, but on air policy they were all in complete agreement. Air support was best used solely beyond the battlefield. On D-Day the Allied cause would pay the price for this line of thinking.

The return of Montgomery's favoured Broadhurst from Italy at the end of March, replacing Dickson at No. 83 Group, did little to change the prevailing policies and attitudes, although at least he was in place, ready with a more sympathetic attitude to battlefield air support should it be wanted or required. The same could be said of Broadhurst's South African counterpart at No. 84 Group, responsible for supporting the Canadian Army. Air Vice-Marshal Leslie Brown was another Desert veteran who had been actively involved in air/ground co-operation since Wavell's successful offensive against the Italian Army in the winter of 1940/41.

In the months leading up to the invasion a new bomb line that was ten miles beyond the coast crept into Allied thinking. This was as far as it was planned to advance on the first day, so clearly anything beyond this could be safely attacked. This also happened to be beyond the range of most army artillery, which is where air force commanders believed aircraft should operate. It was also in line with Montgomery's idea of holding the ring. The 500-yard bomb line was still in the battle plans but was seen as a special case that might be organised in particular circumstances, rather than normal practice.[56] The fading interest in impromptu air support meant less interest in the intensive inter-service training required to create the necessary trust and confidence.

In his plans for the invasion Coningham was looking a lot farther afield than a ten-mile bomb line. He saw the bridges over the Seine, fifty to over one hundred miles from the Normandy beaches, as the key targets for his fighter-bombers. Typhoons did not have the range to reach those targets from Britain, which was why Coningham was so keen for Montgomery to capture the airfield-friendly terrain beyond Caen. Again it was the Air Force expecting the Army to dance to their tune. 'I wasn't fighting to capture airfields; I was fighting to defeat Rommel in Normandy', Montgomery quite reasonably later pointed out.[57] Coningham was right that the Seine bridges were important targets but the Allies were not short of fighter-bombers that could reach them. Coningham's Typhoons did not have the range to reach them but they had ample range to support the troops his Second Tactical Air Force had been set up to support. Significantly, Broadhurst, who was more interested in hitting targets closer to the front line, later made it clear that he never felt airfields were a problem.[58] There were lots of advantages to having airfields in France, and indeed room would be found for them even in the initial rather limited bridgehead. However, not having them was not fatal for close air support. The irony was that by not prioritising Broadhurst army-orientated air support, Coningham was making it more difficult for Montgomery to capture the airfield-friendly country Coningham was so keen to acquire.

All improvisation was being drained from Allied thinking and planning. Leigh-Mallory made it clear that the greater proportion of direct support would be of the pre-arranged variety and only a smaller proportion to meet unexpected developments and these would largely be responding to air reconnaissance, rather than requests from the ground.[59] In effect, on-call air support was becoming a fourth priority after air superiority, interdiction and pre-arranged close air support. The air force saw its primary role as dealing with more distant threats rather than any immediate obstacle the troops on the ground were encountering. This was not what the troops needed as they went ashore when, to use Slessor's colourful phrase, 'there was about as much cover as on the floor of a bird cage'. This was where the landing troops needed the morale-boosting sight of friendly aircraft being guided to enemy targets immediately ahead of them. This was when they needed a Tebaga-style swamping of the battlefield. The same sort of support would be needed to overcome resistance as they pushed inland, if Montgomery's ambitious first-day targets were to be met.

The number of squadrons available for direct army support was soon in decline. The Army were initially told that on D-Day, thirty-eight squadrons (eighteen RAF and twenty USAAF) would be available for Army support. Leigh-Mallory, however, was reluctant to let any of these attack beach defences. As a compromise, Leigh-Mallory suggested twenty-four of them be used to support the first wave of troops as they hit the beaches. Some of those would be circling the control ship awaiting instructions, while those heading for pre-determined targets could be redirected if necessary. It seemed that this had been agreed in principle.[60] Across five beaches, and given the huge resources available, it was scarcely a generous allocation for such a perilous part of the operation, but even this was soon being whittled away.

In April the Army was still assuming that each of the eight British and Canadian brigades involved in the initial assault would have at least one squadron on call for immediate support and were enthusiastically trying to set up affiliation meetings between air and ground commanders to ensure co-operation ran smoothly.[61] However, in May the AEAF informed the Army that there had been a 'slight misunderstanding'.[62] It was argued that, 'from an air point of view', where two brigades were landing on the same beach it would be impracticable to have two squadrons operating in such a small area. The Army might argue that from a ground point of view the five miles of coastal defences on each beach did not look so small. The Army were told only one squadron would operate over each beach with another squadron hitting predetermined targets further inland. This was clarified on 1 June. As the troops hit the beaches, a maximum of twenty squadrons would be available for the entire tactical zone, to a depth of ten miles. One squadron on each beach would attack beach defences and the remainder would attack artillery positions and enemy headquarters in the rear.[63] Montgomery raised no objections. The Army might be denied even this. On the eve of the invasion Leigh-Mallory wanted to hold back all fighter-bomber support from the initial assault so that even more air resources would be available to use against reinforcements moving up to the front. This time the Army made a stand and persuaded Leigh-Mallory to keep the one squadron per beach.[64] All this was coming from an RAF commander who, the Army believed, was on their side.

The final plan for the Anglo-Canadian forces involved one squadron attacking beach defences on Sword, Juno and Gold beaches, five striking artillery positions and two bombing enemy headquarters in the rear. After that there were no plans. Support for the two American beaches was on a similar scale. It would have been quite unthinkable for a Russian commander to send his troops across open ground without the encouraging sight of low-flying assault aircraft striking enemy targets immediately in the infantry's path. In a couple of weeks the Russians would launch their offensive on the Eastern Front, protected by 2,000 fighters and with 1,700 light and medium bombers attacking targets on and behind the battlefield. However, there would also be 1,700 low-flying armoured Il-2 Sturmovik ground-attack planes providing the sort of intimate support many in the War Office had always wanted. These were not tactics that were alien to Allied commanders in the west, as dramatically demonstrated in the 1943 battle for the Tebaga Pass, when fire support was provided from airfields seventy miles away from the battleground. Closer to home Air Ministry dogma would be more strictly adhered to.

The same attitudes prevailed in USAAF circles, although there seemed to be more resistance amongst American land commanders and more effort to lay the foundations for an effective close air support system. For the Canadian and British armies, Coningham was only willing to allocate one Visual Command Post per corps. Even this was not an automatic entitlement, with the deployment being at Coningham's discretion. Bradley made sure every division in his Army had its own visual command post, with armoured divisions sometimes getting two or three.[65] However, none of these formations were any use if there were no aircraft to direct. Bradley's tactical Ninth Air Force fighter groups were commanded by Brigadier General Elwood Quesada. He would become a passionate believer in close army-air co-operation, very much the American Broadhurst equivalent. However, even he confessed that before D-Day he followed the general USAAF line that 'it was not our mission to participate that close in battle'.[66] In the months leading up to the invasion, Ninth Air Force commander Brereton, 'a purist in air matters' in Bradley's words, had no objections to IX ASC fighter squadrons being used to escort American heavies rather than prepare for their army-support role.[67] Exercises involving army units rehearsing for D-day did so without the presence of these squadrons.[68] Bradley was not as submissive as Montgomery and was quick to express his displeasure but the USAAF hierarchy seemed as determined to keep its distance from Army operations as their RAF counterparts.

Early in March Leigh-Mallory tried to get the Ninth Air Force fighter squadrons taken off escort duties, although it would seem mainly with the aim of strengthening the pre-Overlord offensive against communication targets in France rather than allowing them time to prepare for their army support role. Spaatz, however, insisted that escorting his bombers was still the most useful contribution they could make to supporting the invasion. The squadrons were only released weeks before the invasion by which time it was too late to take part in any exercises; the divisions earmarked for the invasion were already moving into their embarkation zones.[69]

There might have been little training or preparation but at least the means to provide front-line troops with support was rapidly expanding. The RAF fighter-bomber contribution was fixed at eighteen squadrons by production schedules but, in the month preceding the invasion, the American IX Fighter Command expanded from ten fighter groups to no fewer than seventeen groups. Each group comprised three squadrons with a nominal strength of twenty-five aircraft each. Furthermore, from 20 May, all Quesada's fighter groups officially became fighter-bomber units, reflecting the growing importance of their ground-attack role. Indeed these were now fully engaged in the campaign against communication targets in northern France.[70] Coningham, who on D-Day itself would control all Allied air units, would have at his disposal well over a thousand American fighter-bombers in addition to the 300 Typhoons of Second Tactical Air Force. There would be no shortage of aircraft to use should the Air Force or Army deem it necessary.

As the day of the invasion approached, with no sign of any Luftwaffe movement into northern France, Leigh-Mallory was beginning to realise the German air threat was entirely imaginary.[71] Yet fears over what the Luftwaffe might do was still inducing near panic amongst his fellow Allied commanders. As late as 3 June, when discussing how the air forces should be used once the invasion was underway, Tedder, Spaatz, Lieutenant General Jimmy Doolittle, commanding Eighth Air Force in the UK, and Bottomley were all urging Leigh-Mallory to switch the focus of Allied air attacks from communications to the German Air Force. Indeed Tedder, having led the campaign for the transportation plan, now believed continuing the attacks on French towns beyond D-Day would just result in a senseless loss of life. Luftwaffe-related targets should have priority. Leigh-Mallory remained adamant that the priority had to remain preventing the movement of German reserves and, in the heated debate that followed, threatened to resign if the Allied air forces did not stick to his plan.[72] An anxious Montgomery rang Leigh-Mallory to make sure the interdiction programme was still going ahead. Again, the first and second priorities (air superiority and interdiction) were attracting all the attention and controversy. No sparks were flying over the plans for battlefield air support.

On the eve of the invasion, with still no sign of the Luftwaffe, Leigh-Mallory was insisting fighters assigned to defensive duties should be used as offensively as possible. Those patrolling well behind the coast were to be encouraged to shoot up any appropriate targets once their patrol was over. He also wanted more squadrons used in the fighter-bomber role from the outset. American Thunderbolts on patrol over the beachhead were to carry bombs so that they could join in these efforts if no Luftwaffe showed up. American fighters operating deeper inside France were to cut off any movement of German reinforcements from Brittany or anything heading north across the Loire, and the Paris-Orleans line,[73] There was no talk of using any of these to help the ground forces achieve the ambitious goals they had been set for the first day.

On the Army side, a lack of interest in close air support seemed to be spreading. Second Tactical Air Force were informed that it would not be possible to get the landmark parties that were supposed to help guide incoming air strikes ashore until the third day of the invasion. Montgomery did not see air support on D-Day as particularly crucial. On the eve of the invasion, with the weather doubtful and Eisenhower considering postponement, Montgomery declared his willingness to go ahead even without any air support. He felt it was sufficient that the air forces had had fine weather for the preparatory phase 'and we must accept the fact that it may not be able to do so well on D-Day.'[74] Tedder was horrified and Eisenhower was none too impressed that the heavy bomber support he had fought so hard to secure and without which he considered the whole venture 'extremely hazardous or even foolhardy' was being so casually dispensed with.[75] Neither Eisenhower nor Tedder were concerned that, whether the invasion was launched on 5 or 6 June, close air support had already been casually dispensed with. Despite Montgomery's apparent indifference, the invasion was postponed twenty-four hours.

The British were viewing close air support scarcely any more sympathetically in 1944 than they had in a previous battle for France in 1940. In that battle the Luftwaffe had demonstrated how air support could substitute for the artillery the German Army lacked after its sixty-mile dash through the Ardennes. In the crossing of the Meuse, it was the continuous attacks of the Luftwaffe on forward positions, both during and after the crossing of the river, that had proved so decisive in pinning down and demoralising the French defenders. With the Royal Navy on hand, the Army was not so reliant on air power for its 100-mile dash across the Channel, but air support was another very different but equally valuable way of substituting for the lack of Army fire power.

From the depths of the 1940 debacle, RAF close air support capability had risen to the heights of the glorious 1943 victory at Tebaga but the wheel had very rapidly turned full circle. Four years after the Battle of France, specialised battlefield close air support was once again not a major part of Allied thinking or planning. The RAF was approaching liberation of France with the same frame of mind as they had approached the Battle of France in 1940, with, arguably, more Army backing for the policy than in 1940.

Chapter Nine

D-Day

On the night of 5/6 June 1944, 6,000 vessels set sail for the coast of Normandy. The invasion of France, the operation which British commanders had viewed with so much foreboding for so long, was finally underway. 'I am very uneasy about the whole operation,' wrote the ever pessimistic Brooke in his diary, as the armada sailed. 'At the best it will fall so very, very far short of the expectation of the bulk of the people, namely all those who know nothing of its difficulties. At the worst it may well be the most ghastly disaster of the whole war'.[1]

The weather was still poor, although not quite as bad as the day before. Tide and moon conditions did allow one more twenty-four-hour postponement but the troops could not be held in a state of readiness any longer. Waiting for the next window would require a substantial delay and the Allies had promised the Russians that the landings would take place before their next offensive on the Eastern Front, set for late June.

The huge armada presented an inviting target for determined air attack and it was assumed that the Germans would throw all their available air resources against it. However, the invasion had the sort of air cover that should have provided reassurance even for Brooke. There was no lack of focus. Of the twenty-nine day-fighter squadrons left to ADGB, only four were stationed north of the London-Bristol line.[2] The twin-boom P-38 was one of the most recognisable Allied fighters and therefore the most likely to escape the unwanted attentions of friendly anti-aircraft fire, so this would be used to protect the invasion fleet as it crossed the Channel. Six groups with around 450 P-38s from the Eighth and Ninth US Air Forces would be available for continuous patrols. Over the beachhead itself there would be a permanent presence of six Spitfire IX squadrons on low patrol covered by three Thunderbolt squadrons at altitude. These would be able to patrol for fifty and sixty minutes respectively.[3] An outer defensive ring would be provided by nine groups of American P-47 Thunderbolts and

P-51 Mustangs, with nearly 700 aircraft, flying patrols up to one hundred miles inland from the landings. It was one of the most extensive aerial umbrellas ever created. Other fighters would be escorting day bombers and transports. Fifteen RAF and another fifteen American squadrons were held back as a reserve, ready to reinforce the defensive patrols if required. It was an extraordinary display of strength. On the first day of the invasion the RAF would fly around 1,500 fighter sorties, an impressive figure but one that was somewhat overshadowed by the 3,500 the USAAF were going to fly.[4]

The Luftwaffe had indeed been involved in frantic efforts to create a 450-strong force of torpedo-bombers and missile-launching aircraft.[5] The Fritz guided bomb and Herschel Hs 293 guided air-to-ground missile had already achieved some notable successes against Allied warships. Much was also expected of the 'Mistel' composite plane, an Fw 190 fighter mounted over an unmanned Ju 88 bomber with a hollow-charge nose cone replacing the cockpit, which could be dived into Allied battleships. For battlefield air support little was available. Almost all the available conventional piston-engined close air support aircraft were deployed in the east, where a Soviet offensive was expected and the vast front needed some sort of mobile air reserve. There were plans to switch around half the home defence day-fighter force to northern France as soon as the invasion was underway. These could be fitted with a couple of under-wing rocket launchers for ground attack, but the degree of air superiority the Allies in Italy had shown themselves capable of establishing scarcely encouraged any belief that these could achieve much. A fighter-bomber version of the Me 262 jet was on the way which might stand a better chance of evading the Allied fighters but this, along with the fighter version and the Arado 234 bomber-reconnaissance jet had not yet reached the squadrons.

The weapons the anti-shipping force carried were no longer so daunting. Ways of jamming the guiding radio signal used by the Fritz X and Henschel Hs 293 guided weapons were becoming available. Both weapons required the launching bomber to fly straight and level while the weapon was being guided, leaving the bomber desperately vulnerable to fighters. The Mistel did not arrive in time for the invasion and when it was used proved far too inaccurate to hit anything as small as a battleship. Even the planned 450-strong force would have dashed itself against the Allied fighter armadas. Along the entire Channel coast the Luftwaffe had fewer than 600 planes of all types, few of which were within range of the Normandy beaches. During the hours of daylight on 6 June, the Luftwaffe flew just one hundred sorties in the Normandy region, mostly by fighters and nearly all were engaged by Allied fighters long before they got anywhere near the beaches. The only aircraft that penetrated the defensive screen were two fighters of JG26, which strafed Sword beach.

The failure of the Luftwaffe to appear in any numbers took everyone, from top generals to the man in the street, by surprise. Newspaper articles speculated the Germans were fiendishly holding their forces back just as Britain had done in the 1940 Battle if France, although to what purpose (in either case) was scarcely obvious.[6] The entire country had been sucked into the mighty, invincible Luftwaffe myth. Amongst Allied commanders the surprise was genuine and the relief immense. There was much talk of the bomber offensive being even more successful than anyone had imagined. The bomber advocates were soon adding another victory to their lengthy but imaginary list of battle honours. What was beyond dispute was that the Allies had air supremacy over the ports the fleet sailed from, the Channel, the beaches where the landings would take place and at least one hundred miles into the German rear. German air reinforcements might yet arrive, but for the first day at least the Allies had undisputed control of the skies.

Could the Allied air forces take advantage, especially on this all-important first day, when so much was expected? The invading armies would have surprise on their side; the Germans thought an invasion unlikely in the prevailing poor weather. There was no lack of ambition. Montgomery hoped not just to capture Caen but take the front line ten miles inland along the entire length of the landings. It was a tall order. Montgomery demanded boldness from his commanders, but if strong defences were to be overcome and the advance inland be as rapid as Montgomery was demanding, his commanders would need fire support as well as boldness.

At dawn on 6 June six American, British and Canadian divisions stormed ashore along the Normandy coast; a further three airborne divisions had landed behind the German coastal defences. In the centre, the British 50th Division landing on Gold beach was to secure Bayeux and link up with the Americans on Omaha beach. To their left, on Juno beach, the Canadian 3rd Division was to drive towards Caen. The British 3rd Division landing on Sword beach was to secure the left flank and join the drive on Caen. The city of Caen, the gateway to the open tank country beyond, was the number one objective.

The initial airborne landings did not go according to plan everywhere. On the eastern flank, Pegasus bridge was captured by British glider-borne forces but in the west many American paratroopers lost their lives when they

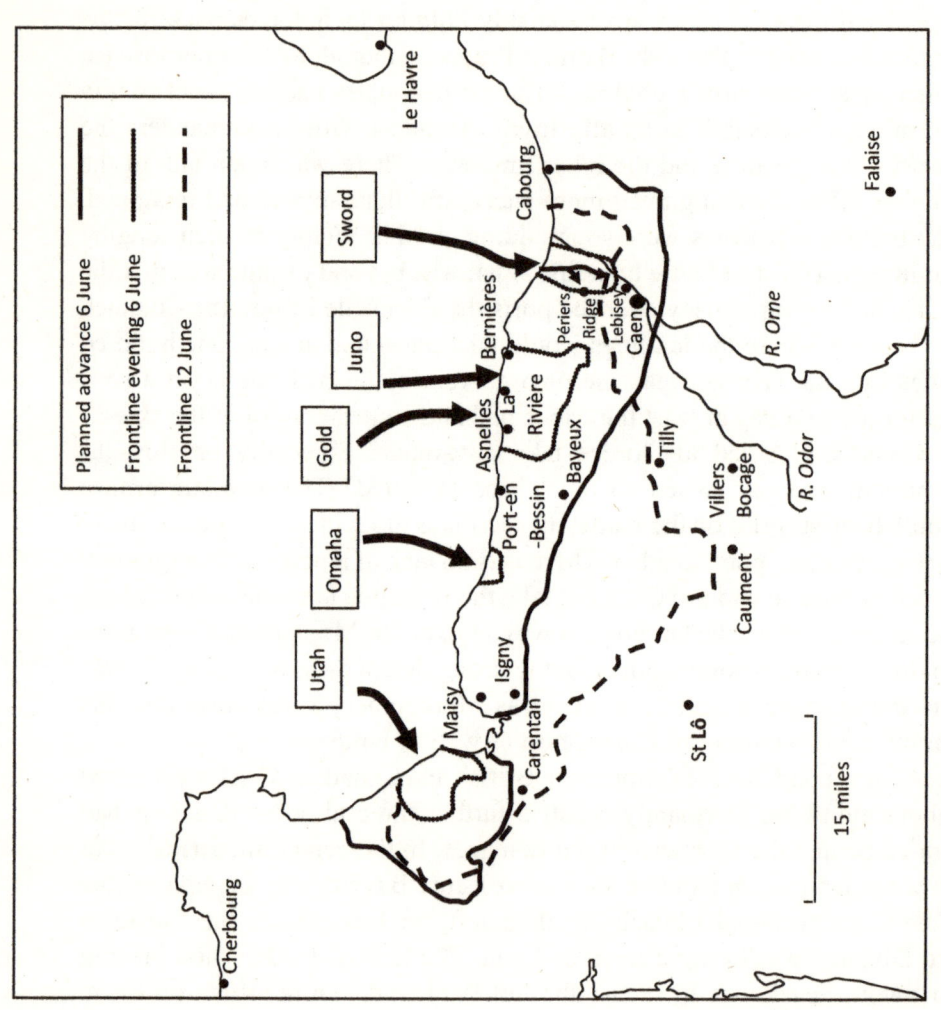

Normandy landing, June 1944.

were dropped in the many marshes behind the American Utah beachhead. Some key objectives were captured and held but for the most part the American airborne forces were reduced to a desperate battle for survival wherever they happened to have landed.

The main landings would benefit from an awesome display of naval firepower. One and a half hours before the troops were due to step ashore, seven battleships and twenty-three cruisers opened fire on the German defences. Twenty minutes later over one hundred destroyers, operating from closer to the shore, began to engage the beach defences, bringing to around 1,000 the number of guns shelling the German positions. Half an hour before the landings, 1,000 American Liberators and Fortresses of the Eighth Air Force and nearly 300 mediums of Ninth Air Force attacked beach defences.[7] The landing craft would also have their own artillery. Of the 4,000 landing craft heading for the shore 350 had been fitted out with a variety of weapons including 105 mm howitzers and various cannon.

Five minutes before landing, craft packed with 1,100 5-inch rockets unleashed their missiles in a single salvo and at about the same time the first tanks were supposed to hit the beaches. At this point the final bombs had been dropped by the American bombers and the heavy naval guns began to direct their fire further inland. As the troops went ashore already some 3,000 bomber sorties had been flown in support of the landing. Approximately two-thirds of these had been aimed at coastal defences and the remainder at artillery and communication targets to the rear. It was all very different from Dieppe when there had been no heavy bomber, battleship or cruiser support whatsoever, just twenty-eight light bombers and the fire of eight destroyers. However, as the troops hit the beaches, the level of air support would be little different from Dieppe. Just one Typhoon squadron was allocated to each of the Canadian and British beaches.[8] The thirty-two sorties they delivered on the three beaches compared to the fifty-eight sorties flown by five Hurricane squadrons as the troops went ashore two years previously on a single beach at Dieppe. It was a similar story on the two American beaches. Just thirty-three fighter-bomber sorties were flown against beach defences as the troops went ashore.[9]

To the dismay of the troops leaving the landing craft, the naval and air assault had not wiped out the defences. The Bomber Command attacks on the ten batteries achieved some success, with half the batteries being at least temporarily put out of action. However, the day bombing had achieved little. Even bombing in perfect conditions in Italy, the heavies of the USAAF had been very inaccurate; it was optimistic to expect any more in the poor weather the invasion was taking place in. The daylight American heavy bombers had to bomb blind, using H2X radar, the American version of H2S Mark III. So great was the fear of their bombs dropping on friendly forces, lead pilots were told to delay an extra thirty seconds after the radar indicated they were over their targets, to make absolutely sure none fell on Allied forces. A bomber would fly a couple of miles in this time so it was hardly surprising most bombs fell into fields well behind the coastal defences. The medium bombers of Ninth Air Force were more successful. Bombing visually from between 3,500 and 7,000 feet, below the clouds, they at least hit the intended target zone along the Utah beaches.

Later investigations revealed that even the naval bombardment had caused relatively little physical damage. Nevertheless, the barrage kept German heads down and, at least for a while, left the defenders disorientated. It was now, as the troops hit the beaches, that the assaulting infantry faced the greatest danger. Ahead of them lay up to one hundred yards of exposed beaches. With the Allied heavy bombers returning to their bases, along with the three squadrons of Typhoons, and the naval barrage seeking targets further inland, fire support on the beaches would now only come from the guns of the landing craft themselves and the tanks that were supposed to precede the first infantry. Now in their moment of greatest need the only Allied aircraft in view were the fighters circling high above.

Air effort against battlefield targets beyond the beach defences was equally scanty. On the British and Canadian fronts, in the hour or so following the landings, six missions, comprising fifty-five sorties, were flown, four against gun positions and two against suspected German headquarters in Bayeux and Saint-Lô. Fewer than one hundred sorties had been flown in support of the three British and Canadian beachheads in the entire tactical zone stretching ten miles into the rear. This, however, proved to be the pinnacle of the morning effort. Only three more missions were flown before mid-afternoon, two patrols were flown in the Bayeux-Caen area and a radar station at le Havre was attacked.[10]

On Juno Beach, just as Ramsay had feared, the landing craft arrived late giving the German defences time to recover from the naval and air barrage. At Bernières and la Rivière the Canadians found themselves in much the same position as their compatriots had two years before at Dieppe. The first wave encountered heavy enemy fire as soon as they left their landing craft, suffering 50 per cent casualties. Elsewhere, however, the bombardment of the defences had proved sufficient to allow the infantry to push rapidly off the beaches. Indeed within two and half hours of landing, German beach defences had been breached along the entire Juno landing area. On Gold the supporting tanks arrived late and a German strongpoint on the Asnelles seafront ('le Hamel' in most accounts) inflicted heavy casualties. It was one of the pre-arranged targets for the Typhoons but they had failed to eliminate it. There was, however, no demand for a repeat attack. It was late afternoon before the position was neutralised. It was precisely the sort of strongpoint the War Office had in mind when they had proposed their intimate support aircraft. Despite these difficulties, here too troops were soon pushing beyond the first line of defence. On Sword things went according to plan, the tanks landed first and were soon clearing a path through German minefields and eliminating German strongpoints.

These landings had not been the disaster some feared. The sight of waves of aircraft shooting up the enemy ahead might have made the task of the disembarking infantry less daunting and Canadian losses less severe. Strongpoints might have been overcome more rapidly. However, the failure to make more use of tactical air support had not had any immediately obvious serious consequences. On Utah beach, too, the lack of air support following the landing was not felt by the American forces going ashore. Accurate bombing by the Ninth Air Force mediums had done much to reduce the level of resistance.

The events on Omaha beach, however, would demonstrate how little margin for error there had been. Here American forces were soon in serious trouble. The first American troops to hit the beaches were cut down by fearful crossfire. Trapped on the beaches, casualties were horrendous. Throughout the day the American commanders viewed the predicament of their forces with growing dismay. Yet despite the seriousness of the situation the USAAF, under Coningham's direction for the day but acting in line with agreed Anglo-American priorities, rigidly adhered to their two priority tasks of maintaining air superiority, even though there was no sign of the Luftwaffe, and interdicting the battle zone, even though there were no significant reserves moving towards the American beach.

By mid-morning casualties on Omaha were running as high as they had in the Dieppe raid. The situation was so serious, evacuating the forces already landed was being seriously considered. As at Dieppe the confusion on the beaches prevented targets being passed to the naval guns. As at Dieppe destroyers braved the enemy batteries and sailed as close as 800 yards to the shore to engage enemy positions over open sights. As at Dieppe little close air support arrived. The Thunderbolts patrolling above Omaha beach were armed with bombs, but their instructions were to use these to interdict the battlefield if no enemy showed up.[11]

As had happened over Dieppe, it occurred to some pilots patrolling high above that perhaps they should be doing something about the tragedy unfolding beneath them. Lieutenant Robin Olds, a future American ace, flying P-38s with the USAAF 479th Fighter Group, was one such pilot. On 6 June, still a relative newcomer to the front, Olds, patrolling over the beaches, struggled to make sense of the specific orders he had been given not to attack targets on the ground. He could clearly see the positions from which Germans were pouring fire on to the beaches. He dutifully obeyed his orders, assuming his superiors must know what they were doing and imagined more specialist ground-attack units were being called in to deal with these positions.[12] His assumption was wrong.

Thirteen requests for air support were received, although none of them were from troops on the beaches. These led to some strikes on artillery and enemy transport in the Isgny, Carentan and Maisy areas, five miles or more from the front. The attacks on artillery pounding the beaches were desperately needed, but equally valuable would have been much closer air support hitting the German defensive positions along the beaches that were preventing the troops from moving inland. Trapped on the beaches, the American troops made a compact target for German artillery.

The situation seemed desperate enough and the targets seemed clear enough. The sort of close air support Allied air forces were capable of delivering might or might not have made a difference. Air support was not a panacea. However, it was an option that was not even tried. The exaggerated fears of what the Luftwaffe might do were still uppermost in most minds. As this fear abated, the long-term danger distant reinforcements might pose replaced it. So far from the action, it was difficult for the commanders in their Uxbridge bunker to appreciate that the danger was not the Luftwaffe, or reinforcement that might arrive in the next few days: it was the guns cutting the Americans down. More control at a lower level of command might have seen the fighters circling above redirected. As happened at Dieppe, the Uxbridge control centre was too distant, both physically and in mindset, to appreciate what was needed and react appropriately.

Quesada, the commander of IX Fighter Command, alone seemed aware of what was happening and what was required. He took it upon himself to try and provide the struggling troops on the ground with the air support they desperately needed. Using a back-up radio net that took Uxbridge out of the loop, from the afternoon of the 6th he began organising missions from his

Middle Wallop headquarters. It was too late to have much effect on D-Day, but he would be ready for day two of the invasion.[13]

By the evening the situation on Omaha beach was not quite as serious as the army commanders feared it might become. Unlike Dieppe, troops kept coming ashore. By mid-morning the first American infantry had managed to infiltrate German lines. Gradually, by weight of numbers and at huge cost, the German defences were beaten back. By late afternoon American troops were beginning to move off the beaches in substantial numbers. By nightfall the Americans were up to a mile inland. The beachhead was still very vulnerable to a vigorous enemy counter-attack but fortunately the Germans had nothing immediately available that might deliver such an attack.

Meanwhile, the British and Canadians were still hoping to reach Caen. A visible and substantial air presence might not have been needed to avert disaster but it might have led to a speedier suppression of the defences and created a more solid foundation for the advance inland. The heavy resistance the Canadians had encountered put them behind schedule but the British were reasonably well placed to push on. Their advance, too, was slowed by fierce and effective resistance. Many of the tanks required for the advance got bogged down helping infantry take various German positions still holding out. Further inland a German strongpoint at Périers Ridge (codenamed Hillman) proved unexpectedly difficult to overcome. The last elements did not surrender until the following morning. With the ridge dominating the surrounding countryside, it was difficult to bypass and push on to Caen.[14]

The network of strongpoints was perhaps a more obvious target for the Navy's big guns, but the naval forward controller had been killed and there was no immediate back-up.[15] At least there had been a naval forward observer in place. What happened to the special air support parties that were scheduled to accompany the troops ashore and relay requests for air support is not clear. There was no satisfactory link established for requesting air support until the normal forward air controllers landed a couple of days later. This did not seem to have caused any inter-service controversy or recriminations. No Army commanders were fretting at the lack of air support. It was not even occurring to anyone to call for it. The application of a fraction of the available airpower available to the Allies to help overcome obstacles like Hillman might or might not have made a difference, but again it was an option that was not even considered.

Some forces braved the fire and pushed on past the German Périers Ridge stronghold. However, early in the evening, these ran into elements of the panzer grenadiers of 21st Panzer Division in Lebisey Wood, just a mile short of Caen. The advancing troops did not expect to meet such strong opposition. An Auster spying out the land ahead might have provided some warning, might even have called in an air strike or Navy guns to disperse the waiting grenadiers. This was why the War Office Air department wanted their 'eye in the sky'. The War Office had shown plenty of enthusiasm for getting Austers into action as quickly as possible and indeed even on D-Day some were already operating from the beaches, spotting for naval guns. Ideally, they were needed to identify obstacles as well as directing fire It was one of the many lessons that did not make its way back from Italy to Britain. The fighter-reconnaissance squadrons operating from Britain were supposed to meet Army tactical-reconnaissance needs. However, operating from distant airfields and operated by a different branch of the armed services, they could not be as responsive as an Army-controlled Auster AOP. Front-line Army commanders needed information with the speed an Auster could contact an artillery battery rather than the time it took to pass information through the normal channels via the RAF.

RAF reconnaissance squadrons had far grander aims than spying out what lay ahead of the advancing troops on the ground. Not that the RAF had the resources for their grander aims. High level photo-reconnaissance was largely ruled out by the weather, but one of the two Spitfire XI squadrons helped out by flying half a dozen low-level tactical missions in the battle area. A handful of sorties were also flown by a Coastal Command Spitfire photo-reconnaissance squadron.[16] However, it was the five Mustang tactical-reconnaissance squadrons the Army was counting on. Three of them were partly employed spotting for naval guns. Along with Fleet Air Arm Seafires, nearly 500 artillery spotting sorties were flown, enabling the Navy to provide valuable fire support. This was undoubtedly one way in which air superiority was well exploited on D-Day but it meant there was not much left for finding out what the enemy was up to. Fewer than fifty reconnaissance missions were flown during the course of the day. Each usually involved a pair of aircraft, sometimes a formation of four. Their main purpose was to seek out distant threats that Typhoons could nip in the bud. In effect, the reconnaissance squadrons were working for the RAF rather than the Army, but this was what Montgomery and Dempsey wanted.

These missions covered a huge swathe of territory as far south as Alençon but the main interest was reinforcements approaching Caen from the south and east. There were not even enough aircraft to cover this area adequately; the movement of the remainder of 21st Panzer from Falaise was not picked up.[17] In the battle zone there was very little coverage. In the morning and early afternoon there were a couple of missions north-west of Caen where elements of 21st Panzer Division lay in wait for the advancing British and Canadians but they apparently spotted nothing. There was no concerted attempt to co-ordinate these missions with specific lines of advance; the hundred-odd sorties flown were almost entirely at the strategic end of the tactical reconnaissance spectrum.

In the air superiority/interdiction/close air support pecking order, reconnaissance did not even qualify for fourth place. Armed reconnaissance by fighter-bombers was supposed, to some extent, to make up for the lack of specialist squadrons but looking for a target to attack, then heading home and keeping an eye out for anything interesting is not quite the same as a specialist intelligence-gathering mission. It was even less useful if the fighter-bombers were not even operating in the battle zone. Short-range tactical reconnaissance was an air resource that needed to be under the immediate control of front-line commanders. Tactical reconnaissance was one of those areas on the fault line between army and air force spheres of responsibility and suffered as a result.

One of the key advantages of air superiority was being squandered. There were plenty of aircraft directing naval guns but not many monitoring German movements in the battle zone. With Allied air superiority, German forces should have found themselves under the microscope, their every move observed and reported. Information is one of the most valuable commodities in any battle and a few more reconnaissance squadrons at the expense of a few fewer heavy bomber squadrons would have paid rich dividends. This, however, was not how any strategically-orientated air force bent on maximising destruction is likely to think. Any squadron equipped for reconnaissance was one squadron fewer carrying bombs.

One of the oddest features of D-day was that both sides were fighting without adequate battlefield air support – the Germans because the Luftwaffe could not get anywhere near the battlefield, the Allies because neither the Air Force nor the Army saw it as important. There was frustration at some Typhoon airfields that one of the greatest military operations was underway yet, come the afternoon, they had still not been asked to fly a single mission. There were no requests for battlefield air support from the three British and Canadian beaches to respond to. The only request for air support in the morning was for the attack on the radar station near le Havre.[18] The first call for battlefield close air support did not come in until mid-afternoon when the airborne forces to the east of the beachhead wanted guns west of

Cabourg silenced. It seems a request was made for air support north-west of Caen late in the day, and this corresponded to where the Canadians from Juno beach were trying to push towards Caen. However, the mission seems to have ended up as an armed reconnaissance south-west of the city. If this was an attempt to support the drive on Caen, it failed.

There were no inter-service recriminations about the lack of air support. On D-Day many things went wrong as might be expected in an operation as complex as Overlord. However, close air support on the battlefield had gone wrong long before D-Day. Without air support, the Allied armies were fighting the battle with one hand tied behind their backs. Eisenhower was in awe of the destructive powers of the Allied heavies but it was the Austers, fighter-bombers and Broadhurst-style close air support that Eisenhower should have seen as his ace in the pack.

While the forces landed on Sword and Juno beaches tried to push on towards Caen without air support, Allied airpower continued to fill the skies above them. A second wave of 500 American heavy bombers set off to hit communications targets in the rear, with another 600 following later in the day. The Ninth Air Force despatched another 500 to similar targets.[19] Ironically, joining this intimidating display of strength were the squadrons that could have supported the troops heading for Caen. Dempsey was more worried about enemy movements towards Caen rather than German forces holding up the Allied advance north of Caen and this was where he wanted air effort focused.[20] In the late afternoon the Typhoon squadrons were sent off on armed reconnaissance sorties along roads leading to Caen from the south. As the British and Canadian forces attempted to overcome stubborn German resistance on the approaches to Caen, the aircraft that could have supported them were flying over them heading for more nebulous threats deep in the enemy rear. Everyone was worrying about a future battle when the current battle still hung in the balance.

The Typhoons were not sent off with any particular targets in mind. Allied reconnaissance planes were bringing back no clear indications of any substantial German reserves moving to the front but, with Caen Montgomery's principal objective, south of the city seemed a useful area to be operating in. In fact, the main body of 21st Panzer Division was on the move from Falaise towards Caen. Some of the Typhoons by chance came across elements of the division and imposed some delay. However, once these German units had joined the units already north of Caen, they were effectively on the safe side of the Allied bomb line.

Brooke was relieved that the landings were not the disaster he feared and Montgomery was well satisfied with progress made. However, it was scarcely a day of triumph. At no point along the front did the Allies achieve the penetration planned for the first day and the beachheads remained unconnected, shallow and vulnerable to counter-attack. Yet the forces that were containing them were sketchy, to say the least. Only where 21st Panzer had intervened could the Germans feel reasonably comfortable.

In so many respects the preparations for the Overlord operation were far more thorough than the 1942 Dieppe raid but on the air side the same mistakes were being repeated. The Allied air forces had kept the Luftwaffe at bay, but there was not much Luftwaffe to keep at bay. Throughout 6 June massive fighter screens were maintained for a Luftwaffe that never came. Some of these Allied fighters could and should have been redirected to relieve pressure on Allied ground forces where things were not going well and to accelerate the advance where the landings were going better. In some respects air support had gone backwards since the Dieppe raid. At Dieppe the available ground-attack squadrons had done everything they could to support the Canadians. By mid-day squadrons had already flown three missions. By mid-day on D-Day some Typhoon squadrons had yet to fly their first.

The Allies were paying a very heavy price for their scrupulous application of the air superiority/interdiction/close air support priority. Throughout the day, the air force emphasis had been on preventing Luftwaffe attacks rather than attacking the enemy. The focus was on preventing the movement of German forces rather than facilitating the advance of Allied units. Allied commanders, air and ground, were still haunted by fears of what the enemy might do to them rather than driven by what they might do to the enemy. Many of the forces at Montgomery's disposal were inexperienced, and they were facing an army that was well led and well-armed. On this first day and indeed the subsequent campaign there was much criticism for a lack of aggression among the British and Canadian forces, but it is so much easier to be aggressive if friendly aircraft are swarming over the enemy. Eisenhower had told the troops they were not to worry about any aircraft they saw in the sky 'They will be ours' he assured them. He was right but they tended to be patrolling high in the sky or heading somewhere else.

One of the many interesting parallels between the battles of France in 1940 and 1944 was that in both cases the Allied use of battlefield air support left a lot to be desired. The difference was that in 1940 the Allies did not have the means nor the method to apply close air support effectively. On D-Day the Allies had both, but failed to take advantage of all the expertise gained since those dark days in 1940. The lack of close air support and effective reconnaissance was a collective Air Force and Army failure. The D-Day landings were not a hastily thrown together operation. They were one of the most meticulously planned military operations ever devised. It seemed nothing had been left to chance. The huge number of sorties flown by the Allies on D-Day gave the impression of air forces doing everything they could to support the invasion but the numbers concealed a flawed attitude and approach. Amidst the overwhelming Allied presence in the air, there was an air support vacuum over the battlefield, The Allies had air supremacy but simply did not take full advantage.

Even when the dust had settled in the calm of the post-war evaluations, the failure went unrecognised. The air effort for Overlord was, as the British official history emphasises, 'the culmination and intensification of our efforts rather than a new campaign'.[21]

Even more damning were the views expressed in the American official USAAF history. D-Day was:

> an anticlimax ... the day proved to be, in one sense, particularly uneventful ... . There were no great air battles ... . The record of air operations in its most significant aspects points chiefly, therefore, to impressive evidence of a victory already won ... The record speaks too of adherence to sound principles of air warfare.[22]

This is describing the day American troops were massacred on Omaha beach. Even with hindsight, the air war was not seen as part of the battle raging on the ground. By securing air superiority and isolating the battle zone the air forces had done their job. Now it was up to the armies to do theirs. Army and air force roles were neatly segregated.

The reality was that, once Allied troops were in action on the battlefield, everything had changed. It was the first day of a very new campaign with very different priorities. Rear communications were worthy targets, but these were not the only targets and, on 6 June, they were not the most important targets. Churchill's maxim that once battle was joined air effort should be focused on winning that battle had been the guiding principle behind the Desert Air Force's early success.[23] It was not a principle applied on D-Day. Battlefield air support had failed to play any part in one of the most crucial days of the war.

D-DAY

D-Day was an opportunity for the Allies. It was on this first day that the Allies had tactical surprise. Airpower is most influential when the situation on the ground is fluid. This was when the Allies had their best chance of shattering the German defences. Their plans were not lacking in ambition and with the available air and naval power they had the means to keep German defences off balance and the advance rolling forward. If airpower had played a fuller part, it might have made a contribution as significant as the Luftwaffe's at Sedan in May 1940 in a previous Battle of France. Airpower could have made the decisive contribution air commanders were constantly claiming it was capable of. It was not to be. The Germans managed to hold the line. By 7 June, the 12th SS Panzer Division had joined the 21st around Caen and the Panzer Lehr Division soon followed.

For years, in all Air Ministry/War Office discussions, the Air Staff had always airily, and perhaps disingenuously, referred to the distant day when an Allied Army might be advancing on the continent, as the only circumstances in which close air support could possibly be useful. On 6 June 1944 that day had arrived and the RAF was found wanting. In British circles the failure passed completely unnoticed.

Chapter Ten

Re-learning Old Lessons

After being largely ignored on D-Day, close air support would slowly claw its way back into Allied thinking. As had happened on every front since the outbreak of war, the reality of actually fighting real battles would force a rethink. It would, however, be a slow process. Air defence and interdiction remained the priorities. Encounters with the Luftwaffe were much more frequent on the 7th, as reinforcements began to arrive, but Allied control of the skies was secure enough for the six RAF Mustang squadrons to be taken off air defence. These too joined the masses of Allied air power attacking targets in the rear. Spitfires continued to be used exclusively for air defence.

On 7 June the Anglo-Canadian forces renewed their attempts to reach Caen but were repelled with heavy losses. Canadian forces ran into the newly-arrived 12th SS Panzer, which was determined to drive the Canadians straight back into the sea. The Germans failed, but the Canadians were pushed back some two miles in considerable disarray. In the air the ten Typhoon squadrons of No. 83 Group continued to perform armed reconnaissance missions along roads leading to Caen from the south. No. 84 Group were operating on similar missions on the Allied left flank, attacking targets as far east as the Seine. The six Mustang III squadrons released from air defence duties had the range Coningham wanted and were despatched to attack targets well to the south-east of Falaise, reaching almost as far as Paris.[1]

So few were the targets in No. 84 Group's area, most of these were switched to the area the Mustangs were operating in. These targets were so distant from British bases that the Typhoon had to operate with half its offensive war load, either four rocket projectiles or just 500lb bombs, in order to accommodate drop tanks. Second Tactical Air Force was going to extraordinary lengths to hit distant targets with insignificant offensive loads, targets that could be attacked far more effectively by some of the longer-range aircraft available to the Allies. At the same time, British and

RE-LEARNING OLD LESSONS

Canadian troops the Second Tactical Air Force squadrons were supposed to be supporting were struggling to deal with German counter-attacks. Again this was not entirely the fault of the Air Force. Squadrons were instructed to check with the HQ ships that there were no more useful targets that needed to be dealt with.[2] Two missions were diverted. The first, flown by eight Typhoons, was directed to patrol the Villers-Bocage/Caen road. At midday four Typhoons were instructed to attack targets just south-west of Bayeux as British troops entered the town. In the afternoon, in response to a specific request, twenty-three Typhoons attacked German positions around Port-en-Bessin as British troops linked up with the still precariously held Omaha bridgehead. Of the 750 fighter-bomber sorties flown by RAF Typhoons and Mustangs, only thirty-five were direct support missions, but there was no demand from the Army for more.[3]

The Americans were moving much faster towards a better interdiction/close air support balance. For 7 June Quesada set aside four fighter-bomber groups, each with three squadrons, totalling some 300 aircraft, for close support. Each hour, three squadrons arrived over the front, ready and available to attack any enemy troops or positions holding up the American advance. With disorganised air support parties on the ground, close co-ordination was still difficult, but Quesada was determined to make the air support as close and as relevant as possible. The lack of pre-invasion training soon showed with unfortunate friendly fire incidents. Where effective, the support was welcome but mistakes led to some American units making it clear they did not want any more air support.[4]

While British Army commanders did not seem to be too concerned by the lack of fighter-bomber close support, they were anxious to get their Auster AOP squadrons operating with the artillery that was now moving into position. The first AOP base was established on the 7th, and the next day Nos. 662 and 652 Squadrons moved in permanently. By the end of June five Auster squadrons were in France. Operating from tiny airstrips within the ranks of the Army, these hybrid Army/Air Force units again proved priceless. As well as directing artillery, they were soon being used for visual and photo tactical reconnaissance. So important did the latter become, each squadron had a specialised photo-reconnaissance flight.[5] The Austers filled a huge gap in RAF capability. As the number of squadrons expanded, the Germans began to fear the Austers as much as the Typhoon fighter-bombers. Just the sight of an Auster could force a German battery to cease fire, for fear of giving away its position and inviting a furious counter barrage.

Calls for close support from the RAF became more common from 8 June when the first proper air support signal units arrived in the Normandy bridgehead. These Rovers acquired the formal title of Visual Control Post, if they were operating within visual range and Forward Control Posts if they were not. Both could call in air support and control cab ranks; the former was more mobile but more limited in the command centres it could contact.[6] The first direct support mission this day was in fact a response to an American request. The American troops were advancing towards Isigny and Carentan from the Omaha beachhead in an attempt to link up with the Utah beachhead. Thirty-two Typhoons in two missions, along with Ninth Air Force fighter-bombers, attacked enemy positions and tanks on the line of advance. On the British/Canadian front there were requests for air support from Canadians under pressure from German forces advancing from Caen and the equally hard-pressed 6th Airborne Division. Three missions were flown, comprising forty-eight sorties, but the reported enemy concentrations of armour were not sighted and most of the aircraft returned with their weapons unused. It was certainly an attempt at very close support; one of the squadrons sighted Allied tanks in the area that were expecting to find the enemy. Clearly much had to be done to match the levels of expertise being achieved in the Mediterranean. The tendency still seemed to be to call for air support when on the defensive whereas the Americans were using it to support an advance. With the fighter-bombers flying 400 interdiction sorties compared to eighty close air support, the balance of Second Tactical Air Force fighter-bomber operations was still weighted heavily in favour of the former.[7]

The actual balance in favour of interdiction was even greater as large numbers of British and American light, medium and heavy bombers were also attacking communication targets. The fighter-bomber, however, was undoubtedly very effective in this role. For all the swathes of destruction the heavy bombers inflicted on communication centres, it was the low-level fighter-bomber that left the biggest impression on German commanders and their troops. To be the target of attack long before getting anywhere near the front was dispiriting to say the least. As more reinforcements were rushed to the Normandy front, there was now much more to be gained by attacks on lines of communication. Even so, air commanders tended to over-estimate the results of interdiction as much as they underestimated the value of close air support. It is extremely difficult for airpower to wipe out entire divisions, tank by tank, truck by truck. Of the early reinforcements Panzer Lehr Division suffered the most, probably losing about 10 per cent of its strength in a ninety-mile move from Chartres.[8] This was a notable achievement, but air commanders would have been disappointed; they believed they were doing much better than 10 per cent. As impressive as this loss was, even this division was still a formidable force when it reached the front.

The delays caused were more important than losses inflicted. The aim of sealing off the battle zone entirely was always over ambitious. Nevertheless, the threat Allied air forces posed meant most German movement had to be made by night, which was bound to cause significant delays. On a non-active front, a delay of a day or two can often be irrelevant; in a fast evolving battle, however, even a delay of a few hours can be crucial. Even reserves covering relatively short distances might arrive more than a day late. Rommel's front line was so precarious that, as soon as any units arrived, he had to commit them to plug the holes in his rickety defences. The attacks on lines of communication leading to the front were paying dividends but to reap the full reward the Allies still had to take advantage on the battlefield. A natural inclination not to act until everything was ready, combined with poor weather and rough seas delaying reinforcements, was hindering the Allied cause. With each passing day the defences were becoming more entrenched.

In the air the Allies remained dominant. Between 7 and 12 June around 500 fighters were transferred to the Normandy front. Luftwaffe fighters in western Europe were now divided fairly equally between the Reich and Normandy The entire force operating from secure bases inside Germany had struggled against the long-range fighters the USAAF could put over Germany. A smaller force operating from airfields within range of the Allied tactical as well as strategic fighter and bomber forces had the odds even more heavily stacked against it. From the 7th the Luftwaffe would fly around 500 sorties a day on the Normandy front. In truth since the invasion of the Soviet Union the Luftwaffe had rarely done much better than this on any western or Mediterranean front. Fighters were often engaged long before they got anywhere near the front. Daylight anti-shipping strikes were soon abandoned after heavy losses. Nocturnal missions only brought limited success. Hit-and-run raids by day and harassing bombing by night were a persistent nuisance but the Luftwaffe was never going to achieve more than this. Allied superiority was so overwhelming that Bomber Command heavies felt confident enough to venture out by day. E-boats operating from le Havre had been causing problems so, on the evening of 14 June, 221 Lancaster bombers, flying in very loose, makeshift defensive formations and escorted by Spitfires, wrecked the harbour for the loss of just one bomber.

The Allies were so comfortably in control of the skies over Normandy that not even the launching of the V-1 offensive had a serious effect. The first V-1 crashed into Bethnal Green on 13 June, killing six people. The Spitfire IX scarcely had the speed to catch the pilotless plane, and many ADGB squadrons still had Spitfire Vs. One of the two Mustang III wings, along with the two Tempest V and three Spitfire XIV squadrons, were transferred from Second Tactical Air Force to ADGB. This left the RAF relying entirely on the Spitfire IX to provide air defence of the beachhead. These, however, along with the American Thunderbolts, Lightnings and, most importantly, the American Mustangs, were more than sufficient to keep the Luftwaffe at bay.

For his next attempt to take Caen, Montgomery planned a pincer movement from the east and west. Montgomery wanted airborne forces dropped to complete the encirclement but this part of the plan was vetoed by Leigh-Mallory. On 10 June 7th 'Desert Rats' Armoured Division struck from the west and on 11 June 51st (Highland) Division advanced from the east of Caen. Poor weather on the 11th prevented any air support but on the 10th and 12th the Typhoons were in action and there was now a much greater effort to fly in the battle zone. Most missions were against rear headquarters, artillery positions or just armed reconnaissance in the general area but there were examples of very close support. On the 10th enemy infantry and armoured vehicles were reported in a wood just 500 yards ahead of Canadian forces covering the left flank of 7th Armoured Division and Typhoons of No.184 squadron were ordered to attack them. No enemy targets could be seen so the Typhoons just fired into the wood. With specific targets hard to see, this became common practice. It was scarcely precision air support, but it was at least taking place in full view of the troops. A second mission in the same area later in the day was cancelled at the last minute because friendly forces had taken the area the aircraft were scheduled to attack.[9] The support was getting very close, although it was still on a very small scale. Neither pincer made much progress and the forces on both sides were demoralised by the heavy losses they were suffering.[10] More such visible air support might have done much to raise Allied spirits and depress even further German morale.

Montgomery's plan had failed, but an opportunity arose farther south when a rapid advance by American towards Caumont opened up the western flank of the German defences. The 7th Armoured Division was now swung round through the stretched German defences and early on the morning of the 13th advanced through Villers Bocage. A handful of Tiger tanks, however, was sufficient to bring the entire advance to a halt, rather dramatically underlining the gap in the quality of both the opposing tanks and the way in which the opposing commanders exploited their resources. One tank commanded by panzer ace Captain Michael Wittman went on the rampage, causing havoc amongst the British forces.[11] The Air Staff had constantly underlined the pointlessness of knocking off tanks one by one on the battlefield when it was so clearly more sensible to destroy the tank factory building them. If ever there was ever one tank that provided the counter argument, it was this one.

Poor weather had prevented any air support being provided on the 13th until late in the evening. The next day the weather was fine and a concerted effort was made to support the troops in the Villers-Bocage area, with eleven squadrons flying repeat missions. By this time some Typhoon squadrons were flying from temporary bases in Normandy, which helped increase sortie rates. The missions on the 14th included attacking targets indicated by army-fired smoke bombs. Again, in practice this often just resulted in fire being directed at a village or wood without any specific enemy being seen. Air commanders were always dubious about the value of this sort of vague targeting but the troops on the ground tended to be very appreciative.[12] It was not enough to get the advance going again, but one small element of the infantry/tank/artillery/air support combined-arms package was falling into place. This, however, would be the last chance to take advantage of the fluid situation that had existed since D-Day. From this point on, German defences would be solid all along the line. Close air support was beginning to get into its stride just as the opportunities for it to make a difference were in decline.

While the British and Canadians were getting bogged down around Caen, the Americans were pushing out from their bridgeheads with more success. On 18 June American forces reached the west coast of the Cotentin peninsula, cutting off Cherbourg. Four days later the remaining German forces found themselves besieged in the French port. The final assault received the most substantial air support yet. This included the might of the might of 9th Air Force with its medium B-26 Marauders and A-20 Havoc light bombers. The aerial assault began at 12.40, with fighter-bomber squadrons, including RAF Mustangs and rocket-firing Typhoons. The light and medium bombers delivered their attacks as the troops began their advance at 14.00 and air support continued, albeit on a reduced scale, until dusk. In all some 1,100 sorties were flown.

Despite the aerial assault initial progress was slow. Again, a price was being paid for the lack of pre-invasion preparation and training. Given the worrying number of friendly-fire incidents that had plagued previous advances, as a precaution troops pulled back 1,000 yards before the first fighter-bomber strikes went in, which was bound to negate to an extent any advantage gained.[13] The co-ordination close air support required cannot be cobbled together at the last minute. Although appreciated by the ground forces there was considerable criticism in American air force circles for the lack of concentration and the failure to have anyone in the front line directing the pilots towards targets. Damage inflicted by aerial attack proved to be disappointing, but German prisoners spoke of the demoralising effects. And progress was being made. In three days Cherbourg fell. Within another five days the entire peninsula was cleared of all German forces.

Perhaps most important of all there was in the American camp a growing recognition that control of close air support needed more decentralised control along the lines of the discredited USAAF FM 31-35 field manual rather than the FM 100-20, partly inspired by the Tedder/Coningham approach, that replaced it.[14] At this stage the Americans were adjusting more quickly than their British Allies to the realities of the campaign they were fighting. The schism between American bomber advocates and the ground force generals was as great as in the British armed services, but having both within the same organisational framework to some extent eased the problem.

With the capture of Cherbourg, the Allies had the port they needed so badly, although so thorough were German demolitions that it was several weeks before the port facilities were even partially restored. Overlord was not going as hoped. Caen had not fallen on the first day and Bradley had not been able to attempt the breakout to the south envisaged by Montgomery. By the time Cherbourg fell, it had been hoped the Americans would have broken through the bocage and advanced beyond Avranches. At least in the west, with the Cherbourg peninsula cleared, progress was being made. The Germans, however, had time to reinforce their defences around Saint-Lô in countryside that heavily favoured the defence. The terrain around Caen was far the more favourable for a breakthrough, though for this reason it was also where German defences were strongest. There were no easy options for the Allies.

Once again frustration was growing in the Allied camp. The Allies clearly had total control of the skies and two huge fleets of heavy bombers that ought to be able to exploit it. These were continuing their demolition of communication targets by day and night over a vast tract of occupied territories from Nantes to Luxembourg and up to Eindhoven in the Netherlands. During planning for Overlord, using them on the battlefield had always been one of the options. With the campaign underway, Eisenhower kept emphasising to Montgomery that all this brute force was available to him and reminded air force commanders that every Army request must be met. Eisenhower wanted Montgomery 'to blast the enemy with everything we have', as if only a reluctance to make use of the air resources available was preventing the decisive breakthrough.[15] Once again the heavy bomber was taking centre stage in the debate about how the Allied armies should make best use of air superiority.

Montgomery had no intention of hurrying his next attempt to take Caen. It would be a typical Montgomery set-piece battle and he would not strike until he had the firepower in place that would guarantee success. The navies were still providing substantial support from the wings and the Army was now moving its own artillery resources into position. However, poor weather in the Channel was seriously delaying the arrival of reinforcements and supplies. There was a particular shortage of artillery shells. An alternative source of firepower would be useful.

On the afternoon of 14 June, Leigh-Mallory, turned up at Montgomery's headquarters with a solution. Anxious to make up for denying Montgomery airborne troops for the previous attempt to take Caen, Leigh-Mallory suggested that the heavies be called out again as they had been on D-Day to blast a 5,000-yard-wide hole in the German defences.[16] For Montgomery, this seemed to revive memories of his Tebaga triumph. Here, too, his initial attempt to advance had failed and the alternative drive through the Tebaga Pass had needed the extra fire support the air force could provide. This would be another opportunity to use these 'blitz' tactics, as Montgomery called them.[17] In fact what was being proposed was entirely different. Light and medium bombers had been used at Tebaga to bomb the battle zone but, far more significantly, low-level fighter-bombers had been directed to their targets by a forward air controller. Leigh-Mallory was offering carpet bombing by heavy bombers from altitude. For Montgomery, however, this was just Tebaga with more bombs.

A meeting at Dempsey's Second Army headquarters in France was organised for the following day to sort out the details. Leigh-Mallory rang Coningham's HQ about the decision but Coningham was out dining and could not be contacted.[18] Tedder, however, got to hear about it, and passed the news on to Coningham who was infuriated that he had not been consulted, and the pair of them immediately set off to France. In fact, Leigh-Mallory was offering no more than Eisenhower was suggesting and indeed Tedder himself had been talking of the need for a 'terrific air punch' against targets near the battle line.[19] The best way of delivering this was all that needed deciding.

On arriving in France, Tedder and Coningham burst into the meeting where Zuckerman, Kingston McCloughry, Leigh-Mallory's deputy Chief of Operations, and Dempsey and his staff were discussing the heavy bomber intervention. They took Dempsey to one side and explained how impractical the project was. They were preaching to the converted. Dempsey had already expressed his fear that, far from encouraging his troops, any inaccurate bombing causing Allied casualties would severely shake their already wavering morale. Dempsey was sent out and Zuckerman and McCloughry were then brought in and told this sort of planning was none of their business and any air support for Montgomery would be organised by Coningham.

Zuckerman argued that the accuracy strategic bombers could now achieve opened up new possibilities in the land battle which ought to be investigated and Kingston McCloughry rather pointedly asked why the Army was still stuck in Normandy if Coningham and Tedder were so sure the tactical air forces were sufficient. 'This remark was also brushed aside,' Zuckerman relates, 'and the class, as it were, dismissed.'[20] McCloughry was making a valid point, and a reasoned discussion might have been useful. This was not forthcoming. Tedder asked Coningham to pass his verdict on the proposed area bombing which, Tedder recorded, 'was speedily done and the operation was cancelled'.[21] It was a humiliating position for Leigh-Mallory to be in; Tedder was giving Leigh-Mallory's subordinate the opportunity to veto his superior's plan. Leigh-Mallory considered resigning but, still convinced the heavy bomber would ultimately have to be used tactically to break the deadlock, bided his time.[22] Once again the heavy bomber was dominating proceedings. Heated debate over its use was diverting attention from more useful ways in which airpower could support the Army and perhaps even distracting attention in Army circles from the many more general non-air issues, tactical and technical, that were hindering the Allied cause in Normandy.

Like everyone else, Leigh-Mallory could not explain why Allied air superiority was not making more difference. Nobody could accuse him of not trying to make it count. He spoke passionately of the need to support the Army; 'I have always taken the view that the Army must be given all the support it desired' but he had been:

up against, more or less since D-Day, the school of thought which takes the view that the air support given to the Army should be the minimum rather than the maximum, on the principle that if you give the Army an inch it will take an ell,

he explained, using the old English version of the expression.[23] He continued,

> This school urges as a principle that really heavy Air Forces should not be used on the immediate battle-front but elsewhere, beyond and outside it.

This, from an Army point of view, might sound promising but again it was the heavy bombers that were dominating Leigh-Mallory's thinking. He seemed to be finding it difficult to break free from the commonly held view in Air Ministry circles that a bomber was a bomber and could be used equally well against any target, strategic or battlefield.

Leigh-Mallory might seem better disposed towards the Army than most but this did not stop him from grumbling that Montgomery did not appreciate the support the air forces were providing. Without air force interdiction, Leigh-Mallory claimed, Montgomery would be facing far more enemy divisions and they would not be the 'very much below strength' divisions he currently faced.[24] Montgomery, according to Leigh-Mallory, was 'profoundly uninterested' by these arguments, perhaps, it might be argued, with some justification. The German formations Montgomery faced did not seem so enfeebled to him or his troops. Indeed, Leigh-Mallory was grossly overestimating how much the Air Force had achieved. Interdiction had slowed arrival but it had not prevented any divisions reaching the front.

Leigh-Mallory was scarcely any more complimentary about the average soldier's vision than Tedder or Coningham. As an air force commander, he suggested, his own view 'was not bounded, as seems to be the case with the Army, by the nearest hedge or stream'.[25] In truth the problem was the opposite. The Army had no problem seeing the advantages offered by air force attacks on targets beyond 'the nearest hedge or stream'. Indeed, Brooke was expecting too much of the offensive against German industry. Army commanders were united in their desire for attacks on German lines of communications; they were simply more realistic about what it might achieve. The problem was that too many air force officers could not see that they also had a role to play in dealing with the enemy closer than the 'nearest hedge or stream'. Leigh-Mallory was not in this camp but, in the favourable circumstances he believed the air force had created, he, like Tedder, could not understand why the Army could not get on with it. It was a measure of the Army-Air Force divide that Leigh-Mallory was considered in Army circles as one of the more sympathetic voices within the RAF. Despite his jaundiced view of Army aptitudes, he wanted to do all he could to support the Army but that meant using heavy bomber support to 'loosen things up'.[26]

Tedder and Coningham were quite right in believing heavy bombers were not the answer, but neither Tedder nor even Coningham were preaching the value of Broadhurst precision style tactical air support on the battlefield as an alternative. Tedder's opposition to using heavy bombers seemed to have as much to do with his disapproval of Leigh-Mallory's pandering to Montgomery and the Army's requirements as to the impracticalities of heavy bombers operating over the battlefield. Tedder and Coningham's personal grudges against Montgomery and Leigh-Mallory were just adding to the toxic mix. In Tedder's books Broadhurst was none too popular either. Broadhurst was livid when Tedder greeted him one day with a cheery 'How's your bloody Army friend today', a jibe, combining in one expression Tedder's dislike of Montgomery and his disapproval of Broadhurst's close association with him. 'Well what do you expect him to be, my enemy?' an exasperated Broadhurst retorted to his superior and stalked off, a comment and reaction which he expected to earn him the sack.[27]

Broadhurst survived, but it was not a happy camp. Everyone was blaming everyone else. As far as Tedder was concerned it was not the fault of the Air Force that Montgomery was still stuck in Normandy; the Army was simply not trying hard enough. Montgomery was infuriated by Tedder and Coningham's veto of Leigh-Mallory's heavy bomber plan. It was yet another example of the air force's unco-operative attitude. Montgomery blamed Dempsey for conceding too easily and not fully understanding how airpower could be integrated into land operations.[28] In fact it was Montgomery who could not see the difference between the heavy bomber support Leigh-Mallory was proposing and the Tebaga-style 'blitz'.

Everyone seemed to be missing the point. What would help was the greater precision Broadhurst on the British side was offering and Quesada on the American side was beginning to apply with some gusto. But the lure of mass destruction on the battlefield was proving as tempting for Army generals as the mass destruction of German cities and industries was for the disciples of strategic bombing. Even the likes of Broadhurst and Quesada were not against the tactical use of strategic bombers. Like everyone else, they too were in awe of the heavy bomber. Neither drew attention to the disadvantages of tactical carpet bombing from high altitude.

Having claimed that Coningham's tactical air force was capable of meeting all Army needs, there was an onus on Tedder and Coningham to prove it could. They did this by providing the Army with exactly what it was asking for – pattern bombing of battlefield targets. The Second Tactical Air Force's six Boston and Mitchell squadrons were not capable of providing this but Coningham had access to Brereton's mighty force of 9th Air Force light and medium bombers. For Montgomery's forthcoming Operation Epsom these would be used to bomb the flanks of Montgomery's intended advance. This was in fact a better option than the heavies Leigh-Mallory and Eisenhower wanted to use. As 9th Air Force had demonstrated on D-Day, medium bombers operating from lower altitudes were far more accurate than the heavies operating at higher altitudes. Tedder and Coningham were giving Montgomery what he wanted, and managing to upset everyone, including Montgomery, in the process. Typhoons striking targets in the path of the advancing forces would provide the true Tebaga-style element. The problem with the scheme was that, even with the more accurate mediums, a 2,500-yard bomb line was deemed necessary, which meant the bombing would be of little immediate value to the advancing forces.

Channel storms from 19 to 23 June delayed the landing of supplies and reinforcements and it was 26 June before Montgomery was satisfied that everything was ready. Montgomery might see Operation Epsom as a re-run of the Tebaga operation but the drive through the Tebaga Pass was an improvised change of plan mid-battle that involved swinging armoured divisions around to attack a front some fifty miles away, catching the Germans by surprise. For Operation Epsom there was going to be no tactical surprise. The plan was to push across the River Odon and outflank Caen from the south. Rommel was ready and waiting.

As it turned out, poor weather in the UK forced the cancellation of most of the air support, including the planned 9th Air Force carpet bombing. This was unfortunate, not just because the Army would be denied useful air support but also because it might have demonstrated to Montgomery that air support was moving in the direction the Army needed, albeit somewhat against the air marshals' better judgement. Instead, the denial of heavy bomber support would fester. In France the weather was fine and fortunately, by the 20th, eight Spitfire and three Typhoon squadrons were permanently based on the continent.[29] Being so close to the front line was not ideal; airfields were within enemy artillery range, but with poor weather in Britain, airfields in France became priceless.

Unfortunately the Typhoon's Sabre engine was not taking kindly to the Normandy dust and the Typhoons were either grounded in France or had been temporarily pulled back to Britain for engine overhauls and the fitting of dust filters. On the opening day No. 83 Group flew around 500 sorties, mostly defensive Spitfire sorties. The Spitfire was not the best of fighter-bombers but it was being used for dive-bombing and perhaps could have filled the void left by the absent Typhoons. With Allied air force units in Britain grounded, there was more opportunity for the Luftwaffe to make its presence felt, making air defence more important. Even so, there was scope for the Spitfires to stand in for the absent Typhoons. However, there do not seem to have been any specific requests for support from the Army.[30] On this first day there was no pressure from the Army to provide more of this sort of air support.

After some initial progress German resistance stiffened until, on the 27th, the Germans counter-attacked. With better weather the Typhoons were able to get back to their bases in France and were on hand to respond to calls for support. During the course of the day seventeen requests for air support were made, leading to 115 sorties, with smoke markers and forward control posts guiding in the fighter-bombers. Another 111 Typhoon sorties were flown on armed reconnaissance missions over the battlefield.[31] On the 28th, the weather remained poor in Britain with No. 84 Group in the UK only able to despatch ninety Spitfires. However, the British were able to renew their advance; 11th Armoured Division pushed across the River Oden, five miles from their start line. The following day II SS Panzerkorps (9th and 10th SS Panzer Divisions) launched a fierce counter-attack. By this time the weather in the United Kingdom had cleared sufficiently for No. 84 Group to play a full part in the battle, Nos. 83 and 84 Groups flying over 1,250 sorties over the battle area. The British again found the German Panther and Tiger tanks a handful, but German commanders were equally troubled by the repeated fighter-bomber attacks and the panzers were repelled.[32] The violence of the German attack convinced Montgomery that no further progress would be made and the offensive was called off.

Both sides had lost heavily. The Allies committed more tanks infantry and artillery yet the Germans were able to hold them. Weather had prevented the Allies making full use of their superiority in the air but clearly a lot more was going wrong than a spell of bad weather. Allied struggles around Caen were in rather stark contrast to what was happening on the Eastern Front.

RE-LEARNING OLD LESSONS

Three days before Montgomery launched Operation Epsom, the Soviets opened their latest offensive. Combining their superior numbers in the air and on the ground, the breakthrough came in days and within weeks the advance stretched hundreds of miles. Defending a sixty-mile front in Normandy was much easier than a 1,000-mile front in Russia. Even so, Soviet success should have been providing food for thought.

The initial Soviet breakthroughs were supported by massed air attacks on German front-line positions, with low-flying armoured Il-2 Sturmoviks, Pe-2 dive-bombers and strafing fighters, all directed by forward air observers, picking out their targets. There was no heavy bomber carpet bombing. Nor was there any debate about the relative value of armoured assault planes, precision dive-bombers and versatile fighter-bombers; the Soviets simply used all three. Soviet interdiction focused mainly on routes into the battle zone. The Soviet Air Force might be criticised for not putting more effort into more distant support but, going by results, it seemed it was better to err on the side of close rather than distant air support. For twelve days the Soviet Air Force flew around 4,500 sorties a day in and around the battle zone.[33]

It was not just air support that was winning the day. High-quality tanks helped and, even more crucially, the Soviets were able to get infantry, tanks, artillery and aviation all working together as one. The British Army only excelled in its infantry/artillery combination. Tanks as good the German Panther or Soviet T-34 were not going to suddenly become available (although the excellent Comet was on the way) and getting tanks and infantry to work together was proving equally problematic. One area, however, where the British could match Soviet expertise was in systems for organising close air support; all that was lacking was a willingness to make maximum use of it. The RAF in France was moving in the right direction. Even so, among too many key air commanders there was a reluctance to accept that such support should be a standard tool available to any modern army. On the Army side, there was too much focus on heavy bomber support.

Following the Epsom failure the mud was flying. Tedder, Coningham and Leigh-Mallory were all blaming the Army in general and Montgomery in particular for the slow progress. Montgomery was not happy with the air support he was getting. The complaints were rather vague, as one might expect from someone who had not made airpower a 'life study'. It was more a complaint about attitude than anything else. Montgomery had huge faith in Broadhurst, believed Leigh-Mallory was broadly sympathetic to the Army cause and doing his best but would be quite happy to see

Coningham gone.³⁴ These were judgements made on willingness to co-operate and indeed personal enmity rather than what they were offering. In Montgomery's eyes, the unco-operative attitude of the air force had been epitomised by the refusal to commit the heavy bombers to the land struggle. In the blame game that followed Epsom it was easy to point the finger at air force intransigence as the reason for failure, rather than look for other explanations. It was not just air/ground co-operation that needed to improve; infantry/tank co-operation and many other issues also needed reviewing. But the heavy bomber was attracting all the attention. This was still an option and the closing stages of Epsom provided some evidence that it was still an option worth investigating.

As British armour pulled back behind the River Odon, a substantial concentration of German tanks was spotted preparing to launch an attack from the Villers-Bocage region. It was such a dense concentration that it was felt that it might be vulnerable to carpet bombing. On the evening of 30 June, 232 heavy bombers of Bomber Command, skilfully directed by a Master Bomber, dropped 1,100 tons of bombs on the German concentration from 4,000 feet. There was no question of aiming the bombs at individual tanks, the aim was to devastate the entire area. It appeared to work; the counter-attack launched next day was successfully beaten off.³⁵ This seemed to justify Leigh-Mallory's suggestion that the heavies should be used to blast a way through German defences.

Eisenhower was once again anxious that Montgomery should throw everything into his next attempt to break the German stranglehold and reminded him that this included 'all resources of the Air', tactical and strategic. Tedder again objected: 'the Air could not and must not be turned on thus glibly and vaguely in support for the Army, which would never move unless prepared to fight its way with its own weapons.'³⁶ It was the sort of comment one might expect from a commander of the strategic bomber forces; it was not what you would expect from the highest ranking RAF officer in an organisation set up to ensure the air force played its part in supporting the Army. It was a comment that highlighted one of the disadvantages of splitting up the armed services into self-contained organisations; rather unhelpful ideas about what weapons are 'ours' and which are 'theirs' tend to develop. It was clearly ridiculous to claim 'The Air' weapon was not an army weapon. It was one of its most important weapons.

In claiming that the heavy bomber was not a tactical weapon, Tedder was on much stronger ground. He pointed out that the success at Villers-Bocage had been against a force concentrating for a counter-attack. Carpet bombing could not be expected to be so successful against a more widely dispersed defensive force. Tedder felt the lessons from Italy, where heavy bombers had caused more problems than they solved, were being ignored. He was right, but he was still showing no interest in championing the other lesson from the fighting in the Mediterranean – the value of well-directed precision attacks on battlefield targets. As far as Tedder was concerned the Army had to learn to stand on its own two feet by fighting its battles with 'its own weapons', not air force weapons. For Tedder battlefield air support was a favour. If ground forces were in trouble the air force was happy to bail out their sister service, indeed took some pleasure in coming to the rescue and saving the day, but that was as far as co-operation went.

Leigh-Mallory was happy to see Montgomery get all the bomber support Eisenhower had in mind. With such huge fleets of heavy bombers readily available it was just too tempting not to try using them to break the logjam. Montgomery was grateful for any way of increasing the firepower available for the initial assault, and, indeed any new ways of breaking through the German defences. The heavy bomber was the ideal quick fix. As far as Eisenhower was concerned, this was the whole point of having the heavy bombers under his control. [37] Tedder, seeing which way the wind was blowing, did not push his reservations.

Carpet bombing slotted nicely into Montgomery's meticulous planning; it was an easy bolt-on to Montgomery's normal approach. It required no initiative or involvement from front-line commanders, apart from getting their own troops out of the way. They could just stand back and watch. To make best use of Broadhurst style air support required initiative and decision making from army commanders at all levels. With far less fanfare and none of the controversy that surrounded the use of heavy bombers, Broadhurst was slowly making this more refined use of air power an integral part of army operations. For the next move forward, Operation Charnwood, aerial reconnaissance would identify enemy tanks, mortar positions, guns and troops and the Army would make extensive use of smoke shells to indicate the positions of targets.[38]

Operation Charnwood was a straightforward concentric attack on Caen. The original plan had been to use the heavy bombers to obliterate the German strongpoints immediately behind the front line. However, it was decided that this posed too great a risk for friendly troops and the bombardment was moved four miles deeper into enemy-held territory. The bombing operation was supposed to take place in the early morning of 8 July, but predicted poor weather brought it forward to the previous evening.[39] The support would not be close in distance or time. Some 467 bombers dropped 2,276 tons of bombs in a rectangle 4,000 yards by 1,500 yards across the northern outskirts of Caen and the open countryside beyond. Many of the bombs were delayed action, designed to go off the following morning when the ground forces started their advance.[40] Army commanders and their troops gathered to watch the spectacle. As at Cassino, the bombardment did much to raise the spirits of the watching Allied ground forces. Broadhurst took Dempsey up in his captured German Storch to get a better view. Everyone was impressed by the scale of the attack – it was difficult not to be.[41] It was far enough away to present no danger to the spectators but it was also far too far behind the front to make the task of the advancing infantry any easier.[42]

Once again direct air support was limited by poor weather; over 750 sorties were flown by French-based squadrons but only one hundred by those based in the UK. Initially good progress was made but, as Allied troops occupied the area obliterated by Bomber Command, there was little evidence that substantial German units had been there. As the British forces reached the outskirts of Caen, as had happened at Cassino, their progress was slowed by the rubble the suburbs had been reduced to. The devastation also created excellent ready-made defensive positions for the enemy to occupy.[43] By the evening of the 9th the Allies had reached the River Odon, 'liberating' what was left of the northern half of the city, but no further advance was possible. Dropping more than two kilotons of explosives to obliterate two square miles of enemy defences anticipated the thinking behind plans to use tactical nuclear weapons a decade or two down the line. It was visually an impressive display of brute force but it did not lead to a breakthrough.

Precision strikes by fighter-bombers were not such a spectacle. No one gathered to watch a Typhoon knock out an anti-tank gun. Nor was the humble-looking Auster an awe-inspiring sight but, by accurately directing artillery fire, they were contributing far more than the heavy bombers. With the Auster the Allies were undoubtedly making full use of air superiority. Slow unarmed planes were far more inviting targets than massed bomber formations with powerful escorts, but it was not the vulnerability of the Auster that made it a top priority target for German fighters; it was the accuracy with which it could direct fire on German positions. No real effort was made against the carpet-bombing heavies; German fighter pilots were told to focus their efforts on the fighter-bombers and Austers.[44] The apostles of airpower tended to obsess about the need to focus air resources to maximise effect, but the Auster was an example where spreading resources thinly maximises value. A single, cheap aircraft could multiply the effectiveness of artillery batteries out of all proportion to the resources expended.

However, on the Allied side, it was still the heavy bomber that was seen as the way forward. The problems encountered in its first use in Normandy seemed to confirm the lessons learned in Italy but the generals were not giving up. As was the case with strategic bombing, there was a grim determination to make the heavy bomber a success. It had not worked for Operation Charnwood but it was hoped that all that was required was to drop more bombs, drop them nearer the front line and have ground forces close at hand to exploit the carnage caused.

Things were not going well for Montgomery. However it was dressed up, the Allies were stuck and frustration was growing. More than a month had passed since the landings. The bridgehead was almost bursting at the seams with military hardware. But, just like Salerno and Anzio, the Allies could not break out and this time there was no overland advance to come and save the day. It was all in very stark contrast to events on the Eastern Front where an entire German army group was disintegrating. Summer was running out and the nightmare scenario of the Allies having to maintain the bridgehead through a difficult winter was becoming a possibility. Tedder was openly campaigning for Montgomery's dismissal and Churchill was quite happy for him to go if that was what Eisenhower wanted.

The invasion of France was not going to plan.

Chapter Eleven

The Bomber War

On the Home Front the media did its best to put a positive spin on events in Normandy, but the sluggish Allied progress in France had to compete with stories of the huge advances and large prisoner counts coming from the Eastern Front. To add to their woes, Londoners now had to deal with the long-awaited missile offensive. On 13 June a solitary V-1 crashed into a railway bridge in Bethnal Green, killing six people. Three others crashed harmlessly in Sussex and Kent. For the British Chiefs of Staff it was an astonishing anti-climax. An initial salvo of at least 400 tons of explosive had been expected.[1] It was indeed a false start. The Germans had decided to open their offensive even though preparations had been severely disrupted by Allied air attacks. Very few of the sixty-four launching sites were operational. Instead of hundreds, just ten flying bombs were launched, six of which crashed before they reached the British coast. This opening salvo underlined both the unreliability and inaccuracy of the weapon.

Two days later the Germans tried again. This time nearly 250 were launched in the first twelve hours. One fifth crashed soon after launch and many more failed to reach London. In the first twenty-four hours of the offensive, seventy-three missiles, each carrying a ton of explosives, hit targets in Greater London.[2] It was a scale of attack that would have scarcely warranted a mention in the Allied air offensive against Germany, yet it made an impression. These attacks were not like conventional raids, where, once it was over, you were safe. The threat was constant, day and night. The randomness and unpredictability was morale sapping for a war-weary population. As soon as the distinctive throbbing pulse jet cut, the missile would begin its terminal dive and anyone in the vicinity had ten seconds to take cover. Actual casualties were often relatively light but there was always the potential for serious loss of life. On 18 June a V-1 crashed into the Guards Chapel in Wellington Barracks, killing sixty-three servicemen and fifty-eight civilians.

THE BOMBER WAR

It might be unreliable and inaccurate but it was cheap. From the German point of view this was the weapon's main asset. The Germans gleefully dropped propaganda leaflets helpfully explaining how, costing just £600, a hundred V-1s could be built for the price of one Lancaster and it had no crew in it to perish, unlike the Lancaster 'thousands [of which] have been shot down'.[3] While Bomber Command crews were dying over Germany, the Luftwaffe could retaliate from the comfort and safety of their launching sites.

It was a powerful argument, if all that was required was indiscriminate destruction. Indeed it was an argument Trenchard had used in the twenties when Britain had been developing its own RAE Larynx flying bomb. Early in July the Luftwaffe added another dimension to the attack by air launching V-1s from Heinkel bombers, enabling London to be attacked from a different direction and putting other more distant cities at risk. The number launched in this way was very small; it was no more than a demonstration of the potential flexibility an air-launched missile system offered. It was another pointer to how future bomber offensives might be conducted.

Harris was most impressed with this 'weapon of the next war'. In his post-war memoirs he described how the V-1 had the potential to deliver, continuously and in all weathers, a weight of bombs his huge Command would find difficult to match. Indeed, if his Bomber Command had not disrupted German plans 'it is difficult to see how an invasion [of France] could have been mounted with London in ruins, Southern England laid waste and every type of communication in disorder' he claimed with characteristic overstatement.[4] How one-ton warheads falling randomly over such a huge area were ever supposed to deliver the level of disruption Harris was envisaging is hard to imagine. In contrast, Albert Speer, writing his post-war memoires in the less salubrious surroundings of his Spandau prison, could not understand how he had ever managed to convince himself Hitler's vengeance weapons could change the course of the war.[5] Victory tends to dull the senses while defeat sharpens the mind.

It was indeed a very efficient weapon for those who believed winning wars was about killing as many people as possible. It was a philosophy from which the Air Ministry had not yet broken free. The capacity of the V-1 to kill was brutally brought home to the Air Staff on 28 June when a V-1 crashed into the Air Ministry, killing 198 people. Air Ministry departments were soon dusting down some of their pre-war thinking on unmanned bombers. Vice-Chief of Air Staff Evill, was sufficiently impressed by the V-1 to suggest it might be worth having another look at the unmanned approach without, he emphasised, 'slavishly' following the V-1 model. He suggested several advantages. Unmanned craft were potentially much faster than manned aeroplanes and, only needing fuel for a one-way trip, range would be far greater. There would always be well-defended targets where it might be more economic to employ pilotless planes. Large targets like fleets in port, or the vast sprawling industrial Ruhr, would be vulnerable to even a relatively inaccurate weapon, he suggested.[6]

Others pointed out its value as a decoy, absorbing the efforts of the defences while the piloted bombers attacked with precision. There might also be tactical uses for pilotless planes. There was no reason why, used en masse, it could not deliver the tactical carpet bombing that was becoming the vogue in Normandy.[7] It was also suggested such a weapon might be launched from aircraft carriers or submarines against Japan and indeed, once Germany was defeated, captured V-1s might be immediately pressed into service against Japan. Another suggestion was that after the war these missiles could be set up aimed at German cities, primed and ready for launch as a means of maintaining control of occupied Germany. At the touch of a button instant retribution could be delivered for any misdemeanour. There was an eerie, spine-chilling air about this most ruthless manifestation of colonial style 'air control'.[8] On reflection, the author decided manned bombers could carry out the punishment just as effectively – less spine-chilling perhaps but no less pitiless. Leaving aside such methods for pacifying a conquered country, there was a consensus that, although it was perhaps not a weapon for this war, it was a weapon for the future. Interestingly, since it was effectively a type of long-range artillery, and perhaps without fully thinking through the implications for the future RAF, it was seen in one assessment as more of an army or naval than an air force weapon.[9] This seemed to be handing the Army and Navy weapons with strategic applications. Long-range unmanned weapon systems posed an interesting dilemma for air forces that saw long-range bombardment as their primary role.

By 5 July flying bombs had caused the deaths of 2,500 Londoners.[10] It was not the apocalyptic death toll some had predicted but, nevertheless, it was another taxing time for Londoners. Some clever disinformation made the V-1 offensive less effective than it might have been. Luftwaffe reconnaissance flights over the British Isles had not been possible for some time, so the Germans had no idea where the V-1s were landing. Selective British announcements on where V-1s had hit and false information supplied to German agents gave the impression they were overshooting. Gradually the average landing point was pulled southwards, with a higher percentage of flying bombs failing to reach the capital. Nevertheless, the offensive was a grim reminder that the war was far from finished. It was serious enough for the government to worry about whether war-weary Britons could take it. Tedder shared these concerns. The apparent lack of any Army ambition to break out of the Normandy bridgehead and clear the Pas de Calais V-1 launching sites was another reason for getting rid of Montgomery, not that Tedder felt he needed any more reasons.

The V-1, flying at a steady speed without altering course, made an attractive target for anti-aircraft fire, once its high speed at low altitude was catered for. Clearly there was no point in trying to shoot them down over London, so the main anti-aircraft defences had to be moved to the coast. The need to launch the V-1s from the Pas de Calais, the nearest point on the continent to the United Kingdom, made it reasonably easy to position the anti-aircraft guns in their path. The new American SCR-584 anti-aircraft gun-laying radar and predictor equipment, the first of which entered service at the end of June, proved particularly effective at tracking the V-1.[11] However, it would take time for the anti-aircraft defences to take up their new positions on the coast and become proficient in the use of these new radars, and generally adjust to the new enemy. Initially fighters would provide the main defence.

Flying at around 400mph at relatively low attitudes the V-1 was not an easy target for fighters. The Spitfire V, still in service with some fighter squadrons, was far too slow, and even the Spitfire IX struggled. Something faster was clearly needed. The fastest fighters available to the RAF were the Mustang III, Tempest V and Spitfire XIV. Second Tactical Air Force had priority with deliveries of these but, with the launching of the V-1 offensive, the three Tempest and two Spitfire XIV Second Tactical Air Force squadrons, soon followed by three squadrons of Mustangs, were transferred to bolster London's defences. Had fighter resources been less plentiful and the struggle for the control of the skies over the beachhead a more finely balanced affair, the decision on whether to transfer these fighter squadrons would have been more difficult and controversial. As it was, Allied air superiority over the Normandy beachhead was so overwhelming that the Tempest and Spitfire XIV squadrons were not missed.

It was also suggested that the handful of pre-production Meteor Is be put to some operational use.[12] These were not considered fit for normal combat operations. Top speed was no higher than the Spitfire IX's, it climbed more slowly and flying characteristics were so poor pilots were not allowed to perform any aerobatics. However, it was faster than any Fighter Command piston-engined fighters at the low altitudes the V-1 flew and intercepting these robot planes would require minimal manoeuvring.[13] With talk of German jets entering service, deploying Meteors operationally would also give the impression the Western Allies were not so far behind. The available Meteors were despatched to re-equip a flight of No. 616 Squadron. The squadron received its first Meteor I on 21 July and on 4 August a Meteor shot down its first flying bomb. The RAF could claim it had a jet fighter in front-line service.

Up to 15 July over 4,300 V-1s had been launched; the defences claimed around 1,200 of these, with 80 per cent claimed by fighters. Of the reminder, 1,270 exploded in the London area.[14] The death toll had risen to around 3,000 with 10,000 seriously injured.[15] However, there was good reason to fear the worst was yet to come. Goebbels had promised the German people that the V-1 was just the first of his vengeance weapons. The press were anticipating the next of these would be a ninety-ton rocket with a ten-ton warhead.[16] The government could give no assurance that this was not the case. Against the rocket it seemed there could be no defence. The best that might be hoped for was the minute's warning radar might provide. Hospitals were already beginning to clear space for the expected wave of casualties. By the end of August 1944 more than 15,000 patients and staff had been evacuated from London. Over 28,000 beds stood ready. Another 8,000 patients were lined up for immediate discharge should their beds be needed.[17] It was September 1939 all over again. As the war approached the end of its fifth year, the authorities could only speculate about how Londoners would cope with an attack by ballistic missiles.

Meanwhile, Bomber Command's offensive against Germany, which had done so much to provoke an acceleration in the development of the V-weapons, was about to step up its own campaign of terror. There was now hope that the Command might be capable of more than just indiscriminate bombing. The pressure to save French lives had forced the Command to try out new ways of improving accuracy. These could now be used to attack targets inside the Third Reich. It was scarcely precision bombing, as the destruction of French towns and city suburbs demonstrated, but it demonstrated that Bomber Command could aim its bombs at particular targets rather than just aiming at cities. Whether more precision was possible over the greater distances involved and with more formidable defences remained to be seen.

In the summer of 1944, a resumption of a full-scale strategic air offensive understandably filled Bomber Command aircrews with apprehension. The scars of the Battle of Berlin were still fresh and the occasional venture into German airspace during the summer months provided ample reminder of the effectiveness of the German night-fighter force. Even over France losses in nocturnal raids had been discouragingly high, far higher than in parallel daylight operations. Despite the new-found skills developed over occupied territories, Harris was anxious to get back to his city-busting programme. The Air Staff were still trying to persuade him to at least concentrate on cities and towns with important targets in them. The latest candidate for precision bombing was oil; the Americans were proving this was a far more attractive target than the Air Ministry experts believed it to be.

Eisenhower had suggested to Spaatz that any surplus bombers available in the run up to the invasion should be directed at oil. The Fifteenth Air Force had launched several heavy raids against the Ploesti plants in Rumania from its bases in Italy. On 12 May 1944, almost four years to the day since Bomber Command launched its first attempt at destroying the German oil industry, the Eighth Air Force re-opened the campaign with 950 bombers attacking five oil installations. The raids appeared to be successful. This would not have been the first time such success had been claimed but this time it was confirmed by alarmed signals Bletchley Park was picking up. It was 28 May before the American bombers could be made available to renew the attack with another 400 sorties. More Ultra intercepts underlined the catastrophic impact the bombing was having.[18]

For Portal events had turned full circle. He had been in charge of Bomber Command in May 1940 when it had failed so miserably to inflict any damage on German oil installations. Four years later there was an opportunity to demonstrate that the idea had been right. Tedder, well aware of German difficulties, was now quite happy to be 'led up this garden path' and was also suggesting that Harris, like Spaatz, should use any excess capacity to strike oil targets. Bufton, the Air Ministry Director of Bomber Operations, feared the American campaign was going so well that they would destroy all the German oil plants before Bomber Command had a chance to contribute and Bomber Command was given ten oil targets to consider. Harris was not enthusiastic but, on 12/13 June, Bomber Command despatched 303 bombers against the Gelsenkirchen synthetic oil plant in the Ruhr. Mosquitoes carrying new improved Oboe equipment marked the plant, but the technique was not so dissimilar to previous area

Bomber Command raids. The main difference was that an oil plant was the aiming point rather than a city centre. Initial night photography suggested only fifteen bombers had hit the plant; it seemed to be the same old story. However, reconnaissance the next day showed that the plant had been very heavily damaged, so damaged it was predicted production would fall to zero.[19] For Harris, such claims had a very familiar ring to them, but those in the know about the Enigma intercepts (Harris was not one of them) had more reason to believe.

On the night of 16/17 June the Sterkrade plant was bombed through cloud, apparently without much success, and an attack on the Wesseling and Schloven plants on the night of 21/22 June also appeared to inflict only slight damage. Yet again the pessimism was not justified. It was scarcely precision bombing – a very high percentage of bombs were missing – but enough were hitting to cause serious damage. Production at the former was reduced by 40 per cent and the latter by 20 per cent. Bomber Command had probably been capable of doing far better than just hitting city centres for some time. Between 150 and 300 bombers were involved in these attacks, the size of a typical Bomber Command raid in the summer of 1942. Churchill had been right when he told Portal the solution to Bomber Command's problems was to get more bombs on target, not build more bombers to compensate for inaccuracy.

The Anglo-American oil campaign turned out to be a triumph. German output of oil products dropped from 733,000 tons in March 1944 to 427,000 tons in June. Production of aviation fuel slumped from 180,000 tons in March to just 54,000 tons in June.[20] Spaatz had predicted a 50 per cent reduction in oil production in six months. The Allied bomber force had come close to achieving this in three months. For aviation fuel this target had been more than achieved. An intelligence appreciation at the end of July suggested that there was a possibility that Germany would not be able to continue the struggle beyond December 1944. It was a staggering turnaround in the fortunes of the strategic-bombing policy. This was not slowing the rate of increase in output; these were real and severe cuts. It was not even a full-scale offensive, just the surplus air effort after commitments to Overlord and the offensive against the V-weapon launching sites had been met.

It was ironic that an attack on the very target system against which the strategic air offensive had been launched with such high hopes in May 1940, as the British Army was being evicted from France, should four years later finally bear fruit as the British Army returned to France. The advocates of strategic bombing might feel they had finally been vindicated, that, in the end, their perseverance had paid off. Allied Army generals and soldiers might view it differently. In May 1940 the Air Staff had promised the German offensive against France would soon grind to a halt when the oil stopped flowing. The French, and indeed the troops defending Dunkirk, might argue success had come four years too late. It was four years in which the bomber war had diverted vital resources from key battles raging across the globe. The success against the German oil industry was remarkable but if the bomber policy was to come out of the war ahead on the advantages/disadvantages ledger, it still had a lot of ground to make up.

Harris was not persuaded by the intelligence reports he was getting. In line with his preference for general more widespread indiscriminate destruction, he was soon using his spare capacity for indiscriminate attacks on cities. On the night of 23/24 July Bomber Command hit Kiel, three raids in five nights wiped out Stuttgart and Hamburg was revisited. There was no shortage of military targets in these cities, but they were not targets on which the Air Staff wanted to focus. Even after the war, when the results of the attacks on oil were well-established fact, Harris remained unrepentant, still claiming he was right to prefer bombing cites to oil plants. 'What the Allied strategists did was bet on an outsider, and it happened to win the race,' was his rather grudging post-war concession.[21] There was, though, an element of truth in Harris's obduracy. The Allies had struck it lucky with their oil campaign. For four years the bomber advocates had been floundering around in search of the German Achilles Heel. It was not the first time oil had been tried. It was scarcely a good advertisement for strategic bombing as a reliable means of winning wars. However, with his belief that just bombing people could win wars, Harris was also betting on a rank outsider.

The problem for Harris was that, as soon as he turned his attention to targets in Germany, whether they be oil plants or cites, his losses rose alarmingly. New methods for deceiving and jamming German radar defences, held back for D-Day, now became available to Bomber Command. Occasionally the counter-measures would work. Thanks to very successful electronic counter-measures, only four of the 629 bombers involved in the Kiel raid were lost (0.6 per cent loss rate), but the next night 4.6 per cent failed to return from the first raid on Stuttgart, 2.2 per cent the next night against the same target, and on the third attack on the city losses rose to an alarming 7.9 per cent. On 12/13 August Brunswick was the target and twenty-seven bombers, 7.1 per cent, were lost. The German night defences were very much alive and kicking.

Attempts were made to knock out the German night-fighter force on the ground. On 15 August a thousand bombers set off for the airfields in Holland and Belgium from which night-fighter squadrons were believed to be operating. Only three aircraft were lost. It made sense to attack the airfields in daylight, when the night-fighters would be on the ground, but even so there was a certain irony about this being the best way of avoiding the night-fighters they were trying to destroy. The assault appeared to have the desired effect; losses were substantially lower on subsequent attacks. Raids on Stettin and Bremen involved losses of 1 per cent or less, but then began to rise again against Russelsheim on 25/26 August (3.6 per cent), Darmstadt on the same night (3.7 per cent), Kiel on 26/27 August (4.6 per cent), Stettin on 29/30 August (5.7 per cent) and Königsberg (7.9 per cent) the same night.

A new approach was needed. Instead of trying to avoid the enemy, Bomber Command had to find a way of taking on the German night-fighter force and defeating it, as the Americans were doing by day. Fighter escorts had been tried but, despite friend-or-foe systems, the escorts had spent too much time chasing friendly aircraft. The only aircraft that had a good chance of encountering an enemy night-fighter were the luckless bombers they were heading for. Somehow the bombers had to be given the ability to take on the interceptors.

The huge numbers of enemy fighters that American bombers were already claiming to have shot down was not going unnoticed in Bomber Command circles. By comparison, the number of German night-fighters shot down by RAF gunners was insignificantly small. American claims might well be exaggerated but gunners of Lancasters, Halifaxes and Stirlings, viewed with envy the 0.5-inch guns available to their American allies. The excellent Rose rear turret, with its heavy machine guns and 60-degree depression, reached the squadrons in May 1944, but the company lacked the means to build the large numbers required and relatively few bombers were ever equipped with the turret. The less satisfactory Fraser Nash twin-gun FN82 would not become available until the end of 1944.

Even with 0.5 guns bombers were still going to be outgunned by the 20mm cannon German night-fighters carried. Even the frightening density of fire in all directions that entire formations of American bombers could throw in the path of enemy fighters had not prevented heavy losses. The lone RAF night bomber with just its own guns to defend itself was scarcely the same daunting prospect as a mass formation of Flying Fortresses. With the blind spot to attacks from below, German pilots did not need to expose themselves to any enemy fire.[22]

Bomber Command was expecting much of the Village Inn airborne gun-laying turret (AGL(T)), which had been under development since 1942. Expectations were perhaps unreasonably high. The system was considered to be the biggest advance in bomber defence since the introduction of the power-operated turret. Gunners would be able to aim at a radar-generated image of the enemy fighter long before it came within visible range. The problem of identifying friendly planes was resolved by carrying an infra-red lamp, which could be detected by a receiver in the AGL turret.[23] However, in practice, the system just gave the gunner a range of vision closer to what was possible in daylight, which had not done American bombers much good. Fitting Village Inn was given top priority in the autumn of 1943 and what were considered to be successful operational trials took place in early 1944. In June an emergency hand-built batch of 100 were ordered to enable two squadrons to be equipped, while preparations were made for the mass production of the system. The first squadron became operational with the turret early in July 1944.[24]

The system proved far from perfect. On the early models the range of the incoming fighter had to be read out by the radio operator, rather than being visually represented in the gunner's gunsight. The tendency of the radar generated dot to drift, which had dogged the use of this display in the earlier AI Mark V, had never fully been sorted out, which meant that the system's potential range of 1,330 yards could not be exploited. However, it was reasonably accurate up to about 700 yards, which still gave the rear gunner the opportunity to take on the attacking fighter before it came within visual range.[25]

The first month of operations did not produce any startling confirmation of the effectiveness of the equipment, with one enemy plane claimed and one AGL(T)-equipped bomber lost. Even with heavy 0.5-inch guns, there was a reluctance to slug it out with a cannon-armed enemy. Violent corkscrew evasive manoeuvres seemed a better bet than flying straight and level to give the gunner a better chance. For the turret to be effective while the aircraft was manoeuvring some sort of stabilising system was required to stop the radar dot jittering all over the place. Work on this was underway, but nothing was expected in the near future.

There were all sorts of technical problems with the system and the shortage of skilled radar technicians to install and service the equipment did not help. There were also doubts about the effectiveness of the 'identification friend or foe' (IFF) infra-red system. The substance on the lamps that prevented the transmission of visible light was being washed off in clouds and the power of the lamps had to be reduced. Gunners were loath to fire on anything that could not be positively identified as enemy. There were many reports of gunners holding fire on targets that were not transmitting the infra-red signal that did indeed turn out to be friendly. Such instances tended to be blamed on pilots forgetting to turn the IFF equipment on, although it was equally likely that they feared giving away their position to the enemy. Whatever the reason, confidence in the Village Inn system was soon on the wane.[26] There was frustration within the Air Ministry that the true potential of the weapon was not being exploited but, in truth, like so much high-tech radar equipment rushed into service, it was temperamental at best. It was nowhere near sufficiently developed to be the solution to Bomber Command's problems. Only the original two trial squadrons were ever equipped with the AGL(T) turret.

Higher-performance bombers would help. Air Ministry fears that a Lancaster replacement would soon be needed were proving justified but there was nothing on the way that might embarrass even the current crop of German night-fighters. The Windsor flew in October 1943 but, far from being the 'fluke design' Portal had hoped for, the prototype was not even achieving its expected performance. Production would not begin until April 1945 and it would be 1946 before it entered service. It was expected to be faster and to fly further than the Lancaster IV but it was such a marginal improvement that no more than a limited order seemed justified.[27] Indeed, its 300mph cruising speed was scarcely likely to worry the German jet night-fighters that were much closer to entering service than the Windsor. The Merlin 61-powered Lancaster IV was supposed to be reasonably similar to the Lancaster, simplifying production but in practice it was effectively a new plane. This was recognised when, in August 1944 it was renamed the Avro Lincoln.[28] Despite the name change, it was scarcely a new generation of bomber. Even this would not become available until well into 1945. Neither the Lincoln nor the Windsor were in the same class as the Boeing B-29 Superfortress, which was already entering service in the USAAF. If the war stretched beyond 1945 Bomber Command was going to be in serious trouble.

The irony for Bomber Command was that, while the night bombers were still encountering fierce and very effective resistance from the German night-fighter force, American bombers, with the Luftwaffe day-fighters hopelessly stretched trying to cover the front in Normandy and at home, not to mention a catastrophe on the Eastern Front, were roaming with increasing freedom over Germany. Bomber Command was already venturing out by day against targets in France. Operating by day on a more permanent basis was now being seriously considered. This would be a remarkable turn of events. Having been hounded out of daylight by day interceptors, Bomber Command might now be hounded from the cover of darkness by the night-fighters. Targets inside Germany would be much better protected by flak and fighters than targets over France. With the Lancaster unable to reach 20,000 feet, Harris feared they would be sitting ducks for flak.[29] German pilots were in no doubt that Lancasters were sitting ducks for fighters.[30] Standard Spitfires had been able to escort missions over France, but the Air Ministry had always insisted it was quite impossible for Spitfires to fly further.

This myth was in the process of being demolished by the Americans. Before the Normandy landings. Arnold, anxious to increase the escorts available for his day bombers and frustrated at Portal's refusal to do anything about increasing the range of the Spitfire, had asked American engineers to see what they could do with the British fighter.[31] They fitted two leading-edge wing tanks with a total of 33 gallons and an extra tank in the rear fuselage with another 43 gallons, nearly doubling the internal fuel. With two Mustang-style 62-gallon wing drop tanks, total fuel carried was increased to 287 gallons, two-thirds more than a standard Spitfire with the rather clumsy 90-gallon slipper tank. This was enough fuel to allow the Spitfire to fly escort missions to Berlin. It seemed an extraordinary achievement but similar ideas for increasing the range of the Spitfire had been circulating in the Air Ministry since 1940.[32] Just to ram the achievement home, the Americans flew the modified Spitfires over the Atlantic, via Greenland. The Americans were so pleased with what they had achieved, they asked for a couple of Tempests to see what they could do with that fighter.[33]

The British however, were ready with a counter proposal. Fearful of what the Americans might achieve, Vickers had already been asked to see what they could do. Their proposal provided for a 70-gallon tank in the rear fuselage which, with the standard 90-gallon slipper tank, increased fuel to 247 gallons. With these modifications a Spitfire IX was sent to Boscombe Down for comparative trials with the American modified Spitfire. On discovering the Americans had done better, Vickers decided that they, too, could add leading-edge tanks and with the slightly larger Spitfire VIII main tank, could match the Americans.[34] Portal, none too pleased at being proven wrong, found himself having to pen a congratulatory note to Arnold.[35] It really was not particularly difficult to increase the range of the Spitfire.

With their huge 70-gallon rear fuselage tank, Vickers were pushing the internal fuel capacity to the very limit, indeed a tad beyond the limit. The American 40-gallon rear-fuselage tank was about as much as the Spitfire could take and still handle reasonably well. Boscombe Down concluded that until the Vickers rear tank was half-empty the plane would not be much fun to fly for inexperienced pilots but, as an Air Ministry report put it, 'no war is fun'.[36]

For not entirely convincing reasons, the British arrangement, initially without the leading-edge or Spitfire VIII tanks, got the go-ahead. Boscombe Down were unhappy with the wing ribs the Americans had removed to make way for their leading-edge tank. As trials in 1943 had demonstrated, the Spitfire's fuselage slipper tank, which the Air Ministry seemed determined to keep, generated more drag than the teardrop-shaped drop tanks the Americans and indeed other British types were using. The American arrangement for attaching the wing tanks was considered only suitable for ferrying purposes, although surely bringing it up to the standard required for combat missions was not an impossible task.[37] Nor was it particularly difficult to fit a more conventional drop tank to the Spitfire fuselage. Fleet Air Arm engineers aboard HMS *Implacable* rigged up their own attachments so that some American drop tanks they acquired could replace the unpopular slipper tanks their Seafires used.[38] The greater internal fuel of the British version was considered an advantage. Indeed, with the American adaptation, the proportion of external fuel to internal fuel was relatively high which meant not all the external fuel could be used to extend range. However, since half the fuel in the rear tank of the Vickers version had to be used on the outward flight to restore reasonable manoeuvrability, this was not the advantage it seemed. The British version was declared the winner but the Americans were quite content to have won the argument.[39]

The effective radius of action of the Spitfire was increased to nearly 500 miles, just short of Berlin. With the leading-edge tanks and Spitfire VIII main tank, it would be able to operate just beyond Berlin. These were distances the Air Ministry had claimed quite impossible just a few months before, yet they were modifications that required no major re-design and could be applied to existing Spitfires. Not only did the modifications give Fighter Command the ability to escort bombers deep inside Germany, it also gave Spitfires the range to support rapidly advancing ground forces, although no one in the Air Ministry was thinking about that particular application. No remarkable new technology had emerged, the proposed changes could have been made at any stage in the Spitfire's career and

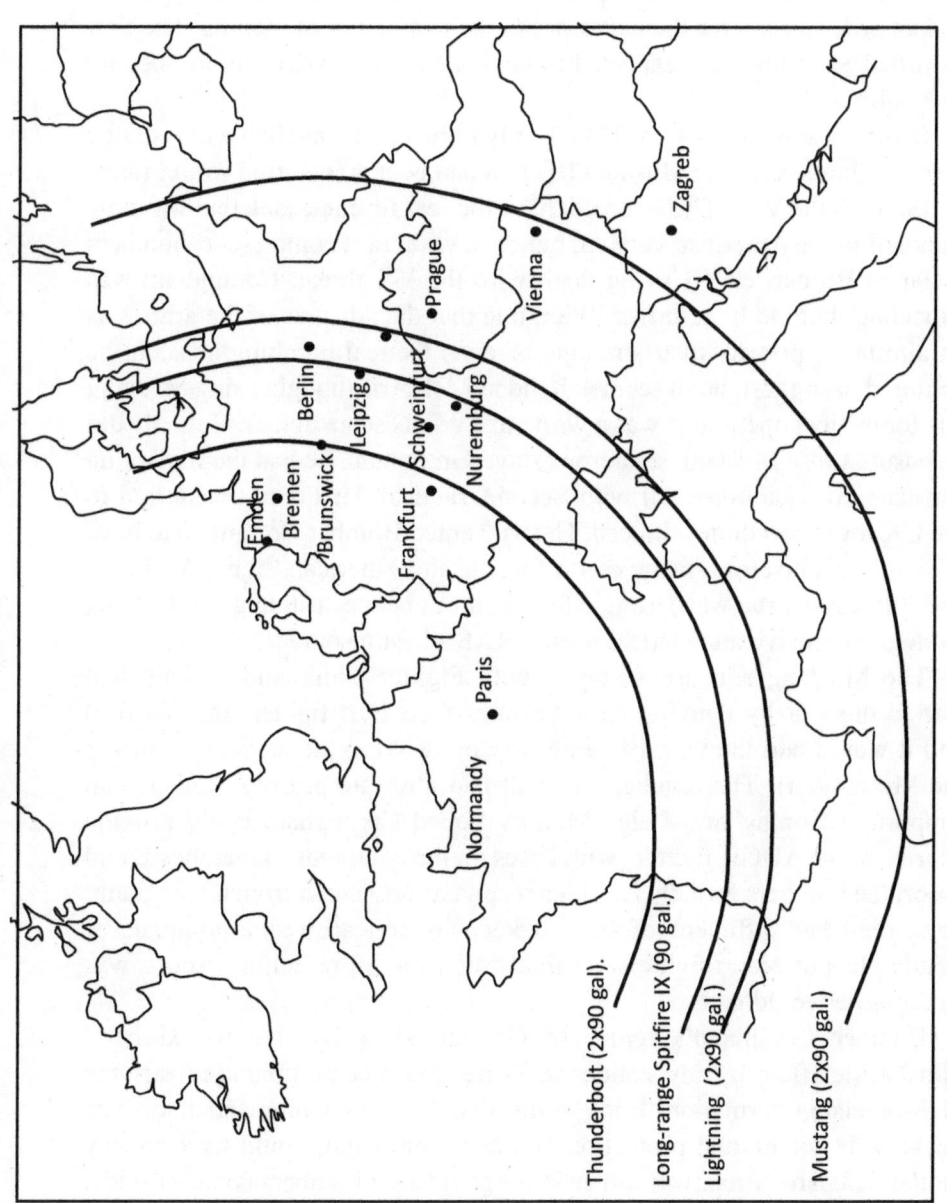

Fighter escort range, 1944.

indeed had been proposed as early as 1940. It was just a question of having the will to do something about the fighter-range problem. In the end, the required modifications to the Spitfire had been completed, tested, approved and an order placed for the necessary tanks in a matter of months. The first modified Spitfires were expected to be available to ADGB before the end of 1944.[40]

In the autumn of 1944, the RAF's only immediately available long-range escort fighters were the Mustang IIIs that had been transferred from France to deal with the V-1s. These did not have the rear fuselage tank that was now standard in the American version, but even without it could escort bombers as far as Brunswick.[41] Having dealt with the V-1 threat, Coningham was expecting them to be returned. 'I assume that the advance of the armies as an aim takes priority over strategic or even tactical bombing as such' he ventured to suggest, but it seemed it did not.[42] Harris thought using Mustang IIIs for tactical operations was a waste of a good escort fighter. Not only did he ensure those Mustang squadrons stayed in Britain, he had the remaining Mustang III squadrons still with Second Tactical Air Force transferred to the UK for escort duties. Indeed, Harris wanted Bomber Command to have its own specialist long-range escort force as the American Eighth Air Force had.[43] It was a three-way struggle for resources between strategic defensive, strategic offensive and tactical for the RAF's best resources.

The Mustang squadrons stayed with Fighter Command. Britain had started the war by denying Allied armies their best fighter (the Spitfire) and it would end the war the same way by denying the tactical air forces the Mustang III. The bomber war still had absolute priority. Rather than supporting Coningham, Leigh-Mallory hoped Coningham could provide shorter-range ADGB fighters with bases on the continent so that they could escort the bombers further. This idea received short shrift from Coningham; he scarcely had sufficient resources to keep his tactical air units going, never mind a fleet of escort fighters. Airfields set aside for refuelling escorts was as far as he would go.[44]

Bomber Command's return to German skies by day would be a ramshackle affair, by any standards. There would be no time to relearn the high-precision formation-flying skills that Bomber Command had once possessed. For mutual protection Bomber Command would have to rely on the defensive firepower rather loose gaggles of bombers could provide. Nor were they easy to escort with the spaced out bombers occupying a stream up to fifteen miles long.[45] Nevertheless, on 27 August 1944, for the first time in the Second World War, a large Bomber Command formation crossed the German frontier in daylight. Some 243 bombers, mostly Halifaxes, attacked a synthetic oil plant in the Ruhr. Sixteen squadrons of Spitfires provided escort. No bombers were lost. The final irony was that heavy cloud cover meant that many of the bombers were relying on Oboe marking by pathfinders. The main advantage of operating by day was the lighter losses rather than the greater accuracy. With American forces also regularly using Oboe and H2S by day, the methods of the two bomber forces were converging.

Whether such loose formations would stand a chance on deeper penetration missions remained to be seen. Even if formation flying skills could be restored, the Lancaster flew lower and slower than the B-17 Fortress and defensive firepower was hopelessly inadequate. To add to their problems the first German jet fighters were appearing. On 26 July, a Mosquito from No. 544 Squadron on a reconnaissance mission over Munich made the first confirmed contact with a German Me 262. The pilot was left in no doubt that the predicted performance of German jet fighters had been no exaggeration. Previously, reconnaissance Mosquitoes had been almost immune to interception. The RAF pilot spotted the jet in plenty of time and opened the throttle to escape but was horrified to discover the German jet closing in on him with ease. Only the most violent manoeuvres enabled the pilot to escape into cloud. Two days later American bomber crews reported sighting tail-less rocket planes rising to intercept. The Me 163 had also arrived. This did not bode well for a daylight offensive. With nocturnal missions looking an equally unattractive prospect, in the late summer of 1944 the future for Bomber Command did not seem bright.

It was events on the other side of the Channel that would come to Bomber Command's rescue. In 1940 the unexpected collapse of the Allied armies in France had thrust Bomber Command back into a central war-winning role. In 1944 it was the success of the Allied armies in France that would go a long way towards enabling Bomber Command to meet the expectations made of it in 1940.

Chapter Twelve

Breakthrough

As Bomber Command prepared to renew its assault over Germany, Montgomery was preparing yet another offensive in Normandy. In mid-July a breakthrough seemed as far away as ever. Despite the huge quantities of military material being thrown into the battle, the Allied armies were still being held within their cramped bridgehead. Montgomery's next attempt on the Caen front, Operation Goodwood on 18 July, was supposed to be followed three days later by a major American drive south from the Saint-Lô region (Operation Cobra). For Montgomery's Operation Goodwood, three armoured divisions with more than 1,000 tanks were lined up to smash through the German defences east of Caen. In the air, there was brute force to match. Once again heavy bombers had a key role to play. Over 1,000 Lancasters and Halifaxes from Bomber Command, together with around 650 Eighth Air Force heavy bombers, would saturate 5,000-by-2,000-yard rectangles on both flanks of the proposed advance. As the aim was to protect the flanks, excessive cratering was considered an advantage. Defences well behind the front line around Soliers and Cagny would also be bombed. In total the heavies would drop over six kilotons of bombs. Half an hour before the forces on the ground began their advance, around 400 medium bombers of the Ninth Air Force began carpet bombing the area the ground forces were to advance into, dropping light and fragmentation bombs to avoid excessive cratering. As the tanks started their advance 300 Second Tactical Air Force fighter-bombers were lined up to strike predetermined targets in their path. In places the German defences were indeed obliterated. Bomber Command attacks were particularly effective against German defences around Colombelles and Mordeville and elements of 21st Panzer were annihilated around Manneville and le Quai.[1] The flanking forces encountered dazed and disorientated defenders. In the centre, where medium bombers had paved the way, for a while the advance went well for the three British armoured divisions, but resistance

BREAKTHROUGH

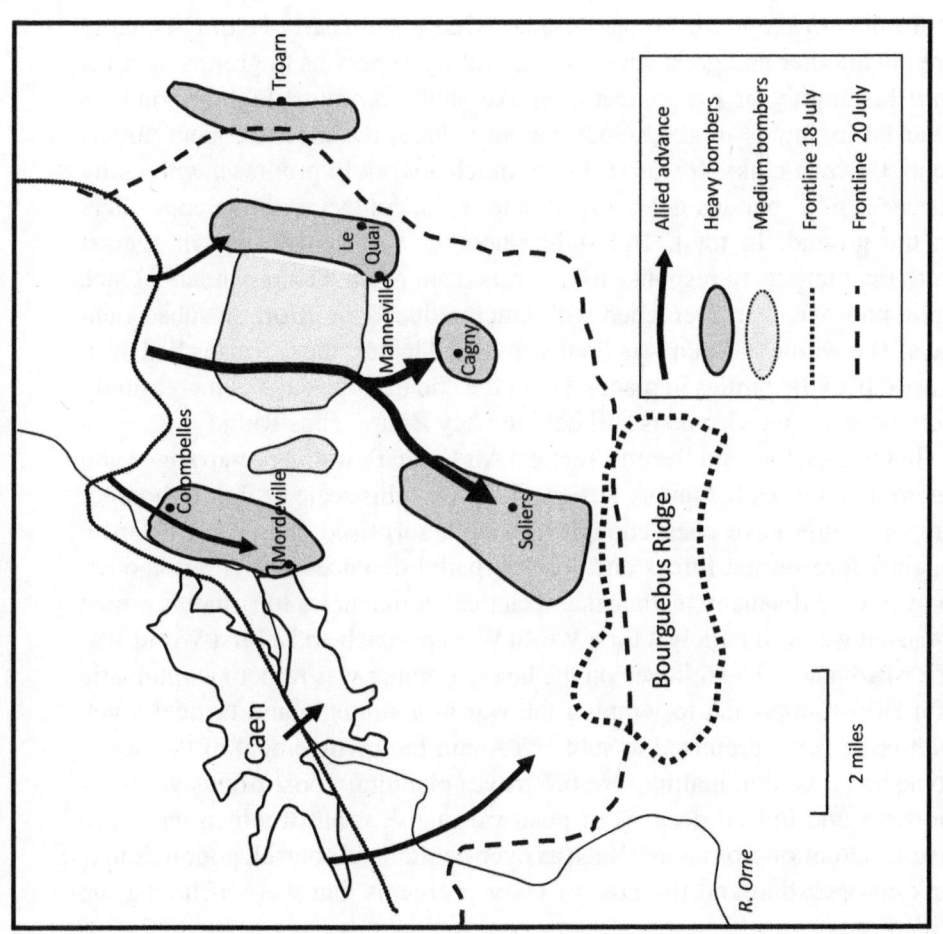

Operation Goodwood, July 1944.

soon stiffened as they reached areas in the rear where the defenders had the time to recover from the bombing.

With American bombers and fighter-bombers responsible for targets beyond the battlefield, the Second Tactical Air Force fighter-bombers were free to focus entirely on air support in the battle zone. Calls for impromptu air support were soon coming in. As an experiment, a couple of Sherman tanks were fitted out as Visual Control Posts in an attempt to enable controllers to keep up with the advance. One was an early victim of enemy fire but another had great success in directing Typhoons to groups of tanks until his supply of red indicator smoke shells ran out.[2] Fighter-bombers attacked in flights of six, sometimes just three, the most frequent targets being German tanks. It was still very much a work in progress, with many instances of Typhoons not being able to make contact with the controllers on the ground. In total, 162 fighter-bomber sorties were flown against battlefield targets in response to requests from ground commanders.[3] Once again poor weather intervened with much reduced air effort on subsequent days. The whole of Caen was finally in Allied hands, the Germans had been pushed back five miles in places, but at the end of three days of increasingly slow progress the Germans still held the key Bourguébus Ridge.

In total, on the 18th Second Tactical Air Force flew 458 pre-arranged and impromptu close air support sorties. On D-Day this scale of fighter-bomber support might have been enough to keep a surprised enemy off balance. Against forewarned forces and well-prepared defences it was not enough to overcome the many technical and tactical deficiencies in Britain's armed forces. It was still largely a First World War approach and a First World War rate of advance. The reliance on the heavy bomber was rather symptomatic of a British approach to winning the war at a strategic and tactical level, with brute force preferred to subtlety. Again the involvement of the heavy bombers was dominating pre-offensive planning, post-offensive post-mortems and indeed decades of post-war analysis, all of which tended to distract attention from issues such as over-centralised control, poor infantry/tank co-operation and the host of other problems that were afflicting the Allied cause.

The Army were full of praise for the work of the heavy bombers. Indeed there was much enthusiasm for developing the heavy bomber as a tactical weapon. There were, however, also some interesting ideas on how the bombing could have been more helpful. Some areas, it was suggested, had been 'overhit' and a less intense bombardment extended over a longer period of time would have been more useful.[4] Again there were interesting parallels with the 1940 French campaign. At Sedan the Luftwaffe had wanted to deliver a single massive blow on French positions, largely because this would be easier to escort, but eventually adopted the Army's preferred option of a less intense bombardment spread over a greater length of time.[5] The aim was to distract and demoralise, not destroy, and the Luftwaffe had done this very successfully. This was what the British Army wanted in 1944. The British Army also felt that safety margins were excessive; the troops on the ground had to be closer to the bomb line to take advantage. All this was more in keeping with a genuine combined arms approach.

Air Force commanders were somewhat taken aback by the Army willingness to accept the friendly fire casualties closer heavy bomber support might involve, indeed a little irritated given it was the air force that would be criticised.[6] Broadhurst was not against carpet bombing support but warned that its use, especially when armies were advancing, had to be approached with great caution. Interestingly, he wanted to avoid the problem of friendly casualties by slowing the advance. He tried to persuade Montgomery to limit the initial advance of his tanks so that the medium bombers had time to turn round and launch a second pattern bombing raid on the defences along Bourguébus Ridge. This was even more of a First World War approach and scarcely in line with Montgomery's hopes of a rapid 'blitz' advance. Montgomery had no intention of waiting for more bombers to arrive and showed no interest in the suggestion.[7] Organising pattern bombing is difficult enough when the front line is fixed; organising a rolling barrage just multiplies the difficulties.

Montgomery might be pleased with the bomber support he was now getting but it was not bringing success proportionate to the huge forces committed. The Allies had finally captured Caen, but what was supposed to be a victory on D-Day had turned into a Pyrrhic victory the best part of two months later. Frustration with Montgomery was growing. Eisenhower complained that the expenditure of 7,000 tons of bombs had brought an advance of seven miles and the Allies could not go on advancing at a 1,000 tons of bombs per mile.[8] Montgomery was not exactly driving the British Army towards a more modern approach to warfare, but the real problem was expecting thousands of tons of bombs to solve all the Allies' woes. In this respect Eisenhower was as guilty as Montgomery.

Montgomery could claim he was sucking German forces onto the Caen front as required by his pre-D-Day plan, although how relevant pre-D-Day plans were seven weeks later is open to question. Eisenhower believed the Allies should now have the materiel advantage to advance just about anywhere they chose. Nevertheless, Goodwood clearly had stretched German resources. The next American push south, Operation Cobra, would also rely on heavy bomber support. So critical was this support considered that the offensive had been put back to 24 July, to provide the heavy bombers with the weather they needed but in so doing lost the advantage of the attack going in while the Germans were still distracted by Montgomery's assault.

The formula was the same as Montgomery had employed around Caen with massive superiority in quantities of equipment and numbers of men all supported by saturation bombing of the German front line. An area more than three miles long and nearly a mile wide along the Périers-Saint-Lô road immediately south of the front line was the designated target for the heavies. To prevent friendly casualties, front-line troops would have to pull back. Bradley needed his troops to be as close as possible to the bombed area and wanted to withdraw just 800 yards. Air force commanders recommended 3,000 yards and, as a compromise, 1,500 yards was agreed.[9] As a further precaution Bradley had demanded the bombers fly parallel to the front line so that at least bombs falling short, the most common source of error, would not hit friendly forces.

It was always galling to surrender hard fought for territory, especially when German soldiers were soon taking the opportunity to occupy the vacated positions in the knowledge that this was probably the best way to avoid the bombing that was coming. But it was a price that had to be paid if the inaccurate heavy bomber was going to be used for close support. The more accurate fighter-bombers would attack enemy positions up to 250 yards beyond the Périers-Saint-Lô Road, the heavy bombers would strike beyond this, or at least try to hit this zone. Once the advance was under way, forward observers in Sherman tanks equipped with VHF radios to communicate with the fighter-bombers above would call in air support when required. The contrast between the two methods could not have been greater. For effective fighter-bomber support it was important to get control systems as far forward as possible in the vanguard of the attack and troops had to get themselves into a position where they needed the air support they could call in. For heavy-bomber close support the first priority for the troops was to get out of the way. The former was an application of combined-arms warfare; the latter was not.

The plan was for the infantry to make the initial inroads into the German defences before the armoured divisions were let loose. On 24 July, with the heavy bombers already on their way, more poor weather caused the

BREAKTHROUGH

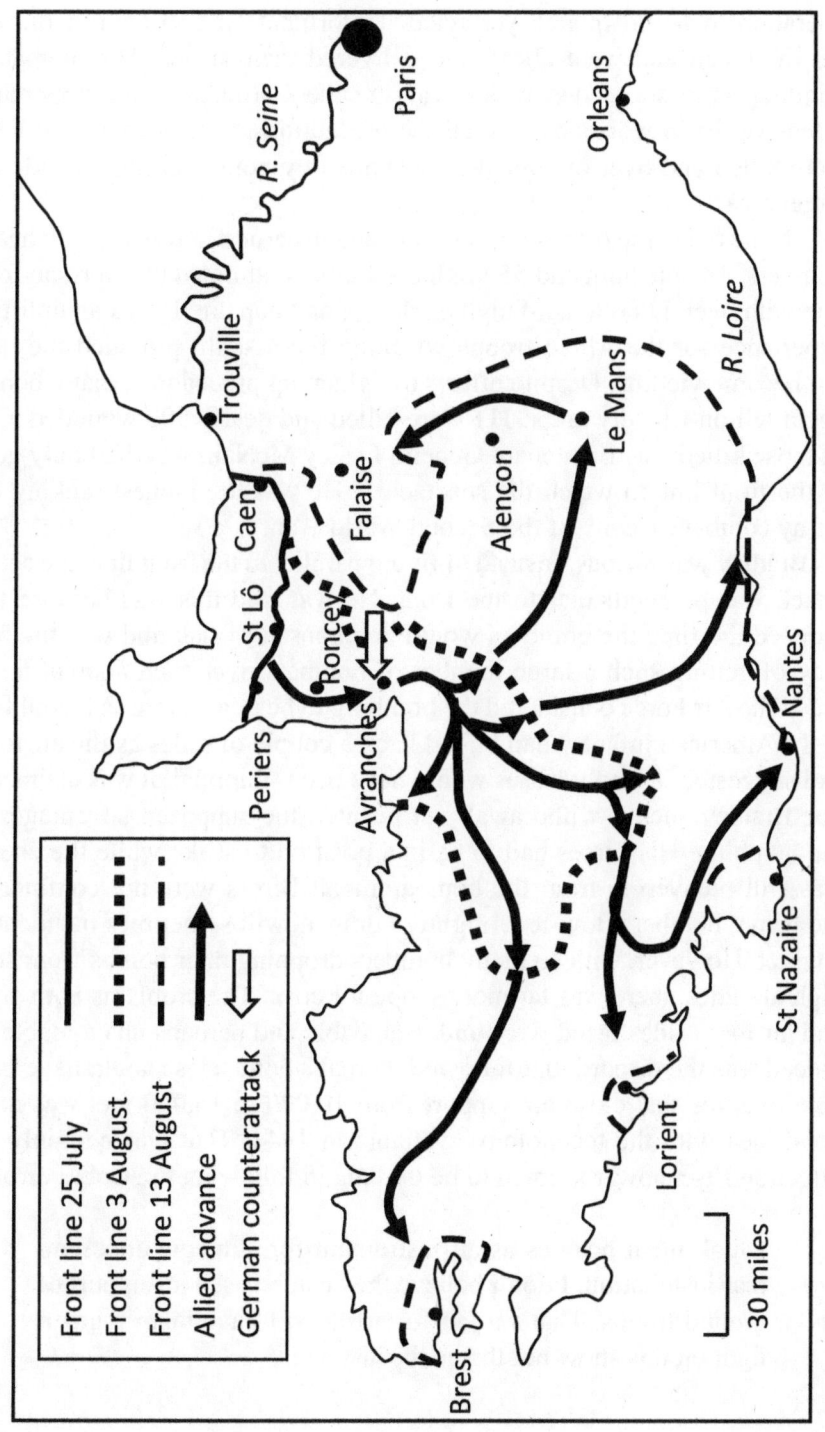

Operation Cobra, July–August 1944.

operation to be postponed yet again. Unfortunately, 550 aircraft did not get the recall and went ahead and delivered their attack. The premature bombing only succeeded in forewarning the Germans of the impending offensive. Even worse, despite all the precautions, twenty-five Americans were killed and over one hundred wounded by bombs falling outside the target area.

The next day the offensive was launched in earnest. Around 1,500 heavy bombers, 380 medium and 550 fighter-bombers saturated the German front line with over 4,000 tons of high explosive and napalm. It was an uplifting experience for the Allied troops watching the assault, provided they did not become victims. Despite efforts to tighten up procedures, many bombs again fell on friendly units; 111 were killed and nearly 500 wounded. One of those killed was Lieutenant General Lesley McNair, who had only gone to the front line to watch the spectacle.[10] He was the highest ranking US Army combat casualty of the Second World War.

Bradley was furious. Instead of flying parallel to the front line, the actual attack was perpendicular to the front. He was told this was because this reduced the time the bombers would be exposed to flak and was the best way of getting such a large number of bombers over such a small target area. The Air Force considered the bombing to be as accurate as it could be. If the American infantry had pulled back a couple of miles as the air force had suggested, friendly losses would have been 'minimal' it was claimed.[11] For Bradley such a withdrawal just negated the supposed advantages of the bombing. His forces had to be in a position to strike while the enemy was still recovering from the bombardment. Errors were not confined to the heavy bombers; low-level fighter bombers will sometimes misidentify a target. However, with so many bombers dropping their bombs from such high altitudes, there was far more scope for error. The problems both army and air force sides faced were understandable and perhaps unavoidable, as indeed was the discord that followed. Perhaps both sides should have been able to agree that close air support from 10,000 to 15,000 feet was not a good idea with the technology available in 1944. That was certainly the direction Eisenhower seemed to be moving in following the Cobra errors.

> I look upon heavies as an instrument for strategic attack on rear installation. I don't believe they can be used in support of ground troops. That's a job for artillery. I gave them a green light on this show but this is the last one.[12]

BREAKTHROUGH

Significantly, Eisenhower did not see fighter-bomber support as another alternative way of supplementing artillery. Everyone was having a problem seeing air options beyond the heavy bomber.

Crude and inaccurate it undoubtedly was and, for some friendly forces, fatal, but where it hit the enemy, it could be devastating. The density of bombing was not uniform. Where few bombs had fallen resistance was immediately stiff. Where bomb density had been high, serious damage was inflicted on the enemy. Panzer Lehr Division was particularly hard hit. Guns and equipment were literally buried, tanks overturned and communications with the rear severed. However, once again, as soon as the carpet bombing was over, even in the most devastated areas, Germans emerged from the churned-up countryside to offer the fiercest of resistance and there were more complaints from the advancing tank commanders that their advance was delayed by cratered roads.[13] At the end of the first day American infantry gains were slight.

Nevertheless the American commander, Major General Collins, decided to commit his mobile forces anyway. Each armoured column was assigned a forward observer in a Sherman tank and would have flights of four fighter-bombers at all times flying 'armour column cover' above it, ready to strike in accordance with instructions from the mobile column below. It was close support of the most intimate kind. The fighter-bombers above the tanks were literally able to warn the tank crews below about what was around the next corner. Enemy tanks just 200 hundred yards ahead of the armoured columns were engaged. It was the 'penny packet' distribution of air forces that attracted the ire of so many air commanders, including Coningham. When a British Army tank commander had suggested something similar to Coningham, he used it as an example of the Army's naïve ignorance.[14]

Attitudes towards decentralising resources depended on how modern warfare was viewed. From an air force perspective, where airpower was seen as the all-important determining factor in war, spreading air resources thinly just meant being weak everywhere. From a combined-arms perspective, however, where the air element was just one component of the overall military package, having a handful of Thunderbolts supporting an armoured column increased military capability out of all proportion to the air resources involved. As was the case with the artillery observing Austers, a small number of aircraft attached to a particular ground unit can make a huge difference to combat efficiency. For the Army, aircraft attacking distant targets while a crucial battle is raging is a wasteful dispersion of resources. Views depend on whether the focus was on airpower as a separate entity or overall military power. What some would view as a dispersion, others would see as a force multiplier.

Control of air resources is always a controversial issue. A healthy dose of pragmatism is usually more useful than dogma. There is no point in centralising Auster resources because they have no value used en masse and army commanders need instant access to the services they offer. Equally, it makes no sense to attach a squadron of Lancasters to each army corps or division. In between these extremes there are grey areas where it depends. Tactically, whenever possible it is better to decentralise control as this increases responsiveness. This is easier to do on the offensive where you have the initiative and know where focus is required. Different circumstances require different thinking. The key is having the control to switch from centralised to decentralised and vice versa as required. By 1918 the Royal Flying Corps and, for the last seven months of the war, the RAF were very good at this. It became more difficult as the two services grew apart and the question of control turned into a turf war. Control becomes a particularly sensitive matter when both services do not believe the other service knows what it is doing.

Under Quesada's system, requests for air support were not going to a command centre in the rear, they were going to an aircraft flying above. The RAF cab-rank system did the same. It was all remarkably similar to the methods No. 8 Squadron RAF was developing in 1918 when it was attached to the Tank Corps. The commander of that squadron was a certain enthusiastic, youthful Major Trafford Leigh-Mallory.[15] It is doubtful such ideas were at the forefront of Leigh-Mallory's mind in 1944. For the commander of the Allied tactical air forces in Normandy such practice belonged to a bygone era when military aviation was in its naive infancy. That naive infancy, however, contained many valuable but long forgotten lessons.[16] In 1944 Leigh-Mallory's 1918 approach was being re-invented as 'armoured column cover' and it would become a standard USAAF mission. For Leigh-Mallory, and many others, the modern approach was the heavy bomber.

The introduction of the tanks into the Cobra offensive did not immediately turn the tide. With some American tanks now equipped to bulldoze their way through the thickest of hedgerows, the Americans were able to gain a greater degree of tactical freedom. Even so, at the end of the second day the desperately outnumbered German forces were still holding on. To the Americans victory seemed as far away as ever. To the German commanders, too, initially the situation seemed no more serious than it had during previous

BREAKTHROUGH

Allied breakthrough attempts. However, the floodgates were creaking. The German defences were not as deep as they were around Caen and fighter-bombers were playing havoc with the reserves attempting to move up to the front. Quite suddenly, resistance began weakening perceptibly. By the 28th one of the American armoured columns had fought its way to the rear of the main German defences south-west of Roncey. The surrounded German forces became the targets for intense fighter-bomber attack. The trapped Germans attempted a breakout to the south-east, but this left the coast free for an American thrust southwards. The Americans were through the last line of German defences and also out of the bocage. By the 30th American forces were in Avranches, the gateway to the French interior. When General George Patton's Third Army poured through the breach Bradley's First Army had created, the Allies had precisely the right commander to take advantage of the situation. The breakthrough was complete

In many ways there was nothing very different about this latest offensive. The assault by the heavy bombers was probably the most successful such assault so far, but by no means decisive. More precise fighter-bomber close air support was growing in scale and precision, but even this cannot claim to be a game-changer. In the end the Germans were simply overwhelmed by sheer weight of numbers. In this final breakout attempt, the Americans had more than 2,000 tanks, the Germans fewer than 200. In the air the odds were even more overwhelming. The continuous build-up of material in the Allied bridgehead was bound to count in the end. It was not a victory for airpower, or Anglo-American strategic or tactical prowess. There was no military finesse, it was just straightforward, simple brute force. For the overstretched German Army it was one defensive battle too many. It was not quick or clever but, in the end, the Allies had succeeded.

Disaster now loomed for the German Army. The dyke had burst and with it went the static warfare in Normandy that negated to some extent the Allied advantage in the air. With the German armies forced into the open in a war of manoeuvre, targets for air attack became more plentiful. American forces were in a position to strike virtually anywhere, but Brittany and the Atlantic ports were still the priority, with a defensive line along the Loire covering the southern flank. Patton ordered his armoured columns to head for Brest, Lorient, Nantes and le Mans. Patton brought with him Brigadier General Otto Weyland's XIX Tactical Air Command. Weyland had been Quesada's deputy and had become another firm advocate of an active air force role on the battlefield. He, too, encouraged the closest possible air support, and was especially aware of the enormous boost to morale such support provided the troops below.¹⁷ He ordered his Thunderbolts to fly ahead of the tanks in search of possible hold-ups, scattering and disorganising German forces wherever they found them.

To the relief of the German commanders, the move they feared most, a pincer around the southern flank of their armies in Normandy, was not actually the initial Allied plan. It was 8 August before the possibility of inflicting a major defeat on the Germans, rather than just occupying territory to the west, was appreciated.¹⁸ By this time many of the American armoured units were scattered over much of north-western France. It gave the Germans time to seal the breach in their lines. To Hitler, the twenty miles that separated the German front line just east of Mortain and the Channel coast looked temptingly narrow. If Avranches could be re-captured the supply lines of the American forces marauding through France would be cut and they could be dealt with at leisure. It looked easy on Hitler's map; in practice it was a tall order. The three panzer divisions extracted from other sectors for the attack mustered just 145 tanks and thity-two self-propelled guns. The failure of the Americans to threaten immediately their southern flank, however, gave the Germans the glimmer of a chance. German commanders made it very clear that, for the counter-attack to have any chance, the German forces would have to be shielded from the Allied fighter-bombers. Maximum flak cover would be provided; the Luftwaffe would do its best

At midnight on 6/7 August the counter-attack was launched. Some early advances were made with German tanks pushing four miles into American positions. Early morning mists proved a more effective counter to Allied air dominance than the Luftwaffe was likely to manage. Once the mist lifted the Allied tactical air forces descended on the German forces. Most German aircraft trying to intervene were engaged by Eighth Air Force fighters operating in the vicinity of their airfields and did not even make it as far as the American IX Tactical Air Command protective ring.

Second Tactical Air Force, with its tank-busting Typhoons, was called in to support the IX TAC, the rocket-armed Typhoons and Thunderbolts concentrating on the armour while other American fighter-bombers took on the supporting columns. The aerial offensive was continuous, with Typhoons attacking, returning to base, refuelling and re-arming, and setting off for the front again. IX TAC flew around 400 fighter and fighter-bomber sorties and Second Tactical Air Force around 300. In the face of fierce resistance on the ground and continuous assault from the air, the German advance ground to a halt. In eight hours the RAF had claimed eighty-four tanks left in flames, thirty-five 'smoking' and twenty-one damaged.[19] If true, the Typhoons had wiped out virtually the entire German tank force.

In fact, the Typhoons achieved nothing like the success they claimed. Days after the assault, Army and RAF survey teams were conducting the first detailed assessment of the effectiveness of the rocket projectile against tanks in combat conditions. Neither team found much evidence of any tanks having been destroyed by rocket fire. The discovery of how few tanks were actually victims of air attack was greeted with disbelief in RAF circles and much ill-feeling between the operational research teams and Second Tactical Air Force commanders ensued. All sorts of arguments were put forward to explain the huge discrepancy between the numbers of tanks RAF pilots had claimed and the wrecks found. These included the suggestion that the very efficient German tank-recovery system had rescued them for repair.[20] The strength of feeling within air force circles was an interesting reaction, given that before the invasion evidence from trials of the ineffectiveness of the fighter in a close air support role had been used to justify not providing such support. The survey of the Mortain battlefield seemed to provide more evidence. However, taking the credit for coming to the rescue and saving the day was just too attractive an opportunity to miss.

The American troops on the ground were in no doubt about the value of the aerial intervention. They were full of praise for the Typhoons. Nor were the Germans in any doubt. The scale of aerial attack was unprecedented. There was very real mayhem caused by the strafing of soft-skinned vehicles and troops. Captured Germans tank crews left their interrogators in absolutely no doubt that they found the rocket projectile a terrifying weapon. Those prisoners who had experienced rocket attacks spoke with awe of the experience, the noise of the diving aircraft, the screeching of the rockets through the air, even the tell-tale igniting flame of the rockets; all had left their mark. Exaggerated talk of the effectiveness of the rocket projectile was clearly rife within the German Army. Many who expressed enormous fear of the weapon had never experienced it personally nor ever seen any damage inflicted by it.[21]

For the tank crews rocket attack was a frightening prospect. They knew it only took one rocket to bring about the certain destruction of even heavily-armoured Tiger or Panther tanks and almost certain incineration for the crew. The fear of air attack restricted movement; no German tank commander was going to expose his crew unnecessarily to rocket attack. There were also signs of panic. Vehicles had been abandoned but often there were no bodies or graves to suggest casualties. The demoralising effect on German troops was far more important than the losses inflicted.[22] The Allies now had their own equivalent of the Stuka. The German dive-bomber had never been that accurate but its screeching air brakes, amplified by sirens, had been the hallmark of the blitzkrieg. Now it was the turn of the inaccurate screeching rockets to have a disproportionate effect on an enemy. The Typhoon was repaying the Wehrmacht in kind. At Mortain the Typhoons had not destroyed many tanks but they had helped win the battle.

The Allied response to the Mortain counter-attack was a classic example of the ability of an air force to focus its effort speedily where it is most required. The American breakthrough had seen close air support used in a decentralised way to speed the advance and a centralised way to defeat a counter-attack. Pragmatism rather than dogma was driving policy. These were the same air forces that had been available to the invading forces on D-Day. The intervention the British and American fighter-bombers were managing in July and August was precisely the sort of intervention that might have made so much difference in June.

It seemed with each new campaign the value of close air support had to prove itself again. There was always a reason why it might have worked in the past but would not work in different circumstances in the future, whether that be terrain, climate or even the nationality of the opposition. Once again, the reluctance to use aircraft on the battlefield was slowly being overcome. But it was still very much a work in progress. Although more than happy to take the credit when close air support was a success, even at a tactical level most air force commanders were still driven by a desire to prove airpower achieved more when operating independently. Developing close air support was still relying on the enthusiasm and drive of front-line commanders like Broadhurst, Quesada and Weyland. In British circles there was still a strong tendency to see close air support as an emergency measure rather than a normal use of airpower.

Throughout the Normandy campaign the fighter-bombers had been the bane of the German armies. They had disrupted German movement and the low-level strafing in particular had sapped morale. However, with the battle becoming more mobile, a healthy respect for Allied airpower was beginning to turn into fear. German troops were beginning to show a greater willingness to surrender. The advancing Allies began to come across increasing numbers of abandoned but undamaged vehicles. There were signs of growing panic. Allied commanders liked to explain the lack of Allied progress by the superiority of the German soldier, rather than the flaws in their own methods and organisation. Germans could fight just as stubbornly and courageously as soldiers from any other nation but, when the pressure became too great, they were as human and vulnerable as any other nationality. Using racial stereotyping to explain setbacks, defeats or victories can distract attention from the real factors that determine success and failure in warfare.

The Allied delay in attempting to close the Normandy pocket from the south had given the Germans the opportunity to strike west, but now that this had failed, and with American forces belatedly swinging round from the south towards Falaise, it was the German forces that were in a precarious position. Switching as much as possible to the Mortain counter-attack meant the situation could not have been more favourable for the Canadians, driving towards Falaise from the north. However, each new attempt to move south still required getting artillery into place and the massive intervention of Allied heavy bombers. Over 1,000 bombers were despatched by Bomber Command on the night of 7/8 August to support the start of the next drive, Operation Totalise. These were followed by around 500 Fortresses. Again there were polite suggestions from the Army that perhaps less intensive bombing over a longer period would be more useful. Again inaccurate bombing was a problem with twenty-five Canadians killed and 131 wounded among the attacking infantry.[23] These problems did nothing to dampen Army enthusiasm, even though there were ample fighter-bombers available with Nos. 83 and 84 Groups flying 2,000 sorties in support of the Canadians from 9 to 12 August.[24] There was simply not the same level of enthusiasm for developing this form of support. The survey teams that investigated the battlefield when the dust had settled were well aware of the lift to morale heavy bombers could provide with their spectacular pre-assault displays of firepower, but insisted they were often causing relatively little damage.[25] In this sense it could be argued that it was no different to fighter-bomber close air support. However, boosting the morale of forces while they are in action is more useful than boosting it while they are waiting to go into action. The effects of heavy-bomber support can wear off fairly quickly on friend and foe.

By the 10th German armoured strength was down to just thirty-five tanks while the Canadians still had 700. Yet the next day the Canadians pulled their armoured units back to regroup for the next move forward. It seemed no advance could be attempted without massive saturation bombing. The Allied armies were not over-reliant on airpower, but they were over-reliant on the heavy bomber. Any form of fire support that required an initial retreat was not setting the right tone for finishing off any enemy who was clearly in desperate straits. Just as ground forces often found themselves battling their way through the rubble and the carnage the bombers had created, so the planners and strategists found it difficult to see through the bomber haze that had descended on Anglo-American military thinking. Army commanders seemed quite happy to accept the problems that came with carpet bombing.

On 14 August the Canadians were supported by another 800 RAF heavies, with short bombing killing thirteen and wounding fifty-three. As a result of depressingly incompetent planning, Bomber Command decided to use yellow target markers, the same colour the Canadian troops were using to indicate their forward positions.[26] Despite Eisenhower's 'last one' avowal following the friendly fire casualties in the Saint-Lô offensive, he seemed to have no objection to his commanders continually turning to the heavies.

Manpower problems encouraged this tendency. All commanders want to minimise casualties but Britain and Canada had good reason to be particularly anxious. The armies of both countries were facing severe manpower crises. Army commanders had to be very mindful of casualties, especially among the infantry. The idea of saturation bombing doing the fighting for the infantry was as much welcomed by the War Office and Canadian authorities as it was by the front-line soldiers. Whether massive firepower saved lives was another matter. There were plenty of examples from the First World War where the heaviest of artillery barrages had just been the prelude to horrendous infantry casualties. Conversely, commanders using initiative and grasping opportunities as they arise do not necessarily incur heavy losses.

No one would have created such a bludgeoning weapon for tactical air support but the bomber fleets were there, ready to use. It was too easy for Allied commanders to turn to the heavy bomber. The result was a vicious circle. Ponderous army tactics lent themselves to ponderous heavy bombing which in turn made any advance even more laboured. The heavy bomber was doing more harm than good. A German assessment of British methods that had fallen into Allied hands picked up on the over-reliance on firepower. The report emphasised the poor offensive qualities of the infantry and the reliance on heavy artillery and air support. Tedder was quick to cite it as support for his own low opinion of the British Army.[27] But what Tedder chose to see as over-reliance on the Air Force and airpower was more accurately an over-reliance on blanket barrages from air and ground. The German army had a very healthy respect for the precision Austers brought to artillery fire and the effectiveness of low-flying fighter-bombers.

BREAKTHROUGH

It was not until the night of 16/17 August that the Germans abandoned any hopes they had of holding the Normandy front and began pulling out of the pocket. Any lingering doubts about the wisdom of this move had been removed by the invasion of southern France on 15 August. The German objective now was to extract as much as possible from southern and western France and hopefully re-establish a defensive line along the Seine. From the south Patton's forces were wheeling round towards Falaise as quickly as they could to join up with the British and Canadians advancing from the north. By this time the American advance meant they had a huge front to cover. As Patton swung north-eastwards, units were still heading west towards the Atlantic. To the south there was the vast front along the Loire to cover. This was where airpower came into its own. Constant patrols along the Loire could warn of any threat developing, removing the need for substantial ground forces to secure the flank. Airpower was providing the opportunity to focus forces where they could do most damage, and Patton was taking full advantage,

It was difficult for the artillery to keep up with the rapid advance but tactical air support was able to make up for this deficiency. The close support advancing forces were getting on all fronts was now far more substantial than at any previous stage of the campaign. Brigadier General Richard Nugent's XIX TAC was the third USAAF tactical air force to join the fray. This was supporting Ninth Army's attempts to defeat German forces holding out in the Brittany ports and Nugent was as keen to provide genuine close air support as Quesada and Weyland. Having aircraft in the air waiting for targets cut response time, special fluorescent panels displayed by forward troops helped reduce friendly-fire incidents and assigning specific units to particular sectors of the front helped pilots become familiar with the local terrain. In vicious house-to-house fighting during the battle for Brest, Thunderbolts were being called in to hit individual houses just 100 to 150 yards in front of advancing American troops.[28]

There had been no major change of heart in USAAF circles; strategic bombing was still most important and full independence from the Army still the long-term aim. It was just that tactical air support was needed, it clearly worked and the Americans had the industrial and manpower resources to deliver it without it wrecking their plans to expand their strategic bomber fleet. The Americans could afford to be pragmatic without abandoning their ideals. Quesada, Weyland and Nugent were happy to ignore the provisions and priorities laid out in their USAAF FM 100-20 field manual and, when necessary, decentralise control by attaching air units to specific ground forces.[29] It was perhaps easier for USAAF commanders to do this, as a temporary expedient, because they were still part of the army and there was no constitutional issue. For RAF commanders it would have been an abrogation of their right to control everything that flew.

Broadhurst was just as enthusiastic as his American counterparts about providing the Army with the closest possible support, but did not have such ample resources at his disposal, nor the independence American commanders seemed to have acquired from their Ninth Air Force commander, Brereton. Nor indeed with Montgomery at the helm, was there the attacking, risk-taking frame of mind in which tactical air support could flourish. However, with his cab-rank system and Visual Control Posts, Broadhurst too was effectively decentralising control.

With Patton driving north towards Falaise, soon just twelve miles separated the British and Canadians in the north and the Americans in the south. If the gap could be closed, it would be the first time the western Allied Armies had surrounded a substantial German force with a twin-prong pincer movement. Yet there was a strange lack of conviction about the need to close the gap. Bradley seemed aware enough of the opportunity that was beckoning. It was he suggested 'an opportunity that comes to a commander not more than once a century', although surely encirclements in the Second World War were a lot more frequent than that.[30] It was not an opportunity Bradley was willing to grasp. Much to Patton's frustration, Bradley ordered him to halt his advance. He feared the encircled forces would be too powerful to contain and spoke of the dangers of Allied units in the two prongs firing on each other as they approached.[31] They were scarcely sound reasons for not taking this 'once a century' opportunity.

With the Canadians struggling to close the gap from the north, and the strongest desire on all sides to minimise infantry casualties, both Montgomery and Bradley were happy to leave the task of finishing off the enemy to their air forces. It was not so dissimilar to Hitler's decision to halt the German advance on Dunkirk in 1940, although then it had been the preservation of the panzers rather than infantry that had been the motivating factor. The Luftwaffe had failed to destroy the BEF and the limitations of airpower operating alone had been exposed as the British and French armies made their escape. Too much had been expected of the Luftwaffe. In 1944 far greater resources were available to the Allied air forces but it still made no sense to try and destroy an army tank by tank, column by column, if the entire force could be encircled and rounded up. Just as Tedder had so often complained, the soldiers were asking the airmen to do their job for them. However, this time it was a task air commanders relished as a chance to show what airpower could do on its own. This was how the RAF commanders liked to fight their battles – clear targets, no need to get too involved with what the forces on the ground were doing and at the end of it a victory the air force could take sole credit for.

On the 17th the focus of fighter-bomber attacks switched from the German forces blocking the advance of the Canadian and American troops attempting to close the pocket to the German columns pulling out of the pocket. A bomb line was established to the east of the Allied forces and Second TAF was given free rein to attack any columns to the east of this line. Effectively the Allies were allowing the Germans to escape and then trying to destroy them. Mists on the morning of the 17th prevented the fighter-bombers operating but when those cleared the fleeing German columns were subjected to continuous attack. With American Lightnings, Thunderbolts and Mustangs joining Spitfires and Typhoons Not all the air strikes were well directed. Between 16 and 18 August the Canadians recorded fifty-two attacks by Allied fighter-bombers on friendly forces advancing east, well to the north of the German pocket.[32] Clearly better ground air coordination was still required.

Attacking retreating columns might look an attractive proposition to the commanders, but it was not quite so attractive to the pilots who had to fly the missions. A compact concentration of high-value targets meant anti-aircraft defences were bound to be strong. Nos. 83 and 84 Groups lost twenty-five planes on the 18th and another fifteen the next day, mostly to flak.[33] Flak was a growing problem that the Air Ministry was still not showing much interest in tackling. Enemy fighters were less of a threat to the fighter-bombers. The Luftwaffe tried to intervene in the battle zone but apparently only succeeded in getting fighters into the Falaise area on one occasion. This was on the 17th when III/JG 27 bounced and shot down four out of seven Typhoons of No. 184 Squadron, a reminder of the inadequacy of the Typhoon as a fighter.[34] The problems of the German fighter force were dramatically illustrated the next day when Mustangs of No. 315 Squadron pounced on a formation of JG 2 taking off from their base, shooting down no fewer than eight.[35] The air threat had been largely dealt with but the Allies could not claim complete air superiority until the flak threat had also been dealt with.

By the evening of the 19th the gap between the Canadians in the north and the Americans in the south had been closed to just three miles. On the 20th what would appear to be the first close-support mission for some days was flown when Typhoons were called in to deal with a group of German tanks attempting to keep the escape route open a little longer. Four squadrons attacked in the afternoon, followed by two more in the evening.[36]

By the evening of the 20th roads out of the pocket had been blocked and by noon the following day all movement out of the pocket ceased. Fifty thousand troops were captured. Perhaps as many as 40,000 escaped. Many of the latter were rear support personnel but there were also battle-hardened veterans. In truth the forces in Normandy were stretched so thinly and had suffered such heavy losses, there was not a huge number of men or much material that could escape. It was a defeat but in terms of prisoner count and lost equipment, not a defeat on the scale being suffered in Russia. The Soviet summer offensive had destroyed the German Army Group Centre with the 200,000 captured. The southern sector of the Russian front then collapsed yielding another 100,000 prisoners.

The Falaise Gap was hailed as a triumph of Allied airpower and in particular the rocket-firing Typhoon. The rows of burnt-out and abandoned vehicles seemed to stand testament to the success of the aerial assault. It was, however, a success that was again soon being called into question by the operational research units, picking their way through the carnage left by the air force. As at Mortain, the investigators found little evidence of tanks or indeed any vehicles that had actually been destroyed by rocket fire. Out of 301 tanks and eighty-seven armoured vehicles examined, only thirteen had definitely been destroyed by rockets. Such was the apparent inaccuracy of the rocket it was estimated that it would require 140 rocket projectiles to have a 50 per cent chance of destroying a Panther. Most of the vehicles were either abandoned or destroyed by their own crews. The carnage inflicted on soft-skinned vehicles had largely been due to machine-gun and cannon fire.[37] It was more evidence that fixed guns were still the most accurate weapon available and more evidence that the 40mm cannon had perhaps been discarded a tad prematurely.

Again, the discrepancy between tanks claimed destroyed and tanks found destroyed caused bitter controversy. RAF commanders bristled at any suggestion that their air force had not wiped out the opposition and won a glorious victory. It was another victory in the tactical domain, but in air force philosophy the key distinction was not so much tactical versus strategic as collaborative versus independent. Falaise was another example of what airpower could do on its own. It was far too precious an achievement for the triumph to be brought into question by scientific analysis. Air Force attempts to explain away the discrepancies highlighted in the Mortain and Falaise studies provoked an irritated response from the scientific investigators. The only alternative explanation, they suggested, was that the 'the fairies in Normandy' had removed destroyed tanks at Mortain and substituted armoured troop carriers for tanks in the Falaise pocket.[38] 'It is a fact that the RPs [rocket projectiles] destroy very few tanks and comparatively few vehicles and [it] is not an accurate weapon.'[39]

The findings of the operational research teams also made little impression on the growing enthusiasm for the rocket projectile within the Army. G (Air) section, the 21 Army Group section responsible for developing and advising on air policy, felt such scientific analysis and arithmetic conclusions were misleading.[40] They had a point. The rocket projectile may have been inefficient in a purely statistical way but this did not make it an ineffective weapon. If crews were being induced to abandon their tanks by the threat of rocket attack then the weapon had achieved its purpose. If the Germans had instituted operational research teams these would have discovered that in the early days of the war the Stuka rarely caused much physical damage and would have come to the same conclusion about the value of the dive-bomber. The Ju 87, however, was indisputably a successful weapon. Allied air commanders spent years trying to persuade troops how ineffective the dive-bomber was but the average soldier remained steadfastly unimpressed by their arguments. Now the experts were trying to persuade the Army and Air Force that the one weapon that really struck fear in enemy hearts was equally ineffective.

Nevertheless, G (Air) was getting a little carried away in its enthusiasm for the weapon. It was wrong to believe the rocket was 'inherently accurate' but it was a weapon that could destroy even the heaviest tank. G (Air) was right to point out that missile systems were in their infancy and the technology had enormous potential. The solution was not to abandon it but to make it more accurate. The Army made it very clear that the current rocket should remain an anti-tank weapon until something better emerged. Despite its inaccuracy, the Americans and Germans were sufficiently impressed to adopt similar weapons, although never on the same scale as the British. Everyone was aware that something better was required.

The Allies had won the Battle of Normandy but it was scarcely a glorious triumph. It was a victory that could and should have been quicker and more decisive. In the closing stages, both Army and Air Force commanders were guilty of seeing air support as a substitute for offensive action on the ground rather than a tool for facilitating offensive action. Both, for their own different reasons, were happy for the air force to have the opportunity to complete the victory.

For Army and Air Force commanders the Normandy campaign had been a triumph for the Typhoon. The aircraft was no longer a failed fighter to be palmed off on any branch of the Air Force that could make do with second best; it was a valuable close-support fighter that was terrorising a resilient foe. With its rugged airframe, cannon armament and excellent lifting capability, it had a lot going for it. Yet, the Typhoon was scarcely ideal for its new role. Like the Hurricane before it, it fell between two stools. It did not have the qualities to fulfil the fighter element of the fighter-bomber role but nor was it the specialist ground-attack aircraft the War Office wanted. A quality fighter-bomber would always be needed – a plane with excellent fighter and ground-attack capabilities – and the Tempest II, with its air-cooled engine and higher performance, would provide this when it became available. The losses to flak reinforced the War Office message that there was also a need for the armoured ground-attack plane to supplement the fighter-bomber, to operate where unarmoured fighter-bombers dare not go.

The immediate short-term need, however, was for more Typhoons. Losses as a percentage of sorties flown had been low, around 1 per cent. However, sortie rates were high; in intense periods pilots might fly several sorties a day, so losses soon built up. With tactical-reconnaissance losses also heavier than expected, a replacement for the Allison-powered Mustang I/II was also becoming more urgent and the Typhoon was lined up as the replacement. It had not been so long ago that the Air Ministry had been wondering what it could possibly do with all the Typhoons it was acquiring. The plan was to phase out the Typhoon just as soon as the Meteor was ready to enter production. Tempests were supposed to take over from the Typhoon but labour shortages were slowing Tempest V deliveries and the Tempest II was not expected for some time. The Air Force needed more Typhoons.

Even before the invasion Coningham was becoming concerned about a possible shortage of Typhoons.[41] Spitfires were being prepared for fighter-bomber duties to make up for the potential shortage, but they were not as rugged, did not provide such a stable gun platform and could not carry as many bombs or rockets as a Typhoon. Coningham thought it 'ridiculous' that his best fighter-bomber was being siphoned off into reconnaissance squadrons and he was being asked to make do with less satisfactory Spitfires instead.[42] Just to add to the controversy, No. 268 Squadron, the first tactical-reconnaissance squadron to get the Typhoon, was making it clear that they considered the fighter unsuitable and wanted Mustangs or Spitfire XIVs.[43]

With full-scale fighting underway and reconnaissance squadrons playing a vital role, the case for providing these squadrons with the best available aircraft was much stronger. Coningham wanted them to have Meteor jets. He was told they lacked the range, although a more obvious problem was that the handful of existing Meteor Is were scarcely suitable for any combat duties and the planned production version, the Meteor III, had only just taken to the air.[44] The next best option was the Spitfire, preferably the latest Mark XIV or, failing that, the Mark IX. The former were like gold dust. The arrival of the Packard-built Merlin 61s from the United States was easing the shortage of the latter but even so there were still not enough quality single-seater fighters.

One of the complications in the debate over whether the Typhoon should be used for reconnaissance or as a fighter-bomber was that the fighter-bomber version was not one of the 'designated types' – the five aircraft (Lancaster, Halifax, Mosquito, Spitfire, Tempest) the production of which could not be reduced for any reason. The photo-reconnaissance version of the Typhoon, however, had been added to the list, ensuring anyone working on them was not called up. Hawkers were reluctant to start turning out Typhoons as fighter-bombers if it risked having their workforce sent off as infantry replacements. Nor did there seem much chance of getting the fighter-bomber version of the Typhoon 'designated' as, the MAP would argue, its replacement, the Tempest, was on the designated list.[45] In the summer of 1944 Britain found itself in the rather odd situation where the one aircraft that was making the most significant contribution to winning the battle in Normandy could not make its way into the 'designated' category.

An active front in north-west Europe was exposing Britain's rather dubious production priorities. Being on the designated list was no guarantee that sufficient were being built; it just meant existing production was not going to be cut. The Spitfire and Mosquito were the two outstanding British designs of the Second World War and both were on the designated list but neither was being built in sufficient numbers to meet Britain's needs worldwide, as Arnold discovered when he decided the USAAF could do with a few Mosquitoes. In 1943 he wondered if he could have 'a few hundred' for reconnaissance, not, he felt, an unreasonable request given the thousands of aircraft the Americans were supplying to the British. It is not clear who was the more stunned, Portal by the casual request for such a huge number or Arnold by Portal's offer of two.[46]

Britain was fortunate to have a more generous ally on her side. Substantial Lend-Lease supplies of fighters, light and medium bombers to RAF and Commonwealth squadrons in Europe and the Far East, not to mention a host of aircraft for the Fleet Air Arm, helped make up for the aircraft the four-engine bomber priority was preventing Britain from building. Without American generosity the error would have been more glaring. It was too late for Britain to alter production priorities, but there were some signs that now the armies in north-west Europe were in action, attitudes were changing. Common sense prevailed over the use of the Typhoon and these would now be delivered solely as fighter-bombers. The tactical-reconnaissance squadrons would get their Spitfires – not time-expired Spitfire Vs, but Spitfire IXs and, in an even more dramatic change of attitude, the very latest Griffon Mark XIV version.

Meanwhile, on the Western Front, the German retreat continued. By the time the Falaise Pocket was closed American forces had already established a bridgehead over the Seine. There was now a desperate race between the advancing Allies and German forces pulling out of all regions of France. The Germans soon abandoned any attempt to make a stand on the Seine. It became a race for the German frontier where the defences of the Siegfried Line and the natural barrier of the Albert Canal running through Belgium provided the Germans with the best chance of re-establishing a defensive line. Even this was soon beginning to look optimistic. Allied armoured forces were advancing along the entire front virtually unopposed. With total control of the skies, Allied commanders could operate with the sort of freedom German commanders had possessed in the Wehrmacht's heyday. On 25 August Paris was liberated. The V-1 units were swept out of France and beyond range of London. On 3 September Allied forces reached Brussels

The advance was so rapid, the air forces had difficulty keeping up. The introduction of 'contact cars' helped. These were armoured cars or half-tracks with sufficient radio equipment to operate as a Visual Control Post. However, the limited radius of action of the Spitfire and Typhoon meant that there were not many aircraft for them to control. Coningham fumed at not having more planes with the range of the Mustang. Indeed, his remaining Mustang III squadrons had been transferred to the UK for bomber escort missions.[47] Coningham often found himself having to ask the Americans for help. Even for the longer-range American fighter-bombers, the situation was not ideal; with airfields so far in the rear, response time was bound to suffer. It took days to prepare or repair the large airfields high-performance combat aircraft required by which time, at the rate the Germans were retreating, airfields even further forward were required. The only RAF aircraft capable of a rapid move forward were the Austers, with their ability to operate from any reasonably-sized field. An Auster-type aircraft with a combat capability, as the War Office Air Department had wanted, would have been ideal.

On 4 September, the major prize of Antwerp fell, its occupation so rapid that the normally thorough Germans did not have the time to destroy the port facilities. A bridgehead was established across the Albert Canal and farther east American patrols crossed into German territory near Aachen. It was an astonishing advance with all sorts of negative consequences for the Germans. Not only had they lost the V-1 launching sites, they would not now be able to deploy their V-2 ballistic missiles from France. Indeed, it was difficult to see how the Allied armies pouring towards the German frontier from northern and southern France could be stopped.

Allied politicians and military commanders began talking of the war being over before Christmas. Montgomery was suddenly willing to throw caution to the wind by focusing everything on a single drive through Holland and Germany to Berlin. On the face of it, Holland, with its intricate canal systems, not to mention the massive Maas and Waal waterways, looked the least attractive way of entering Germany. However, beyond these obstacles lay the tempting tank-friendly plains of northern Germany. There were plenty of problems with such a plan, not least of which was supporting the rapidly advancing spearhead with the RAF's short-range fighter-bombers. One hundred miles across the Channel had been a reasonably comfortable distance, the rapid 250 mile advance to Brussels was causing problems. A further 400 mile leap to Berlin would be impossible to cover. Either Montgomery did not appreciate the problems or he did not see air support as a crucial factor in such an extensive and rapid advance.

Eisenhower showed no interest in the project, so Montgomery came up with a less ambitious, but still audacious plan. Since the initial involvement of Allied airborne forces on D-Day these elite formations had been kicking their heels, waiting for another opportunity to demonstrate their value. Suddenly there was a possibility the war might end without them ever having another chance. Brereton had been transferred from Ninth Air Force to command the British, American and Polish First Allied Airborne Army, with Lieutenant General Frederick Browning commanding the I British Airborne Corps. Montgomery's plan was to use these to capture bridges over the various waterways between the Allied front line and Arnhem. This would create a clear run for Lieutenant General Brian Horrocks's Second Army XXX Corps, supported by VIII and XII Corps, to drive as far as the Zuyder Zee, cutting off any German forces in western Holland and providing the ideal launch pad for the envelopment of the Ruhr. The proposal gained a new significance when, on 8 September, from launch sites in western Holland, the first V-2 ballistic missile crashed into London. If Montgomery's plan succeeded, these launching sites would fall into Allied hands. It was bold, so bold that it never occurred to the Germans that this was one of the options the Allies were considering. The Allies would certainly have surprise on their side.

It was assumed that the broken forces of the Wehrmacht would not be able to put up any effective opposition. Intelligence was picking up information that elements from two panzer divisions were refitting in the Arnhem area, but the warnings were not taken seriously enough for them to be passed on to the commanders directly involved in the operation. Even if they had, it is doubtful that they would have dampened enthusiasm for the operation. The Allies, apparently on the brink of outright victory, would be committing their toughest troops, which would surely prove too strong for any remnants of the German armies that had survived the 300-mile retreat to the German border.

On 10 September, Montgomery got the go-ahead from Eisenhower for Operation Market Garden. Both knew the operation would have to be launched as soon as possible if the Allies were to take advantage of the existing confusion within the German ranks. Montgomery assured Eisenhower that provided his armies were given priority with supplies, the operation could begin in as little as five days. Plans for the operation were drawn up in great haste. The operation was planned and controlled by First Allied Airborne Army based in Britain. The outline of the plan was agreed the same day Eisenhower had given his approval. Detailed planning followed, but not with any representatives from Second Tactical Air Force. Apparently bad weather had prevented anyone flying over.[48]

Crucial decisions made at this meeting included the restriction that No. 83 Group would not be allowed to operate in the same area that troops were being dropped or re-supplied. It was feared that there might be confusion between the British- and continental-based formations and, perhaps more justifiably, there was the risk that troops dropped in the wrong area might

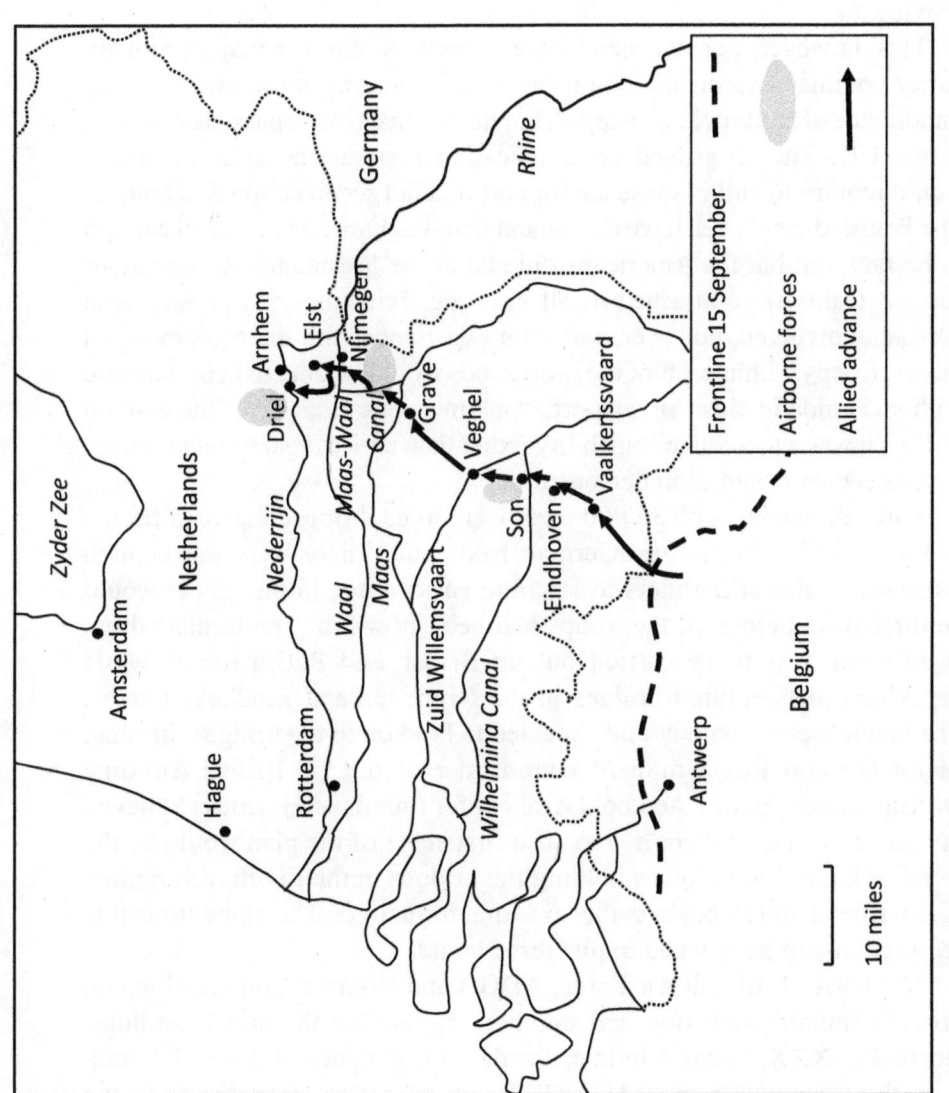

Operation Market Garden, September 1944.

come under attack. It was a very significant restriction. Without the full range of artillery support, the airborne forces would need all the air support they could get. It was going to take three days to land all the troops and the need to re-supply the forces landed, would limit the opportunities to provide it.

This, however, was not seen by the airborne forces as a major problem. Army commanders on the continent were becoming more aware of the importance of battlefield air support but this seems to have passed unnoticed in the UK. The air/ground communication systems the airborne forces would require to call in close air support had not received much attention. The British did not even have equipment that was light and powerful enough to be flown in but the Americans did and at the last minute American air support teams were attached to all airborne formations.[49] The American personnel involved, however, had little experience with the equipment. In theory, troops within each of the drop zones would be able to communicate with and guide in close air support attack missions but, as was the case on D-Day, it was a theoretical capability rather than a tried, tested and practised one, as events would soon demonstrate.

Three divisions, with 35,000 men, were to be dropped between fifteen and sixty miles behind the German front line. There were not enough transport planes and gliders to land the entire force in one go; it would be three days before all the troops had been flown in. The farthest drop, at Arnhem, was to be carried out by British and Polish troops while the Americans captured bridges in the Nijmegen and Eindhoven areas. The paratroopers could not be expected to hold on to the bridges for long. Major General Roy Urquhart, commander of the 1st British Airborne Division, believed he could hold Arnhem for four days. Horrocks believed his forces would be there in two. The first stage of the plan would be the relief of the airborne forces holding the bridges in the Eindhoven region, some fifteen miles beyond the existing front line. The tight timetable required this to be reached in just three hours.

The USAAF Eighth Air Force, ADGB and Bomber Command would provide fighter protection and bomber support for the aerial landings. Horrocks' XXX Corps would have the full support of No. 83 Group with the Canadian Army's No. 84 Group, now also operating from the continent, on standby to help if required. However, it was not a clear-cut division in responsibilities between British- and continental-based air units. Elements of No. 83 Group were also expected to operate over the landing zones.

BREAKTHROUGH

Again as on D-Day, most attention focused on actually getting the troops there. There was good reason to be concerned; the slow transports would be extremely vulnerable to fighters and flak. The most meticulous preparations were made to ensure known flak sites in the path of the lumbering transports were suppressed if they could not be avoided. Luftwaffe bases would also be targeted and the heaviest possible fighter escort would be provided. These precautions were all justified but, once again, defensive requirements tended to draw attention away from the equally urgent need to support the troops once they were on the ground.

During the night 16/17 September, nearly 300 aircraft of Bomber Command attacked flak batteries on the route and Luftwaffe bases in the general area. The next morning there were more attacks on flak batteries by over 800 B-17s of the Eighth Air Force. Another one hundred planes from Bomber Command struck coast batteries in Walcheren. On the morning of the 17th, just before the first troops landed at Arnhem, Typhoons flew around 100 sorties against gun positions in the area. One thousand five hundred transport planes and nearly five hundred gliders transported the first wave of troops. It was a daylight operation, mainly because dispersion had been a problem during the Normandy nocturnal drops. Another advantage was that, rather conveniently, the German day-fighter force was now much less of a threat than the night-fighter force. Nearly 1,200 escort fighters were on hand to ensure there was no Luftwaffe revival. The Allied air forces were making extraordinary efforts to ensure the airborne forces arrived safely but once the troops were on the ground and at their most vulnerable, the air support would end. It was all very reminiscent of the Normandy landings. Amongst other difficulties the airborne troops had to contend with was an active Luftwaffe. German efforts rose to over 300 sorties a day on the 18th. It could make no impression on the hordes of fighters escorting the transports but succeeded in adding to the confusion on the ground with strafing and bombing attacks.[50]

Horrocks' land forces driving towards them were more fortunate, with effective air support from the start. The plan was for Guards Armoured Division to advance behind a creeping artillery barrage. As soon as this was lifted a Typhoon squadron would attack any targets on the road ahead of the Guards. Then ten fighter squadrons would form a cab rank, which would be called in as required by the Forward Control Post in an armoured vehicle with the lead tanks. Once the guards passed beyond Valkensvaaard the air support would become more problematic as operations would be too close to the drop zone for the American 101st Division in the Eindhoven area.

At 14.35 on the 17th Horrocks launched his drive north. Swift progress was anticipated against the relatively weak opposition expected. The initial objective, Vaalkenssvaard, was about six miles beyond the existing front line, nearly halfway to Eindhoven. It was not long before the Typhoons were required. After just ten minutes the Guards' tanks were taken by surprise by intense anti-tank fire. In minutes, nine tanks were knocked out. It was not a good start. The tanks called in the Typhoons. Directed to their targets by the forward controller, continuous eight-strong flights of Typhoons struck the German positions. In all 116 sorties were flown with targets as close as 100 yards to the leading tanks. The resistance was eliminated and the advance continued, with Typhoons continuing to attack targets ahead of the column until the division reached Valkenswaard.[51] It was a textbook demonstration of close air support and another example of what might have been achieved against German strongpoints holding up the Allied advance three months before on D-Day. It was early evening before the Guards reached Valkenswaard and it was decided not to push on towards Eindhoven until the following day. The Guards were already well behind schedule.

The American 101st Airborne Division had been dropped between Eindhoven and Veghel and pushed north and south to capture the bridges between these two towns. The bridge at Veghel was quickly captured but there was strong opposition around Son and the central span of the Son bridge was blown before it could be secured. Further north at Nijmegen the American 82nd Airborne Division were also encountering some fierce resistance. Typhoons were called in to silence batteries firing on American positions and deal with German counter-attacks from the Reichswald Forest to the east. Around one hundred sorties were flown but the frustrated Visual Control Post wireless operators were unable to make any contact with the aircraft overhead so were not able to direct them on to their targets. The radio sets landed with the airborne troops were proving useless. It transpired that such was the speed with which the air support parties were organised, the American operators had ended up broadcasting on the wrong frequency.[52] Bridges over the Maas at Grave and Maas-Waal canals south of Nijmegen were captured intact but the Germans retained control of the bridge over the Waal north of the town.

At Arnhem the British airborne division was already in serious trouble. To avoid the heavy flak defences in Arnhem, the airborne forces had been landed six miles to the west of the town. Unfortunately, many of the gliders containing the vehicles that were supposed to lead a rapid drive into Arnhem did not make it. Three battalions took three separate routes towards Arnhem and its all-important bridge. All encountered far stiffer resistance than expected, with opposition coming in the form of heavy mortar fire, tanks and assault guns. These were the shattered panzer divisions the ignored intelligence reports had been referring to. Elements of Urquhart's force fought their way to the northern end of the bridge, suffering heavy losses in the process but the majority of his force was held in the outskirts of Oosterbeek, just to the east of Arnhem. The Army investigation into the failure of the operation would later pinpoint the lack of cab-rank close air support the Guards had benefited from, as a key factor in the failure to reach the bridge in sufficient strength.[53] It was all very clear with hindsight. In truth, the commanders of the airborne forces had not shown much interest in ensuring they had such air support.

As it turned out, poor communication would have scuppered attempts at providing air support. No signals were getting through from the airhead and Brereton at Allied Airborne Army HQ had no idea how much trouble the British troops were in. It was not just long-range communications that was proving inadequate. The individual battalions found it extremely difficult to communicate with each other. Urquhart was getting so little information on the position and plight of his own forces, he felt obliged to abandon his headquarters and set off to find out what was happening at first hand. Urquhart had neither the means nor the information to call in the air strikes his troops so desperately needed.

On 18 September Horrocks' XXX Corps continued their advance towards Eindhoven. Once again the Guards were held up by fierce resistance but the Typhoons earmarked to support them were grounded by fog. Meanwhile the American 101st Division had moved into Eindhoven but the Guards would be involved in much fierce fighting before they finally fought their way through to join them in the early evening. After the best part of two days the Guards were still more than forty miles short of Arnhem. To add to their problems a heavy Luftwaffe raid on Eindhoven on the evening of the 19th caused considerable damage and disruption. It was probably the most effective Luftwaffe intervention on the western front since D-Day. Air cover along the entire drop zone was not as comprehensive as it had been in the Normandy campaign. The fighters did an excellent job protecting the transports; German fighters found it almost impossible to fight their way through the escorts. The one occasion when they succeeded demonstrated how vital this work was. On 21 September Fw 190s from JG 26 savaged a re-supply mission, shooting down most of the twenty-nine C-47 Dakota and Stirling transports lost. Although clearly necessary, the effort put into escorting these aircraft meant less was available to provide cover for the forces on the ground. With frequent German hit-and-run raids, and little sign of any similar support from their own air forces, to the troops on the ground it did not seem like the Allies had air superiority. Clearly it did not help relying so heavily on squadrons based in the UK but Fighter Command Spitfire squadrons would have been able to patrol the drop zones for far longer if the Vickers long-range Spitfire, with the rear fuselage tank, had been available.

At Nijmegen further attempts to take the bridge over the Waal were delayed by continuing German counter-attacks from the east. By the morning of the 19th, however, the bridge at Son had been repaired and the Guards were able to link up with the American 82nd Division. With so much effort being diverted to meet the continuing counter-attacks, even the combined British-American force lacked the strength to break through the German defences defending the Nijmegen bridge. Again poor weather prevented much air support; on the 19th only fifty-nine sorties were flown in support of XXX Corps.[54]

On the 20th weather again affected operations. Typhoons were supposed to support a daring crossing of the 400-yard-wide Waal downstream from the Nijmegen bridges. The Typhoons took off despite the atrocious weather but were unable to find any targets.[55] Nevertheless, the crossing was a success and the bridge was taken from the north. Meanwhile, Guards' units were still struggling to hold off the German attempts to recapture the bridges to the south of Nijmegen. Typhoons were called in to help, 115 sorties being flown against gun positions, tanks and troops, but the tenuous link between Eindhoven and Nijmegen was cut and would not be fully restored until the 25th.[56] The diversion of effort to secure the rear continued to weaken the drive north attempting to reach Arnhem.

In Arnhem a somewhat improvised force was fighting a desperate defensive battle to hold on to the northern end of the bridge while the rest of the force sought to fight its way through to help them. Communications with First Allied Airborne Army HQ remained poor; the first message did not get through until the 19th. These included a request for air support but bad weather continued to dog the operation. Poor weather was also delaying the landing of further troops and supplies. First priority had to go to re-supply operations and with Second Tactical Air Force grounded while these operations were taking place there were very few opportunities for the Typhoons to intervene.

BREAKTHROUGH

Even if communications had been more reliable, close support would have been difficult. In confused fighting the paratroopers were often unaware of the position of friendly forces and on occasion fired on each other. Identifying enemy targets for air strikes in such circumstances would have been fraught with difficulty. It was not impossible as Nugent's XXIX TAC was demonstrating many hundreds of miles away in Brest, but it required good ground/air communications and this the airborne forces did not have.

The valiant resistance of the force holding the northern end of the Arnhem bridge finally ceased on the 21st. Other elements of 1st Airborne Division had been forced back into a small bridgehead on the Nederrijn just north of Driel. The Guards were now ordered to make an all-out effort to get to Arnhem but, at Elst, halfway between Nijmegen and Arnhem, a strong force of German tanks stopped the advance in its tracks. Again cab-rank Typhoons were on hand but the radio equipment in the RAF contact car had broken down and no contact could be made with the Typhoons.[57] Without reinforcements further progress along the route into Arnhem was not possible. However, through the marshy land to the west of the main Nijmegen-Arnhem route, progress was made towards Driel, where, on the 23rd, the Polish brigade was going to be dropped.

By the 21st, communications with the remnants of Urquhart's beleaguered force had improved considerably and with XXX Corps artillery now within range, they were getting more effective support. Such was their plight Urquhart's men were willing to risk calling in artillery support from eleven miles away to strike targets just hundreds of yards from their positions. There was considerable frustration that the more conservative RAF, which could deliver such support much more accurately than distant artillery, were reluctant to strike unless they could identify a clear enemy target. On 22nd twenty-four Typhoons hit a factory in Arnhem from which snipers were reported to be operating, but by this time the troops in Arnhem itself had surrendered. Better weather enabled around 500 sorties to be flown but they were against communication targets distant from the front, to the north-west of Arnhem.[58] It was not until the 23rd that German gun and mortar positions around the shrinking Nederrijn perimeter became the primary target. On the 24th, the defenders were treated to a three-hour procession of Typhoons arriving to strike enemy positions hemming in the airborne forces. Often no specific targets were seen, it was just a case of firing at suspected German positions, but nevertheless, the intervention did much to raise morale.[59] Allied forces eventually reached the south bank of the

Nederrijn but by this stage it had turned into a rescue mission rather than an attempt to reinforce the bridgehead and on the night of the 25/26th, the surviving airborne forces were pulled back across the river.

After the battle, the First Allied Airborne Army post mortem emphasised that, in the circumstances, attacks on distant communications targets were a wasted effort as they could have no effect on the immediate plight of front-line troops. More direct support should have been the priority. The RAF may have considered attacking targets where no enemy was visible a waste of time but the ground forces tended to rate the results of such missions as excellent. The RAF, like the USAAF, had had its fair share of friendly-fire incidents and had been heavily criticised by land commanders, so the caution of the pilots was understandable. The balance of risk is always difficult to assess. Troops coming under friendly fire will take it a lot harder when they are chasing a beaten enemy, as was the case with some of the Canadian incidents in August. When soldiers are in imminent danger of being wiped out, as was the case with Urquhart's force, the mindset is very different.

To Urquhart's men, it seemed the RAF had not been willing to expose the paratroopers to risks they accepted as part and parcel of war. For the RAF, not intervening was always the safer option. The risk/gain balance was especially difficult for RAF pilots to judge because of the history of mistrust between the services. It would have been easier for pilots from the same service to make the judgement, without the baggage that comes with inter-service strife, an advantage the US Marine Corps had in their Pacific operations. Morale was another misunderstood element. Air force commanders did not see it as part of their job to boost the morale of friendly ground forces; indeed the very idea that ground forces needed their morale boosted just confirmed the low Air Force opinion of their Army brethren. The importance and value of morale in any military engagement can never be overestimated, a point the Army had been making since the War Office Bartholomew Report, written in the wake of the 1940 debacle in France.[60]

After the battle, both Urquhart and Montgomery would complain that with such overwhelming air superiority more effective air support ought to have been available. However, neither Urquhart nor Montgomery had made a determined effort to secure it before the operation. Indeed, both had agreed to a plan which necessarily ruled out close air support from operating for much of the time. They had also overseen preparations which sent Allied forces into action with poorly or non-functioning radio equipment. The problems of providing the airborne forces with adequate close air support had not been addressed by Army or Air Force. The lack of air support was by no means the only reason why the Market Garden operation failed, but it was one of them.

Once again the fault lines in British military thinking and planning had been laid bare. Too many Army commanders did not see battlefield air support as their business, which was not entirely surprising since the Air Force had constantly insisted that these things were none of their business. On the other hand, providing the Army with air support was scarcely an Air Force priority. Too many in the Air Force did not see it as their job to advise the Army on how airpower could help achieve Army objectives. It was up to the Army to state what it wanted and it was for the Air Force to decide how to meet these requirements if indeed they could be met. They were not there to offer help and advice. This sort of segregated approach was deliberately designed to accentuate the separate identities of the two services. The result was a customer/provider relationship rather than a team effort. Close air support suffered from having to exist in the artificially created inter-service void that Air Force independence had generated.

The priority given to Market Garden exacerbated an already critical supply situation, which made it easier for the German defences to consolidate their positions elsewhere. The port of Antwerp had been taken intact, but until the German forces along the Scheldt estuary leading to the port could be eliminated, the port was useless. This would have been a simpler task in the early days of September before the German forces had time to organise their defences. The Allies now faced a tough task just to clear the Germans from these positions before they could even consider tackling the main defensive line along the German frontier.

The previous two months had seen the most dramatic swings in fortunes for the Allies. In early July it had seemed there was no end to the stalemate in Normandy and victory over Germany seemed a distant prospect. The American breakout at Avranches had broken the stalemate. The defeat of the German forces in Normandy had resulted in the rapid eviction of all German forces from France and Belgium and brought the defeat of Hitler tantalisingly close. The defeat at Arnhem changed all that. The defeat was more psychological than material but it had lifted the spirits of the German nation. Intricate waterways, dense forests and Siegfried Line casemates provided a sound basis for a strong defence of the homeland. Suddenly progress was being measured in yards rather than miles. It now looked like the war would stretch well into 1945. The nightmare scenario was that come the following summer a still formidable German Army would be getting effective air support from a new generation of jet aircraft.

While the army generals were filled with dismay, air force commanders saw an opportunity. For Harris and the bomber fraternity there would be one last chance to prove their case. The Allied advance through France and Belgium had swept aside the Luftwaffe's night-fighter early-warning system. There was less enemy airspace to penetrate to reach key targets. Navigational radar aids could now direct bombers from the continent, making precision strikes much farther east much easier. Air Force commanders would never now be able to claim the bomber had won the war on its own but if they could force a German surrender while the German Army was still holding a solid front, then they could claim that they had had the final and arguably decisive say in the outcome.

Conclusion

Four years after an ignominious retreat from France, British forces, supported by new Allies, had returned to recover the ground lost. Four years to switch from a defensive posture on the Channel front to an offensive posture was a long time, especially when the enemy was locked in battle with a mighty foe on a distant front. The delay was not due to a lack of resources; it was a direct result of decisions made long before the war over which of two rival theories of war best met Britain's defence needs. One saw bombers winning wars on their own, either by terrorising the enemy population into defeat or destroying the means to carry on the fight. The other believed the future of war belonged to air-supported mechanised armies.

In the inter-war years the bomber advocates argued that, with the bomber as an alternative, there was no need for British forces to intervene on the continent. Bombing, it was claimed, would win wars in months, even weeks, possibly days. Knockout blows would provide a much speedier way of deciding wars than endless trench warfare. There would be no need for the youth of the country to relive the horrors of the Somme and Passchendaele. Their words seemed to have been heeded, but the reality of fighting a real war soon forced a rethink and another British Expeditionary Force was despatched to France. The subsequent humiliation of a hasty retreat via Dunkirk seemed a vindication for the bomber advocates. There was no need to repeat the mistake. No invasion of Europe would be required to defeat Hitler. Bombing would win the war, and win it quickly.

The bomber offensive launched with such high hopes in May 1940 soon proved incapable of living up to expectations. Reasons for the failure were analysed, new technologies and tactics introduced. Fresh starts were made; the clock was constantly being reset. Victory by bombing was always just around the corner. The bomber barons seemed oblivious to the passing years. The talk was still of knockout blows, but the reality was that the knockout blow had mutated into the long drawn-out First World

War style battle of attrition, the sort of campaign bombing was supposed to replace. Although mechanised armies were furiously battling it out on four continents, the Air Ministry still clung to the belief they were in the midst of a bomber war.

With the bomber offensive struggling, the bomber advocates needed more time to prove an invasion of France was not necessary. Every opportunity was taken to make an invasion look as difficult as possible. It would be much easier, they insisted, once the bombers had been allowed to finish their work. This delaying action was not a devious plot hatched by individuals, it was more of an institutional conspiracy, generated by an unshakeable collective belief in the ability of bombers to win wars. With army generals struggling to work out why the Wehrmacht was so difficult to defeat, they had a very receptive audience. There was, however, a point beyond which the politicians were not willing to wait; the invasion could not be put off beyond 1944. Expectations of what the bomber offensive might contribute to Overlord had to be reined in. In the end all the bombers could offer was air superiority. It was a fig leaf for failure. The Allies had possessed air superiority over northern France for some time and had more than ample air resources to ensure there could be no Luftwaffe revival.

Once serious preparations for the invasion were underway, the air force had no choice but to contribute; but it ensured its contribution was as distinct and separate as possible, as befitted an independent service. The air force was not there to collaborate with the other armed services; it was there to fight its own separate war. Tactical air support would be restricted to air-only campaigns where the air force could fight its own battle, set its own goals and achieve them quite independently of what armies and navies might be doing. It would do battle with the Luftwaffe high in the skies above the battlefield and attack targets beyond the battlefield, but the battlefield itself was no place for an air force. Instead of the destruction of German industry, air superiority and the wrecking of German communications became the air force contribution to Overlord. Tactical operations had to match the air force's grandiose status. Air superiority meant the destruction of the Luftwaffe. Interdiction would not be simply restricting the flow of reinforcements to the front; the aim would be the destruction of entire enemy communication systems. Airpower had to be seen as the facilitating factor. The Air Force role was determined by the need to demonstrate its credentials as the decisive factor in wars, rather than the needs of the British armed forces.

CONCLUSION

These were aims worthy of an independent air force but, like the strategic air offensive, they were also hopelessly over-ambitions. In the end the RAF was overburdened by the ambition of its commanders. Ironically, by choosing such ambitious objectives, the Air Force were throwing away the chance to make the decisive contribution it so desired. More limited aims in closer co-operation with ground forces were more easily attainable, cost less and had far more impact on the course of the war. There was absolutely nothing revolutionary about battlefield close air support. The technology had changed since 1918 but in essence the method was the same. It was an application of air warfare the Air Ministry had been so quick to ditch after the First World War and Trenchard's acolytes had been attempting to suppress ever since but, such was its obvious value, it kept re-emerging. On the world stage it was only the air force leaders of the RAF and USAAF who were so stubbornly holding out against what other countries, and indeed RAF commands beyond the reach of Air Ministry dogma, saw as an obvious use of airpower. Battlefield interdiction and the battle for air superiority fell neatly into the category of independent air operations; battlefield close air support did not.

In the planning for and execution of Overlord the heavy bomber both dominated and distorted thinking. Army commanders were as seduced by the destructive power of the bomber as their Air Force colleagues. There is nothing in the least bit unsound about unloading large quantities of high explosives on a powerful enemy, but with the technology available at the time there were too many disadvantages to using heavy bombers to do so. The controversy over the use of heavy bombers diverted attention from more useful tactical applications of airpower and indeed from the changes both Army and Air Force needed to make in their approach to fighting a modern war. As the battle for Normandy progressed, as had happened in every active theatre, reality forced closer co-operation on the battlefield, but it still ran counter to the instincts of air force commanders. The need to demonstrate and justify independence was a constant barrier to developing a truly integrated multi-service combined-arms approach.

The Air Ministry was trapped in its own self-created universe where airpower was the dominant factor in warfare. In fact it was this overestimate of the importance of airpower that was limiting horizons. Air Force commanders genuinely believed they were more progressive than their army counterparts. The Air Ministry constantly ridiculed War Office thinking but on fundamental air related issues the War Office got more right than the Air

Ministry. The need for a full-scale invasion of France had demonstrated the fallacy of the idea that bombing alone could win wars. The fighting in Normandy was yet another demonstration that airpower was required on as well as beyond the battlefield. Dismissive terms for the way the Army believed airpower should be used were themselves discredited by events in Normandy. Air forces 'tied to armies' (integrated with army), 'penny packets' (decentralised control), 'air umbrellas' (combat air patrols) all turned out to be perfectly sound ideas and crucial to success in Normandy. In Normandy the air commanders were constantly complaining that the Army would not move until bombing had removed all obstacles. Yet it was the air force that encouraged the idea that the invasion should not take place until German military production had been slashed, communications leading to the invasion zone destroyed and air superiority over the beachhead guaranteed.

It should not have taken four years to switch from the defensive on the Channel front to the offensive. That does not mean an earlier invasion would have succeeded. The dominant bomber strategy with all the implications for personnel and materiel resources and even more importantly mindset was bound to retard the development of the tools and skills required for an invasion. Even in 1944 the UK-based RAF was far from ready for the challenge of a modern tactical air battle. The Allies seemed doomed to go through a painful learning process whenever they chose to invade. Arguably, the sooner the invasion, the sooner this process would be set in motion and the shorter the war would be.

In the end the delay did not enable the bombers to make a useful contribution to the invasion but it did allow such a huge material advantage to be amassed that it did not matter that the armies and air forces were not working together as one. These were scarcely the best reasons for delay. It was the price that had to be paid for being so totally seduced by the bomber fantasy. Events could only have turned out differently if British defence thinking had chosen to go down a different path in the interwar years. If Britain had chosen to build on the combined-arms approach being developed in 1918, an invasion of France would have been possible much sooner. But then again, it would have been a very different British force that counter-attacked at Arras in May 1940 and there would probably never have been a need to invade France. The past cannot be changed but examining alternatives puts mistakes in clearer focus. In the end, a longer war was the price Britain had to pay for following the bomber path so diligently.

CONCLUSION

In September 1944 the western Allies had still only managed to regain the territory they had held in September 1939. The war was far from won. All was not yet lost for the Bomber Barons. With the Allied advance stalled on the German frontier, there would be one last chance to prove bombers could bring down a nation.

To be continued

Bibliography

Aders, G., *History of the German Night Fighter Force 1917-1945* (London: Janes, 1979).
Air Ministry, *The Rise and Fall of the German Air Force* (London: Air Ministry, 1948)
Air of Authority, www.rafweb.org.
Alanbrooke, Lord, *Alanbrooke War Diaries 1939-1945* (London: Weidenfeld & Nicolson, 2001).
Army Doctrine Publications – Land Operations (2005) https://vdocuments. mx/irectorate-general-evelopment-and-doctrinearmy-doctrine-publication-land-operations.html.
Arnold H., *Global Mission* (Blue Ridge Summit: TAB, 1989).
Bateson, R., *Stuka* (London: Ducimus Books, 1972).
Baughen, G., *Blueprint for Victory* (Stroud: Fonthill, 2014).
Baughen, G., *The RAF in the Battle of France and the Battle of Britain* (Stroud: Fonthill, 2016).
Baughen, G., *The Rise of the Bomber* (Stroud: Fonthill, 2015).
Bekker, C., The Luftwaffe War Diaries (London: Macdonald, 1966)
Bowlby, A., (London: Leo Cooper, 1995)
Bowman, M., *USAF Handbook 1939-1945* (Stroud: Sutton Publishing, 1998).
Bowyer, M., *Aircraft for the Many* (Sparkford: Patrick Stephens, 1995)
Bowyer, M., *No. 2 Group RAF* (London: Faber and Faber, 1974).
Brookes, A., *Air* War over Italy (Shepperton: Ian Allan, 2000)
Brookes, A., Photo-Reconnaissance (London: Ian Allan, 1975).
Budiansky, S., Air Power (London: Penguin, 2003)
Buttler, T., British Secret Projects, Fighters and Bombers 1935-1950 (Hinckley: Midland, 2004)
Caldwell, D., JG 2 War Diary (London: Grub Street, 1998)
Campbell, J., *The Bombing of Nuremburg* (London: Futura, 1974)

BIBLIOGRAPHY

Carrington, C., *Soldier at Bomber Command*, (London: Lee Cooper, 1987)
Churchill, W., *Vol. 3, Grand Alliance* (London: Reprint Society, 1952).
Churchill, W., *Vol. 4, The Hinge of Fate* (London: Reprint Society, 1952)
Churchill, W., *Vol. 5, Closing the Ring* (London: Reprint Society, 1952)
Clark, R., *Tizard* (London: Methuen, 1965).
Clarke, R., *British Aircraft Armament Vol.1* (Sparkford: Patrick Stephens, 1994)
Clarke, R., *British Aircraft Armament Vol.2* (Sparkford: Patrick Stephens, 1994)
Clostermann, P., *The Big Show*, (London: Chatto and Windus, 1958)
Collier, B., *The Defence of the United Kingdom* (London: IWM, 1995).
Copp,(Waterloo: Wilfrid Laurier University, 2000)
Craven, W., Cate, J., *The Army Air Forces in World War II, Vol. 1, 2* (Chicago: University of Chicago Press 1948, 1949).
Crosley, R., (Shrewsbury: Airlife, 2001)
D'Este, C., *Decision in Normandy* (London: Penguin, 2001)
D'Este, C., *Fatal Decision* (London: Fontana, 1991)
Divine, D., *The Broken Wing* (London: Hutchinson, 1966)
Douglas, W., Wright, R., *Sholto Douglas*, (London: Collins, 1966)
Ellis, L., 2, (London: HMSO, 1962)
Embry, B., *Mission Accomplished*, (London, Methuen, 1957)
Ethell, J., Price, A., *Target Berlin*, (London: Jane's, 1985)
Fahey, J., https://ses.library.usyd.edu.au/bitstream/2123/664/2/adt-NU20050104.11440202whole.pdf
Farrar-Hockley, A., *The Army in the Air*, (Stroud: Alan Sutton Publishing, 1994).
Rein, C., *Forging the Ninth Army-XXIX TAC Team*, (Leaveworth Papers No. 24, 2019)
Frankland, N., *History at War*, (London: Giles de la Mare, 1998)
Freeman, R., *The Mighty Eighth* (London: Cassell, 2000)
Freeman, R., *The Mighty Eighth War Diary* (London: Jane's, 1981)
Furse, A., *Wilfred Freeman* (Staplehurst: Spellmount, 1999)
Galland, A., *The First and Last*, (London: Methuen, 1955)
Gibson, C., Buttler, T., *British Secret Projects Hypersonics, Ramjets, Missiles.* (Hersham: Midland, 2007)
Golley, J., *The Day of the Typhoon* (Stroud: Wrens Park Publishing, 2001)
Gooderson, I., *Air Power at the Battlefield* (London: Frank Cass, 1998)
Goulding, A., (Manchester: Goodall, 1996)
Goulding, J., *Interceptor* (Shepperton: Ian Allan, 1986)

Goulter, C., *A Forgotten Offensive* (London: Frank Cass, 1995).
Greenhous, B., Harris, S., Johnston, W., Rawling, W., *The Ceucible of War, 1939-1945*, (Toronto: University of Toronto Press, 1994)
Grigg, J., *The Victory That Never Was* (London: Penguin, 1999)
Gunston, B., *Rolls-Royce Aero Engines* (Frome: PSL, 1989)
Hallion, R., *Strike from the Sky* (Shrewsbury, Airlife, 1989)
Hamilton, N., , (London: Hamish Hamilton, 1983)
Hancock, W,. *Statistical Digest of the War*, (London: HMSO, 1951)
Hardesty, V., *Red Phoenix,* (Shrewsbury: Airlife Publishing, 1982)
Hardy, M., *The North American Mustang*, (London: David and Charles, 1979)
Harris, A., *Bomber Offensive* (London: Greenhill Books, 1990)
Harrison, G., *European Theater of Operations, Cross-Channel Attack* (Washington: Centre of Military History, 1951)
Hastings, M., *Bomber Command,* (London: Pan Books, 1981)
Hastings, M., *Overlord*, (London: Pan, 1999)
Hill, A., *The Great Patriotic War of the Soviet Union, 1941-45* (London: Routledge, 2009)
Historical Section (Canadian) Army Report No 74, 5 July 1955, https://publications.gc.ca/collections/collection_2016/mdn-dnd/D63-5-74-1955-eng.pdf
Hooton, E.R., *Eagle in Flames* (London: Arms and Armour Press, 1997)
Hughes, T., *Overlord* (New York, The Free Press 1995)
Irving, D., *The Mare's Nest* (London: Corgi, 1966).
Irving, D., *The Rise and Fall of the Luftwaffe* (London: Futura 1976)
Irving, D., *The Trail of the Fox* (London: Futuraa 1978)
Jackson, B., Bramall D., *The Chiefs* (London: Brassey's, 1992).
James, D,. *Gloster Aircraft*, (London: Putnam, 1987)
Johnson, J., E., *Full Circle* (London: Pan, 1969)
Joint Doctrine Publication, 0-30 UK Air and Space Power (London: MOD, 2017)
Jones, R.V., *Most Secret War* (London: Coronet 1981)
Keegan, J., *Six Armies in Normandy* (Harmondsworth: Penguin, 1983)
Kesselring, , (London: William Kimber, 1953)
Kohn, Haraham, Air Interdiction in World War II, Korea, and Vietnam https://media.defense.gov/2010/May/25/2001330268/-1/-1/0/AFD-100525-070.pdf
Kosin, R., *The German Fighter Since 1915* (London: Putnam, 1988).
Latham, C., Stobbs, A., *Radar a Wartime Miracle* (Stroud: Sutton Publishing, 1996)

BIBLIOGRAPHY

Leasor, J., *War at the Top*, (London: Michael Joseph, 1959)
Lewis. J., *Changing Direction* (London: Frank Cass, 2003)
Lloyd, I., Pugh, P., *Hives and the Merlin* (Cambridge: Icon Books, 2004)
Longmate, N., , (Barnsley: Pen & Sword, 2009)
Lovell, B., *Echoes of War* (Bristol: Adam Hilger, 1991).
Lyall, G., *The War in the Air* (London: Arrow, 1971)
Mead, P., *The Eye in the Sky* (London: HMSO, 1983).
Meekcoms, K.J., Morgan, E.B., *The British Aircraft Specifications File* (Tonbridge: Air Britain Publication, 1994).
Mets, D., *Master of Airpower*, (Novata: Presidio Press, 1988).
Middlebrook, M., Everitt, C. *The Bomber Command War Diaries* (London: Penguin, 1990).
Montgomery, B., *Memoirs* (London: Collins, 1958)
Montgomery, B., *The Memoirs of Field-Marshal the Viscount Montgomery of Alamein* (London: Collins, 1958).
Morgan, F., *Overture to Overlord* (London: Hodder and Stoughton, 1950)
Muller, R., *The German Air War in Russia* (Baltimore: Nautical and Aviation, 1992)
Newton Dunn, B., *Big Wing* (Shrewsbury: Airlife, 1992)
Olds, R., *Fighter Pilot* (New York: St Martin's Griffin, 2010)
Orange, V., *Coningham*, (London: Methuen, 1990).
Overy, R., *The Bombing War* (London: Penguin, 2014)
Parham, H. J., Belfield, E. M. G., *Unarmed into Battle* (Chippenham: Picton Publishing, 1986)
Peret, G., *Winged Victory*, (New York: Random House, 1993)
Pitt, B., , (Paulton: Purnell, 1967)
Postan, M,. *British War Production*, (London HMSO, 1952)
Price, A., *Focke Wulf 190 at War* (Shepperton: Ian Allan, 1977)
Price, A., *Instruments of Darkness* (London: Macdonald and Jane's, 1977).
Price, A., *The Spitfire Story* (London: Jane's, 1982)
Price, A., *World War II Fighter Conflict* (London: MacDonald and Jane's, 1975)
Probert, H., *Bomber Harris* (London: Greenhill Books, 2001)
Probert, H., *High Commanders of The Royal Air Force* (London: H.M.S.O., 1991).
Probert, H., *The Forgotten Air Force* (London: Brasey's, 1996)
Richards, D., *Portal of Hungerford* (London: Heinemann, 1977)
Ryan, C., *A BridgeToo Far* (London: Coronet, 1977)
Salavrakos, I., (Athens University)

Santoro, G., *L'Aeronautica Italiana Nella Seconda Guerra Mondiale Vol. 1, 2* (Rome: Apollon, 1957)

Sharp, M., Bowyer J. F., *Mosquito* (London: Faber and Faber, 1971)

Sherry, M., *The Rise of Ameriacn Air Power*, (New Haven, Yale University Press, 1987)

Shores, C., *Ground Attack Aircraft of World War II*, (London: Macdonald and Jane's, 1977)

Shores, C., Massimello, G., *A History of the Mediterranean Air War 1940-45 Vol. 4*, (London: Grub St, 2018)

Shores, C., *Second Tactical Air Force* (Oxford: Osprey, 1970)

Slessor, J., *The Central Blue* (London: Cassell, 1956)

Spaight, J., *Bombing Vindicated*, (Glasgow, The University Press, 1944)

Speer, A., *Inside the Third Reich* (London: Sphere Books, 1975)

Spires, D., *Air Power for Patton's Army* (Washington: Air Force History and Museums Program, 2002)

Stocker, J., , (London: Frank Cass, 2004)

Tedder, Lord, *With Prejudice*, (London: Cassell, 1966)

Terraine, J., *The Right of the Line,* (Sevenoaks: Sceptre, 1988)

Tooze, A., *The Wages of Destruction* (London: Penguin, 2007)

Trevor-Roper, H., *Hitler's War Directives 1939-1945* (London: Pan Books, 1973)

Webster, C., Frankland N., *The Strategic Air Offensive Against Germany 1939-1945 Vol. 2,3, 4* (London: HMSO, 1961)

Whitford, R., *Fundamentals of Fighter Design*, (Ramsbury: Airlife, 2004)

Wilmot, C., *The Struggle for Europe* (Ware: Wordsworth Editions, 1997)

Wilson, T., *Churchill and the Prof.* (London: Cassell, 1995)

Appendix 1

Aircraft deliveries July 1943–September 1944

(A-Airframe only, B-bomber, C-Coastal, F-fighter versions)

	British Aircraft Production July 1943-September 1944														
	1943						1944								
	Jul	Aug	Sept	Oct	Nov	Dec	Jan	Feb	Mar	Apr	May	Jun	Jul	Aug	Sep
Auster	46	43	50	49	37	7	12	74	87	65	50	50	31	72	58
Barracuda	58	52	76	83	80	76	99	95	112	111	122	115	75	110	13
Beaufighter(F)	131	140	146	147	138	129	125	121	125	109	100	90	100	85	90
Beaufort	30	29	37	24	33	33	26	21	22	25	24	18	12	8	10
Buckingham	-	-	-	-	-	-	-	1	1	3	2	3	7	7	12
Firebrand	-	-	-	-	-	-	-	-	-	-	1	1	4	0	5
Firefly	8	8	1	5	9	9	13	12	25	26	27	16	28	24	29
Halifax	156	132	155	150	159	167	196	215	218	208	205	211	198	159	216
Hurricane	200	242	240	194	256	184	145	147	148	87	63	60	38	-	-
Lancaster	145	140	187	198	189	181	224	199	257	228	259	260	217	298	266
Meteor	-	-	-	-	-	-	-	1	1	3	0	3	4	7	0
Mosquito (B)	12	6	15	7	5	6	7	12	16	11	27	28	12	10	19
Mosquito (F)	77	110	92	97	121	83	103	178	234	159	155	150	168	173	196
Seafire	23	18	16	17	30	32	39	51	57	63	63	70	74	59	90
Spitfire	292	379	383	384	306	354	353	378	432	432	442	471	392	424	396
Stirling	65	83	86	91	74	72	58	37	45	33	22	16	13	11	4
Sunderland	15	17	18	18	16	17	23	16	21	11	20	20	13	12	17
Swordfish	51	55	55	60	56	55	60	55	60	55	55	62	45	27	-
Tempest	-	-	-	3	0	0	8	12	27	23	32	49	51	56	60
Typhoon	93	80	110	98	108	98	111	110	115	103	121	115	96	85	90
Warwick (R)	-	-	-	-	-	-	-	1	1	3	6	7	9	10
Welkin	-	-	2	3	0	0	0	0	0	6	4	4	0	2	13
Wellington	207	185	207	217	215	192	210	216	225	203	211	215	155	205	200

Arrivals in UK from USA and Canada

	1943						1944							
	Jul	Aug	Sep	Oct	Nov	Dec	Jan	Feb	Mar	Apr	May	Jun	Jul	Aug	Sep
Avenger	14	0	22	4	26	29	76	18	26	10	24	19	5	21	4
Boston	6	3	3	-	-	-	1	0	12	27	15	18	56	-	-
Catalina	2	2	17	23	14	2	6	8	21	32	20	13	24	13	32
Corsair	8	0	2	1	20	0	12	25	22	34	154	155	29	17	56
Fortress	-	-	-	-	-	-	-	8	15	3	12	10	14	2	6
Hellcat	37	2	17	9	14	16	27	33	17	4	26	6	59	45	56
Hudson	6	2	0	6	0	0	-	-	-	-	-	-	-	-	-
Lancaster	-	-	1	0	4	1	8	1	17	10	17	8	12	18	18
Liberator	22	21	1	2	17	10	5	15	11	6	26	41	11	31	19
Mitchell	11	7	11	0	51	21	48	19	31	9	18	18	5	36	45
Mosquito (B)	-	5	0	0	0	0	0	0	7	18	27	9	27	7	42
Mustang I/II	35	-	-	-	-	-	-	-	-	-	-	-	-	-	-
Mustang III/IV	-	-	3	74	90	105	53	46	3	16	56	51	3	71	71
Thunderbolt	-	-	-	-	-	-	-	-	-	2	-	-	-	-	-
Vengeance	0	2	0	0	0	17	9	14	26	44	34	5	78	27	60
Ventura	7	7	1	0	7	3	4	1	8	11	2	-	-	-	-
Wildcat	28	3	5	10	64	35	20	9	23	16	33	29	21	2	10

American Deliveries to the Mediterranean

	1943						1944							
	Jul	Aug	Sep	Oct	Nov	Dec	Jan	Feb	Mar	Apr	May	Jun	Jul	Aug	Sep
Baltimore	64	69	64	16	69	71	69	45	52	77	34	36	16	5	-
Boston	-	-	-	-	-	-	-	-	-	-	-	7	26	-	-
Kittyhawk	9	132	23	24	120	31	75	14	1	-	-	-	-	-	-
Liberator	-	-	-	4	17	6	16	10	4	20	46	47	18	27	18
Marauder	-	-	-	39	20	5	3	18	9	1	92	76	27	2	25
Mustang	-	-	-	-	-	-	-	14	11	54	14	30	35	39	17
Thunderbolt	-	-	-	-	-	-	-	-	--	-	-	-	-	-	18
Vengeance	-	-	-	-	-	-	-	-	-	-	-	7	13	8	7
Ventura	-	-	-	21	35	36	48	30	11	8	1	7	6	1	1

AIRCRAFT DELIVERIES JULY 1943–SEPTEMBER 1944

	American Deliveries to India														
	1943						1944								
	Jul	Aug	Sep	Oct	Nov	Dec	Jan	Feb	Mar	Apr	May	Jun	Jul	Aug	Sep
Avenger	-	-	-	-	-	22	32	-	-	-	-	-	-	-	-
Corsair	-	-	-	-	-	-	20	0	42	6	0	0	90	11	0
Hellcat	-	-	-	-	-	7	12	0	3	-	-	-	-	-	-
Liberator	-	-	-	2	46	20	29	21	18	23	52	55	34	7	25
Mohawk	-	-	-	-	-	-	8	16	-	-	-	-	-	-	-
Sentinel	-	-	-	-	-	-	-	-	-	-	-	-	-	20	40
Thunderbolt	-	-	-	-	-	-	2	0	0	0	114	82	104	52	10
Vengeance	35	53	37	8	2	0	5	21	6	14	8	0	22	38	0
Wildcat	-	-	-	-	-	18	30	0	17	-	-	-	-	-	-

Appendix 2

Aircraft Performance

(Unless otherwise stated, mg refers to 0.303 calibre machine guns.)

Fighters

	First flight	Engine	Speed (mph)/altitude (ft)	Range (miles) (with external)	Climb (ft/min-sec or initial rate ft/sec)	Ceiling (ft)	Empty Weight (lbs)	Loaded Weight (lbs)	Wing area (sq ft)	Armament Guns Bombs RP=rocket projectile
Curtiss P-40K Warhawk	25/11/1941	1,325hp Allison V-1710-73	362/15,000	700 (1,400)	20,000/11-12	28,000	6,400	8,400	236	6x0.5in. mg 700lb
De Havilland Vampire	26/09/1943	2,700lb st. t. Goblin I	506	730	4,200 ft/min		6,370	8,580	266	4x20mm cannon
Focke-Wulf 190A-8	01/06/1939	1,700hp BMW 801D-2	408/20,600	500	16,400/4-50	37,400	7,000	9,750	197	2 mg, 4x20 mm cannon
Gloster Meteor I	24/07/1943	2 x 1,700lb st. t. Welland 1	410/30,000		2,155 ft/min	40,000	8,140	11,800	374	4x20mm cannon
Gloster Meteor III	11/09/1944	2 x 2,000lb st. t. Derwent	483/30,000	450 (1,340)	3,980 ft/min	44,000	8,810	13,300	374	4x20mm cannon
Hawker Hurricane II	01/06/1940	1,460hp Merlin XX	342/22,000	460	20,000/8-24	36,500	5,500	7,000	258	4x20mm cannon 1,000lb
Hawker Tempest II	28/06/1943	2,530hp Centaurus V	440/15,900	775 (1,700)	20,000/5-36	37,000	9,300	13,900	304	4x20mm cannon 2,000lb or 8 RP
Hawker Tempest V	21/06/1943	2,200hp Sabre IIB	435/17,000	820 (1,480)	20,000/6-06	36,000	9,250	11,400	302	4x20mm cannon 2,000lb or 8 RP
Hawker Typhoon	24/02/1940	2,180hp Sabre IIA	405/18,000	610 (1,000)	15,000/6-12	34,000	8,800	11,400	279	4x20mm cannon 2,000lbs or 8 RP

Fighters

	First flight	Engine	Speed (mph)/ altitude (ft)	Range (miles) (with external)	Climb (ft/min-sec or initial rate ft/sec)	Ceiling (ft)	Empty Weight (lbs)	Loaded Weight (lbs)	Wing area (sq ft)	Armament Guns Bombs RP=rocket projectile
Lockheed P-38F Lightning	27/01/1939	2 x 1,225hp Allison V-1710-49/53	395/25,000	400 (1,750)	20,000/8-48	39,000	12,260	15,900	328	20mm cannon, 4x0.5in. mg
Heinkel He 280	02/04/1941	2 x 1,540lb st. t. Heinkel-Hirth HeS 8.4	578/19,685	435	4,920 ft/min	49,200	7,100	9,410	232	3x20mm cannon
Messerschmitt Bf 109G-2	1941	1,475hp DB 605A	398/20,670	340	19,685/5-06	39,370	4,968	6,834	174	2 mg, 1x20mm cannon
Messerschmitt Bf 110G-4	1942	2 x 1,475hp DB 605B	342/22,900	565	18,000/7-54	26,000	11,220	20,700	413	2 mg, 2x20 mm 2x30mm cannon
Me 262	18/07/1942	2 x 1980lb st. t. Junkers Jumo 004B	538/29,560	300	3,940 ft/min	37,570	9,741	14,100	234	4x30mm cannon, 24 R4M missiles, 1,100lbs bombs
North American Mustang II	26/10/1940	1,200hp Allison V-1710-81	390/20,000	1,000	20,000/9-06	31,350	6,433	8,600	233	4x0.5in. mg 1,000lb bombs
North American Mustang III	09/1942	1,620hp Packard V-1650	440/30,000	550 (2,200)	20,000/ 7-00	42,000	6,840	9,200	233	4x0.5in. mg 2,000lb
Republic P-47D Thunderbolt	06/05/1941	2,300hp Pratt and Whitney R-2800-21	433/30,000	640 (925)	20,000/11-00	40,000	9,900	13,500	300	8x0.5in. mg 2,000lb or 10 RP
Supermarine Spitfire V	20/02/1941	1,470hp Merlin 45	371/20,000	470 (1,135)	15,000/ 4-36	37,000	5,033	6,525	242	4 mg, 2x20mm cannon
Supermarine Spitfire IX	04/1942	1,720hp Merlin 61	403/27,400	434 (1,650)	20,000/ 6-30	42,000	5,800	7,500	242	4 mg 2x20mm cannon 500lb
Supermarine Spitfire XIV	1943	2,050hp Griffon 65	448/26,000	450 (850)	20,000/ 7-0	44,000	6,600	8,500	231	4 mg and 2x20mm cannon 1,000lbs

Bombers

	Prototype first flight	Engine	Speed (mph) /altitude (ft)	Range (miles)	Ceiling (ft)	Empty Weight (lbs)	Loaded Weight (lbs)	Wing area (sq ft)	Bomb load (lbs) Armament
Arado Ar 234	15/6/1943	2 x 1,980lb st. t. Junkers-Jumo 004B	461/19,690	1,000	32,810	11,460	18,540	284	3,300lbs 2x20mm cannon
Avro Lancaster I	09/01/1941	4 x 1,460hp Merlin 22	281/11,000	2,250	20,000	36,900	68,000	1,297	14,000lbs 8 mg
Avro Lincoln	09/06/1944	4 x 1,750hp Merlin 85	300/18,000	3,560	27,800	42,590	82,000	1,421	22,000lbs 6x0.5 in. mg
Boeing B-17E Flying Fortress	28/07/1935	4 x 1,200hp Wright Cyclone 9	317/20,000	2,000	36,600	32,250	53,000	1,420	8,000lbs internal 1 mg, 12x0.5in. mg
Boeing B-29 Superfortress	21/09/1942	4 x 2,340hp Wright-Cyclone 18 R-3350-23	358/25,000	5,000	31,850	70,140	134,000	1,740	20,000lbs 10x0.5in. mg 1x20mm cannon
de Havilland Mosquito	25/11/1940	2 x 1,250hp Merlin 21	380/17,000	1,795	33,000	13,400	21,462	454	2,000lbs
Douglas Boston III	26/10/1938	2 x 1,600hp Wright Twin Cyclone	304/13,000	1,020	24,250	12,200	25,000	465	2,000lbs 8 mg
Handley Page Halifax III	25/10/1939	4 x 1,675 Bristol Hercules XVI	281/13,500	2,000	20,000	38,320	54,600	1,275	13,000lbs 9 mg

Bombers

	Prototype first flight	Engine	Speed (mph) /altitude (ft)	Range (miles)	Ceiling (ft)	Empty Weight (lbs)	Loaded Weight (lbs)	Wing area (sq ft)	Bomb load (lbs) Armament
Heinkel He 177	19/11/1939	2 x 2,975hp Daimler-Benz DB 610A-1	317/19,300	3,480	23,000	35,500	66,140	1,100	14,400lbs 3 mg, 2x13mm mg, 1x20mm cannon
Messerschmitt Me 264	12/1942	4 x 1,700hp BMW 801D	339/20,000	9,320	26,250	46,627	123,460	1,375	4,400lbs 4x13mm mg, 2x20mm cannon
Martin Baltimore	14/06/1941	2 x 1,600hp Wright-Cyclone GR-2600	301/10,400	1,030	23,500	15,900	21,340	539	2,000lbs 8 mg
Martin B-26 Marauder	25/11/1939	2 x 1,850hp Pratt & Whitney R-2800	315/15,000	1,000	25,000	21,400	32,000	602	4,800 8 x 0.5in. mg
North American B-25 Mitchell	01/1939	2 x 1,700hp Wright Twin Cyclone	284/15,000	1,500	21,200	20,300	34,000	610	3,000lbs 5 mg (3x0.5in.)
Short Stirling III	14/05/1939	4 x 1,640hp Hercules VI	270/7,000	2,010	17,000	45,000	70,000	1,460	14,000lbs 8 mg
Vickers Wellington III	15/06/1936	2 x 1,500hp Hercules XI	255/12,500	2,200	18,500	19,000	29,500	840	4,500lbs 8 mg
Vickers Windsor	23/10/1943	4 x 1,635hp Merlin 65	317/23,000	2,890	27,250	38,600	54,000	1,248	8,000lbs

Army co-operation/Naval/Ground attack

	Prototype First flight	Engine	Speed (mph)/ altitude (ft)	Range (miles)	Ceiling (ft)	Empty Weight (lbs)	Loaded Weight (lbs)	Wing Area (sq ft)	Bomb Load Guns
Focke-Wulf 190	01/06/1939	1,700hp BMW 801D-2	394/18,000	500	34,780	7,330	9,700	197	1,100ls 2 mg, 2x20mm cannon
Grumman TBF Avenger	07/08/1941	1,900hp Wright Twin Cyclone CR-2600-20	275	1,000	30,100	10,545	17,890	490	2,000lbs 2 mg 1x0.5in. mg
Hawker Hurricane IV		1,640hp Merlin 24	284/13,500	470	32,600	5,900	8,500	258	1,000lbs or 8 rockets or 2x40mm cannon
Henschel HS 129	1939	2 x 700hp Gnome-Rhone 14M	253/12,570	428	29,530	8,400	11,570	312	770lbs 2xmg, 2x20mm, 1 x 30mm cannon
Ilyushin Il-2 Sturmovik	02/10/1939	Mikulin 1,700hp AM-38F	250/4,900	475	14,850	9,750	14,00	414	1,329lbs, 2 mg, 1x12,7mm mg, 2x23mm cannon
Junkers Ju 87 D-2	1940	1,400hp Jumo 211D	255/13,500	510	15,520	8,598	12,880	343	3,968lbs 4 mg
Martin-Baker Tankbuster	project	1,760hp Griffon II	270				12,000	470	1x57mm cannon
Taylorcraft D Plus	1939	55hp Lycoming	110	275	15,000	700	1,200	155	None
Vultee Vengeance	30/03/1941	1,650hp Wright Twin Cyclone CR-2600	275	1,500	22,500	9,725	14,300	353	1,000lbs 6 mg

Endnotes

Chapter One

1. Endnotes. AIR, AVIA, WO, CAB, and HO are National Archives files Webster, Frankland, Vol. 2, p 11
2. Webster, Frankland, Vol. 4, Appendix 23
3. Webster, Frankland, Vol. 4, Appendix 20
4. Webster, Frankland, Vol. 4, Appendix 23.
5. AIR20/2673, 14 May 1943
6. AIR8/327, February-March 1942
7. Freeman, *Mighty Eighth War Diary,* p. 66
8. Perret, pp. 260-1, 270
9. Webster, Frankland, Vol. 2, p. 31
10. Hooten, p. 266
11. Webster, Frankland, Vol. 2, pp. 273-4
12. Speer, p. 390
13. Freeman, *The Mighty Eighth*, pp. 80-3
14. Middlebrook, Everitt, p. 425
15. AIR14/1735
16. AIR14/1647, August-November 1943; AIR14/1736 3 November 1943
17. AIR14/1646, 1 May 1944; AIR14/1647, 1, 5 April 1944
18. AIR14/1735, 28 October 1943
19. AIR14/1735, 29 October 1943
20. AIR2/3126, November 1941
21. AIR14/1735, 3 November 1943
22. AVIA15/1405, 8 September 1941
23. AVIA15/1405, 11, 18, 22, 30 May 1942
24. AIR14/1735, 24 June 1943
25. AIR2/7742, 23 April 1943, 27 March 1944
26. Clarke, Vol. 1, p. 149

27. AVIA9/44, 18 October 1942
28. AVIA9/44, 18 October 1942
29. AVIA9/44, October 1942
30. AIR8/451, 17 April 1943
31. AVIA15/1744, August 1942-January 1943
32. AVIA15/1744, 25 September 1942
33. AVIA15/1744, 20 December 1942
34. Churchill, Vol. 5, p. 523
35. AVIA15/1744, 20 December 1942; Buttler, p. 135
36. AVIA15/1968, 27 September 1943

Chapter Two

1. AIR41/55, p. 9; Irving, *The Mare's Nest*, pp. 155, 158
2. SUPP6/510, 5 October, 26 November 1936
3. Irving, *The Mare's Nest*, p. 77
4. AIR41/55, p. 9
5. Irving, *The Mare's Nest*, p. 155
6. Webster, Frankland, Vol. 2, pp. 158-60, 283-4
7. Jones, pp. 448-9
8. AVIA7/1518 (July -October 1941)
9. AIR41/55, pp. 17-18; Irving, *The Mare's Nest*, p. 153-63
10. AIR41/55, p. 8; Irving, *The Mare's Nest*, p. 133
11. Millgate, p. 221; Longmate, pp. 115, 122, Clostermann, p. 76
12. Baughen, *Blueprint for Victory*, Chapters 8, 10, 14
13. Irving, *The Mare's Nest*, p. 91
14. Speer, p. 385
15. Speer, p. 390
16. Speer, pp. 383-8
17. AIR40/1207; Webster, Frankland, Vol. 4, Appendix 49
18. *The Rise and Fall of the German Air Force*, p. 240
19. *The Rise and Fall of the German Air Force*, p. 236
20. Collier, pp. 327, 520
21. Sharp, Boywer, pp. 168-71; Collier, p. 520
22. *The Times*, 23 February 1944
23. AIR41/55, p. 42
24. AIR41/55, pp. 39, 213; Latham, Stobbs, pp. 13, 45-7
25. Stocker, p. 22

26. Longmate, p. 312
27. Longmate, pp. 126-7
28. Irvine, p 172
29. AIR9/209, 11 March 1943
30. AIR9/209, 11 March 1943
31. AIR9/177, 11 September 1943
32. AIR9/177, 11 September 1943
33. AIR20/3739, spring-summer 1942
34. Lewis, p. 21
35. Spaight, pp. 25-6, 145, 152
36. Lewis, p. 7
37. Lewis, p. 7
38. AIR9/209, 15 December 1943
39. AIR9/209, 5 January 1944
40. Lewis, p. xxv
41. Lewis, p. 86
42. Lewis, p. 350

Chapter Three

1. Overy, p. 524
2. Craven, Cate, Vol. II, pp. 463-4; Overy, p. 527;
3. Shores et al., p. 330; AIR41/34, p. 106; The A-36 is sometimes erroneously referred to as the Apache. This was the name North American gave to their original NA-73 fighter project, but it was not used by the USAAF.
4. AIR41/34, pp. 106-11
5. Gooderson, pp. 203-6
6. Baughen, *Blueprint for Victory*, pp. 88, 185, 186, 189
7. Parham, Belfield, p. 46
8. AIR41/34, pp. 110-11
9. AIR41/34, pp. 110-12; AIR41/59, p. 66
10. AIR41/34, p. 158
11. Brookes, *Air War Over Italy*, p. 27
12. Hooton, p. 231; AIR41/34, Appendix 4
13. AIR41/34, p. 141; AIR23/1701; Craven, Cate, Vol. 2, p. 530
14. AIR23/1701
15. AIR41/34, pp. 127-8

16. Tedder, pp. 458-63
17. Tedder, p. 461
18. AIR41/34, p. 123, 140
19. AIR41/34, p. 146; Shores et al. pp. 354-5
20. Craven, Cate, Vol. 2, p. 523
21. Craven, Cate, Vol. 2, pp. 527-8
22. Craven, Cate, Vol. 2, pp. 525-6
23. AIR41/34, pp. 151-2; AIR23/6337, pp. 59-60; Craven, Cate, Vol. 2, pp. 530-1
24. AIR41/34, pp. 153-4, Craven, Cate, Vol. 2, pp. 534-5
25. Parham, Belfield, p. 47
26. AIR41/34, p.168
27. AIR41/34, p.128
28. WO 32/10403, 6 September 1943
29. AIR41/34, p.181
30. Brookes, *Air War Over Italy*, p. 33; AIR41/34, pp. 182-3
31. AIR41/34, p. 202
32. AIR41/34, p. 203
33. Parham, Belfield, pp. 48-9
34. Bowlby, pp. 38-9
35. AIR40/304, 5 December 1943, pp. 33-6
36. Slessor, pp. 121-2, Appendix B.
37. AIR40/304, 5 December 1943, pp. 33-6
38. AIR41/34, pp. 211-12
39. AIR41/34, p. 233
40. MOD Joint Doctrine Publication, UK Air and Space Power, p. 2
41. AIR41/34, p. 229
42. Craven, Cate, Vol. 2, p. 557
43. AIR20/2671, 13, 14, 20 October 1943
44. Tedder, p. 488
45. Tedder, p. 398
46. Brookes, *Air War Over Italy*, p. 44
47. Coningham, p. 178

Chapter Four

1. WO205/443, 5 August 1943
2. WO205/443, 1 September 1943

3. AIR41/66, p. 130
4. AVIA15/1013, 30 May 1943
5. AVIA15/2722, 29 April, 25 May 1943
6. AIR20/4617, 14 August 1943
7. AVIA15/1747, 23 November 1943
8. AVIA15/1747, 29 February 1944
9. AIR20/4617, 8, 18 August 1943
10. Price, *The Spitfire Story*, pp. 217-20
11. AIR20/4617, 8, 13 October 1943
12. Price, *The Spitfire Story*, Appendix C, pp. 244-4
13. AIR19/226, 2, 8 November 1943
14. AIR19/226, 8 November 1943
15. AIR41/24 Appendix 4
16. AIR23/1921, p. 9
17. AVIA46/134, 1 March 1943
18. Price, *World War II Fighter Conflict*, pp. 119-20
19. AIR8/327, February-March 1942
20. AIR2/3037, March-June 1940
21. AVIA15/1013, 28 November, 3 December. 1942
22. Churchill, Vol. 3, p. 600; NA AIR20/2925, 3 June 1941
23. AIR37/166, 20 April 1943
24. AIR37/159, July 1943
25. Tedder, p. 463
26. AIR37/166, 20 April 1943
27. Morgan, pp. 149, 159

Chapter Five

1. Webster, Frankland, Vol. 3, p 11
2. Webster, Frankland, Vol. 4, Appendix XX, p. 492
3. Webster, Frankland, Vol. 2, pp 244-262
4. Webster, Frankland, Vol. 4, Appendix 49, p. 466
5. Fahey, for a rigorous analysis
6. Webster, Frankland, Vol. 4, Appendix XX; Tooze, p. 660. Tooze arrives at a 0 per cent increase from May 1943 to February 1944 by comparing an above-average month (May 1943) with a below-average month (February 1944)
7. AIR14/2481, 19 October 1943

8. AIR20/2673, 7 December 1943
9. AIR20/2673, 23 December 1943
10. AIR20/2673, 1 January 1944
11. Craven, Cate, Vol. 3, Chapter 5
12. Hastings, *Bomber Command*, p. 311
13. Craven, Cate, Vol. 3, p. 11
14. AIR20/3343, 29 September 1943
15. AIR20/3343, 14 October 1943
16. AIR20/3343, 28 October 1943
17. AIR20/3343, 31 October 1943
18. AIR20/2673, 14, 24 October 1943
19. AIR16/119, 6 April 1939.
20. AIR41/49, p. 281.
21. AVIA6/11516, May 1943
22. AIR20/888, 9 September 1943; AIR20/2212, 18 October 1943
23. Webster, Frankland, Vol. 2, p. 46.
24. AIR20/2673, 11 November, 1944
25. AIR20/2673, November 1943
26. Air 20/2673, 12 November 1943
27. AIR20/2673, 5 January 1944
28. AIR20/2673, 17 January 1944
29. Craven, Cate, Vol. 3, p. 8
30. Air37/511, undated January 1944
31. Webster, Frankland, Vol. 4, pp. 160-1
32. Middlebrook, Everitt, pp. 456-66
33. AIR20/2673, 27 January 1944
34. Richards, p. 314; Webster, Frankland, Vol. 3, pp. 69-70
35. Webster, Frankland Vol. 3, pp. 271-6
36. Middlebrook, Everitt, pp. 484-5
37. Middlebrook, Everitt, p. 487
38. Harris, p. 267
39. Middlebrook, aggregated figures from November 1943 to March 1944
40. Frankland, pp. 100-1
41. Craven, Cate, Vol. 3, p 43
42. Webster, Frankland Vol. 4, Appendix 49
43. Hooton, approximations based on pp. 262, 268-9
44. AIR40/1207
45. AIR40/1207

ENDNOTES

Chapter Six

1. Morgan, p. 51
2. AIR37/166, 27 October 1943
3. AIR8/327, 3 March 1942
4. AIR20/888, 17 December 1943
5. AIR20/888, 12, 17 December 1943
6. AIR20/888, 25 February, 7, 10 March 1944
7. AIR20/888, 17 December 1943, 13 February 1944
8. AIR20/3343, 25 April, 1944
9. AIR20/3312, 17 March 1944
10. AIR51/373, 2 March 1944
11. AIR51/373, 29 February 1944, 30 March 1944
12. Shores, *Second Tactical Air Force*, p. 196
13. AIR20/2690, 19 July 1943; AIR16/630, September 1942
14. AIR20/2690, 19 July 1943
15. AIR20/2690, 19 July 1943
16. AIR20/3310, 28 September, 14 October 1943
17. AIR20/2690, 6 October 1943
18. Goulding, J., pp. 146-7
19. AVIA15/1923, 5 October 1943
20. AIR2/5870, 19, January 1945; James, pp. 250-2
21. AVIA15/1923, 5, 30 October 1943
22. AVIA15/1923, 30 October 1943
23. AIR8/784, 29 October-3 December 1943
24. Avia15/1627, 19 September 1942
25. AVIA15/1490, 30 September 1941
26. AVIA15/1627, 5 June, 19 September, 14 December 1942
27. Orange, pp. 189-90
28. AIR20/3030, 4, 7 June 1944
29. AIR20/3030, 7 June 944
30. AIR41/66, pp. 130-1
31. WO232/56, 5 May 1943
32. AIR41/66, p. 131
33. Copp, p. 22
34. WO205/102, 11 April 1944
35. AIR16/705, 3 August 1943
36. Copp, p. 22
37. AVIA10/381, 4 November 1942, 15 November 1943

38. AIR16/705, July-August 1943
39. AIR20/889, 29 June 1943
40. AVIA15/1640, 4 April 1943
41. AVIA15/1640, 12 April 1943
42. AIR16/705, 8 August 1943
43. Clostermann, pp. 76-82
44. AIR37/636, 10, 11, 21 November 1943
45. AIR37/636, 27 September 1943
46. AIR20/3312, 5 September 1943
47. AIR20/3312, 29 September 1943
48. AVIA10/381, 5, 12, 13 August 1943
49. AIR23/1921, November 1943
50. AVIA10/381, 9 December 1943
51. WO 232/56, 3, 5, 26 May 1943
52. WO232/56, 5 May 1943
53. WO232/56, 5 May 1943
54. WO 232/56, May - September1943
55. WO232/56, letter from Sorley 6 August 1941
56. WO232/56, May-July 1943
57. AIR 2/690, 30 January 1941
58. AIR37/91, 11 November 1943
59. AIR51/373 3 July, 30 August 1943
60. AIR51/373, 3 July, 24 August, 1943, 2 January 1944
61. See Baughen, *The Fairey Battle,* pp. 35, 51-3, 58
62. AIR37/91, 24 November 1943
63. AIR51/373, 11 March 1944; AIR20/3030, 27 May 1944
64. WO232/56, 18 November 1943
65. WO232/56, 10 August 1943
66. WO232/56, July 1943
67. WO 232/56, 27 October 1943
68. AIR37/636, 12 February 1944
69. AIR37/636, 12 February 1944
70. AIR37/636, 21 October 1944
71. AIR37/91, 11 November 1943
72. AIR37/636, 12 February 1944
73. AIR51/322, 10 March, 3 May; AIR20/4617, 25 May 1944
74. Air20/4617, 25 May 1944
75. AIR37/636, May-July 1944; AIR51/373, 10 March, 3 May 1944
76. AIR37/1175, 19 January 1944

ENDNOTES

Chapter Seven

1. Brooke, pp. 468, 486
2. Brooke, p. 460
3. Brooke, p. 465
4. Brookes, *Air War Over Italy*, p. 52; Hooton, p. 236
5. AIR41/34, p. 252
6. Brookes, *Air War Over Italy*, pp. 49, 52
7. Shores et al, Volume four, pp. 501-7
8. AIR41/34, p. 253
9. D'Este, *Fatal Decision*, pp. 147-50
10. Malony, p. 685
11. Brookes, *Air War Over Italy*, p. 68; d'Este, *Fatal Decision*, p. 260
12. Craven, Cate, Vol. 3, p. 365
13. AIR41/34, p. 288
14. Pitt, Vol. 4, No. 13, p. 1696
15. Craven, Cate, pp. 355-7, AIR41/34, p. 261
16. AIR41/34, p.262; Brookes, *Air War Over Italy*, pp. 56-7
17. AIR41/34, p.262; Parham, Belfield, pp 56-57
18. Craven, Cate, pp. 366-7
19. AIR41/34, p. 297
20. Brookes, *Air War Over Italy*, pp. 68-71
21. Orange, p. 185
22. Slessor, p. 573
23. Slessor, p. 573
24. Slessor, p. 571
25. Slessor, p. 572
26. Kesselring, p. 200
27. Slessor, pp. 575-6
28. AIR41/34, p. 331
29. Craven, Cate, Vol. 3, p. 390
30. AIR41/34, p. 339
31. Brookes, *Air War Over Italy*, pp. 90-4; AIR41/34, p. 343
32. AIR41/34, p. 346
33. Brookes, *Air War Over Italy*, p. 96
34. AIR41/34, p. 343; Gooderson, p. 28.
35. AIR41/34, p. 347
36. Slessor, p. 575
37. AIR10/5547, Appendix 9

Chapter Eight

1. See Baughen, *Blueprint for Victory*, pp. 179, 184
2. AIR41/66, p. 72
3. Perret, p. 283; Craven, Cate, p. 109
4. Hamilton, p. 588
5. Spires, p. 48; Hamilton, p. 599
6. D'Este, *Decision in Normandy*, p. 91
7. Tedder, p. 522
8. Craven, Cate, Vol. 3 p. 75; Mets, 201
9. Tedder, p. 517
10. AIR41/66, p. 134
11. AIR41/66, p. 121
12. Mets, p.190; Craven, Cate, Vol. 3 pp. 5, 75
13. AIR41/66, pp. 125-6
14. Countless personal accounts, including my Dad
15. Craven, Cate, Vol. 3, p. 76
16. AIR8/1217, 13, 18 April 1944
17. Air41/66, pp. 156-9; CAB65/46/1, 3 April 1944
18. Tedder, p. 516
19. Webster, Frankland, Vol. 3, pp. 32-3
20. Middlebrook, Everitt, p. 486
21. AIR41/66, p. 156
22. CAB65/46/1, 3 April 1944
23. Middlebrook, Everitt, pp. 492-4
24. Webster, Frankland Vol. 4, Appendix XXXIV, p. 160
25. Webster, Frankland Vol. 4, Appendix XXXVIII, pp. 167-70
26. AIR41/66, p. 170
27. Overy, pp. 573-6; Churchill, Vol. 5, pp. 410-11
28. Webster, Frankland Vol. 3, pp. 154-5
29. Overy, p. 574
30. Hooton, p. 278
31. Freeman, *Mighty Eighth War Diary*, April-May operations
32. Hooton, p. 268
33. WO205/182
34. AIR 41/66, p. 136
35. Dunn, p. 104
36. Hallion, p. 167

ENDNOTES

37. AIR51/322, 14 January-April 1944
38. AIR51/322, 4 February 1944
39. WO 205/182, 18 December -February 1944
40. WO 205/182, March 1944
41. WO 205/182, February 1944
42. WO 205/182, 8 March 1944
43. WO205/553, 25 February 1944
44. WO205/553, 24 March 1944
45. WO205/553, 24 March 1944
46. WO205/553, 24 March 1944
47. AIR20/888, February 1944
48. Shores, *Second Tactical Air Force*, p. 139
49. WO32/10403, April-May 1944 report
50. *Airpower Review*, Vol. 19, No 1, p. 57
51. Copp, pp. 21-2
52. Hamilton, p. 600
53. Terraine, p. 380
54. Gooderson, p. 36; Spires. p. 48
55. Hamilton, pp. 598-9
56. AIR51/322, January–April 1944
57. Montgomery, p. 257
58. D'Este, *Decision in Normandy*, p. 223
59. WO205/182, 23 April 1944
60. AIR 41/66, pp. 136-7
61. WO 205/182, 30 April 1944
62. WO 205/182, 16 May 1944
63. WO 205/182, 16 May 1944; AIR41/66, p. 185
64. AIR41/66, p. 43
65. Gooderson, pp. 42-3
66. Hamilton, p. 598
67. Hughes, pp. 156-7, Hamilton, p. 598
68. Hughes, pp. 118-20
69. Spires, p. 48-49, Rein, p. 8
70. Craven, Cate, Vol. 3, p. 125
71. AIR41/66, p.129
72. AIR 41/66, pp.129, 184, AIR41/24, p. 59
73. AIR 41/66, p. 185
74. Montgomery, p. 248
75. Tedder, p. 545

Chapter Nine

1. Brooke, p. 554
2. AIR 41/24, Appendix 4
3. AIR41/24, p.141
4. AIR41/24, p.143; Freeman, *Mighty Eighth War Diary*, p. 259
5. *The Rise and Fall of the German Air force*, p. 321
6. *Daily Mail*, 8 June 1944
7. AIR41/24, p. 61
8. AIR27, relevant squadron records.
9. Craven, Cate, Vol. 3, p.192
10. AIR27, relevant squadron records
11. Kohn, Harahan, p. 24
12. Olds, pp. 51-2
13. Hughes, pp. 7-10
14. D'Este, *Decision in Normandy*, pp. 130-6
15. Keegan, p. 126, Hastings, *Overlord*, p. 135-6
16. Bowyer, *Aircraft for the* Many, pp. 227, 296
17. Hastings, *Overlord*, pp. 132-3; D'Este, *Decision in Normandy*, pp. 123-9
18. AIR41/24, p. 147
19. AIR21/41, p. 190
20. Ellis, p. 203
21. Ellis, p. 72
22. Craven, Cate, Vol. 3, p. 185
23. Churchill, Vol. 3, p. 393

Chapter Ten

1. AIR41/24, p. 151
2. AIR41/24, p. 151
3. AIR41/24, pp. 152-3
4. Hughes, p. 178
5. Bowyer, *Aircraft for the Many*, p. 215; Shores, *Second Tactical Air Force*, p 275; Parham, Belfield, p. 74; Mead p. 210
6. *Report No 74, Historical Section (Canadian) Army*, 5 July 1955, pp. 12-13

ENDNOTES

7. AIR41/24, pp.155-6; AIR 27 squadron records
8. Hastings, *Overlord*, p 313
9. AIR27/1138/21, 22
10. Hastings, *Overlord*, pp. 154-5
11. Hastings, *Overlord*, pp. 157-8
12. AIR27, squadron records, June 1944
13. AIR41/67, p. 12-13
14. Spires, pp. 55-6
15. Tedder, pp. 554-5
16. Dunn, p 131; D'Este, *Decision in Normandy*, p. 225
17. Hamilton, p. 680
18. D'Este, *Decision in Normandy*, p. 227
19. Tedder, p. 552
20. D'Este, *Decision in Normandy*, pp. 226-7
21. Tedder, p. 552
22. 'D'Este, *Decision in Normandy*, pp. 228-9
23. Dunn, p. 156
24. Dunn, p. 131
25. Dunn. p. 131
26. Dunn, p. 131
27. D'Este, *Decision in Normandy*, p. 220
28. Hamilton, p. 673
29. Shores, *Second Tactical Air Force*, pp. 13-15
30. AIR41/67, p. 15; Caldwell, p. 292
31. AIR41/67, p.16
32. AIR41/67, p.19
33. Hardesty, pp. 194-6
34. Hamilton, pp. 692-3
35. AIR41/67, pp. 20-1
36. Tedder, pp. 557-8
37. AIR41/67, p. 22
38. AIR41/67, p. 24
39. Gooderson pp. 134-5; AIR41/67, p. 23
40. AIR41/67, pp 22-3
41. D'Este, *Decision in Normandy*, p. 318
42. Gooderson, p. 135
43. AIR41/67, p. 24
44. Caldwell, p. 296

Chapter Eleven

1. Irving, *The Mare's Nest*, p. 235
2. Irving, *The Mare's Nest*, pp. 235-6
3. HO 199/292, 7 November 1944
4. Harris, p. 216
5. Speer, p. 492
6. AIR 9/195, 22 August 1944
7. AIR 9/195, 22 August 1944
8. AIR9/125, 4, 7 September 1944
9. AIR 9/195, 22 August, 4 September 1944
10. Irving, *The Mare's Nest*, p. 243
11. Collier, p. 384
12. AIR2/5870, 20 May 1944
13. AIR20/3030, 26 June, 12 August 1944
14. Collier, p. 523
15. AIR41/55, p. 112
16. Millgate, pp. 248-9
17. AIR41/55, p. 211; O'Brien, p. 664
18. Murray, pp. 246-7
19. Webster, Frankland, Vol. 3, p. 49
20. Webster, Frankland, Vol. 4, pp. 322-3, 516-17
21. Harris, p. 220
22. AIR14/1735, 22 June 1944
23. AIR14/1273, October 1943-February 1944
24. AIR2/5594, 5 August 1944
25. AIR2/5594, 25 June 1944
26. AIR2/5594, February-April 1945
27. AIR 2/7742, 4, 27 March 1944
28. AIR 20/1799, 30 June-8 August 1944
29. Webster, Frankland, Vol. 3, p.148
30. Caldwell, p. 314
31. AIR20/3312, 13 July 1944
32. AIR2/3037, March-June 1940; see Baughen, *The RAF in the Battle of France and the Battle of Britain*, pp. 29, 68-70; *RAF on the Offensive*, p.196
33. AIR20/3312, 8 August 1944
34. AIR16/327, 12 September 1944
35. AIR20/4617, 19 July 1944

ENDNOTES

36. AIR16/327, 12 September 1944
37. AVIA6/11516 May 1943
38. Crosley, pp. 158-9, 165
39. AIR16/327, 12 September 1944
40. AIR16/327, 13 December 1944
41. AIR2/5655, 4 October 1944
42. AIR37/634, 9 September 1944
43. AIR2/5655, 30 August, 3 September 1944
44. Orange, p. 214, AIR37/609, 10 September 1944; AIR37/880, 13 September 1944
45. AIR37/880, 13 September, 1944

Chapter Twelve

1. AIR41/67, p. 51
2. Greenhous et al, p. 312
3. AIR41/67, pp. 46-50
4. WO205/556, 3 August 1944
5. Bekker, pp. 118-19
6. AIR37/459, 29 July 1944
7. AIR37/459, July 1944
8. D'Este, *Decision in Normandy*, p. 394
9. Craven, Cate, Vol. 3, p. 232
10. Craven, Cate, Vol. 3, pp. 232-6, Hastings, *Overlord*, pp. 298-300
11. D'Este, *Decision in Normandy*, p. 403
12. D'Este, *Decision in Normandy*, p. 403
13. Gooderson, pp. 147-8
14. Orange, p. 112
15. Baughen, *Blueprint for Victory*, p. 179
16. Baughen, *Blueprint for Victory*, Chapters 12, 13
17. Spires, p. 66
18. D'Este, *Decision in Normandy*, p. 424
19. AIR41/67, pp. 85-9
20. WO205/556, 28 October 1944; Copp, p. 24
21. WO 106/4348, pp. 24, 41, 63, 88, 101; WO 205/556, August–September 1944
22. WO205/556 9 August, 7 September 1944
23. Freeman, *Mighty Eighth War Diary*, p. 319

24. AIR41/67, p. 99
25. Copp, p. 101
26. Middlebrook, Everitt, p. 562
27. Tedder, pp. 570-1
28. Rein, pp. 83-7
29. Spires, pp. 73-6
30. D'Este, *Decision in Normandy*, p. 424
31. D'Este, *Decision in Normandy*, p. 430
32. Gooderson, p. 33.
33. AIR41/67, pp. 107-8
34. Shores, *Second Tactical Air Force*, p. 62
35. Caldwell, p. 326
36. AIR41/67, p. 108
37. WO 106/4348
38. WO205/556, 28 October 1944
39. WO 106/4348
40. WO 205/556, 30 October 1944
41. AIR37/91 15 May 1944
42. AIR37/636, 15 June 1944
43. AIR37/880, 13 September 1944
44. AIR37/880, 13 September 1944
45. AIR37/636, 21 June 1944
46. Arnold, pp. 377-8; AIR23/7772, 15 April 1943. The Americans would eventually acquire more than 100
47. AIR37/634, 9 September 1944; AIR37/876, p.40
48. Terraine, pp. 669-70; Ellis, Vol. 2, p. 53
49. AIR37/1214
50. AIR41/67, p.151
51. AIR41/67, p 150; AIR37/1249, p.38
52. AIR37/1214, Index E; Gooderson, pp. 96-7
53. AIR37/1214
54. AIR41/67, p.151
55. AIR27/1489/25
56. AIR41/67, pp. 151-2
57. Ryan, pp. 433-4
58. AIR37/1249, p. 61
59. AIR37/1249, p. 67; Gooderson, p. 98
60. CAB106/220

Index

Admiralty, 120
Air Control (colonial), 37–8, 214
Air Defence of Great Britain
  (ADGB), 121, 126–7, 179, 198,
  226, 254
Air Ministry, 5, 10, 22, 32, 48,
  69, 71–2, 74, 79, 84–5, 96,
  121, 146, 165, 175, 213, 222,
  245, 248
  on tactical air power, vii–viii, xi,
    30, 33, 36, 58, 87, 111–12,
    113–15, 117, 119–27, 193,
    203, 266
  RAF independence, xi, 46, 93,
    264–5
  post-war policy, xii, 33–9
  bomber policy, 9, 25, 30, 33–4,
    36, 68, 92, 217, 264
  bomber defence, 12–13
  bomber development, 14–21
  jet aircraft, 20, 100, 107–10
  fighter range, 45, 74–6, 103,
    106, 223–4
  air superiority, 67–8
Air Position Indicator, 9
Air Staff, 18, 41, 81, 121–2,
  149, 212
  bomber policy, vi–viii, xii, ix,
    2–3, 20, 93, 217, 219

tactical air support, x, 147–8,
  193, 199
  post-war policy, 19, 39
Air support controls, 43
Air Support Team, 254
Airborne radar,
  Mk IV, 85
  Mk V, 221
  Mk VII, 26
  Mk VIII, 26
  Mk X, 30
  German Lichtenstein
    B/C, 85
  SN2, 84
Alexander, Gen. H., 136–7
Allied Expeditionary Air Force
  (AEAF), 82, 105, 121, 122,
  149, 160, 166, 168–70,
  172, 174
Antwerp, importance of, 251, 261
Anzio, landing (Shingle), 61, 105,
  130–5, 142, 145–6, 156, 164,
  211
  fighter cover for, 131–2
  air support for, 132–5
  German attack (February 1944),
    137–9
Arado 234, 180
Armour column cover, 235

Army, British, vii, ix–x, 38, 46, 67–8, 78, 111–12, 119–24, 143, 147, 178, 187–9, 242–3, 264
  relations with RAF, ix, 45, 49, 55, 58–9, 67, 120, 123, 137–41, 171–4
  on close air support, 54–5, 111–12, 119–21, 130, 148, 167–9, 177, 187, 192, 195, 206–207, 235, 247, 254, 257, 260–1
  carpet bombing, 136–7, 139–40, 201–202, 205, 207, 210, 230–1, 241–2, 265
  G(Air), 168, 247
Army, German ix, 27, 29, 37, 60, 154, 191, 237, 242, 250, 252, 264
Army, American, x, 1, 56, 175, 243–4
Army, Canadian, 64, 172, 254
Army, French, 35, 145
Army, Soviet, viii, ix, 38–9, 78, 102, 129
Arnhem, (Market Garden), 252–61
Arnold, Gen. H., 5, 86, 90–1, 93–4, 103, 136, 141, 249–50
  on escorts, 5, 86–90, 223
Avro Lancaster, 12–13, 17, 41, 81, 83, 126, 197, 213, 249
  qualities, 9–10, 14, 18
  vulnerability, 10, 84–5, 223, 227
  obsolescence, 18, 222
Avro Lincoln (Lancaster IV), 17–20, 222
Avro Manchester, 13–14
AWACS, 123–4

Battle of Britain, vii, 35, 67, 86, 98, 101
Battle of France (1940), 35, 67, 112, 127, 148, 156, 177–8, 181, 191, 193, 219, 227, 231, 244, 260, 266
Battle of the Atlantic, 35, 80
Berlin, raids on, 9, 83–5, 91, 94–6, 98–101
Big Week, 94, 97–8
Blitzkrieg, vi, 59–60, 162, 240
Blohm & Voss BV 40, 8
Boeing B-17 Flying Fortress, 6–7, 14, 19, 51, 220
Boeing B-29, Superfortress, 14–16, 18–20, 222
Boeing B-47, 20
Bomber Command, 5, 18, 20–1, 41, 79, 80, 93–4, 111, 152, 157–61, 168, 213, 216–22
  strategic role, vii, 2–3, 28, 37, 81–2, 164, 183, 216, 217–19, 228
  battlefield role, 208, 210, 241, 228, 242, 254–5
  casualties, 9, 85, 97, 101, 219–20
  Battle of Berlin, 83–6, 91, 94–6, 99
  daylight operations, 197–8, 222–3, 226–7
Bomber defence, 10–13, 16, 18–19, 220–2
Bomber, future designs, 14, 15–21, 35
Bomber offensive, viii, 171, 213, 263
  required for Overlord, viii, ix, 1–2, 65, 91–3
  value of, 6–7, 27–8, 79–80, 91, 97–8, 101–102, 163–4, 181, 264
  as war winner, 35, 41, 48, 76, 129

INDEX

for air superiority, 45, 47–8, 68, 93, 98, 106, 149, 152
oil offensive, 156–8, 163–4, 217–19
Bottomley, AM M., 81, 91, 94, 176
Boulton Paul Defiant, 10, 69
Bradley, Lt. Gen. O., 150, 175, 200, 232, 234, 237, 244
Brereton, Lt. Gen. L., 82, 150, 175, 205, 244, 251, 257
Brest, battle for, 243, 259
Bristol,
    Centaurus, 15, 73, 116, 121
    Beaufighter, 69, 85
    Blenheim/Bisley, 112
British Air Forces in France (1940), 112
Broadhurst, AVM H., x, 40, 43–5, 54, 56–9, 62–4, 114, 124, 137, 171–3, 175, 190, 204, 207, 209–10, 231, 240, 244
    cab rank, 57–8
Brooke, Gen. A., x, 61, 67, 129, 130, 144, 149, 157, 159, 164, 179, 191
    on bomber offensive, x, xi, 1, 65, 77–9, 82, 129, 203
    post-war policy, 38–9
Brown, AVM L., 172
Browning, Gen. F., 252
Burma theatre, 63–4, 73, 116

Cannon, Gen. J., 62–3, 142
Carpet bombing, 40, 51, 136, 140–1, 201–202, 205, 208–10, 214, 228–35, 241–2
Casablanca, conference, 1, 3, 78, 149, 151
Cassino, 130, 140–2, 146–7, 164, 210
bombing of monastery, 135–7
second battle for, 137
third battle for, 139–40
fourth battle for, 144–5
Chain Home, 31–2
Cherwell, Lord, 22–3, 25, 159
Churchill, W., viii, 5, 20, 26, 31, 42, 60–1, 83, 108, 129, 130, 136, 152, 192, 211
    bombing policy, viii, 2, 26, 83
    transportation plan, 158–60
    fighter range, 75, 105
Close air support, x, xi, 49, 59, 122, 132, 134, 137, 140–1, 148, 195–6, 199–200, 207, 230, 234, 257, 261, 265
    specialised aircraft for, 113–21
    priority for, xi, 41, 45, 46, 50, 53, 63, 111, 130, 191–3, 254, 260
    value of, 40, 44, 55, 239–41, 256, 259
    for D-day, 111, 149, 167–78, 185–6, 189–93
    weapons for,
        cluster bombs, 112
        rockets, 112–5, 118, 121–2, 238–40, 246–7
        cannon, 113–15, 118, 170, 246
Collins, Maj. Gen. J., 235
Combat air patrol, 46, 266
Coningham, AM A., xi, 56, 63–4, 149, 166, 176, 185, 194, 200, 204, 226, 235, 248, 250
    air policy, xi, 41, 57–9, 62–4, 140–1, 172–3, 175, 204–205
    dislike of Montgomery, 170, 172, 207
    jets, 110, 249
    reconnaissance, 126–7, 175, 249
    carpet bombing, 140, 201–202

Consolidated B-24 Liberator, 43, 47–8, 83, 131
Convair B-36, 15, 17, 19–20
Crawford, Maj. Gen. K., 117, 119–20, 123
Crossbow, 32
Crow, A., 22–3, 25
Curtiss P-40,
    Tomahawk, 125
    Kittyhawk, 43–4, 54, 131, 135

D'Albiac, AM J., 64, 168
Dambusters, 24, 27–8
De Gaulle, C., 160
De Havilland,
    Mosquito, 10, 22, 26, 83, 85, 114, 126–7, 155, 161, 166, 217, 227, 249
    Vampire, 108
    Goblin, 108–109
Decentralised control, 58, 200, 210–11, 235–6, 240, 243–4, 266
Dempsey, Lt. Gen. M., 64, 150, 188, 190, 201–202, 204, 210
Desert Air Force, ix-xi, 40–1, 44, 46, 53–4, 56, 131, 137, 141, 147, 192
Dickson, AVM W., 115, 172
Dieppe raid, 110–11, 117, 122, 165, 167–8, 183, 184–7, 191
Dodecanese campaign, 60–1
Dornier Do 217, 9
Douglas A-20 Boston (Havoc), 43, 155, 199, 205
Douhet G., 92
Drop tanks, 4–5, 7, 45, 76, 86–7, 89–90, 103, 105, 107, 121, 194, 223–4

Eaker, Gen. I., 2, 63, 79, 136, 139, 141
Eisenhower, Gen. D., 40, 47, 61, 64, 82, 136, 150, 152–3, 161, 172, 177, 190–1, 201–202, 205, 208, 217, 251–2
    on air power, 40, 53, 59, 151, 160–1
    interdiction, 48, 155, 159
    carpet bombing, 53, 40, 165, 209, 231, 234–5, 242

Fairey Battle, 121
Falaise, German retreat, 245–6
Fighter Command, vii, 26, 70, 88–90, 121, 216, 224, 226, 258
Fighter roles,
    air superiority, 68–9, 74, 92, 110
    escort, 4–5, 85–90, 96–101, 103, 105, 152, 162–3, 176, 220, 223, 226
    interceptor 4, 10, 26, 68–9, 74, 87, 89, 97, 100, 109–10
fighter-bomber,
    on battlefield, 55, 66, 138, 148, 199, 206, 230, 235, 238–40, 246–7, 256, 259–60
    beyond battlefield, 157, 196–8, 240, 246–7
Firestorms, 8, 83
First Tactical Air Force, 56
Flak as air superiority tool, x, 40, 57, 146, 245
Fleet Air Arm, 46, 89–90, 120, 165, 188, 224, 250
Focke-Wulf Fw 190, 31, 69, 71–2, 74, 86, 97, 113, 121, 180
Foreign Office, 37–9, 157

INDEX

Forward Control Posts, 43, 46, 53, 57–8, 132, 140, 144, 169, 187, 196, 206, 255–6
   Rover, 43, 46, 54, 57, 140, 145, 250
Fraser Nash turrets, 11–12, 220
Freyberg, Gen. B., 136–7, 139
Friendly-fire incidents, 55, 138–9, 145, 166, 195, 200, 231, 234, 241–3, 245, 260
Fritz X, 50, 67, 132, 180

Gammell, Lt. Gen. J., 147
Geddes, Air Cdre. A, 124–5
GEE, 25
Gloster,
   Meteor, 20, 107, 116, 121, 248
      Mk I, 108–109, 215–16, 249
      Mk II, 108–109
      Mk III, 108–109, 122, 249
   Gladiator, 66
   Ace, 110
Goddard, R., 23
Goodwin-Austen, Gen. A., 123
Gotha raids (1917), 27
Graham, AVM R., 66, 149
Groom, AVM V., 168
Ground Position Indicator, 9

H2S, 7, 9, 11, 83–4, 184, 227
Hamburg, bombing of, ix, 8–9, 27, 83, 96
Handley Page Halifax, 9–11, 13–15, 80, 83, 95, 126, 220, 249
Harris, ACM A., viii, 7, 35, 79–80, 82, 93–6, 99, 101, 155, 158–61, 213, 223, 226
   bomber strategy, xi, 2–3, 8–9, 27, 35, 83, 92, 101, 217–19, 262
   attitude to Overlord, xi, 92, 129, 151–3
   bomber defence, 10–13
   conflict with Air Staff, 80–2, 94
Hawker Tempest, 73, 126, 223, 245, 249–50
   Mk I, 73
   Mk II, 73, 116, 121, 125, 248
   Mk III, 73
   Mk IV, 73
   Mk V, 73, 108, 121, 198, 215, 248
   qualities, 73–4, 245
   range, 106, 223
Hawker Hurricane, 66, 113–18, 183, 248
Hawker Typhoon, 69, 73, 88, 113, 121, 176, 189–91, 194–5, 206, 238–9, 246–9
   qualities, 114–16, 173, 248
   production, 116, 122, 248
   for reconnaissance, 125–7, 248–50
Heinkel,
   He 177, 28, 31
   He 280, 107
Helicopter, 120–1
Henschel,
   Hs 129, 113
   Hs 293, 50, 61, 67, 132, 180
Hitler, A., vi, 21, 26–7, 30, 40, 54, 60–1, 130, 213, 238, 244, 261, 263
Horrocks, Lt. Gen. B., 252, 254–7

Ideal Bomber, 15
Inglis. Air Cdre. F., 81

Japan, 17, 20, 214
Japanese Air Force, 4, 75
   Mitsubishi Ki-46, 73

Jeschonnek, Gen. H., 29
Junkers
    Ju 87 (Stuka), 59, 61, 112, 118, 240, 247
    Ju 88, 10, 180
    Mistel, 180

Knockout blow, 23, 25, 37, 47, 95, 263
Korten, Gen. G., 29

Leigh-Mallory, AM T., 70, 71–3, 82, 87–8, 114–15, 121, 149–50, 152–5, 170, 172–7, 198, 201–205, 226
    on fighter range, 89–90, 105
    on jets, 108
    First World War, 149, 236
    on army air support, 149, 166, 168–9, 172–4, 202–204
    relations with Americans, 150, 154
    carpet bombing, 201–202, 204, 208–209
    attitude to Army, 202–204, 207
Lizzie, 23
Lockheed P-38 Lightning, 4, 45, 60, 62, 69, 101, 103, 179, 186
    as escort, 4–5, 86, 88, 96–7, 103
Lubbock, I., 23, 25
Lucas, Gen. J., 130–4
Luftwaffe, 6, 14, 26, 30, 45, 55, 74, 98, 127, 162, 180–1, 222, 262
    effectiveness, 6–7, 40, 49, 59–60, 66–8, 96, 100–101, 138, 189, 197
    strategic bombing policy, 28–9
    Allies overestimate, 66, 150–2, 154, 176–7, 161, 186

Marshal, Gen. G., 41
Martin B-26 Marauder, 51, 144–5, 199
Martin Baker tank-buster, 114
Master bomber, 24, 158, 208
Mediterranean Allied Air Force, 62, 105
Messerschmitt,
    Bf 109, 69, 71–2, 74, 86, 97, 100, 107
    Bf 110, 10, 86
    Me 163, 227
    Me 209, 69, 71, 74
    Me 262, 107, 110, 180, 227
    Me 264, 17
Metropolitan-Vickers F.2, 20
Milch, E., 97
Ministry of Aircraft Production, 13, 17–18, 70, 75, 105, 112–14, 116–17, 122, 126, 170
    jet aircraft, 20, 109, 110
    designated types, 126, 249
Ministry of Supply, 22–3
Mitchell, W., 93
Monica, 11, 84
Montgomery, Gen. B., xi, 54–7, 64, 151, 173, 181, 190–1, 198, 200–207, 211, 228, 231–2, 244, 251–2
    relations with air commanders, 45, 170, 172, 207–208
    on air support, 54, 59, 151, 171–2, 174, 176–7, 188, 191, 201, 203–205, 207, 209, 231, 251, 260
Morale as battlefield factor, 53, 55, 136, 138, 148, 173, 177, 191, 198, 200, 202, 231, 237–41, 259–60

INDEX

Morgan, Lt. Gen. F., 64–5, 92–3, 106, 149
  on fighter range, 74, 76–7, 89, 106, 103–105
  on air support, 66–7, 110–11, 114
Munich agreement, 34
Mussolini, B., 4, 42

Napier Sabre, 15, 19, 73, 116, 121, 126, 206
NATO, 37
Normandy battles,
  Villers-Bocage, 199
  Cherbourg, 199–200
  Epsom, 205–206
  Charnwood, 209–10
  Goodwood, 228–30
  Cobra, 232–7
  Mortain, 238
  Totalise, 241
  Falaise, 245
North American,
  B-25 Mitchell, 43, 51, 155, 205
  P-51 Mustang, 43
    range of, 86, 103, 105–106, 109
    for reconnaissance, 125–7, 165, 188, 249
    for ground attack, 194, 199, 250–1
    Mk I/II, 76, 87, 125, 248
    A-36 Invader, 43, 45, 48–51, 54, 131
    Mk III, 69–71, 74, 87–8, 96–7, 99–100, 108, 125, 162, 180, 194, 198, 215, 226, 245, 250
    Mustang Mk F/G, 125

Nugent, Brig. Gen, R., 243, 259
Nuremburg raid, 95–6

Oboe, 25, 217, 227
Olds, Lt. R., 186
Overlord,
  Morgan's plan, 65–6
  Montgomery's plan, 150–1

Pantelleria, 40–1, 136, 164
Patton, Gen. G., 237, 243–4
Peenemunde, 22–5, 158
Pizzo, battle, 44–6
Pointblank, 3–4, 29, 32, 62, 77, 79, 81–2, 91–2, 94, 101–102, 136, 142, 150, 152
Portal, ACM, C., 2, 38, 47, 92–3
  bomber offensive, 2, 5–6, 9, 46, 81–2
  fighter range, 5, 103, 105
  jets, 108, 110
Post-Hostilities Planning Committee, 37–8

Quesada, Brig. Gen E., 175–6, 186, 195, 204, 236–7, 240, 243

RAE Larynx, 25, 31, 213
Ramsay Adml. B., 82, 165, 184
Rebecca/Eureka, 118
Republic P-47 Thunderbolt, 5–7, 62, 69, 86, 88, 90, 96, 99, 103, 116, 142, 177, 185, 235, 238, 243, 245
Robb, AVM J., 149
Rolls-Royce,
  production problems, 17, 71–2
  Merlin XX, 17, 72
  Merlin 27, 115, 117

Merlin 60 series, 16–18, 69–71, 74–5, 86, 222, 249
Merlin 100, 70
Griffon 61, 70–3, 250
Welland, 108–109
Rommel. FM E., viii, 113, 164, 130, 170, 173, 197, 205
Roosevelt, F., 2, 160
Rose turret, 12-3, 220
Royal Air Force,
   independence issue, vii, xi, 27, 93, 142, 146, 158, 192, 208, 235–6, 240, 244–6, 261, 264–5
   Air/Army relations, 49, 59, 63–4, 67, 119–21, 137–8, 143, 203–204, 208–209, 260–1, 264–5
Royal Flying Corps, 236
Royal Navy, 46, 49, 61, 67–8, 78, 119–20, 152, 177, 187–8, 214

Salerno, 41, 43, 76, 105, 130, 132, 211
   fighter cover for, 45, 48–9
   close air support for, 46
   battle, 48–54
Sandys, D., 22, 25
Sangro, battle for, 57–8
Savannah, USS, 50
Schweinfurt, 3, 5–6, 8, 27, 82–3, 94–5
SCR-584, 215
Second Tactical Air Force, x, 64, 82, 149–50, 166, 168, 173, 176–7, 194, 196, 198, 230, 238–9, 252, 258
   equipment, 74, 121, 125, 129, 140, 215, 226

Short,
   Stirling, 9–11, 13–15, 80, 83–4, 95
   Super Stirling, 15
Sicily campaign, lessons, 54, 130
Slessor, AM J., 58, 63, 89, 142–4, 160, 171, 173
   attitude to army support, 141, 147–8
Slim, Lt. Gen. W., 63
Smuts, J., vii, xi, 36
Soviet Air Force, 163, 175, 197, 175, 207
Soviet aircraft, 146
   Ilyushin Il-2 Sturmovik, 113, 175, 207
   Petlyakov Pe-2, 207
Soviet Union, viii, 19, 39–40, 68–9
   armed forces, ix, x, 38, 102, 207, 175, 246
   as future enemy, 36, 38
Spaatz, Lt. Gen. C., 92, 141, 151–3, 155–7, 160–1, 163, 176, 217–18
Spaight, J., 37
Specifications,
   B.1/39, 15
   B.5/41, 16
   E.6/41, 110
   B.8/41, 15–16
   B.3/42, 16, 18
   E.5/42, 110
   F.6/42, 68, 74, 92
Speer, A., 27–8, 97, 123
Stalin, J., viii, 42, 65, 91, 129
Steinbock, operation, 30–1
Strangle, operation, 61, 141–3, 154–5, 160
Supermarine Seafire, 46, 48–9, 165, 188, 224

INDEX

Supermarine Spiteful, 71, 109
Supermarine Spitfire, 5, 67, 69
   endurance, 5, 45–6, 74–6, 88–90, 105–107, 223–6, 250, 258
   deployment, 33, 40, 66, 73, 116, 226
   ground attack, 55, 169–70, 206, 248, 250
   development, 69–71, 74
   production, 72–3, 117, 249
   reconnaissance, 75, 88, 125–7, 188, 249–50
   Mk V, 69, 72, 215
   Mk IX, 74, 198, 215
   Mk XIV, 71
   Mk 21, 71, 73

Taylorcraft Auster AOP, 44, 51–3, 55–6, 119–120, 122–4, 127, 144, 167, 188, 190, 195, 210, 235–6, 242, 251
Tebaga, battle, 40–1, 43, 141, 173, 175, 178, 201, 204–205
Tedder, ACM A., 41, 45, 49, 56–7, 59, 63–4, 149–50, 155, 157–8, 164, 172, 176–7, 200–202, 209, 217
   attitude to army air support, 41, 45–6, 59, 204–205, 208–209
   bomber as decisive weapon, 46–8, 61–3, 163–4
   attitude towards Army, 46, 170, 204, 207–209, 211, 215, 242, 244
Tentacles/ASSU, 43, 54, 167–8, 196
Termoli, battle, 54–5
Torch, operation, 4

Transportation Plan, 154–62, 176
Trenchard, influence of, vi–vii, xi, 25, 31, 34, 36–7, 48, 93, 142, 153, 166, 171, 213, 265

United States Marine Corps, 166, 170, 260
Urquhart, Maj. Gen. R., 254, 257, 259–60
USAAF, xi, 5–6, 8, 27, 41, 56, 61, 88, 98–9, 101, 136, 162, 180, 183, 197, 222, 249
   air policy, 2–7, 14, 42, 56, 151, 185, 192, 200, 243, 265
   army support, 56–7, 149, 175, 185–6, 236, 243–4

Vickers,
   Warwick, 15, 17
   Wellington, 17, 47–8, 51, 62, 125, 156
   Windsor, 16–20, 222
Village Inn, 11–12, 221–2
Visual control post, 169, 175, 196, 230, 244, 250
Vultee Vengeance, 112
V-weapons, 21–2, 26, 33, 216
   threat to Overlord, 32–3, 92, 154
   V-1 (Fieseler Fl 103), 24–6, 32, 109, 198, 212–16, 226, 250
   V-2 (A-4), 22, 24, 26, 28, 31–2, 251–2

War Office, x, 33, 39, 41, 118, 124, 156–7, 185, 188, 193, 242, 248, 251, 260, 265–6
   relations with RAF, 33, 67, 118, 120, 265

Air Department, 117–20, 123, 188, 251
air requirements, 54–5, 111, 112–13, 117–20, 122–3, 132, 145–6, 152, 164, 166–71, 175, 185
Warspite, HMS, 50
Westland,
   Welkin, 109
   Whirlwind, 69
   Lysander, 124

Weyland, Brig. Gen. O., 237, 240, 243
Wilson, Gen. H., 136, 147
Window, 8, 30, 84

Z-batteries, 22
Zeppelin, 10, 33
Zuckerman, S., 61, 154–5, 202